HOW TO READ
SHAKESPEAREAN
TRAGEDY

HOW TO READ SHAKESPEAREAN TRAGEDY

EDWARD QUINN, Editor

With contributions by:

MAURICE CHARNEY
Rutgers University

JAMES J. CLARK
San José State University

R. J. DORIUS
San Francisco State University

JAMES J. GREENE
City College, CUNY

J. W. HOUPPERT
University of Maryland

WILLIAM G. LEARY
California State University, Los Angeles

STEPHEN ROGERS
University of Notre Dame

Harper & Row, Publishers
NEW YORK   HAGERSTOWN   SAN FRANCISCO   LONDON

Sponsoring Editor: Paula White
Project Editor: Richard T. Viggiano
Designer: Howard S. Leiderman
Production Supervisor: Kewal K. Sharma
Compositor: Maryland Linotype Composition Co., Inc.
Printer and Binder: The Maple Press Company

HOW TO READ SHAKESPEAREAN TRAGEDY

Library of Congress Cataloging in Publication Data

Main entry under title:
How to read Shakespearean tragedy.
    Includes bibliographies and index.
    1.   Shakespeare, William, 1564-1616—Tragedies.
I.   Quinn, Edward G., Date-   II.   Charney, Maurice.
PR2983.H66   822.3'3   77-21215
ISBN 0-06-160043-1

CONTENTS

CONTENTS

PREFACE

How should Shakespearean tragedy be read? The aim of this book is to demonstrate that there is no one correct way, no royal road to the understanding and enhanced appreciation of these plays. In a fundamental and unchangeable sense, reading Shakespeare or any other form of literature is a unique experience. Each of us brings to the poems, plays, stories, movies, and television dramas that we read or watch a point of view as singular and distinctive as our own fingerprints: no two are alike. The experience of literature is, after all, the product of the encounter between the text and the reader, and it is the reader who is the variable factor. Although this individual element is true of literary experience in general, it is particularly true of Shakespeare. Shakespeare, above all other writers, seems to demand that readers and viewers give accounts of the worlds they experience in his plays. And these accounts are as varied and diverse as there are readers.

Now, for some people this uniqueness of literary experience suggests that any effort at discussion or criticism is a waste of time. "One opinion is as good as another" goes the current rendering of the ancient Latin axiom, *de gustibus non est disputandum* ("concerning taste there is no argument"). But such assertions of relativism fail to perceive the critically important distinction between experience and the understanding of experience. All of us experience life individually, but we understand and communicate with each other in terms that assume a common shared experience. We speak of birth, death, growing up, growing old, falling in love, or listening to music as common, even universal, events available virtually to everyone. And the process of communicating with others is the process of discovering more about our experience—its universality as well as its uniqueness. So discussions of literature are not mere examples of *de gustibus;* they are attempts to enlarge and enhance and unlock those experiences that would otherwise be felt but not necessarily understood.

In this sense, then, the present volume sets out to provide you with a set of keys to unlock that very special, yet universal, experience that is Shakespearean tragedy. Each key is designed for a particular room—the specific play being discussed in each chapter—but it is not the only key to that room, nor is it a key that can work only in that room. In other words, the keys are simply methods of approaching these plays. We want to demonstrate that it is a rich and varied and diverse world open to a wide range of perspectives and approaches. In an important sense these approaches are rooted in the subjective experience of the reader. However, equally important (perhaps more important) is the fact that the understanding of that experience requires alertness, sensitivity, and special mental skills that can be acquired by anyone willing to make the effort.

The effort, your effort, is the ultimate goal of this volume. The commentaries of the different authors are designed in various ways to help you encounter the problems and the questions that the plays raise. Each author approaches his subject from a different angle. In James Clark's chapter on *Romeo and Juliet,* for example, you will approach the play from the standpoint of the playwright. What was the material Shakespeare used in fashioning this play? What were the attitudes of his time toward the behavior that the play depicts and the theme that it suggests? What were the conventions of his theater, the accepted ways of presenting action onstage? What innovations in language and verse did Shakespeare introduce in the play and to what purpose? Answers to all of these questions are offered in the text, but the final answers must be given by you as you attempt to envision Shakespeare at work in the making of *Romeo and Juliet.*

On the other hand, you will be set a decidedly different task in dealing with that most questionable and questioned of all plays, *Hamlet.* For one thing, you will be asked to look at the mystery of the play not from the traditional view of the character of the hero, but from a close scrutiny of the significant passages from the play. Through the comments of the author, Maurice Charney, you will be introduced to the technique of "close reading," a challenging and valuable strategy of literary analysis. You will also be asked to ponder the larger question of the relationship of the parts to the whole in the play.

In Stephen Rogers' essay on *Othello* you will be asked to consider the play in terms of three fundamental categories: (1) as an imitation of life in which a truth of the human condition emerges from the portrayal of men in action; (2) as a "dream of passion," the expression of a profound conflict within the mind of Shakespeare, evident from a comparison of the play to the sonnets; and (3) as a "public dream," a structure that reflects in symbolic form certain fundamental desires and fears that all people share.

Two of these basic themes—love and death—provide the focus of J. W. Houppert's discussion of *King Lear*. Professor Houppert explores the moral atmosphere of the play, emphasizing its profound paradoxes and the human and divine mystery that underlies those paradoxes. He traces in this great play—commonly regarded as Shakespeare's greatest—the pattern of the hero in quest of his own identity, moving from human society to nature, through an "underworld" of suffering and recognition, to death and, perhaps, "resurrection."

In the chapter on *Macbeth* you will be asked to shift to a comprehensive view of the "world" of the play. The term *world,* as defined by the author, William Leary, refers to "the total environment that at once surrounds, impels, conditions and reflects the actions of dramatic characters." Thus, in the course of the discussion you will be asked to consider the physical, psychological, political, and moral dimension of the "world" of *Macbeth*. After that you will be given a scene-by-scene commentary, along with a complementary series of questions. Included as well is a set of wide-ranging and provocative topics for various writing assignments.

In R. J. Dorius' treatment of *Antony and Cleopatra* you have the opportunity to view the play both from a distance and in close-up. In the opening section some of the larger questions concerning tragedy, heroism, and love are examined in relation to the play. From this broad, theoretical springboard you move to a detailed consideration of the play's characters and themes.

Finally, you are offered a strikingly contemporary view of two plays. James Greene provides insights into *Julius Caesar* and *Coriolanus*, based upon the male-female relationships in these dramas. These two essays provide effective examples of perceiving elements in Shakespeare that are "modern" without doing violence either to the letter or to the spirit of the plays. The questions at the end of these essays are designed to elicit a similar effort from you.

That effort, as we have said, is in fact the final goal of this volume. It is a book that contains more questions than answers, more exploration than information. These features have been created quite deliberately, because the book's authors—however diverse their approaches—

all agree on this one point: Shakespeare is a writer who demands action—the physical and psychological action of his characters, the mental and imaginative action of his audience. His enemy is the passive reader or viewer who wants to sit back and be entertained, and only entertained. Shakespeare will entertain us, to be sure, but the richer, more rewarding experience will only be ours if we are willing to "entertain" him in the other sense of that word: to hold in our minds for consideration and reflection, as when we entertain an idea. When we have made that effort with patience and skill, we find ourselves given entrance into a new world, a world that allows us to experience—if only for the moments we are there—what it means to be "not of an age but for all time."

E. Q.

PART ONE

SHAKESPEARE: AN INTRODUCTION

EDWARD QUINN

1

THE IDEA OF SHAKESPEARE

He has been dead for over 400 years. In his lifetime he was not particularly famous, powerful, or wealthy. He founded no religion, invented nothing that improved the lot of mankind, created no philosophical or scientific system, made no great discoveries (at least of the geographical kind). He was simply a poet, playwright, and actor who spent 25 years of his life writing for a popular audience and achieving what can most accurately be described as modest success.

His personality, from all accounts, was cheerful and lively ("gentle" was the word his friends used), apparently devoid of those tempestuous and tormented features we like to think inherent in all poets. Sometime before his fiftieth birthday—an age when most writers feel they are in their prime—he gave up his profession altogether and retired to his home town. In retirement he apparently made no attempt to publish or even preserve the 37 (or more) plays he had written. In all likelihood he did not regard them as his property at all, but as belonging to the acting company for whom he had labored most of his life. It was not until seven years after his death that the first collected edition of his work was published. Had it not been for the efforts of two fellow actors who served as the editors of that edition, nearly half of the plays we identify as his would doubtless have been lost.

How is it then—given these facts and reasonable surmises—that his name would appear on any list of the ten greatest men who ever lived? The answer to that question might well be the goal of anyone setting out to study the works of William Shakespeare. To answer it is to ascertain, for oneself at least, the role that literature plays in the lives of men. Sooner or later, thinking about Shakespeare leads to problems like this because for most people—whether they are "serious" about literature or not—he is the supreme example of the literary tradition of the West.

The centrality of Shakespeare's position in our literary culture was more apparent than ever a few years ago when college students across the country erupted in a series of protests over a number of issues, one of which was the content of the college curriculum. At the time it seemed that students were intent on a total rejection of the past, that their sole interest was in contemporary subjects, the "now." A rare exception to this massive rejection of tradition was the traditional Shakespeare course. Even at the height of the movement students continued to register for courses in Shakespeare.

On the surface such a reaction is difficult to understand. Shakespeare after all is not an easy writer to read. The beginning student encounters considerable linguistic, cultural, moral, and aesthetic difficulties. Despite these problems and despite the fact that one is *expected* to like Shakespeare (an expectation that arouses the rebel in many students) he maintains his popularity. Thus the paradox of Shakespeare continues to be reflected in the response to him: he is not only the great exemplar of the tradition, he is the great exception to it.

But this does not mean that his work is beyond criticism or that it represents some sort of sacred relic that exists only to be venerated. Reading Shakespeare is not a religious experience. To be sure, it relies on belief, an assent of the imagination, but it also encourages intellectual challenge. We are asked not merely to become emotionally and imaginatively involved, we must also be critically alert, prepared to ask ourselves at the right moments that most fundamental of critical questions: "What's going on here?" Shakespeare, the product of an age of belief, continues to challenge and intrigue us, the products of an age of skepticism.

This confirms the insight of Shakespeare's contemporary, friend and rival, Ben Jonson. Jonson commented a number of times on Shakespeare, not always in the most complimentary fashion, but one observation stands out as being among the two or three most important comments ever made about him: "He was not of an age but for all time."

OBSTACLES TO SHAKESPEARE

The foregoing discussion has tried to suggest that the act of reading a Shakespeare play has certain cultural and historical implications we are necessarily involved with whether we are aware of them or not. However, we should try not to be too conscious of these associations, lest our knowledge of the reputation of the plays interfere with our pleasure in them. We should never lose sight of the fact that, whatever else they provide us with, the plays are there for our pleasure. Of course there are pleasures and pleasures, simple and complex, physical and mental, fleeting and durable. Shakespeare's plays can and do provide both types. One summer evening's visit to New York's Central Park or to any of the popular festivals around the country will convince you of this. Achievement of the more permanent pleasure in Shakespeare, however, requires some effort on the part of the student. He must be willing to hurdle an external barrier of language and an internal barrier representing certain assumptions of his own time that he has assimilated.

WORDS, WORDS, WORDS

Although we must never lose sight of the fact that Shakespeare's dramas should be thought of in a theatrical context, it remains true that for most people (James Baldwin's essay is a case in point) our reaction to Shakespeare is governed by our reaction to his language. We accept or reject him on the basis of our response to his words, many of which provide us with problems. A very small minority are simply archaicisms, obsolete terms and phrases, words like *meiny* ("retinue") or *peize* ("balance"). More numerous and troublesome are those words that look familiar but whose meanings have shifted in the more than 350 years that separate Shakespeare's times from ours. Sometimes the shift has been so radical that a word means precisely the opposite of what it meant in the seventeenth century. When Hamlet tells his friends who are attempting to restrain him from pursuing the ghost "I'll make a ghost of him that lets me," it is important for us to know that *lets* means "prohibit," not "allow." More usually, however, the words in Shakespeare bear a rough approximation to our use of them, but relying on our meaning causes us to lose the concrete and forceful quality they exhibit. Thus *kindly* means *"natural,"* not "benevolent"; *favour* means *"appearance,"* not "a concession"; and the *extravagant and erring* ghost in *Hamlet* is one that "wanders around," not one that "wastes his money and makes mistakes."

Obviously the best cure for these linguistic barriers, and for the related obstacles of obscure allusions, is an adequate glossary. Most decent editions of Shakespeare provide such glossaries, usually on the same page as the text. Do not attempt to save money by reading the plays in the edition available in the supermarket. There are a number of excellent one-volume editions, notably those edited by Kittredge and Ribner (Xerox), Neilson and Hell (Houghton Mifflin) and Craig and Bevington (Scott, Foresman). There are, as well, quite a few excellent paperback editions of individual plays, notably the Pelican and the Signet. These series also have been collected in one volume by their respective general editors, Alfred Harbage (Pelican) and Sylvan Barnet (Signet/Harcourt, Brace). An outstanding but incomplete one-play-per-volume edition is the *New Arden Shakespeare*, edited by Brooks and Jenkins, and available in hard cover and paperback. All of these facilitate the overcoming of linguistic barriers in as painless a fashion as possible.

"THE FATAL CLEOPATRA"

One feature of Shakespeare's use of language that even his admirers are inclined to criticize is his propensity for puns. Samuel Johnson, one of the most sympathetic and intelligent readers Shakespeare ever had, called the pun "the fatal Cleopatra for which he lost the world and was content to lose it." Johnson felt that Shakespeare engaged in puns not only too often but often inappropriately. It is one thing to pun in a comic context but quite another to engage in puns when the action is serious, even tragic. Mercutio's dying remark in *Romeo and Juliet* ("ask for me tomorrow, and you shall find me a grave man") and Hamlet's already quoted injunction ("I'll make a ghost of him that lets me") at a moment of intense drama are just two examples of Shakespeare's willingness to play with words at any point in a drama. However, they are also good examples of his ability to complicate and intensify experience through the fusion of two directly opposing elements, in this case tragic fact and comic language. The result for the reader is the illusion of the fullness and contradictoriness of life. There is no finer verbal expression of the paradox that life is both a tragedy and a comedy than the Shakespearean pun.

CONVENTIONS: SHAKESPEARE'S AND OURS

Every Shakespearean play contains at least one character or scene that offers problems to modern readers. Our sense of probability is severely strained by the ghosts in *Hamlet* and *Julius Caesar,* by the witches in *Macbeth,* by the movement from noble love to insane jealousy in a matter of minutes in *Othello,* by Iago's lack of motivation, by the Dover Cliff scene in *King Lear,* by the frequent reliance on disguises and asides. Our usual response is to adjust to these seeming inadequacies for the sake of the work as a whole. Generally, this is the best procedure to adopt, provided we do it in a nonpatronizing manner.

Too many modern readers and audiences look upon such elements as strains of "primitive" or crude art in Shakespeare, examples of some of the naive conventions of the Elizabethan theatre.

The truth is that Shakespeare's conventions are not less sophisticated than ours, merely different. Many of our theatrical conventions are based upon the criterion of physical feasibility and psychological consistency. We expect events to be presented within the terms of what we have learned to think of as probable or credible and expect characters' actions to be explained in terms of internal motivations.

By and large, our expectations have been conditioned by the standards of naturalist or realist drama, whose chief principle is that drama should imitate life as we ordinarily experience it. Features such as ghosts or disguises we relegate to the realm of horror movies or children's literature. Before accepting this convention, however, we should keep in mind that it is relatively new in the history of literature and drama and, in fact, has existed for only about a hundred years. Even now it appears on the way to being replaced by a new convention that bears as strong a resemblance to Shakespeare's theater as it does to naturalism.

The purpose of drama, according to Hamlet, is "to hold the mirror up to nature" which sounds like a perfect description of naturalist theater. But Hamlet's idea of a mirror is not that of an instrument that reflects the external surfaces of life but one that probes beneath the surface to uncover the very "form and pressure" of the age.

Such an approach suggests not just the imitation of life as we know it but the representation of its significance. In the achievement of this goal Shakespeare relies partly on the conventions of the theater of his time, derived directly from the religious, allegorical drama of the Middle Ages. However he never employs these conventions mindlessly or as easy solutions to his problems as a playwright. Rather he uses them to open up a symbolic dimension to his work, to suggest that the full extent of the form and pressure is not to be measured by ordinary observation alone but by moral imagination as well.

READING DRAMA

Beyond specific obstacles of language and theatrical convention are others of a more general nature. One of these is that Shakespeare's plays are *plays*, written to be performed. The magnificence of their language sometimes obscures, but should never obliterate, this fact. To be properly read they must be staged, literally when possible, but always, in any case, performed in the mind's eye. Reading Shapespeare requires a capacity to exercise our visual as well as our verbal imaginations. We are not given descriptions of people and places, as we are in a novel. We must provide these ourselves. As a result our collaboration, so to speak, with the author is much greater and our sense of reality much stronger, always provided that we have made the required imaginative effort.

SHAKESPEARE, OUR CONTEMPORARY?

We have already touched upon the phenomenon of Shakespeare's seemingly universal appeal. Nevertheless we should remember that although Shakespeare may be our contemporary, we are not his. To put it less cryptically: There are values and insights and revelations of the human condition in Shakespeare, as in all great art, that are as true today as they ever were; on the other hand, there are attitudes in the plays that appear to be outmoded and, in a few cases, even abhorrent to many modern readers.

There is for example the attitude toward women in *The Taming of the Shrew*, toward Jews in *The Merchant of Venice*, toward blacks in *Othello* and *Titus Andronicus*. Moreover some critics have discerned sexual disgust in *Measure for Measure* and *Troilus and Cressida*, a contempt for democracy in *Julius Caesar* and *Coriolanus*, military jingoism in *Henry V*, and smug paternalism in *The Tempest*.

Most of these charges are grossly overstated, but it is very unlikely that all are untrue. Shakespeare after all was a man before he became a monument, and it was the man not the monument who wrote the plays. As a man he shared some of the prejudices and limitations of his age. We should resist the occasion to become self-righteous until we understand the implications of life in that time. Beyond that we should try to remember that it is not his "attitudes"—whether they be Elizabethan or modern—that we honor him for but his creative imagination. No more eloquent statement of this position ever has been made than in the essay by James Baldwin, "Why I Stopped Hating Shakespeare."

This essay touches on a number of serious and significant points. Basically it is about the interaction of language and experience. Specifically it deals with the struggle of James Baldwin as a black American writer to articulate his experience in a language he identified as alien and hostile, as the language of the oppressor. As Baldwin records it, Shakespeake stands as a critical element in that struggle. Shakespeare's language—"its candor, its irony, its density and its beat"—provided a model of possibility and a connecting link with Baldwin's own experience that enabled him to resolve his conflict:

> My relationship, then, to the language of Shakespeare revealed itself as
> nothing less than my relationship to myself and my past. Under this light,
> this revelation, both myself and my past began slowly to open, perhaps the

way a flower opens at morning, but, more probably, the way an atrophied muscle begins to function, or frozen fingers to thaw. The greatest poet in the English language found his poetry where poetry is found in the lives of the people. . . . And, though I, and many of us, have bitterly bewailed (and will again) the lot of an American writer—to be part of a people who have ears to hear and hear not, who have eyes to see and see not!—I am sure that Shakespeare did the same. Only, he saw, as I think we must, that the people who produce the poet are not responsible to him: he is responsible to them. That is why he is called a poet. And this responsibility, which is also his joy and his strength and his life, is to defeat all labels and complicate all battles by insisting on the human riddle, to bear witness, as long as breath is in him, to that mighty, unnameable, transfiguring force which lives in the soul of man, and to aspire to do his work so well that when the breath has left him, the people—*all people!*—who search in the rubble for a sign or a witness will be able to find him there.[1]

2
CRITICAL APPROACHES TO SHAKESPEARE

Sooner or later the student of Shakespeare discovers the statistic that can be the source of either despair or exhilaration, depending upon his frame of mind: over a thousand books and articles on Shakespeare are published every year. Sitting down to write his term paper the student feels that "everything has been said." The Shakespeare industry, he finds, turns out interpretations the way General Motors produces Chevrolets. What chance has he against this corporation? Furthermore, why bother, since there is nothing new to be said?

The student's despair is easy to understand, but it is based on a fundamental misunderstanding. He is thinking of Shakespearean criticism as a mountain to be scaled, an enormous obstruction designed to hinder and intimidate. He is wrong. Rather, he should think of Shakespearean commentary as a series of broad avenues converging upon one central plaza from a variety of directions. Each avenue offers a driver direct access to the center, provided he knows where he is going. If, however, he lacks a sense of direction, he is liable to turn onto one of the many side streets, all of which are dead ends.

Another point to keep in mind about these avenues is that they are always under construction. The processes of paving and repaving, widening and narrowing, go on constantly. The task is never completed. A consequence of this continuous repair is that traffic does not move as freely as it might. (In the jam, some drivers lose their tempers and fights break out.) But another more important effect is the knowledge that there is always room for improvement and that everyone can contribute to that task. This section provides a brief introduction to these broad avenues, the major critical approaches to the study of Shakespeare.

For Discussion

Many people feel that close attention to criticism can become a substitute for close attention to one's personal experience of the work. How can one avoid this pitfall? What procedure does it suggest in studying the plays?

CHARACTER CRITICISM

Shakespeare always has been celebrated as a master of character portrayal. In the nineteenth century in particular, readers and critics outdid themselves in their praise of great Shakespearean characters such as Falstaff, Iago, Hamlet, and Cleopatra. Romantic critics, Coleridge and Hazlitt in particular, eloquently testified to the psychological depth and credibility of his creations. Eventually however the character approach to the plays became excessive: characters were treated as if they were historical personages with a life of their own, independent of the plays of which they were a part. A book, *The Girlhood of Shakespeare's Heroines;* a German poem, the translated title of which is "Germany is Hamlet"; an insistence by a Southern lady that Othello must have been a white man—these are just a few of the distortions that emerge when a character in a play (who therefore has no existence outside the limits of that play) is treated as a real person. Even so notable a character critic as A. C. Bradley was given to occasional lapses in this regard. In the appendices to his great book on Shakespearean tragedy, Bradley speculated on such questions as "Where was Hamlet at the time of his father's death?" and "When was the murder of Duncan first plotted?" In 1933 this type of conjecture was satirized by L. C. Knights in a speech titled "How Many Children Had Lady Macbeth?" Knights' speech had the effect of signaling a new approach to Shakespeare's plays that tended at first to subordinate character. The tendency to de-emphasize character persisted during the hegemony of New Criticism with its emphasis on language and imagery. More recently, however, character criticism has reemerged in a somewhat altered form. Many modern critics now see characters less as representations of real people and more as embodiments of intense personal experience.

11

The Motiveless Malignity of Iago

Act. I. sc. 3. Iago's speech:

Virtue? a fig! 'tis in ourselves, that we are thus, or thus, &c.

This speech comprises the passionless character of Iago. It is all will in intellect; and therefore he is here a bold partizan of a truth converted into a falsehood by the absence of all the necessary modifications caused by the frail nature of man. And then comes the last sentiment,—

Our raging motions, our carnal stings, our unbitted lusts, whereof I take this, that you call—love, to be a sect or scion!

Here is the true Iagoism of, alas! how many! Note Iago's pride of mastery in the repetition of "Go, make money!' to his anticipated dupe, even stronger than his love of lucre: and when Roderigo is completely won—

I am chang'd. I'll go sell all my land—

when the effect has been fully produced, the repetition of triumph—

Go to; farewell; put money enough in your purse!

The remainder—Iago's soliloquy—the motive-hunting of a motiveless malignity—how awful it is! Yea, whilst he is still allowed to bear the divine image, it is too fiendish for his own steady view,—for the lonely gaze of being next to devil, and only not quite devil,—and yet a character which Shakespeare has attempted and executed, without disgust and without scandal! . . .

Finally, let me repeat that Othello does not kill Desdemona in jealousy, but in a conviction forced upon him by the almost superhuman art of Iago, such a conviction as any man would and must have entertained who had believed Iago's honesty as Othello did. We, the audience, know that Iago is a villain from the beginning; but in considering the essence of the Shakespearian Othello, we must perseveringly place ourselves in his situation, and under his circumstances. Then we shall immediately feel the fundamental difference between the solemn agony of the noble Moor, and the wretched fishing jealousies of Leontes, and the morbid suspiciousness of Leonatus, who is, in other respects, a fine character. Othello had no life in Desdemona:—the belief that she, his angel, had fallen from the heaven of her native innocence, wrought a civil war in his heart. She is his counterpart; and, like him, is almost sanctified in our eyes by her absolute unsuspiciousness, and holy entireness of love. As the curtain drops, which do we pity the most?

Samuel Taylor Coleridge, *Lectures and Notes on Shakespeare*

HISTORICAL CRITICISM

Historical criticism is the most scholarly approach to Shakespeare. It operates from the assumption that the true meaning of a Shakespearean play is intimately related to the ideas, beliefs, and general culture of the Elizabethan Age. Historical criticism began in the early part of the twentieth century as a counterattack against the character critics who concentrated on the psychology of Shakespeare's characters as if they were characters in a modern novel rather than figures in a Renaissance play. The historical critic brings to his approach a detailed knowledge of at least one aspect of Elizabethan life or thought and tries to illuminate the background, and sometimes the foreground, of the play itself.

This concentration on the exclusively Elizabethan character of Shakespeare's work had drawn the charge that it fails to come to terms with the timeless aspects of the plays, with the experience they represent for the modern reader. It is further charged that historical criticism subordinates the aesthetic aspect of the works to its role in the history of ideas.

> I hope I have made it clear, that the idea of man which lay behind Shakespearean tragedy was, in the first place, inextricably interwoven with the ideas of the state and the world as a whole to a degree which it is difficult for us to realize, and, in the second place, that this interwoven pattern was threatened by an implicit and an explicit conflict. At the time when Shakespeare wrote *Hamlet* there were available for emotional contemplation and for dramatic representation two views of man's nature, two views of the world, two views of the state. Drama could be not merely the conflict between romantic love and external forces, as in *Romeo and Juliet;* it could represent conflict far more complicated and far more profound. . . . The creation of dramatic suspense by an internal conflict in a mind aware of the evil reality under the good appearance is the core of the greatness, the originality of *Hamlet.* . . .
>
> . . . Hamlet's disillusionment is a partial expression of a general predicament; the emotions he gives voice to were shared in his own time and have been shared ever since, by many people less miraculously articulate than himself. [His discovery of the difference between appearance and reality, which produced in his mind an effect so disillusioning that it paralyzed the sources of deliberate action, was a symptom that the Renaissance in general had brought with it a new set of problems, had opened new psychological vistas, which the earlier views of man had not explored.]
>
> Theodore Spencer, *Shakespeare and the Nature of Man*

PSYCHOANALYTIC CRITICISM

Initially based on the insights of Sigmund Freud, psychoanalytic criticism has focused consistently on the plays as the expression of buried motives and drives in the individual psyche of Shakespeare or in the collective psyche of his readers. Thus in the most famous example of psychoanalytic criticism—Ernest Jones' *Hamlet and Oedipus*—the analysis of Hamlet's Oedipal fixation is traced to a similar conflict alleged to exist within Shakespeare himself. Further, the representation of this conflict in dramatic form accounts for the universal popularity of the play.

Most readers have found that psychoanalytic interpretation is too often based upon an arbitrary and irresponsible system of symbolization. Nevertheless, despite its excesses, it has generated a number of provocative and interesting insights in approaching the plays.

> How if, in fact, Hamlet had in years gone by, as a child, bitterly resented having had to share his mother's affection even with his own father, had regarded him as a rival, and had secretly wished him out of the way so that he might enjoy undisputed and undisturbed the monopoly of that affection? If such thought had been present in his mind in childhood days they evidently would have been "repressed," and all traces of them obliterated, by filial piety and other educative influences. The actual realization of his early wish in the death of his father at the hands of a jealous rival would then have stimulated into activity these "repressed" memories, which would have produced, in the form of depression and other suffering, an obscure aftermath of his childhood's conflict. This is at all events the mechanism that is actually found in the real Hamlets who are investigated psychologically.
>
> Ernest Jones, *Hamlet and Oedipus*

ARCHETYPAL CRITICISM

Archetypal or mythic criticism explores the relationship of literature to primitive myth and ritual. It operates primarily on the idea of "archetypes," a term developed by the psychologist C. G. Jung. An archetype is an image of human experience that lies embedded within the "collective unconscious." The Shakespearean critic who employs the archetypal approach attempts to root the tragedies in the ritual of the sacrificial agent, the leader of society whose death constitutes an atonement for the ills of that society.

One weakness of archetypal criticism is the tendency to generalize in dealing with a play and consequently to overlook precisely those individual features of a work that characterize its uniqueness as well as its universality. At its best, however, it lends a sense of the profound reverberations incorporated in Shakespearean drama.

> Disruption in the kingdom, disruption in the family, linked by tradition, were facets of that universal disruption of Nature, that Descent into Chaos, which for millennia had been a standing dread of mankind and at the same time one of mankind's convictions about providential history in the future.
>
> *King Lear* is an exploration of this potentiality to quite a different degree from, say, *Macbeth*. The nadir of that play, the point at which Macbeth's own evil nature seems to diffuse evil throughout his whole country, falls

short of what happens even at the very start of *Lear*. In *Macbeth*, the evil emanates from one man (or one couple) quite alone. In *Lear* it seems, from the first, like an infection spreading everywhere, affecting a general change in human nature, even in all nature. . . . Its status as decisively misguided or evil is not in doubt; and it is the established sign or first step in a movement which threatens chaos or actually brings it. The direction and nature of what is to happen in *Lear* need not be inferred by the spectator through his detailed response to the behaviour and dialogue of the actors. Richly as it may be confirmed and elaborated in these things, its essence stands starkly before him in the stylization of a known kind of opening event. The intricate complication of the story, the detailed characterization, do nothing to obscure what is clear in the almost folk-tale quality of how the play begins. '*We have seen* the best of our time.'

John Holloway, *The Story of the Night*

THEATRICAL CRITICISM

Theatrical critics of Shakespeare focus on the "plays in performance," drama as conceived and worked out in their original theatrical context. They emphasize Shakespeare's role as a practical man of the theater dealing with the problems that face any practising playwright. The limitations of the stage, the range and particular abilities of individual actors, the expectations of the audience, the relative popularity of certain genres (revenge tragedy, for example) and the degree to which meaning is conveyed by unspoken gesture are problems that have been frequently overlooked in the past because they have been regarded as irretrievable, in Shakespeare's words "insubstantial pageants [leaving] not a rack behind." Although this is by and large true, patient work on the part of theatrical scholars has enabled us to learn more and consequently to bring to bear more light on the plays when approached from the angle of theatrical experience.

> The study of Shakespeare as a "philosophic poet rather than a man of the stage" is symptomatic of an intellectual attitude which divorces literary criticism from the theater. . . . Literary critics must learn to consider the full theatrical life of the plays they study, so that they can analyse and judge a play as well as a poem, and speak of an image of life as well as of a theme, or pattern, or moral statement. If they could do this, theater directors, actors, and audiences would recognize their own interests in the critics' deliberations, and would share in them.
>
> John Russell Brown, "Theatrical Research of Shakespeare and His Contemporaries."

SYMBOLIC AND THEMATIC CRITICISM

This is a broad term designed to cover a significant development in twentieth-century criticism of Shakespeare. It is related on the one hand to early studies of the imagery of the plays and on the other to the attempt to integrate the linguistic and poetic elements of the play within a broad philosophical or ethical framework. It presupposes that each play constitutes a unified, organic entity in which every element stands in dynamic and coherent relationship to the whole. The pioneer in this form of criticism is G. Wilson Knight, a critic of extraordinary imagination and sometimes highly idiosyncratic judgments. Knight's strengths and weaknesses as a critic represent in a particularly emphatic manner the virtues and dangers of this critical approach.

> *King Lear* is roughly analogous to Chekov where *Macbeth* is analogous to Dostoevsky. The wonder of Shakespearean tragedy is ever a mystery—a vague, yet powerful, tangible, presence; an interlocking of the mind with a profound meaning, a disclosure to the inward eye of vistas undreamed, and but fitfully understood. *King Lear* is great in abundance and richness of human delineation, in the level focus of creation that builds a massive oneness, in fact, a universe, of single quality from a multiplicity of differentiated units; and in a positive and purposeful working out of a purgatorial philosophy . . . .
>
> . . . The core of the play is an absurdity, an indignity, an incongruity. In no tragedy of Shakespeare does incident and dialogue so recklessly and miraculously walk the tightrope of our pity over the depths of bathos and absurdity.
>
> G. Wilson Knight, *The Wheel of Fire*

3

THE LIFE OF SHAKESPEARE:
FACT FROM FANTASY

What follows is not a narrative account of Shakespeare's life but a selection and transcription of the principal documents upon which such a narrative must be based. Even for experienced scholars and researchers none of these documents is without problems. They raise as many questions as they answer, forcing one to piece together the facts in as careful and responsible a manner as possible. They also tempt us to speculate, to supply the missing answers out of our own imaginations. This exciting and challenging activity can be a dangerous one if we stray too far from the facts or begin to alter or distort them to fit our preconceived theory. At all times we must keep our eyes firmly rooted on the known before sailing off into the unknown.

The items transcribed in this section constitute a significant part of the known. They include official records of Shakespeare's baptism, his marriage, the baptism of his children and his will. They also include various references to him as a member and part owner of an acting company, The Lord Chamberlain's Men, or, as they were known after 1602, the King's Men. Together they provide the basic scaffolding of any reconstruction of Shakespeare's life.

The items are presented in chronological order. As you read, you will be asked questions that will refer you to certain published biographies of Shakespeare. In examining these biographical accounts keep in mind that the important principle is the separation of fact and conjecture. The facts in themselves reveal certain basic data but not nearly enough to satisfy our curiosity about Shakespeare. However, any departures from those facts must be labeled as such. Keep that distinction clearly in mind as you attempt to answer the questions.

Examine one of the following Shakespeare biographies with an eye to distinguishing facts from theory. Is it clear from the language of the author that the conjectures are not being presented as facts? List those words used to identify the conjectural nature of these statements.

REFERENCES

Chambers, E. K. *William Shakespeare: A Study of Facts and Problems,* 2 vols., Oxford: Oxford University Press, 1930.

Hotson, Leslie. *Shakespeare vs. Shallow,* Boston: Little, Brown, 1931.

————. *Mr. W. H.,* New York: Knopf, 1964.

Bentley, G. E. *Shakespeare: A Biographical Handbook,* New Haven: Yale University Press, 1962.

Rowse, A. L. *William Shakespeare,* New York: Harper & Row, 1963.

Schoenbaum, Samuel. *Shakespeare's Lives,* Oxford: Oxford University Press, 1970.

Schoenbaum, Samuel. *William Shakespeare: A Documentary Life.* New York: Oxford University Press, 1975.

Burgess, Anthony. *Shakespeare,* New York: Knopf, 1970.

1564 APRIL 26

[FROM THE REGISTER OF THE DIOCESE OF WORCESTER]

Gulielmus filius Johannes Shakspere

The above entry is taken from the Register of Baptisms of the Church of the Holy Trinity in Stratford. Like many official and legal documents of the time it was recorded in Latin.

For Research: Notice that Shakespeare was baptized on April 26, but that there is no record of the actual date of his birth. Why is his birthday celebrated on April 23?

1582 NOVEMBER 27

[MARRIAGE LICENSE]

Item eodem die similis emanavit licencia inter Willelum Shaxpere et Annam Whateley de Temple Grafton. [On this same day was issued a license between William Shakespeare and Anne Whateley of Temple Grafton.]

1582 NOVEMBER 28

[BOND OF SURETIES SIGNED BY FULK SANDELLS AND JOHN RICHARDSON, FRIENDS OF THE HATHAWAY FAMILY]

> The condicion of this obligacion ys suche that if herafter there shall not appere any Lawfull Lett or impediment by reason of any precontract consanguinitie affinitie or by any other lawfull meanes whatsoeuer but that William Shagspere on thone partie, and Anne Hathwey of Stratford in the Dioces of Worcester maiden may lawfully solemnize matrimony together and in the same afterwardes remaine and continew like man and wiffe according vnto the lawes in that behalf prouided, and moreouer if there be not at this present time any action sute quarrell or demaund moved or depending before any judge ecclesiasticall or temporall for and concerning any such lawfull lett or impediment, And moreouer if the said William Shagspere do not proceed to solemnizacion of mariadg with the said Anne Hathwey without the consent of hir frindes, And also if the said William do vpon his owne proper costes and expenses defend & save harmles the right Reverend father in god Lord John bushop of Worcester and his offycers for Licencing them the said William and Anne to be married togither with once asking of the bannes of matrimony betwene them and for all other causes which may ensure by reason or occasion thereof, That then the said obligacion to be voyd and of none effect or els to stand & abide in full force and vertue.

For Research: Notice the descrepancies between the sureties of November 28 and the marriage license of November 27. Are Anne Hathwey and Anne Whately of Temple Grafton the same person? The orthodox position is that they are (compare the Chambers or Bentley biographies). A minority opinion is offered by Anthony Burgess. Which of these explanations is more convincing?

1583 MAY 26

[BAPTISMAL REGISTER]

> Susanna, daughter to William Shakspere

For Research: Notice that Susanna was born within six months of the wedding. Must we necessarily conclude from this that Shakespeare and Anne had had premarital sexual relations in our sense of the term and that the marriage was a "shotgun" affair? What alternative explanation have some scholars offered? How convincing is that explanation?

1585 FEBRUARY 2

[BAPTISMAL REGISTER]

C. Hamnet and Judeth sonne and daughter to William Shakspere

For Research: The choice of Hamnet as a name for his son and the fact that "Hamnet" and "Hamlet" were interchangeable in Elizabethan England have excited the imagination of many people. (See the explanation given in Chapter 9 of James Joyce's *Ulysses*.) What is the less romantic but more plausible explanation offered by scholars?

1585–1592

These are the so-called "lost years" of Shakespeare's life. During this period the only reference to him is a mention in a legal dispute. The principal in the case was his father who was attempting to recover land that he previously had mortgaged. Beyond that nothing is definitely known of Shakespeare's activities. Conjectures abound, but none has gained general acceptance. Suggestions offered as to his profession during this period have included: soldier, gardener, sailor, printer, lawyer, schoolmaster, scrivener, apprentice actor and barber-surgeon.

Consult one of the following works and consider the strengths of the arguments in it:

Baker, O. *In Shakespeare's Warwickshire and the Unknown Years,* London: Simpkin Marshall, 1937.
Duff-Cooper, A. *Sergeant Shakespeare,* London: Rupert Hart-Davis, 1949.
Everitt, E. B. *The Young Shakespeare,* Copenhagen: Rosenkilde and Bagger, 1954.
Keen, A. and Lubbock, R. *The Annotator,* London: Putnam, 1954.
Knight, W. K. *Shakespeare's Hidden Life,* New York: Mason and Lipscomb, 1973.

1592

[FROM "GROATSWORTH OF WIT"]

Base minded men all three of you, if by my miserie you be not warnd: for vnto none of you (like mee) sought those burres to cleaue: those Puppets (I meane) that spake from our mouths, those Anticks garnisht in our colours. It is not strange, that I, to whom they all haue beene beholding: is it not like that you, to whome they all haue been beholding, shall (were yee in that case as I am now) bee both at once of them forsaken? Yes trust them not: for there is an vpstart Crow, beautified with our feathers, that with his *Tygers hart wrapt in a Players hyde,* supposes he is as well able to bombast out a blanke verse as the best of you: and beeing an absolute *Johannes factotum,* is in his owne conceit the onely Shakes-scene in a countrey. O that I might intreat your rare wits to be inploied in more profitable courses: & let those Apes imitate your past excellence, and neuer more acquaint them with your admired inuentions.

For Discussion: "Groatsworth of Wit" was a pamphlet allegedly written by Robert Greene, a playwright and popular pamphleteer. Greene had died shortly before the publication of the pamphlet and it was, as a result, "edited" by a friend, another playwright, Henry Chettle. Recent scholarship has produced evidence to suggest that Chettle was the real author of the pamphlet and that Greene's name was used in order to profit from the greater fame of the dead writer. In any case Chettle subsequently apologized for this attack on Shakespeare and commended his "uprightness." What does the attack and the subsequent apology suggest about Shakespeare's reputation at this early stage of his career?

1593

[DEDICATION TO "VENUS AND ADONIS"]

To the Right Honorable Henry Wriothesley
Earl of Southampton and Baron of Titchfield
Right Honorable,

I know not how I shall offend in dedicating my unpolished lines to your Lordship, nor how the world will censure me for choosing so strong a prop to support so weak a burden; only, if your Honor seem but pleased, I account myself highly praised, and vow to take advantage of all idle hours, till I have honored you with some graver labor. But if the first heir of my invention prove deformed, I shall be sorry it had so noble a godfather, and never after ear so barren a land, for it yield me still so bad a harvest. I leave it to your honorable survey, and your Honor to your heart's content; which I wish may always answer your own wish and the world's hopeful expectation.

Your Honor's in all duty,
William Shakespeare.

1594

[DEDICATION TO "THE RAPE OF LUCRECE"]

To the Right Honorable Henry Wriothesley
Earl of Southampton and Baron of Titchfield

The love I dedicate to your Lordship without end; whereof this pamphlet without beginning is but a superfluous moiety. The warrant I have of your honorable disposition, not the worth of my untutored lines, makes it assured of acceptance. What I have done is yours; what I have to do is yours; being part in all I have, devoted yours. Were my worth greater, my duty would show greater; meantime, as it is, it is bound to your Lordship, to whom I wish long life still lengthened with all happiness.

Your Lordship's in all duty,
William Shakespeare

Notice the difference in tone between the two dedications, written to the same man within a year. What does that difference suggest about the relationship of Shakespeare and his patron?

Why does Shakespeare refer to "Venus and Adonis" as "the first heir of my invention" if, as "Groatsworth of Wit" makes clear, he had already written some plays?

1598

[FROM *PALLADIS TAMIA* BY FRANCES MERES]

As *Plautus* and *Seneca* are accounted the best for Comedy and Tragedy among the Latines: so *Shakespeare* among the English is the most excellent in both kinds for the stage; for Comedy, witnes his *Gentlemen of Verona*, his *Errors,* his *Love labours lost,* his *Loue labours wonne,* his *Midsummers night dreame,* & his *Merchant of Venice:* for Tragedy his *Richard the 2, Richard the 3, Henry the 4, King John, Titus Andronicus* and his *Romeo and Juliet.*

As *Epius Stolo* said, that the Muses would speake with *Plautus* tongue, if they would speak Latin; so I say that the Muses would speake with *Shakespeares* fine filed phrase, if they would speake English.

For Research: Notice the reference to *Loue labours wonne.* Does this refer to a lost play or to a play which we know under another name? (Consult T. W. Baldwin, *Shakespeare's Love's Labor's Won* [1957].) *Palladis Tamia* ("Wit's Treasury") was the title of a collection of essays by Francis Meres printed in 1598. The reference to Shakespeare occurs in a section devoted to a comparison of classical and English poets.

1601

[DEPOSITION OF AUGUSTINE PHILLIPS]

The Examination of Augustyne Phillypps servant vnto the L. Chamberlyne and one of hys players taken the xvij[th] of Februarij 1600 vpon hys oth.

He sayeth that on Fryday last was sennyght or Thursday S[r] Charles Percy S[r] Josclyne Percy and the L. Montgegle with some thre more spak to

some of the players in the presans of thys examinate to have the play of
the deposyng and kyllyng of Kyng Rychard the second to be played the
Saterday next promysyng to gete them xls. more then their ordynary to play
yt. Wher thys Examinate and hys fellowes were determyned to have played
some other play, holdyng that play of Kyng Richard to be so old & so long
out of vse as that they shold have small or no Company at yt. But at their
request this Examinate and his fellowes were Content to play yt the
Saterday and had their xls. more than their ordynary for yt and so played yt
accordingly.

Augustine Phillips.

The deposition of Augustine Phillips is in reference to a performance
of *Richard II* given on the day before the abortive attempt by the Earl
of Essex to overthrow Queen Elizabeth. The deposition affirms that
supporters of Essex paid Shakespeare's company 40 shillings extra to
perform the play. What was the motive of the Essex plotters in having
the play performed? What other connections existed between Essex
and Shakespeare? (Consult John Dover Wilson, *The Essential Shakespeare* [1932].)

1603

[ROYAL LETTERS-PATENT]

Knowe yee that Wee of our speciall grace, certeine knowledge, & mere
motion haue licenced and aucthorized and by theise presentes doe licence
and aucthorize theise our Servauntes Lawrence Fletcher, William Shakespeare, Richard Burbage, Augustyne Phillippes, John Heninges, Henrie
Condell, William Sly, Robert Armyn, Richard Cowly, and the rest of theire
Associates freely to vse and exercise the Arte and faculty of playinge
Comedies, Tragedies, histories, Enterludes, moralls, pastoralls, Stageplaies,
and Suche others like as theie haue alreadie studied or hereafter shall vse
or studie, aswell for the recreation of our lovinge Subjectes, as for our
Solace and pleasure when wee shall thincke good to see them, duringe our
pleasure. And the said Commedies, tragedies, histories, . . .

These letters-patent signify the transition for Shakespeare's company
from the Lord Chamberlain's Men to the King's Men. James I, who
succeeded Elizabeth upon her death in 1603, became the patron of
the troupe. As a result the company gave special performances at court
much more frequently than it had during Elizabeth's reign. It is generally thought that many of the features in *Macbeth* reflect Shakespeare's attempt to please James. Summarize the argument for this
position as given by H. N. Paul in *The Royal Play of Macbeth* (1950).

1609

[DEDICATION TO THE FIRST EDITION OF SHAKESPEARE'S SONNETS]

TO THE ONLIE BEGETTER OF
THESE INSVING SONNETS
Mʳ. W. H. ALL HAPPINESSE
AND THAT ETERNITIE
PROMISED
BY
OVR EVER-LIVING POET
WISHETH
THE WELL-WISHING
ADVENTVRER IN
SETTING
FORTH
T. T.

"T. T." is Thomas Thorpe, the publisher of the edition. The identity of "Mr. W. H." is one of the most celebrated mysteries in Shakespearean biography. The list of candidates for this position constitutes a tribute to the ingenuity, if not the good sense, of a vast number of Shakespearean commentators. Consult the Variorum Edition of the sonnets, edited by Hyder Rollins (1944, II) for a comprehensive list of possible W. H.'s. For further ingenuity see Leslie Hotson's *Mr. W. H.* (1964). Having looked at these compilations of evidence decide upon the most probable candidate and write an essay defending your choice.

1612

[BELLOTT–MOUNTJOY SUIT]

William Shakespeare of Stratford vpon Aven in the Countye of Warwicke gentleman of the age of xlviij yeres or thereaboutes sworne and examined the daye and yere abouesaid deposethe & sayethe

1. To the first interrogatory this deponent sayethe he knowethe the partyes plaintiff and deffendant and hathe know[ne] them bothe as he now remembrethe for the space of tenne yeres or thereaboutes.

2. To the second interrogatory this deponent sayeth he did know the complainant when he was servant with the deffendant, and that duringe the tyme of his the complainantes service with the said deffendant he the said complainant to this deponentes knowledge did well and honestly behaue himselfe, but to this deponentes remembred he hath not heard the deffendant confesse that he had gott any great profitt and comodytye by the service of the said complainant, but this deponent saithe he verely

thinkethe that the said complainant was a very good and industrious servant in the said service. And more he canott depose to the said interrogatory.

3. To the third interrogatory this deponent sayethe that it did evydentlye appeare that the said deffendant did all the tyme of the said complainantes service with him beare and shew great good will and affeccion towardes the said complainant, and that he hath hard the deffendant and his wyefe diuerse and sundry tymes saye and reporte that the said complainant was a very honest fellow: And this deponent sayethe that the said deffendant did make a mocion vnto the complainant of marriadge with the said Mary in the bill mencioned beinge the said deffendantes sole chyld and daughter, and willinglye offered to performe the same yf the said complainant shold seeme to be content and well like thereof: And further this deponent sayethe that the said deffendantes wyeffe did sollicitt and entreat this deponent to move and perswade the said complainant to effect the said marriadge, and accordingly this deponent did moue and perswade the complainant thervnto: And more to this interogatorye he cannott depose.

4. To the ffourth interrogatory this deponent sayth that the defendant promissed to geue the said complainant a porcion (of monie and goodes) in marriadg[e] with Marye his daughter, but what certayne (some) porcion he rememberethe not, nor when to be payed (yf any some weare promissed,) nor knoweth that the defendant promissed the plaintiff twoe hundered poundes with his daughter Marye at the tyme of his decease. But sayth that the plaintiff was dwellinge with the defendant in his house, and they had amongeste tham selues manye conferences about there marriadge which [afterwardes] was consumated and solempnized. And more he cann [ott depose.]

5. To the vth interrogatory this deponent sayth he can saye noth [inge] touchinge any parte or poynte of the same interrogatory, for he knoweth not what implementes and necessaries of houshould stuffe the defendant gauve the plaintiff in marriadge with his daughter Marye.

Willm Shakp

Shakespeare's testimony in this case reveals that sometime between 1602 and 1604 he was a lodger in the home of Christopher Mountjoy. The case centered around a dispute between Mountjoy and his son-in-law, Stephen Bellott. Bellott claimed that he had been promised a dowry of a certain amount as a condition of marrying Mountjoy's daughter. Shakespeare was called upon as a witness. His testimony states that he had, at the request of Mrs. Mountjoy, helped to arrange the marriage but that he was unable to recall the specific financial arrangements.

1616 FEBRUARY 10

M.[arriage]: Tho. Queeny tow Judith Shakspere

1616 MARCH 25

[SHAKESPEARE'S WILL]

T[*estamentum*] W[*illil*] mj Shackspeare.
R[*ecgnoscatu*] r. In the name of god Amen I William Shackspeare of
Stratford vpon Avon & Ordayne this my last will & testament in manner &
forme followeing. . . .

. . . Item I Gyve & bequeath vnto my saied daughter Judith One Hundred
& ffyftie Pounds more if shee or Anie issue of her bodie be Lyvinge att
thend of three Yeares next ensueing the daie of the date of this my will,
during which tyme my executours to paie her consideracion from my
deceas according to the Rate aforesaied. And if she dye within the saied
terme without issue of her bodye than my will ys & I doe gyve & bequeath
One hundred Poundes thereof to my Neece Elizabeth Hall & the ffiftie
Poundes to be sett fourth by my executours during the lief of my Sister
Johane Harte & the vse & profitt thereof Cominge shalbe payed to my saied
Sister Jone, & after her deceas the said I^{li} shall Remaine Amongst the
children of my saied Sister Equallie to be devided Amongst them. But if
my saied daughter Judith be lyving att thend of the saied three Years or
anie yssue of her bodye, then my will ys & soe I devise & bequeath the
saied Hundred & ffyftie poundes to be sett out *by my executours &
overseers* for the best benefitt of her & her issue & *the stock* not *to be*
paied vnto her soe long as she shalbe marryed & covert Baron (by my
executours & overseers,) but my will ys that she shall have the consideracion
yearelie paied vnto her during her lief & after her deceas the saied stock
and consideracion to bee paied to her children if she have Anie & if not
to her executours or assignes she lyving the saied terme after my deceas.
Provided that yf such husbond as she shall att thend of the saied three
Yeares be marryed vnto or attain after doe sufficientlie Assure vnto her &
thissue of her bodie landes Awnswereable to the porcion by this my will
gyven vnto her & to be adiudged soe by my executours & overseers then
my will ys that the said cl^{li} shalbe paied to such husbond as shall make such
assurance to his owne use. . . . *Item I gyve vnto my wief my second best
bed with the furniture.*

For Research: Shakespear's will was first drawn up in January, 1616,
and revised shortly before his death. In the interim Shakespeare's
younger daughter Judith had married Thomas Quiney and at the same
time it was revealed that Quiney had been involved in an illicit relationship with another woman, who had died giving birth to a child.
How does Shakespeare's will reflect his disapproval of his new son-
in-law?

The bequest of the "second best bed" has caused much speculation
that Shakespeare's marriage was an unhappy one. What explanations
do scholars offer to explain this strange item?

4

CHRONOLOGICAL TABLE

1558
Death of Mary Tudor; accession of Elizabeth

1564
Birth of Galileo
Deaths of Calvin and Michelangelo
Literary and Dramatic Events
Births of Shakespeare and Marlowe

1571
Battle of Lepanto

1572
Massacre of St. Bartholomew
Literary and Dramatic Events
Births of John Donne and Ben Jonson

1586
Battle of Zutphen
Literary and Dramatic Event
Death of Philip Sidney

1587
Death of Mary, Queen of Scots
Literary and Dramatic Event
Marlowe's Tamburlaine, Part One, performed

1588
Defeat of Spanish Armada
Literary and Dramatic Event
Tamburlaine, Part Two, performed

1593
Plague Year in England
Literary and Dramatic Events
Death of Marlowe
Publication of Venus and Adonis

1594
Literary and Dramatic Events
Publication of The Rape of Lucrece and Titus Andronicus

1597
Literary and Dramatic Events
Publication of King Richard II, King Richard III, Romeo and Juliet

1598
Rebellion in Ireland
Literary and Dramatic Events
Publication of King Henry IV, Part One; Merchant of Venice; Love's Labor's Lost, Meres' Palladis Tamia

1599
Birth of Oliver Cromwell
Essex sent to Ireland to quell rebellion, fails and returns to England.
Literary and Dramatic Events
Death of Spenser
Construction of Globe Theatre

1600
Literary and Dramatic Events
Publication of King Henry V; King Henry IV, Part Two; Much Ado About Nothing; Midsummer Night's Dream

1601
Essex's rebellion and execution

1602
Defeat of Irish rebels

Literary and Dramatic Event
Publication of Merry Wives of Windsor

1603
Death of Elizabeth; accession of James I
Literary and Dramatic Event
Publication of Hamlet ("bad" quarto)

1604
Hampton Court Conference
Literary and Dramatic Event
Publication of Hamlet ("good" quarto)

1605
Gunpowder Plot

1608
Literary and Dramatic Events
King's Men move into Blackfriars Theatre
Publication of King Lear and Pericles

1609
Literary and Dramatic Events
Publication of Shakespeare's Sonnets

1616
Literary and Dramatic Event
Death of Shakespeare

NOTES

CHAPTER 1

[1] James Baldwin, "Why I Stopped Hating Shakespeare," *The Observer* (London), April 19, 1964.

CHAPTER 3

Samuel Schoenbaum, *William Shakespeare,* Cf. pp. 129–130.

FOR DISCUSSION

CHAPTER 1

1. The term used to describe an uncritical adulation of Shakespeare is "bardolatry," a phenomenon that reached its height in Victorian England. That period also happened to be the high point of prestige and power in the history of the British Empire. To what extent can you see a connection between these two events, one cultural, the other political? Similarly it might also be interesting to explore the extent to which contemporary critical views of Shakespeare in England reflect the decline of Britain as a world power.

2. "Literature begins in joy and ends in knowledge" (Robert Frost). Try to keep that formula in mind as you turn to a specific passage or scene in one of the plays that has given you the most pleasure. See if you can determine what the source of your pleasure was. Try to be as specific as possible. Do not be content merely to describe it as funny or moving. Particularize your description.

3. Consider the following lines from *Hamlet:*

    Hamlet: I should have fatted all the region kites with this slave's offal. (II, ii, 606–607)

    What is the meaning of the words "kites" and "offal"? What is gained by the use of the adjective "fat" as a verb? How does this passage demonstrate that Hamlet's imagination is vivid and concrete rather than hazy and abstract?

    The dominant image in *Hamlet* is that of decay and cancerous sickness feeding on the body politic of Denmark. How do these lines contribute to that image? In what way do they represent a variation as well as a reinforcement of that idea?

4. Shakespeare's puns are frequently sexual in nature, particularly in the sonnets. Read sonnets 57 and 138 and list the puns that have sexual overtones.

5. Consider the distinction between the terms "dramatic poem" and "poetic drama." Which offers the better approach to the reading of Shakespeare? If you ever have seen a staged or filmed version of a play that

you already had read, describe those features of the play that were enhanced in performance and those that were more satisfactory when read.

6. Look at the quotation from James Baldwin. How does he relate the poet's responsibility to the love of the people?

CHAPTER 2

Consider the opening scene of *Hamlet* from the perspective of each of the six critical schools included in this section and deal with the following problems:

1. *Character.* To what extent and in what manner does the scene reveal to us the character of Horatio?
2. *Historical.* What Elizabethan ideas about ghosts are evident in this scene?
3. *Psychoanalytic.* How might the account of the death of the elder Fortinbras and the activities of young Fortinbras support a Freudian interpretation of the play?
4. *Archetypal.* What is the significance of the prominent references in the scene to Julius Caesar and to Jesus Christ?
5. *Theatrical.* What is the most effective way of presenting the ghost to a modern audience? How might the presentation have been done on the Elizabethan stage?
6. *Symbolic* or *thematic.* What is the significance of the fact that the opening line of the play ("Who's there?") is both a question and an attempt to establish identity?

FOR FURTHER REFERENCE

CHAPTER 2

Criticism

Berman, Ronald. *A Reader's Guide to Shakespeare's Plays: A Discursive Bibliography,* Scott, Foresman, 1965.

Eastman, Arthur M. and Harrison, George B., eds. *Shakespeare's Critics: From Jonson to Auden: A Medley of Judgments.* University of Michigan Press, 1964.

Halliday, F. E. *Shakespeare and His Critics,* London: G. Duckworth, 1950, 1958 revised edition.

Quinn, Edward; Ruoff, James; and Grennen, Joseph. *The Major Shakespearean Tragedies: A Critical Bibliography,* Free Press, 1973.

Character Criticism

Hazlitt, William. *Characters of Shakespeare's Plays* (1819), 2nd. ed. Oxford University Press, 1929.

Knights, L. C. "On the Question of Character in Shakespeare," *Some Shakespearean Themes,* Stanford: Stanford University Press, 1960.

Palmer, J. L. *Political Characters of Shakespeare,* London: Macmillan, 1945.

————. *Comic Characters of Shakespeare,* London: Macmillan, 1946.

————. *Political and Comic Characters of Shakespeare,* St. Martin's Press, combined edition, 1967.

Sewell, Arthur. *Character and Society in Shakespeare,* Oxford University Press, 1951.

Historical Criticism

Craig, Hardin. *The Enchanted Glass,* New York: Oxford University Press, 1936.

Ornstein, Robert. "Historical Criticism and the Interpretation of Shakespeare," *Shakespeare Quarterly* X, 1959.

Spencer, Theodore. *Shakespeare and the Nature of Man* (1941), 2nd ed. Macmillan, 1949.

Stoll, E. E. *Art and Artifice in Shakespeare* (1933), 2nd ed. Barnes & Noble, 1968.

Psychoanalytic Criticism

Freud, Sigmund. "The Theme of the Three Caskets," (1913). Reprinted in *Collected Papers.* London: Hogarth Press, 1950, IV, pp. 244–256.

Holland, Norman. *Psychoanalysis and Shakespeare,* New York: McGraw-Hill, 1966.

Jekels, Ludwig. "The Riddle of Shakespeare's *Macbeth*" (1925), reprinted in *Psychoanalysis and Literature,* ed. by H. M. Ruitenbeek, New York: Dutton, 1964, pp. 142–167.

Archetypal Criticism

Barber, C. L. *Shakespeare's Festive Comedy,* Princeton: Princeton University Press, 1959.

Frye, Northrop. *Fools of Time,* Toronto: University of Toronto Press, 1967.

Holloway, John. *The Story of the Night,* London: Routledge & Kegan Paul, 1961.

Murray, Gilbert. "Hamlet and Orestes," in *The Classical Tradition in Poetry,* Cambridge: Harvard University Press, 1927.

Theatrical Criticism

Beckerman, Bernard. *Shakespeare at the Globe, 1599–1609,* New York: Macmillan, 1962.

Brown, John Russell. "Theatrical Research and the Criticism of Shakespeare and His Contemporaries," *Shakespeare Quarterly,* XIII (1962), 451–461.

Harbage, Alfred. *Shakespeare's Audience,* New York: Columbia University Press, 1941.

————. *As They Liked It,* New York: Macmillan, 1947.

————. *Shakespeare and the Rival Traditions,* New York: Macmillan, 1952.

————. *Theatre for Shakespeare.* Toronto: University of Toronto Press, 1955.

Sprague, Arthur Colby. *Shakespeare and the Actors,* Cambridge: Harvard University Press, 1944.

————. *Shakespearean Players and Performances,* Cambridge: Harvard University Press, 1953.

Symbolic and Thematic Criticism

Heilman, R. B. *Magic in the Web: Action and Language in Othello,* Lexington: University of Kentucky Press, 1956.

Levin, Harry. *The Question of Hamlet,* New York: Oxford University Press, 1959.

Mack, Mayard. *King Lear in Our Time,* Berkeley and Los Angeles: The University of California Press, 1965.

Walker, Roy. *The Time is Free: A Study of Macbeth,* London: Dakers, 1949.

PART TWO
STYLE AND CONVENTION IN ROMEO AND JULIET

JAMES J. CLARK

FOR THE STUDENT

Romeo and Juliet is a play that throughout the years since its composition has suffered from too much popularity. Many persons who have never read a line of Shakespeare know that he wrote at least two plays, *Hamlet* and *Romeo and Juliet;* and if they have ever heard any of the lines from the latter play, these lines have been parodied out of all recognition, in speeches such as "Parting is such sweet sorrow," or "O Romeo, Romeo, wherefore are thou, Romeo." Many local productions scarcely help the casual students' appreciation of the play because this work seems especially attractive to those groups which wish to capitalize on the passion and bold sex of the teenage drama and too often forget the lovely message of the wonder and rapture of first love. Such productions often sacrifice the beauty of the play's poetry for the broad comedy lines or for the spectacle of the love and fight scenes. At the same time, and perhaps for the same reasons, many serious students often reject the play for its failure to meet the later high standards of the author for both comedy and tragedy, and tolerantly accept it only as a product of Shakespeare's apprenticeship days. Despite all of these handicaps, *Romeo and Juliet* has survived for audiences and critics alike; there are pleasures still to be found in it, pleasures which fortunately can make us forget the parodies and distortions of various productions. In itself it is still fresh and alive for new audiences, and like the lovers who died still young, the play will never grow old.

Romeo and Juliet may be considered one of the last of Shakespeare's early plays or one of the first of his more mature dramas. It is a play which shows very clearly how Shakespeare the artist develops as a poet and as a dramatist, at times using poetry for its own sake and not for its dramatic usefulness (see, for instance, the speech of Friar Lawrence in II, iii), but at other times employing his poetry brilliantly to create a believable tale of love and family violence (note, for instance, the scene when Juliet and Romeo part after their wedding night, III, v).

In this play Shakespeare uses his poetry experimentally and, I would suggest, largely successfully, in creating characterizations and dramatic effects by using verse forms other than the conventional blank verse. The play is therefore a fascinating study of an artist at work, creating from old forms and from conventional attitudes and behavior new ideas and new dramatic expressions.

It is this part of the play *Romeo and Juliet* with which this study is primarily concerned. We will look at the play as the experiment Shakespeare was developing, noting how he used the two-line rimed iambic pentameter verse, the rimed couplet, and the sonnet; how he applied the courtly love convention to his portrait of Romeo; and how he adapted his source, a long dramatic poem by an earlier poet, Arthur Brooke. Finally, we will explore the curious and ambiguous relationship that exists between comedy and tragedy. Attempts to establish *what Romeo and Juliet* is can be frustrating and inconclusive, but few critics deny that the play is a tragedy, and no critics deny the comedy in the play.

The present study goes only this far into an analysis of the components that make *Romeo and Juliet* a successful drama. Obviously much is left out: we will not study the complex attitudes toward love we find in the play (Mercutio's, the Nurse's, Capulet's, as examples) and the contrast of these attitudes with those of the two lovers; nor will we seek to explain the characterizations found in the play and Shakespeare's reasons for these characterizations (except in the comparison of these portraits with those in his source). The atmosphere— established on one side by the setting of Verona and the feud, and on the other side by the candlelight and moonlit scenes where the lovers meet—is mentioned briefly only when the dramatist creates scenes different from those in his source. There is no attempt to analyze this play and its themes from a specific orientation (Jungian and mythical, Freudian, sociological, and so forth). These interpretations are suggestive, fruitful, and necessary in a full critical study, but cannot be part of our goals in this brief analysis. Here we will focus on the ingenuity of the play's composition, which is only one way to gain further insight into the meaning of *Romeo and Juliet.*

INTRODUCTION

When he began the writing of *Romeo and Juliet*, most likely between 1594 and 1596, William Shakespeare was at a critical point in his career. He had completed his apprenticeship as a poet with the poetic narratives *Venus and Adonis* and *The Rape of Lucrece* (both probably written in 1592–1593) and, if we accept the assumptions of many Shakespearean scholars, was in the midst of his sonnet writing. Already he had to his credit a series of history plays (the three parts of *Henry VI*); a melodrama (*Titus Andronicus*); a history play with overtones of tragedy as well as of melodrama (*Richard III*); and four comedies (*Comedy of Errors, Love's Labor's Lost, Two Gentlemen of Verona,* and *The Taming of the Shrew*).

Between 1594 and 1596, in addition to *Romeo and Juliet*, he wrote *A Midsummer Night's Dream*, and *Richard II*. These plays utilize poetry more heavily than did earlier plays and all employ that imaginative faculty of man we call the lyrical or poetic to effect new dramatic responses. His two great narrative poems and the sonnets he quite possibly composed in 1592–1593 turned his creativity to new experimental forms of composition. The three plays he wrote soon thereafter demonstrate his new interests and are historically important as transition pieces, dramatic markers leading toward his major comedies and tragedies.

Romeo and Juliet is therefore important in Shakespearean studies because it is one of these important transitional plays. In some respects it is technically more interesting than *A Midsummer Night's Dream* or *Richard II*. In this one play the student can discover how the playwright used a variety of material from many literary and other sources and drew it together into a remarkably successful unified dramatic production. He still used blank verse, of course, but now was capable of a new lyrical beauty in the iambic pentameter form, particularly in the love speeches of Juliet. The rimed couplet spoken by Romeo and Benvolio became for the writer a deft instrument to satirize, very gently but effectively, an entire literary convention. The sonnet he introduced briefly, and with remarkable success, at a critical moment in the play. The wit passages of Romeo and Mercutio became devices not only to entertain but to establish characterizations and to change the play's mood.

Shakespeare worked conservatively through conventions to new ideas and new forms. The convention of "courtly love," a fascinating and radical elitist set of ideas and rules of behavior governing love relationships, was well known to Shakespeare's contemporaries. The portrayal of characters affected by the artificialities of this convention was therefore not original with Shakespeare, although he added new dimensions to its dramatic use. The convention served as a workable vehicle to establish dramatic contrasts: Romeo quickly undergoes a transformation, credible for us, the audience, because we saw him as a courtly lover who, when prompted by Juliet, forgoes manners for serious action. Just as important, courtly love in history provided new psychological and ethical responses toward love as emotion and passion. "Romeo and Juliet" capitalizes on these responses and the love-death relationship in the play contributes new and richer possibilities for those seeking to understand the complex world of love.

In a detailed study of *Romeo and Juliet* we naturally are interested in the playwright's composition technique. We are fortunate in having available the competently written source which Shakespeare very carefully and without condescension adapted. In Arthur Brooke's narrative poem, "The Tragicall Historye of Romeus and Juliet," the playwright found his plot, his characters, suggestions for characterizations, imagery, and atmosphere, and he relied more heavily on this work than on any source for his other plays. Shakespeare, however, did make important changes in his source material which, when analyzed, reveal much about Shakespeare the craftsman and artist. We are justified, therefore, in carefully examining the Arthur Brooke story of the two famous lovers.

Finally, we must ask serious questions about the play's generic nature. Is it a tragedy or a comedy? What part does comedy have in this story which ends in the deaths of the two lovers? Are the characters tragic or pathetic? We do not wish simply to discover a basic definition of tragedy or comedy or pedantically to catalogue the play in a simplistic category. We are interested in audience response. At tragedy must we only weep, or at comedy only laugh? Are our sympathies toward the hero and heroine respect or pity? How do the various incidents of the play, serious or comic, affect our final response? How does the language affect it? These questions at least deserve consideration to help us in identifying our own responses to the work.

Although this study concerns itself technically with style and with the conventions influencing style, it must not conclude with an impression that *Romeo and Juliet* is here considered an incomplete work, or an immature work, or simply an experiment with form and language. The play is, of course, one of the most popular literary creations of all time. It is also technically a successful fusion of comedy and tragedy, of the lyrical and the dramatic, of the conventional and of the real. It is, above all, a beautiful story of two lovers and the triumph of their love, a story which never will be relegated solely to classroom study.

5

STRUCTURE AND STYLE

Even in his first reading of *Romeo and Juliet* a student becomes aware that Shakespeare is taking pleasure in displaying his skill and versatility as a poet. The play is in large degree an experiment in the use of language and verse form for dramatic goals: it contains three sonnets; the rimed couplets spoken in the first scene by Benvolio and Montague, preparing the reader for Romeo's more extensive use of rimed couplets when he speaks to Benvolio; Mercutio's poetic trip into Queen Mab's fairy world, and his wit; and Friar Lawrence's blank verse descriptions of the morning and the herbs and weeds, in which even he grows eloquent, and at times perhaps tedious. The poetry of *Romeo and Juliet* is of some importance and therefore deserves a separate investigation.

Romeo and Juliet can be divided structurally into two large dramatic movements, whose perimeters are determined by the love relationship that develops between the two principals. The first movement of action ends in the balcony scene when Romeo and Juliet exchange vows and each makes the decision to share the other's love and fate. After a brief transition in II, iii, in the speech of Friar Lawrence, the action of the second movement begins with Romeo's entrance.

The two parts of the play differ in many ways. The first part characterizes Romeo and Juliet as searching, each in a special way, for what they find when they touch hands. After their exchange of vows in the balcony scene they are changed, and can no longer return to what they were. The dramatic pace of the first movement is somewhat leisurely, with the reader's interest directed first to the feud, then to Romeo's love concerns, to Mercutio's long speech about Queen Mab, and finally to the feast. After the balcony scene each bit of stage action, to be acceptable, must now relate to the central action of the play, the love story as it evolves within the context of the feud.

The differences found in the characterization and dramatic pace of the two movements of action are not as prominent as the difference found in the poetry Shakespeare employs for some of his principals, particularly Romeo. His use of language and verse form for Romeo in the first two acts places on this play a distinction that sets it apart from most of his others. We can almost call this great experiment with language a *tour de force* except for the implication in this term of something less than success. The experiment succeeds because Shakespeare deftly creates the atmospheric context within which the language can move. Romeo half-humorously affects a pose of the courtly lover and uses language befitting his image of that lover, an ironic parody of his later real self. In the beginning of the play when he first enters, Romeo speaks with Benvolio about the feud: "Why then, O brawling love, O loving hate,/O anything of nothing first created." (I, i, 176–177.) In his next speech he complains of his frustrations in love:

> Grief of mine own lie heavy in my breast,
> Which thou wilt propagate to have it press'd
> With more of thine. This love that thou hast shown
> Doth add more grief to too much of mine own.   (I, i, 186–189)

This is not realistic dialogue like, for instance, the speech which begins the next scene, with Capulet speaking to County Paris: "But Montague is bound as well as I/ In penalty alike, and 'tis not hard, I think/ For men so old as we to keep the peace." (I, ii, 1–3.) Romeo retains his affectations of speech and manner up to and including the scene at the balcony.

It is significant that only in her first sonnet speech with Romeo is Juliet given a stylized speech. In the balcony scene Romeo continues to speak in couplets for most of his dialogue, but Juliet does not turn again to rime. She is treated realistically from the beginning. Her speeches are made delightfully humorous by her self-indulgent consciousness of her own words and images in expressing her newly discovered feelings. In the balcony scene Juliet speaks without mannerisms while Romeo is self-conscious still in many of his lines. Juliet asks

Romeo to "not impute this yielding to light love," and Romeo speaks with his usual flourishes: "Lady, by yonder blessed moon I vow,/ That tips with silver all these fruit-tree tops." (II, ii, 107–108.) Juliet interrupts with scarcely concealed impatience: "O swear not by the moon." Romeo asks: "What shall I swear by?" After her next speech Romeo again begins: "If my heart's dear love." Again Juliet interrupts: "Well, do not swear." (II, ii, 108, 111, 116, 117.) For this moment she seems so delighted by the occasion she scarcely can listen to him. Her language realistically portrays her emotional excitement.

Following the scene at the balcony, Mercutio and Benvolio think that Romeo is his old self. He no longer needs a pose to affect emotions; his feelings are real and require no advertisement and, indeed, must remain his alone. His game now is dissimulation and his wit is turned outward to cover what is within. From now on Romeo speaks in blank verse and the next movement in action begins. No longer does Shakespeare need his rimes and rhetorical flourishes.

Romeo and Juliet begins with a sonnet. Chorus enters and speaks the Prologue, which explains the situation existing in Verona as the play opens, announces the feud and explains that "From forth the fatal loins of these two foes/ A pair of star-crossed lovers take their life." (Prologue, 5–6.) At the beginning of Act II, just after the two have met and prior to the scene at the balcony, Chorus enters for the last time, his speech another sonnet, to summarize briefly what has happened and to anticipate what is to come. These poems are not the conventional sonnets we recognize from Shakespeare's sonnet cycle. They are, first of all, descriptive poems designed to introduce and later to advance the play. But they are nonetheless different. The first is descriptive only and announces this plan:

> The fearful passage of their death-marked love . . .
> . . . Is now the two hours' traffic of our stage.　　　　(Prologue, 9, 12.)

The second sonnet speaks of emotion and thereby arrives closer to a conventional sonnet expression with these lines: "And she steals love's sweet bait from fearful hooks," (II, Prologue, 8) and the final couplet:

> But passion lends them power, time means, to meet,
> Temp'ring extremities with extreme sweet.　　　　(II, Prologue, 13–14)

Neither is a true Shakespearean sonnet. Each serves a minor dramatic function and both can be dispensed with, as they often are, in dramatic productions.

Another sonnet, a dialogue, appears at a crucial place in the play, the moment when Romeo and Juliet meet. For a brief time Romeo has observed Juliet and he now moves across the dance floor to speak to her:

ROMEO: If I profane, with my unworthiest hand
    This holy shrine, the gentle sin is this:
  My lips, two blushing pilgrims, ready stand
    To smooth that rough touch with a tender kiss.
JULIET: Good pilgrim, you do wrong your hand too much,
    Which mannerly devotion shows in this;
  For saints have hands that pilgrims' hands do touch,
    And palm to palm is holy palmers' kiss.
ROMEO: Have not saints lips, and holy palmers too?
JULIET: Ay, pilgrim, lips that they must use in prayer.
ROMEO: Oh, then, dear saint, let lips do what hands do!
    They pray; grant thou, lest faith turn to despair.
JULIET: Saints do not move, though grant for prayers' sake.
ROMEO: Then move not while my prayers' effect I take.   (I, v, 92–106)

In the next lines he kisses her twice, the action a continuation of the emotions aroused in the dialogue but no longer part of the stylized mood established by the sonnet.

The sonnet quoted accomplishes several purposes. All the action to this point had been in anticipation of the meeting of the two principals, and the sonnet form appears to be an appropriate instrument of expression for this crucial scene. The dialogue is similar to that of the wit contest Romeo later has with Mercutio but in the lovers' scene the words are more serious and the stakes are higher. The lovers seem to enjoy the sustaining of the pilgrim and palmer metaphor which Romeo initiates, and each advances a syllogism, "if such and such is so, then such is so," followed by reasons explaining its conclusion. Each character is defined for the other and they discover quickly that they are meeting on equal grounds. The scene is brief, but like Mercutio's wound, " 'tis enough, 'twill serve," and their fates are sealed.

Dramatically the moment is a pause and during it nothing exists outside their confined experience of pleasure and wonder. The other dancers pause in their dancing, the world for an instant ceases to move. Like any other stylized expression the sonnet creates an objective stance to a moment of emotion and, like the symbolic fourth wall of a play's setting, an aesthetic distance is created which allows critical perception. We are capable of enjoying their emotions, this "love at first sight," with a sense of credibility that allows us to accept all the events which follow. And the moment is eighteen lines only, the sonnet and the four lines providing Romeo his opportunity for his first kisses. A dramatic impact is created by the brevity itself; only in Juliet's final lines before her suicide does Shakespeare accomplish so much in such a short space.

Finally there is the wit contest of Mercutio and Romeo, placed strategically in the play on the morning after the Romeo-Juliet meeting at

Juliet's balcony. His previous conversations with Romeo left Mercutio remembering the lovesick youth willing only to grieve over his frustrated affair with Rosaline. Although Benvolio and he are not aware of Juliet, they notice immediately the new Romeo who stands before them. Mercutio issues the challenge in prose:

MERCUTIO: Sure, wit, follow me this jest now till thou hast worn out thy pump, that, when the single sole of it is worn, the jest may remain, after the wearing, solely singular.
ROMEO: O single-soled jest, solely singular for the singleness.
MERCUTIO: Come between us, good Benvolio! My wits faints.   (II, iv, 61–67)

After further dialogue Mercutio exclaims:

Why, is not this better now than groaning for love? Now art thou sociable, art thou Romeo; now art thou what thou art, by art as well as nature.
(II, iv, 88–91)

According to Mercutio, Romeo has returned to himself. The audience knows that Romeo has shed his courtly lover cloak and presumably his pretenses, his "groaning for love," but, the audience also knows that he is no longer the Romeo Mercutio seems to recognize.

QUESTIONS

Discuss the irony of this scene. After having met Juliet, why is Romeo not portrayed as lovesick? What is the difference between his previous speeches about Rosaline and his conversation now with Mercutio? Why doesn't he mention his newly found love, Juliet, to his friends?

From this point on the play's dialogue is in blank verse. The poetic experiments are over now that Romeo has accepted his rightful place in his drama with Juliet. The play must then proceed, in blank verse, to its promised conclusion.

THE CONVENTION OF COURTLY LOVE

Shakespeare has carefully prepared his audience for Romeo's entrance in the first scene of *Romeo and Juliet* by a brief dialogue between old Montague and Benvolio in a meeting at which Lady Montague is present. Romeo's friend, Benvolio, tells Montague and Lady Montague that he has seen their son walking early in the morning in an isolated place "underneath the grove of sycamore/ That westward rooteth from his city side." (I, i, 121–122.) Montague follows this comment by repeating that he had heard that "Many a morning hath he there been seen,/ With tears augmenting the fresh morning's dew" (I, i, 131–132.) and that at the rise of the sun he "Away from light steals home . . ./ And private in his chamber pens himself,/ . . . And makes himself an artificial night." (I, i, 137–140.) A few lines later Romeo enters and, to allow Benvolio to determine Romeo's grievance, old Montague and Lady Montague depart. The dialogue that follows between Benvolio and Romeo is highly formal, particularly in Romeo's lines, all in rimed couplets:

> Alas that love, whose view is muffled still,
> Should without eyes see pathways to his will! (I, i, 171–172)

Romeo, in highly mannered paradoxes, describes the fight that occurred between the two families in the first part of the scene, using phrases such as "brawling love," "O loving hate," "heavy lightness," "bright smoke," "cold fire," "sick health." Throughout the discussion he assumes the pose of the sad lover who, because of a mistress to whom he is devoted and who is unresponsive to his suit, cannot find surcease to his sorrow:

> She'll not be hit
> With Cupid's arrow. She hath Dian's wit,
> And, in strong proof of chastity well armed,
> From love's weak childish bow she lives uncharmed.   (I, i, 208–211)

He is in despair not only because of her inaccessibility but because her beauty is such he cannot find her equal and therefore never will be able to forget her.

In examining this important introduction to Romeo the reader notices specific deliberate moves by the playwright. Romeo has assumed a highly affected pose and the author is, of course, gently making fun of him because he seems to be taking the pose seriously. The reader is aware also that the hero has enough intelligence, wit, and charm to realize that it is a pose. Part of the reader's delight is his understanding that in the course of the play Romeo will be divested of the trappings of the pose (another example of Shakespeare's dramatic use of the unveiling of self-deception). But many of the members of the Elizabethan audience recognized another feature of the playwright's art: Romeo is following the format of the highly sophisticated and artificial "courtly love" convention that was a cultural and literary phenomenon of some of the later medieval and Renaissance courts. In this and other scenes up to the balcony scene Romeo lives and acts on this artificial level, his affectations betrayed by his mannered language. In the balcony scene Juliet cuts through all self-deception and poses to the real stance of love, awakens him, and at the end of the scene we see a new mature Romeo. But our picture of this new man is seen against the "courtly lover" image of the previous scenes. The rest of the play develops this maturity of Romeo, but always with our memory of the immature and adolescent Romeo who began the play. Involved in our understanding of this scene is the conception of what a "courtly lover" is and the part the convention of courtly love plays in our understanding of the character Romeo and the play. What is courtly love and, specifically, as a literary convention what part does it play in this work? What is Shakespeare satirizing in his portrait of Romeo in these first scenes? What does the convention do to our response to the central situation and the conclusion of the play?

Courtly love is one of the most curious literary and dramatic conventions used by Elizabethan writers. It established and codified to an explicit degree the relationship between a lover and his lady; it proposed to dictate rules of behavior a lover must follow during courtship; it suggested attitudes the lover must take toward his lady, her husband, the institution of marriage, and the moral as well as spiritual problems implicit in this act of devotion and in a consummation of the love that developed. It exalted passion, commitment based on a true love relationship, and sacrifice, the effect of that commitment. It proposed ideals of behavior and propriety which became accepted as ideals for the Renaissance man, the Elizabethan courtier, as it did for the works of the Elizabethan dramatist.

The convention had its first clear and explicit literary expression in the courts of Eleanor of Aquitaine and her daughter Marie, Countess of Champagne, in twelfth-century France. According to scholars of the movement, various poets and court figures prepared the ground for the great literary exponents of the courtly love ideal. The first was the poet Ovid, who lived in Rome at the time of Emperor Augustus and who wrote the most important early treatises on love in his *The Art of Love, The Cure for Love,* and *Amours.* All the medieval writers on love were indebted to him. In eleventh-century Spain, itinerant poets carried the message to the Moorish and Christian courts; more important, the Provençal troubador poets expressed the sentiments later to be embodied in the code of etiquette of courtly love. But it was in the courts of Eleanor and Marie that the code assumed the proportions of a formal and almost institutionalized statement in the manifestos of Andreas Capellanus and the literary expression of the works of Chretien de Troyes. Its influence was very strong in the next three centuries and permeated literature in Italy in the works of Dante and Petrarch, in France in the works of Ronsard and the Pleiades, and finally in England in the poetry of the sonnet writers from 1560 until Shakespeare's time and in the stories and plays of John Lyly, Robert Greene, and other contemporaries of Shakespeare.

This summary does not pretend to suggest the complexities of the various threads that wove through the literature of three centuries in at least three countries or to show the effect of the courtly love ideal on the conduct and ethics of the polite society of these countries. The interest here is only in the ideal as used by Shakespeare in his description of Romeo as a lover-hero and in the way it was connected with certain dramatic and poetic stylistic conventions, such as the writing of the sonnet. In this very general treatment of the convention, therefore, much will be left out: the neoplatonic idealism as revealed in the poetry of Petrarch and Dante and later Italian and French writers; the importance of the adultery theme to the courtly love tradition; the so-called "liebestod," or death wish, which, according to many writers (Denis de Rougemont is a popular exponent of this theme), accompanies the courtly ideal of love, particularly in the works of Chretien de Troyes. These ideas, attractive as they are in themselves, do not apply closely enough to *Romeo and Juliet* that we need study them to better understand the play. To some degree the death wish thesis is appropriate and in time will be mentioned, but the major concern of this approach to the play is Shakespeare's treatment of Romeo, Romeo's attitude toward love in general, and his changing attitudes toward Juliet during the course of the play. It may be worthwhile, therefore, to look more closely at a few of the premises of the courtly love tradition that seem to have influenced the writing of the play.

The most useful introduction to courtly love is in *The Art of Courtly Love*, by Andreas Capellanus, who was court chaplain to Marie, Countess of Champagne, and possibly to her mother, Eleanor of Aquitaine, as well. It describes with great seriousness a set of rules of behavior for those lovers in the polite courts of northern France who aspire to a relationship of passion and love. A curious paradox in this work is that the writer is a churchman who reveals in the last chapter, in a complete reversal in his comments on love between man and woman, that a physical relationship must finally not conflict with man's spiritual obligations. The sections preceding this conclusion are, however, deeply concerned with descriptions of relationships which rely solely on the passion of love.

In the medieval period the doctrine of the Catholic Church ignored the fact of passion in the theology of the church; in general, it condemned passion as such, admitting sexuality only if "innocent," that is, without strong sexual desire, and only if conducted within the bonds of marriage. C. S. Lewis in *The Allegory of Love* states:

> The general impression left on the medieval mind by its official teachers was that all love—at least all such passionate and exalted devotion as a courtly poet thought worthy of the name—was more or less wicked. The writer of courtly love, however, is writing of a "passion" which works a chemical change upon appetite and affection and turns them into a thing different from either. About "passion" in this sense Thomas Aquinas has naturally nothing to say—as he has nothing to say about the steam engine. He had not heard of it. It was only coming into existence in his time, and finding its first expression in the poetry of courtly love.[1]

The new attitude toward love is seen most clearly in a categorical judgment of marriage made by the Countess of Champagne (quoted by Andreas Capellanus):

> We declare and we hold as firmly established that love cannot exert its powers between two people who are married to each other. For lovers give each other everything freely, under no compulsion of necessity, but married people are in duty bound to give in to each other's desires and deny themselves to each other in nothing.[2]

Romantic love is the goal but, strangely enough, as an aid to the development of character:

Besides, how does it increase a husband's honor if after the manner of lovers he enjoys the embraces of his wife, since the worth of character of neither can be increased thereby, and they seem to have nothing more than they already had a right to? And we say the same thing for still another reason, which is that a precept of love tells us that no woman, even if she is married, can be crowned with the reward of the King of Love unless she is seen to be enlisted in the service of Love himself outside the bonds of wedlock.[3]

These declarations of the Countess of Champagne were written in 1174, according to the account of Andreas Capellanus, and were reprinted later by him accompanied by many stories as illustrations and many rules and judgments pronounced by the court. These judgments embody the essential features of the courtly love ethos, the parts Lewis lists as "Humility, Courtesy, Adultery and the Religion of Love."[4] It may be convenient to use these categories as definitions for our study of courtly love in *Romeo and Juliet*.

Humility for the courtly lover was manifested by his willingness to assume and carry out the demands of his loved one, particularly of patience. The lover must not only accept but must also desire that the difficulty of attainment of his love be a factor; one of the stated rules of love is that "the easy attainment of his love makes it of little value; difficulty of attainment makes it prized"[5] and "a true lover considers nothing good except what he thinks will please his beloved."[6] The rule of courtesy is, of course, a necessary qualification for any true knight worthy of love. Other rules insist on the lover's concern for the beloved: "Every act of a lover ends in the thought of the beloved."[7]

QUESTIONS

In what respects does Romeo observe humility and courtesy in the mention of his meetings with Rosaline? In his first meeting with Juliet?

The third rule, adultery, is at first glance scarcely relevant to Shakespeare's play. Without seeking to force a connection, or to strive to prove that Shakespeare's play received its plot suggestion from the courtly love theory, this may be said: although adultery plays no part in Shakespeare's drama, there is a relationship between the love of Romeo and Juliet and an adulterous love which deserves a brief mention. Juliet insists on marriage, but the marriage must remain secret. When we consider adultery without its moral implications and gauge it in the way it affects participants psychologically, we tend to place some importance on the secretive nature of the relationship. Traditionally, adultery has been a violation of social as well as moral law and therefore has pitted its participants against the conservative segments of society. This fact of secrecy was an important element of the dramatic and suspense features of courtly love literature. Andreas'

Rule No. XIII states: "When made public love rarely endures."[8] The love of Romeo and Juliet was secret because of their families' feud; it was portrayed by the dramatist as being even stronger and more passionate because in it was embodied their defiance of the society around them. One may be tempted to say that they preferred their love to remain private. In one sense the adultery thesis is irrelevant in that the lovers were enjoying the benefit of an adulterous relationship without the necessity of the situation itself. The psychology behind the arguments of Andreas, and presumably Marie, for adultery was that adultery is necessary in order to establish a true passionate relationship, divested of any security consideration. Marriage for Juliet was taken to be an outward symbol of Romeo's sincerity; its security therefore was the assurance of a true commitment. The future, represented in conventional marriages by contracts and a dowry, was not considered by the lovers. Adultery then is not a necessary ingredient to the dramatic structure, but the fact of a secret liaison is important in the delineation of the intensity of the affair and the poignancy of their love.

QUESTIONS

Does the secret nature of the love affect our attitudes toward it? Would you have felt the same toward a dutiful love for Paris from Juliet?

One piece of evidence points to a closer relationship of early troubadour poetry and Shakespeare's work. The love poetry of the troubadours contained many beautiful examples of the *aubade,* or "morning song," traditionally sung by the watchmen awakening lovers who must part in the early morning after a night spent together. A particular touch of pathos is achieved by the fact that the affair cannot be observed publicly. The beautiful scene between Romeo and Juliet following their wedding night achieves its effectiveness for many of the same reasons as did the aubade of the troubadours.

QUESTION

How does the aubade accomplish the pathos of their parting?

The final category, the religion of love, is complex in its nature, perhaps inconclusive in its thematic import, and in some respects is an indication that a paradoxical element lies at the base of the convention itself. This "religion" associates the desire for the beloved with the desire for something beyond the beloved, for an experience transcending the immediate love experience, perhaps even for "a rapturous embrace of death in the name of love,"[9] to quote a writer on love conventions, Leonora Leet Brodwin. She claims that the lover does not, however, have a "love of death," as Denise de Rougemont,[10] suggests, "but of the Absolute, the Infinite, all that is beyond the sphere of mortal contingency. Rather he despises death because it is the final proof of the hated contingency and limitations of human life from which he wishes to disassociate himself."[11] From her study of courtly love her conclusions are that:

> Courtly Love is a peculiar outgrowth of a broad Platonic tradition, that it is directed to union with the Absolute, that it adores and desires the beloved as a manifestation of the Absolute, that such a desire is defeated by temporal possession as an end in itself but is purified and ennobled through the intensification of obstruction, and that, in its tragic form, it achieves its true end, union with the Absolute, through a paradoxical embrace of death.[12]

QUESTION

In what ways does *Romeo and Juliet* indicate that it contains an expression of the "religion of love"?

The courtly love code is important for its recognition and romanticization of the passionate nature of love and for its set of rules for a court society in the complex area of love relationships. The entire Western world, as Rougemont and others have demonstrated, and, in particular, the literary world of Shakespeare and other writers, have benefited from this radical conception of love as passion. But the set of rules for the courtly lover has suffered another fate—that of satire. Shakespeare was sympathetically amused by the posture of the courtly lover who was thus self-conscious and self-indulgent in his love tribulations. In *Love's Labor's Lost* Shakespeare humorously exposes the superficial emotions of the King and his three dukes; in *As You Like It* Rosalind puts her lover Orlando through a parody of the required courtly love trials; in *Twelfth Night* the Duke assumes the genial posture of a courtly lover and is satirized thereby; in *Troilus and Cressida* the satire becomes less genial when the love achieves the reality of the physical relationship; in *Much Ado About Nothing* the comment on the courtly lover Claudio, although ambiguous, is still less than flattering. Shakespeare the dramatist recognized the dramatic possibilities in the courtly lover attitude and often exploited the concept for purposes of humor. But he was not fooled, and the courtly lover achieved importance only because he was a convenient dramatic foil to the real lover.

Romeo is a courtly lover who becomes a real lover. In this we see the comment on the courtly lover; more important, we seen Romeo achieve maturity. But as interesting to our study of the play is the effect that the description of the courtly lover has on our conception of the character Romeo and on the play itself. Present in this con-

vention was a style attractive to the imagination and its romantic subject. Romeo has the sophistication and imagination to strike the pose
of the courtly lover and thus distinguishes himself from his peers, the
more worldly Mercutio and the less daring Benvolio, and borrows
sympathy and charm from his actions. He is willing to take a pose, to
play the game, as it were. When the game changes to something more
real, he transfers some of the courtly love ideals to the real love relationship. Courtly love gives a quality to his actions as well as to the
play's. We realize then that in his gentle satire of the courtly love
convention Shakespeare actually used it for a reexamination of love
itself. Romeo's love is on a plane above the lover of the others, even
if the exact manifestation of his love is artificial. The same level is
retained, however, when he ascends to Juliet's balcony. Only the
manifestation has changed.

QUESTIONS

How does Mercutio's attitude toward love compare with Romeo's love
for Rosaline? With his love for Juliet?

Even more important, when he ascends to the plane of the real
lover, Romeo obeys a more profound mandate of courtly love in his
acceptance of love as "religion" (to use the vocabulary of those who
write of this phenomenon). His full surrender to Juliet, his fate an
acceptance of his commitment to her, includes the dangers of death.
He tells Juliet:

> My life were better ended by their hate
> Than death prorogued [deferred], wanting of thy love. (II, ii, 77–78)

And when Juliet tells him

> My bounty is as boundless as the sea,
> My love as deep; the more I give to thee,
> The more I have, for both are infinite. (II, ii, 133–135)

we feel she speaks for them both, and most certainly for the Romeo
who dies with her in the tomb.

Courtly love in its various forms was a departure point for this
dramatist who saw through these many forms to the primitive nature
of love itself, for even though he was able to exploit many of the
features of courtly love for dramatic purposes, he was yet able to
conform to its more romantic and noble message. The judgment of
Brodwin is that "*Romeo and Juliet* is not a tract against courtly love,
but a supreme expression of its spiritual mystique."[13] The affectatious
promises of the courtly lover who rhetorically consigns his fate to his
loved one are ironically transposed to fateful predictions of the deaths
that must climax their triumphant love.

THE SOURCE

In writing *Romeo and Juliet* Shakespeare used one source primarily, a long poetic narrative by Arthur Brooke, *The Tragicall Historye of Romeus and Juliet* (1562). Brooke himself used one source primarily, a 1559 French adaptation by Pierre Boiastuau of a novella written in 1554 by the Italian writer, Matteo Bandello. And Bandello had his primary source, a story by Luigi Da Porto published in 1530, and so on. The story is an old one, with part of the legend of the two lovers dating as far back as the fifth century. Early versions of it included the major plot and many of the same characters and incidents we recognize from Shakespeare's play: the family feud, the clandestine lovers, and the Friar. With each new version came additions, so when Brooke started his poem he found in his models Capulet's tyranny over his daughter in insisting on her marriage to Paris; the acceptance of a Montague at the feast of the Capulets; the Nurse's involvement in the marriage and her final betrayal of Juliet; the apothecary's role in giving poison to Romeo; the Friar's inability to deliver the letter to Romeo; and other incidents. Shakespeare was fortunate in having a source with all the material he needed—not only the plot and separate incidents in the story, but also hints as to characterization, imagery and atmosphere. Since he used Brooke liberally, it is to his work we need to turn for our comparison of source and play.

Brooke's poem, a sequence of rimed couplets of iambic lines alternately twelve and fourteen syllables in length, is often verbose and tedious, a "leaden work which Shakespeare transmuted to gold,"[1] as Geoffrey Bullough, a prominent Shakespeare scholar on sources, stated. According to Bullough, Brooke does succeed in creating scenes of "homely realism" and in drawing a rich picture of Verona and city life,[2] material which Shakespeare found useful. Brooke also created attitudes toward the lovers and the other characters in his poem which Shakespeare was able to utilize, even though the reader may be unable to anticipate such an influence when he reads the prose "Address to the Reader" which prefaces Brooke's poem. In this passage Brooke announces that he will describe:

> A couple of unfortunate lovers thralling themselves to unhonest desire, neglecting the authority and advice of parents and friends, conferring their principal counsels with drunken gossips, and superstitious friars (the naturally fit instruments of unchastity) attempting all adventures of peril for the attaining of their wished lust, using auriculer confession (the key of whoredom and treason) for furtherance of their purpose, abusing the honorable name of lawful marriage to cloak the shame of stolen contracts; finally, by all means of unhonest life, hasting to most unhappy death.[3]

The lovers' "most unhappy death" is the natural result of the "unhonest life" and "unhonest desire," and the reader is led to believe that Brooke will describe the lovers unsympathetically. After all, they neglected "the authority and advice of parents and friends" and succumbed to "wished lust." In actuality Brooke manipulates his plot so that the lovers' actions are excusable, and perhaps even praiseworthy. The love of the two as described by Brooke may be labeled by some as foolhardy and impetuous but not criminal, and if "a lust of the blood," one acceptance and honorable by normal standards. Romeo in the Brooke version is a man of integrity and acts with a composure not shared by others in the play (Capulet, for instance); Juliet is portrayed as a modest young girl who observes the proprieties even if she rejects society's sanctions. They are legitimate hero and heroine.

It is Brooke's passage about fate or fortune that appears to illustrate his objective stated in the "Address to the Reader." He placed even more emphasis on Fortune than he inherited from his sources. The Shakespearean scholar, H. B. Charleton, cites fifteen passages in Brooke's poem which include the word "fortune," such as "froward fortune," "fortune's cruel will," "false fortune," and "fierce fortune."[4] The imagery of fortune's wheel is prominent as well:

> My Juliet, my love, my only hope and care,
> To you I purpose not as now, with length of words declare,
> The diverseness and also the accidents so strange,
> Of frail inconstant Fortune, that delighteth still in change,
> Who, in a moment, heaves her friends up to the height
> Of her swift turning slippery wheel, then fleets her friendship straight.
> O wondrous change, even with the twinkling of an eye,
> Whom else her self had rashly set, in pleasant play so high,
> The same in great despite, down headlong does she throw.... (1543–1551)

In all these references Fortune appears as a force as if by plan, creating accidents and coincidences leading to the tragic end.

Although Shakespeare retained references to fortune, its actual influence does not appear to be as prominent. In Shakespeare's play, when Juliet reacts to the news of Romeo's exile, she exclaims:

> O Fortune, Fortune! all men call thee fickle.
> If thou art fickle, what dost thou with him
> That is renown'd for faith? (III, v, 60–62)

Then she adds:

> Be fickle, Fortune
> For then I hope thou wilt not keep him long
> But send him back. (III, v, 62–64)

QUESTIONS

In what way is Shakespeare's use of Fortune different from Brooke's? Does he use it for didactic purposes? Is his Fortune capricious and arbitrary?

Romeo and Juliet have premonitions of their fate. As Romeo enters the house of Capulet to attend the party where he is soon to meet Juliet, he pauses before the door:

> my mind misgives
> Some consequence yet hanging in the stars
> Shall bitterly begin his fearful date
> With this night's revels, and expire the term
> Of a despised life closed in my breast
> By some vile forfeit of untimely death.
> But he that hath the steerage of my course,
> Direct my sail. (I, iv, 106–113)

After the wedding night, as Romeo is leaving her, Juliet looks down upon him from her balcony:

> O God! I have an ill-divining soul,
> Methinks I see thee, now thou art so low,
> As one dead in the bottom of a tomb. (III, v, 54–56)

QUESTIONS

How do these passages affect the play? How do these words affect the characterization of the two?

There are other reasons for these premonitions of misfortune. In the balcony scene Juliet, fearful of her own impetuosity in love and the suddenness of their marriage compact, says to Romeo:

> Although I joy in thee
> I have no joy of this contract tonight.
> It is too rash, too unadvis'd, too sudden,
> Too like the lightning, which doth cease to be
> Ere one can say "It lightens."   (II, ii, 116–120)

QUESTIONS

What additions has Shakespeare given to the fatalism imagined in the form of premonitions by the two lovers? In what way is this a suggestion that the two may be responsible for what happens to them?

Fortune seems arbitrary or capricious in two crucial moments in Shakespeare's play: when Friar John fails to deliver Friar Lawrence's letter announcing the subterfuge death of Juliet, and at the play's end when Juliet awakens only minutes after Romeo has poisoned himself. Shakespeare followed the sources closely in both incidents.

QUESTIONS

In what ways do these "accidents" affect our judgment of the play? Is the play less of a tragedy, for instance, because of them?

The feud is another instrument of Fortune. Shakespeare accepts the feud in most essential details from Brooke but differs in his seriousness of its treatment. Brooke takes no attitude toward the feud except to announce it; between the two families "black hate and rancor grew." (I, 34) At Capulet's banquet when Romeo enters:

> The Capulets disdain the presence of their foe
> Yet they suppress their stirred ire, the cause I do not know.
> Perhaps to offend their guests the courteous knights are loth
> Perhaps they stay from sharp revenge, dreading the Prince's wrath.
>   (184–188)

Brooke uses the feud as background to the lovers' story and the central obstacle to their lovers' fulfillment. Shakespeare makes it more human, often even humorous. The play opens with the fight between factions of each house, and Lady Montague and Lady Capulet try to dissuade their husbands from fighting. Capulet calls for a sword and Lady Capulet is scornful: "A crutch, a crutch! Why call you for a sword?" (I, i, 76.) Montague's wife tells Montague: "Thou shalt not stir one foot to seek a foe." (I, i, 80.) There is Capulet's refusal to allow Tybalt to drive Montague from the Capulet party. The feud is only serious when Mercutio and Tybalt are killed and Romeo is exiled, but the reader's attitude toward it remains detached, concentrated so vividly as it is on the love story. The feud victimizes the lovers, but it can be argued that, unlike the evil of Iago, which destroys another love relationship, it does not capture the dramatic imagination in a significant degree.

QUESTIONS

Is the fact that the feud is not more prominent an argument of the play's weakness? Is the feud only a silly example of the foolishness of society? Can it be taken as another instrument of fortune?

Shakespeare relies heavily on Brooke in the plot and descriptions, and makes his significant changes primarily in style, poetry and dramatic structure. For instance, Shakespeare changes the time period of the incidents. In Brooke, Romeus and Juliet do not speak for a week after their first meeting, although they see each other daily. After their marriage Brooke gives them a summer of married love before Romeus's exile. Shakespeare, however, compresses his entire action to five days; in one day's time the two are married, Romeo kills Tybalt and is exiled, and the lovers share their wedding night.

QUESTION

How does this compression of time in the structure of the play influence the theme and the final effect of the play?

Shakespeare borrowed characterizations from Brooke such as Capulet's habit of alternately pampering and tyrannizing over Juliet. The Nurse is another adaptation, the humor of her personality a direct loan from the early work. Brooke describes her as tedious, one of the Beldames who loves a "tedious long discourse." At her meeting with Romeus to learn of his plans for the marriage, she speaks of Juliet:

> A pretty babe (quoth she), it was when it was young,
> Lord how it could full prettily have prated with its tongue,
> A thousand times and more I laid her on my lap,
> And clapped her on the buttock soft and kissed where I did clap
> And gladder then was I of such a kiss forsooth,
> Than I had been to have a kiss of some old lechers mouth.
> And thus of Juliets youth began this prating nurse,
> And of her present state to make a tedious long discourse.
> For though he pleasure took in hearing of his love,
> The message answer seemed to him to be of more behove.   (653–662)

Similarly Shakespeare establishes the character of the Nurse in her first appearance when she describes Juliet to Lady Capulet, reminding her that Juliet was weaned on the day of the earthquake:

> And she was weaned (I never shall forget it),
> Of all the days of the year, upon that day;
> For I had then laid wormwood to my dug,
> Sitting in the sun under the dovehouse wall.
> My lord and you were then at Mantua.
> Nay, I do bear a brain. But, as I said,
> When it did taste the wormwood on the nipple
> Of my dug and felt it bitter, pretty fool,
> To see it teachy and fall out with the dug.   (I, iii, 24–32)

QUESTIONS

In what ways are the Nurse portraits similar? In what ways different?

Brooke included in his story the model for Rosaline who is not identified by name but is described:

> But she that from her youth fostered evermore
> With virtues food, and taught in school of wisdoms skillful lore,
> By answer did cut off the affections of his love,
> That he no more occasion had so vain a suit to move.
> So stern she was of cheer, (for all the pain he took)
> That in reward of toil, she would not give him a friendly look.
> And yet how much she did with constant mind retire
> So much the more his fervent mind was pricked forth by desire.   (65–72)

In Shakespeare's equivalent scene Benevolio asks Romeo: "Then she hath sworn that she will still live chaste?" And Romeo answers:

> She hath, and in that sparing makes huge waste;
> For beauty, starv'd with her severity,
> Cut beauty off from all posterity.
> She is too fair, too wise, wisely too fair,
> To merit bliss by making me despair.
> She hath forsworn to love, and in that vow
> Do I live dead that live to tell it now.   (I, i, 218–224)

QUESTIONS

What effect is gained by the use of rimed couplets for Romeo's speech? In what way is this speech similar to some of the sonnets in the section on sonnets? Is his verse similar in its effect to Brooke's?

In Brooke, Romeus has been courting the fair and chaste lady for many months but now in despair thinks of leaving Verona. He complains:

> Perhaps my eye once banished by absence from her sight,
> This fire of mine, that by her pleasant eye is fed
> Shall little and little wear away, and quite at last be dead. (86–88)

But he despairs of forgetting her and:

> He moans the day, he wakes the long and weary night,
> So deep has with piercing hand engraved her beauty bright
> Within his breast, and hath so mastered quite his heart
> That he of force must yield as thrall, no way is left to start. (93–96)

QUESTIONS

In Chapter 6 there were equivalent quotes from Shakespeare (I, i, 124–148). From what you learned of courtly love there, what features of this convention can be found in Brooke? What is the difference in reader response between a description of the hero conveyed by the relatives and friends of Romeo in Shakespeare and by a narrative description of him in Brooke?

A friend described in Brooke as the trustiest of Romeus's friends and "riper of his years" (102), the model for Benvolio, rebukes Romeus and persuades him to go to parties to test the beauty of his love against that of other girls of the town. Romeus agrees to this and, as in Shakespeare, at the feast discovers the person he is seeking.

The next crucial scene takes place at the festivities at the house of Capulet. Brooke describes Romeus's first view of Juliet:

> At length he saw a maid, right fair of perfect shape
> Which Theseus, of Paris would have chosen to their rape,
> Whom before he ever saw, for all she pleased him most.
> Within himself he said to her, thou justly may thee boast
> Of perfect shapes reknown, and Beauties sounding praise,
> Whose like nor hath, nor shall be seen, nor lives in our days. (197–202)

Juliet is now aware of him and his attitude to her and Romeus moves close to her:

> At one side of her chair, her lover Romeus
> And on the other side there sat one called Mercutio
> A courtier that everywhere was highly had in price
> For he was courteous of his speech, and pleasant of device
> Even as a Lion would among the lambs be bold,
> Such was among the bashful maids, Mercutio to behold.
> With friendly grip he seized fair Juliets snowish hand.
> A gift he had that nature gave him in his swathing band,
> That frozen mountain ice was never half so cold
> As were his hands, though never so near the fire he did them hold.
> As soon as had the knight the virgins right hand raught [reached]
> Within his trembling hand her left has loving Romeus caught. (253–264)

QUESTION

How did Shakespeare use these suggestions for his portrait of Mercutio?

By his trembling and blushing, Juliet knew Romeus's feelings for her and after a brief silence says, "O blessed be the time of thy arrival here." After an interruption caused by the dance, he is again near her and asks why his coming there was blessed. She answers:

Mercutio's icy hand had all too frozen mine
And of thy goodness thou again hast warmed it with thine.   (289–290)

Romeus responds:

For I of God crave, as price of pains forpast
To serve, obey, and honor you, so long as life shall last. . . .   (289–290)

But if my touched hand, have warmed you some deal,
Assure yourself the heat is cold, which in your hand you feel
Compared to such quick sparks and glowing furious gleade [gladness]
As from your beauties pleasant eye love caused to proceed
Which have so set on fire, each feeling part of mine,
That lo, my mind doth melt away, my outward parts do pine
And but thou help all whole, to ashes shall I turn,
Wherefore (alas) have pity on him, whom you do force to burn.   (301–308)

Juliet realizes she must part from Romeus:

His hand she clasped hard, and all her parts did shake,
When intensely with whispering voice thus did she answer make
You are no more your own (dear friend) than I am yours.   (311–313)

This ends their first conversation in Brooke. They are separated and, as in Shakespeare's version, each discovers the other's name and realizes the peril of the situation but realizes also that it is now too late.

QUESTION

In the pilgrim sonnet quoted in the section on sonnets, what hint did Shakespeare receive for this first meeting of the two?

In Brooke a week passed before they again spoke, although Romeus often passed by her window and she observed him. Finally on a moon-lit evening she noticed him below her balcony and spoke to him:

Oh Romeus (of your life) too reckless sure you are
That in this place, and at this time to hazard it you dare,
What if your deadly foes, my kinsmen, saw you here?
Like Lions wild, your tender parts asunder would they tear.
In grief and in disdain, I weary of my life,
With cruel hand my mourning heart would pierce with bloody knife.
For you mine own once dead, what joy should I have here?   (491–497)

Romeus answers:

> Fair lady my dame Juliet my life (quoth he)
> Even from my birth committed was to fatal sisters three.
> They may in spite of foes, draw forth my lively thread
> And they also, who so says nay, asunder may it shred.
> But who to attempt my life, his rage and force would bend,
> Perhaps should try unto his pain how I it could defend.
> Even if I love it so, but always, for your sake,
> A sacrifice to death I would my wounded corpse betake.   (499–506)

Juliet answers that "But as you suffer pain, so I do bear in part/ (Although it lessens not your grief), the half of all your smart." (527–528.) She continues:

> For if you do intend my honor to defile
> In error shall you wander still, as you have done this while,
> But if your throught be chaste, and have on virtue ground,
> If wedlock be the end and mark which your desire hath found ...
> ... Both me and mine I will all whole to you betake
> And following you where so you go, my fathers house forsake.   (533–540)

Romeus protests that his intentions are honorable and:

> Since Lady that you like to honor me so much,
> As to accept me for your spouse, I yield myself for such.   (553–554)

He tells her his plan to ask Friar Lawrence's advice the next day and he leaves. The next day Juliet confides in the Nurse who is sent to Romeus to learn the friar's advice. When he sees the Nurse Romeus announces the plans made for the marriage "On Saturday . . . She shall be shrived and married." (634)

In Shakespeare the identical scene is as follows:

> JULIET: If they [her kinsmen] do see thee, they will murder thee.
> ROMEO: Alack, there lies more peril in thine eye
>   Than twenty of their swords! Look thou but sweet
>   And I am proof against their enmity.
> JULIET: I would not for the world they saw thee here.
> ROMEO: I have night's cloak to hide me from their eyes;
>   And but thou love me, let them find me here.
>   My life were better ended by their hate
>   Than death prorogued [deferred], wanting of thy love.   (II, ii, 70–78)

After Juliet declares her love to Romeo and he begins to swear his vows, she speaks:

> **Juliet:** Well, do no swear. Although I joy in thee,
>   I have no joy of this contract tonight.
>   It is too rash, too unadvised, too sudden;
>   Too like the lightning, which doth cease to be
>   Ere one can say it lightens.   (II, ii, 116–120)

Juliet hears the Nurse, enters the house, and returns to the balcony quickly:

> **Juliet:** Three words, dear Romeo, and good night indeed.
>   If that thy bent of love be honorable,
>   Thy purpose marriage, send me word tomorrow,
>   By one that I'll procure to come to thee,
>   Where and what time thou will perform the rite.
>   And all my fortunes at thy foot I'll lay
>   And follow thee my lord throughout the world.   (II, ii, 143–148)

She is called within and returns a third time, despite the finality of her previous words. Then follows the final exchange of parting.

Here is a good example of a situation treated by both authors down to many details. A student can see similarities between the words of Brooke and those of Shakespeare, and yet a major difference of effect is obtained.

QUESTIONS

How did Shakespeare reach this effect? An answer may be found not only in differences in the style of the poetry itself, but in the characterizations and the excitement conveyed to us by the lovers as they find themselves alone for the first time. Discuss how Shakespeare manages to accomplish these effects. How is Juliet's characterization portrayed in these specific scenes?

In Brooke's work, the two return to their respective homes after the marriage vows to await evening. He describes this wait:

> How long these lovers thought the lasting of the day,
> Let other judge that wonted are like passions to assay.
> For my part, I do guess each hour seems twenty year
> So that I trust, if they might have (as of Alcmena we hear)
> The sun bond to their will, if they the heavens might guide,
> Black shade of night and doubled dark should straight all over hide.
>
>   (821–826)

In Shakespeare Juliet is alone waiting for Romeo:

> **Juliet:** Gallop apace, you fiery-footed steeds,
>   Toward Phoebus' lodging! Such a wagoner
>   As Phaeton would whip you to the west
>   And bring in cloudy night immediately.
>   Spread thy close curtain, love-performing night,
>   That runaways' eyes may wink, and Romeo
>   Leap to these arms untalked of and unseen.   (III, ii, 1–7)

In Brooke, Romeus arrives and he and Juliet embrace and talk until the Nurse becomes impatient, emerges from the bedroom and interrupts their conversation:

> Who takes not time (quoth she) when time well offered is,
> An other time shall seek for time, and yet of time shall miss,
> And when occasion serves, who so doth let it slip,
> Is worthy sure (if I might judge) of lashes with a whip.
> Wherefore, if each of you hath harmed the other so,
> And each of you hath been the cause of others wailed woe,
> Lo here a field, (she showed a fieldbed ready dight)
> Where you may, if you wish, in arms, revenge yourself by fight.   (891–898)

Shakespeare echoes the imagery of the Nurse's words in Juliet's speech while she waits for Romeo:

Juliet: Come, civil night,
> Thou sober-suited matron all in black,
> And learn me how to lose a winning match,
> Played for a pair of stainless maidenhoods.   (III, ii, 10–13)

QUESTION

What effect does the Nurse have on this important love scene?

Brooke tell us that:

> To light the waxen candles, the ancient nurse is pressed,
> Which Juliet had before prepared to be light,
> That she at pleasure might behold her husband's beauty bright.   (836–838)

Shakespeare has Juliet continue the wish for night to darken everything around her but he seems to have retained the idea of Romeo's beauty in Juliet's imagination:

Juliet: Come, night; come, Romeo; come, thou day in night;
> For thou wilt lie upon the wings of night
> Whiter than new snow upon a raven's back.   (III, ii, 17–19)

QUESTION

In both Brooke and Shakespeare we have reference to the physical body of Romeo. What is the difference?

As mentioned, Shakespeare compressed the time period between the wedding and Romeo's exile. In Brooke, the lovers continue their nightly meetings in Juliet's room throughout part of the summer:

> The summer of their bliss, doth last a month or twain
> But winters blast with speedy foot doth bring the fall again.   (949–950)

On one day in the fall the fight between the Montagues and the Capulets occurs which ends in the death of Tybalt and the exile of Romeus. On the eve of their parting Juliet begs to be allowed to go with him into exile. He dissuades her, saying he will arrange things so that he can return in four months and openly and without disguise take her away "as my wife and only companion, in garment of thine own." (1682) They again exchange vows and promises and:

Thus these two lovers pass away the weary night,
In pain and grief, not (as they wont) in pleasure and delight.
But now (somewhat too soon) in farthest East arose
Fair Lucifer, the golden star that Lady Venus chose,
Whose course appointed is, with speedy race to run,
A messenger of dawning day, and of the rising sun.   (1701–1706) . . .

. . . Then Romeus in arms his lady gan to fold,
With friendly kiss, and sorrowfully she gan her knight behold.
With solemne oath they both their sorrowful leave do take;
They swear no stormy troubles shall their steady friendship shake.
Then careful Romeus, again to cell returns,
And in her chamber secretly our joyless Juliet mourns.   (1715–1720)

In condensing the action by scheduling the fight on the day of the wedding, and by having Romeo come to Juliet after killing Tybalt, Shakespeare creates in this announced exile a poignant background to the lovers' feelings on their wedding night. Romeo's words have the note of warning, the implications and sentiment of the early troubadors' aubade. Juliet tells Romeo:

It was the nightingale and not the lark
That pierced the fearful hollow of thine ear.   (III, v, 2–3)

Romeo corrects her:

It was the lark, the herald of the morn;
No nightingale. Look, love, what envious streaks
Do lace the severing clouds in yonder East.
Night's candles are burnt out, and jocund day
Stands tiptoe on the misty mountaintops.
I must be gone and live, or stay and die.   (III, v, 6–11)

Finally, when he teases her by agreeing with her that it is not the lark and that he will welcome death, Juliet urges:

It is, it is! Hie hence, be gone, away!
It is the lark that sings so out of tune,
Straining harsh discords and unpleasing sharps. . . .   (III, v, 26–29)

. . . Some say the lark and loathed toad change eyes;
O, now I would they had changed voices too,
Since arm from arm that voice doth us affray,
Hunting thee hence with hunt's-up to the day.
O, now be gone! More light and light it grows.   (III, v, 31–35)

QUESTIONS

How did Shakespeare manage this scene successfully? Does Brooke succeed in conveying any of the feeling Shakespeare manages to attain?

Following the departure of Romeo, Lady Capulet and then Capulet enter Juliet's room to notify her of her coming wedding to Paris. Shakespeare kept much of what Brooke describes in particular the scolding and browbeating of Juliet by Capulet, who ends his tirade with a threat:

> Not only will I give all that I have away
> From thee, to those that shall me love, me honor, and obey,
> But also too so close, and to so hard a jail,
> I shall thee wed, for all thy life, that sure thou shall not fail
> A thousand times a day to wish for sudden death,
> And curse the day, and hour when first thy lungs did give thee breath.
>
> (1977–1982)

Shakespeare's Capulet says:

> But, and you will not wed . . .
> Graze where you will, you shall not house with me.
> Look to't, think on't; I do not use to jest.
> Thursday is near; lay hand on heart, advise:
> And you be mine, I'll give you to my friend;
> And you be not, hand, beg, starve, die in the streets,
> For, by my soul, I'll ne'er acknowledge thee,
> Nor what is mine shall never do thee good.   (III, v, 187–194)

In Brooke, Juliet seeks advice from Friar Lawrence, obtains the sleeping potion, and returns ostensibly to prepare for the wedding day, pretending to her parents and Nurse that she will marry Paris. The Nurse suggests the interesting arrangement that after marrying Paris, should Romeo return she could enjoy both.

> This one shall use her as his lawful wedded wife,
> In wanton love, with equal joy the other lead his life.
> And best shall she be sped of any townish dame,
> Of husband and of paramour, to find her change of game.   (2305–2308)

The Nurse in Shakespeare says only that:

> **Nurse:** Romeo is banished; and all the world to nothing
> That he dares ne'er come back to challenge you;
> Or if he do, it needs must be by stealth.
> Then, since the case so stands as now it doth,
> I think it best you married with the County . . .   (III, v, 213–217)

> . . . I think you are happy in this second match,
> For it excels your first; if it did not,
> Your first is dead—or 'twere as good he were
> As living here and you no use of him.   (III, v, 222–225)

In both versions Juliet rejects the Nurse, but in Shakespeare she calls her "O most wicked fiend!"

The final comparison recounts Juliet's feelings just before she swallows the sleep potion. Here Brooke gives a particularly vivid description of her fears:

> The force of her imagining anon did wax so strong
> That she surmised she saw out of the hollow vault,
> A grisly thing to look upon, the carcass of Tybalt,
> Right in the selfsame sort that she few days before
> Had seen him in his blood embrewed, to death also wounded sore.
>   (2378–2382)

With these thoughts:

> Her golden hairs did stand upright upon her childish head.
> Then pressed with the fear that she there lived in,
> A sweat as cold as mountain ice pierced through her tender skin,
> That with the moisture hath wet every part of hers.   (2388–2391)

In Shakespeare's play, Juliet fears first that on awakening she may suffocate in the tomb before Romeo reaches her:

> Or if I live, is it not very like
> The horrible conceit of death and night
> Together with the terror of the place—
> As in a vault, an ancient receptable,
> Where for this many hundred years the bones
> Of all my bury'd ancestors are pack'd,
> Where bloody Tybalt yet but green in earth
> Lies fest'ring in his shroud . . .   (IV, iii, 36–43)

Then she fears that she will be driven mad:

> And madly play with my forefathers' joints
> And pluck the mangled Tybalt from his shroud
> And in this rage with some great kinsman's bone
> As with a club dash out my desp'rate brains.   (IV, iii, 51–54)

Shakespeare follows the rest of Brooke's story closely: the grief over Juliet's death, her burial, the delay of Friar Lawrence's letter to Romeo caused by the messenger's detention because of the plague, Romeo's servant telling of her death, Romeo's trip to the tomb (Shakespeare added Paris's trip to the tomb and his death by Romeo's sword), the gathering of the people of Verona at the tomb, Friar Lawrence's summary of the events (explained more quickly in Shakespeare), and the reconciliation of the families.

Arthur Brooke's poem is important to a student of Shakespeare, for in no other work did Shakespeare rely so heavily upon his source. A study of Brooke's and then of Shakespeare's adaptations discloses Shakespeare's workmanship as a poet, dramatist, and theater craftsman. It is to Brooke's credit that Shakespeare could use his poem so much and so successful. But to see what Shakespeare did to this work of Brooke is, to echo Bullough's words, to see lead turned to gold.

8

THE PLAY: TRAGEDY? COMEDY?

A major problem in our study of *Romeo and Juliet* is definition: Is the play a tragedy? A comedy? A tragi-comedy? It has many comedy elements—the wit contests in the early part, the farcical actions of the servants of both houses, the comic portraits of the Nurse, old Capulet, Peter and others, the comedy underlayer in the banquet scene when Romeo meets Juliet—all suggesting that the play can be labeled a comedy. Yet there are the deaths of the hero and heroine at the play's end, the feud, Romeo's exile and separation from Juliet, and the deaths of Mercutio and Tybalt. Clearly there are contradictions between these definitions if we demand secure categories. Since we cannot, we must be satisfied finally that no clear answer will emerge. Yet the problem needs discussing. We must review our definitions of tragedy and comedy to seek at least partial answers to our questions.

A study of tragedy must begin with the definition by the Greek philosopher Aristotle (384–322 B.C.) who rested his consideration of tragedy on his analysis of the Greek plays he knew and, in particular, the works of Sophocles. The most important passage in the *Poetics,* in the most famous translation, by S. H. Butcher, is brief:

> Tragedy, then, is an imitation of an action that is serious, complete, and
> of a certain magnitude; in language embellished with each kind of artistic

ornament, the several kinds being found in separate parts of the play; in the form of action, not of narrative; through pity and fear effecting the proper purgation of these emotions.[1]

Aristotle is seeking to identify a feeling—a climax or culmination of emotions—which he calls a purgation, or catharsis, of the emotions of pity and fear. This purgation results from a combination of factors. The viewer or reader must find in the work a character with whom he can sympathize or identify. He must have aroused in him pity for this character (a feeling *for,* an understanding leading toward compassion) and fear at what happens to the character (a feeling *with,* an understanding and sympathy arising from identifying with the character's feeling of being endangered by something outside or inside himself). In order to accomplish this moment of catharsis properly and to create the necessary sympathy for the character, the work of art must be large enough ("of a certain magnitude") and must be serious. Aristotle says much more about the language necessary in the work and about the importance of form, but not all of what he says applies to all of tragedy or to Shakespeare in particular.

QUESTION

In what respects does *Romeo and Juliet* fit Aristotle's definition?

Another critic to consult in this brief review of the definition of tragedy is A. C. Bradley, an English writer who developed his theories with specific references to Shakespeare's great tragedies. In his work *Shakespearean Tragedy* (1904) Bradley claims at the outset that a tragedy

> is pre-eminently the story of one person, the "hero," or at the most of two, the "hero" and "heroine." Moreover, it is only in the love-tragedies, *Romeo and Juliet* and *Antony and Cleopatra,* that the heroine is as much the centre of the action as the hero. The rest, including *Macbeth,* are single stars.[2]

Bradley's primary interest is with those of Shakespeare's tragedies concerned with the single figure only, but parts of what he is discussing can apply to *Romeo and Juliet.* He says first that Shakespeare followed the medieval models in writing of men who " 'stood in high degree' happy and apparently secure," and who suffered "a total reverse of fortune."

> Tragedy with Shakespeare is concerned always with persons of 'high degree'; often with kings and princes; if not with leaders in the state like Coriolanus, Brutus, Antony; at the least, as in *Romeo and Juliet,* with members of great houses, whose quarrels are of public moment.[3]

In his concern for those of "high degree" the irony in the fall that occurs is implicit:

> His fate affects the welfare of a whole nation or empire; and when he falls suddenly from the height of earthly greatness to the dust, his fall produces a sense of contrast, or the powerlessness of man, and of the omnipotence— perhaps the caprice—of Fortune or Fate, which no tale of private life can possibly rival.[4]

QUESTION

"West Side Story" was an adaptation of *Romeo and Juliet.* If you know the play or film, what change was effected in moving the story to a New York ghetto and in creating the hero and heroine from a Puerto Rican girl and an Irish boy?

Thus far this much of Bradley's definition can apply to *Romeo and Juliet:* We have a hero and heroine, members of great houses, whose fall "produces a sense of contrast, or the powerlessness of man" and we have the suggestion of the power of "Fortune or Fate" in their lives which helps to determine their actions. We will first discuss the hero (and heroine), whose character, according to Bradley, need not be good,

> though generally he is "good" and therefore at once wins sympathy in his error. But it is necessary that he should have so much of greatness that in his error and fall we may be vividly conscious of the possibilities of human nature.[5]

QUESTIONS

Are the characters of Romeo and Juliet "good" in the sense Bradley means, or do they have the "possibilities of human nature" that would make us sympathetic with their error? What then is their error?

At the end of the tragedy we must be aware of the possibilities rather than the deficiencies of human nature. Our final feeling after reading or viewing the play can never be depression:

> No one ever closes the book with the feeling that man is a poor creature. He may be wretched and he may be awful, but he is not small. His lot may be heartrending and mysterious, but it is not contemptible.[6]

QUESTIONS

What qualities in the personalities of Romeo and Juliet keep them from being mean or petty? Are any of the other characters petty? Are the characterizations of the lovers affected by the meanness or pettiness of the other characters?

We now have this picture of our hero and heroine: they are members of great houses (whose falls affect many others), they are sympathetic (good, not petty), and in their characterizations they have so much of greatness that in their errors we can recognize "the possibilities of human nature." The last is important because Bradley claims that in the action of a tragedy, "the dominant factor consists in deeds which issue from character."[7] The action of a play has other forces determining it—chance, the supernatural, an abnormal state of the hero's mind—but "character" must of necessity direct its important events. In *Romeo and Juliet* we must now question carefully the place of character in the determination of what happens in the play.

QUESTIONS

What in the characters of Romeo and Juliet helps precipitate the final tragedy of their deaths? What "errors" issuing from "character" are they guilty of? Did the love they felt for each other have any relationship to the character traits which proved their failing?[8]

We should also consider the attitude of the principals toward death and this attitude's place in the study of the "religion of love" discussed in Chapter 6. Death is mentioned by Juliet and Romeo soon after their first meeting and often thereafter, always in reference to the strength of their commitment to each other. At the play's beginning Romeo is willing to face death to speak with Juliet and at its end he in reality finds this goal. Juliet has premonitions of death, thinks she sees Romeo as if in a tomb, counterfeits death and joins Romeo in the final wedding of death. But even though the two fuse images of death with the visions of their shared love, neither seems to desire death in itself. On the contrary, in their reaches toward a wedded life both want to live to enjoy life's and love's experiences. Chapter 6 asserted that what the lovers sought as a final experience was a search for the infinite. Critic Leonora Leet Brodwin explained that for Romeo death "is the infinite freedom experienced in the ecstatic instant of self-annihilation."[9] But, according to Brodwin, Romeo goes even further in his words: "Then I defy you stars! . . . Well, Juliet, I will lie with thee tonight." (V, i, 24, 34.) She states that "Romeo defies the stars and all mortal contingency by accepting the worst they have to offer, thereby transmuting it into a spiritual triumph."[10] Romeo is not seeking death but defying it, and in accepting it as he did he actually triumphs. "The ecstasy of self-annihilation at its profoundest level, then, is not due to a feeling of surrender to death but to the triumph of the unconquerable spirit over death, achieving the Infinite in its assertion of ultimate freedom."[11]

QUESTION

Do we end this love tale with a feeling that love has triumphed and that no real tragic emotion is left with us?

From our study of the play we have seen that Romeo and Juliet are being affected by forces outside themselves, that, in fact, these forces may be said to control their lives, their "fates," even though both willfully set themselves above their families and their society in order to satisfy their love. But what are the natures of the obstacles imposed against them? There is the feud. There is Capulet's tyrannical treatment of his daughter. There are the chance accidents—the delay of the letter to Romeo explaining Juliet's assumed death, the unfortunate timing of Juliet's awakening and Romeo's early suicide. Juliet and her Romeo are victims of these misunderstandings and accidents. Are they tragic victims? To answer this question we must pose another proposition. We must of necessity respect the forces affecting the characters in the same degree that we respect the characters. The question now is: How much dignity can we accede to the forces and accidents that help to determine the fate of the lovers?

Let us consider the feud. At the occasion of the first struggle between the families, cowardly servants begin the quarrel. When Capulet enters and calls for a sword, Lady Capulet answers that he should be asking for a crutch. As Montague seeks to enter the fight, Lady Montague halts him with a word. Romeo, told of the fight by Benvolio, dismisses it briefly; it is only an interruption in his thoughts of the fair Rosaline. When Romeo enters Capulet's house during the dance, only Tybalt is disturbed by his presence. Although the fight between Mercutio and Tybalt is more serious, the events of the day begin almost casually. Benvolio seeks to draw Mercutio from the streets for fear of a "brawl," "For now, these hot days, is the mad blood stirring." (III, i, 4.) Mercutio is killed, of course, then Tybalt, and Romeo is exiled. The feud, therefore, is a family quarrel waged by old henpecked husbands, by churlish and cowardly servants, and by hotheaded boys maddened by a sultry day. How seriously, then, can we accept it as a force worthy to contest the love of the hero and heroine?

Juliet's father, old Capulet, is another agent of an outside force. Stubborn and irascible, he accepts as his right the donation of his daughter to whomever he chooses. He intends to force her to accept a wedding to Paris; he actually forces her to take Friar Lawrence's potion, the first act toward her death. Since he is drawn as a comic character, it is difficult for us to accept old Capulet as a dark and sinister agent of a malignant power, even though the final effect of his actions is the death of his only child.

Let us next consider the chance accidents. Friar John is held up from his journey to Mantua by a sudden quarantine; he fails to deliver his letter to Romeo, therefore, and a fatal misunderstanding results. Is this now our example of a malignant fortune determining the fate of the hero and heroine? If so, how can we characterize it as "blind" fortune, or "arbitrary" fortune? As we noted in Chapter 7, Shakespeare followed the lead of Brooke in his references and use of fortune, but made significant changes. And in these changes we must seek the answer to this important question: Did Shakespeare's work leave us with the impression that the outside forces were everything and the victims' will to make their own fates was of no importance? Are the two lovers powerless to act against these forces? If so, how is it that at the end of the play, they retain our sympathy?

Let us return to A. C. Bradley in our search for answers. He claims that the heroes of Shakespeare's tragedies are not victims of a blind fate. "We find practically no trace of fatalism in its more primitive, crude and obvious forms."[12] Bradley then asks the question: "What, then, is this 'fate' which the impressions already considered lead us to describe as the ultimate power in the tragic world?" He presents this answer:

> It appears to be a mythological expression for the whole system or order, of which the individual characters form an inconsiderable and feeble part; which seems to determine, far more than they, their native dispositions and their circumstances, and through these, their action. . . . And whether this system or order is best called by the name of fate or no, it can hardly be denied that it does appear as the ultimate power in the tragic world, and that it has such characteristics as these.[13]

In a later passage Bradley refers to this outside influence as a "moral power" that works according to its own laws, seemingly impartial to good and evil, destroying evil but doing so only at great expense: "an evil which it [the moral power] is able to overcome only by self-torture and self-waste."[14]

QUESTIONS

Bradley's definition fits more nearly the later four great tragedies of Shakespeare, *Hamlet, Macbeth, Othello,* and *King Lear.* How closely does this definition of fate apply to *Romeo and Juliet?* In the great tragedies the individual's assertion of his will often reaches ironic consequences: "What they achieve is not what they intended; it is terribly unlike it . . . They fight blindly in the dark, and the power that works through them makes them the instrument of a design which is not theirs."[15] Can this definition also apply to Romeo and Juliet's assertion of their wills?

Finally, let us consider atmosphere. In a tragedy the atmosphere must be appropriate to the tragic theme. And atmosphere in each of Shakespeare's four great tragedies is dominated by a character or contrivance that in effect becomes a dramatic device; in *Hamlet* it is the ghost, in *Macbeth* the witches, in *Othello* the character Iago, and in *King Lear* the storm. There are many other effects in the setting of atmosphere in each play—imagery in the language, actors' reactions to the ghost and the witches—which help also to impress the atmosphere upon our imaginations. In these four plays the tragic atmosphere thus established is not seriously affected by the presence of comedy. In *Macbeth* the Porter scene helps change the mood of the play, and the Fool's gibes in *King Lear* actually heighten the dramatic tension. In *Antony and Cleopatra,* the comedy is more prominent than in the four plays just mentioned, and is an essential contributor to the seductive attraction of Egypt that debilitates Antony. Comedy in *Romeo and Juliet* poses a more serious problem. A play that includes Mercutio, Capulet, the Nurse, Peter, and the other servants, must include in its analysis a rationale for a comedy that exists apart from its tragic action. Even the feud can be taken only with a modified degree of seriousness as a device for dramatic motivation. The kind of activity we find in the play is circumscribed by the streets and people of Verona. We sense the vitality in the community scenes, the exuberance of the young who are as anxious to fight as to make love, the rich family life of the Capulets, the joy in the flowers and the sunrise and the singing birds of dawn. Back of these scenes are Juliet's visions of death and the poisonous darkness of the apothecary's shop and later the tomb, but these scenes of darkness and gloom affect only part of our imagination; the bright streets of Verona remain with us.

QUESTIONS

How is Shakespeare able to merge the comedy with the tragic as in Mercutio's death? What is the final dramatic effect of his death scene?

How can we identify this comedy in *Romeo and Juliet?* Is it "comic relief"? Critic Susanne Langer defines comic relief as "the introduction of trivial or humor interludes in the midst of serious, ominous, tragic action."[16] In tragedies there is a comedy frame, a "comic substructure" which, according to Langer, may be taken more seriously:

> In *Macbeth* (and, indeed, all Shakespeare plays) there is a large, social, everyday life of soldiers, grooms, gossips, courtiers, and commoners, that

provides an essentially comic substructure for the heroic action. Most of the time this lower stratum is subdued, giving an impression of realism without any obvious byplay; but this realism carries the fundamental comic rhythm from which grotesque interludes may arise with perfect dramatic logic.[17]

In our analysis of tragedy we must include this structure:

Tragedy can rest squarely on a comic substructure, and yet be pure tragedy. This is natural enough, for life—from which all felt rhythms spring—contains both, in every mortal organism. . . . Even while each individual fulfills the tragic pattern it participates also in the comic continuity. The poet's task is, of course, not to copy life, but to organize and articulate a symbol for the "sense of life"; and in the symbol one rhythm always governs the dynamic form, though another may go through the whole piece in a contrapuntal fashion. The master of this practice is Shakespeare.[18]

QUESTION

Is Susanne Langer's definition appropriate for *Romeo and Juliet?*

Accepting the conclusion that in *Romeo and Juliet* the essential rhythm is tragedy and the substructure comedy, do we conclude that the substructure is trivial and irrelevant, or is it, as in *Antony and Cleopatra,* a dramatic necessity to the play? Is the young rapturous love of Romeo and Juliet the more valid and believable because it exists in the midst of the brawling Veronese city streets? Are the deaths of Mercutio and Tybalt understandable consequences of the town's atmosphere of hate and the play's atmosphere of summer days and hot youthful blood? Finally, are the deaths of Romeo and Juliet different in essentials from the deaths of Tybalt and Mercutio—in the establishment of a tragic tone to the play, for instance? Or in the change of the society that comes about because of their deaths?

The last question introduces new considerations. Critics often have noted that tragedy and comedy differ in the degree of importance they give to the individual or to the individual's society. In comedy, for instance, an audience's attention is more often directed to the social environment of the hero and heroine; in tragedy its attention is on the individual. In comedy we often find disorder in the social surroundings, or, if order, a status quo that needs changing, and the hero and heroine are placed in opposition by necessity. Part of the resolution of this comedy is that by their triumph (their marriage, the success in their defiance) society is reformed, its values changed and health is restored. In tragedy the movement may prove to be from order to disorder (the hero, as in *King Lear,* creating the disorder), with a final order established by the hero's death, either as a sacrifice or as a qualification for order to be established. Also in tragedy the progression often is toward a state of isolation for the hero; at the play's end he perhaps suffers death in more or less complete isolation (as do Macbeth and Othello) or is reconciled just before death (as is Lear).

Returning to *Romeo and Juliet* we note the hostile, disordered environment at its beginning, the gradual isolation of the lovers because of their actions, the reformation of the society at the play's end because of their deaths. They are the victims, not the cause of the disorder of their society; but by their deaths they help to reestablish the proper order. Do they then qualify as tragic and heroic figures because of their sacrifice?

QUESTIONS

Do we consider their fate heroic because they were the means of reconciliation of the families? Are we seriously enough interested in this kind of reconciliation at the expense of the lovers' deaths? If the families had continued their enmity, would the play be less or more a tragedy?

From the answers to these questions we may arrive at a clearer opinion of that part of the play we as audience feel is the most serious.

Earlier in this chapter we mentioned the place of Fate and Fortune in the definition of tragedy. Susanne Langer creates distinctions in Fortune and Fate, allowing these distinctions to identify tragic and comic works. To her, "comic destiny is Fortune—what the world will bring, and the man will take or miss, encounter or escape; tragic destiny is what the man brings and the world will demand of him. That is his Fate."[19]

QUESTION

How does this distinction help us in our attempts to categorize *Romeo and Juliet?*

Langer mentions Kismet, another idea of Fate which may apply to our play:

> There is another mythical conception of Fate that is not a forerunner of tragedy, but possibly of some kinds of comedy: That is the idea of Fate as the will of supernatural powers, perhaps long decreed, perhaps spontaneous and arbitrary. It is the "Fate" of the true Fatalist, who takes no great care of his life because he deems it entirely in the hands of Allah (or some other God), . . . the will of a god who gives and takes away, casts down or raises up, for inscrutable reasons of his own, is Kismet, and that is really a myth of Fortune. Kismet is what a person encounters, not what he is.[20]

QUESTION

Is Kismet part of *Romeo and Juliet?*

In these brief critical excerpts three points about the relationship between comedy and tragedy are discussed: the comic substructure, the individual versus society, and Fortune and Fate. We can see in these discussions that *Romeo and Juliet* is often a confusing example of the tragedy-comedy relationship. It contains the active community life(the comic substructure), the conflict that exists when the love of Romeo and Juliet seeks expression in the midst of the feud (the individual-society conflict), and the victimizing of the two by external forces (Fortune and Fate). It is quite possible that in seeking answers to our questions, we may still be unclear in our answer to the central question—Is *Romeo and Juliet* a comedy or tragedy?—or perhaps to the fairer question—What part does comedy assume in the tragedy of *Romeo and Juliet?* And is the confusion not shared by the playwright? One scene may serve as an example to point up difficulties for the student, actor, or director of the play. In IV, v, in which Juliet swallows the potion, we have a curious reaction to what is supposed, by the actors on the stage, as Juliet's death. Each speech by Capulet, Lady Capulet, Paris, and the Nurse, is artificial to the point of parody. The speeches of the Nurse and Paris perhaps are more exaggerated in their rhetorical flourishes than those of the others on stage, but they are yet typical:

> NURSE: O woe! O woeful, woeful, woeful day!
> Most lamentable day, most woeful day
> That ever, ever, I did yet behold!
> O day, O day, Oday! O hateful day!
> Never was seen so black a day as this.
> O woeful day! O woeful day!

> PARIS: Beguiled, divorced, wronged, spited, slain!
> Most detestable Death, by thee beguiled,
> By cruel, cruel thee quite overthrown.
> O love, O life! not life, but love in death!   (IV, v, 49–59)

Capulet speaks in similar vein, as had Lady Capulet before the Nurse's speech. Shakespeare creates a realistic speech only for the Friar. Following the departure of the principals, Peter enters to converse with the musicians who had remained behind. A lengthy scene, notable only for a number of puns on instruments and music, ends with the speech of the Second Musician: "Hang him, Jack! Come, we'll in here, tarry for the mourners, and stay dinner." (V, v, 145–146.)

Many directors cover possible embarrassment with this scene by eliminating it from production. Can the student of the play dismiss the scene as easily? The audience knows, of course, that there is no true cause for grief, as Juliet is actually alive. And yet the situation is painful enough. What is apparent is that the playwright was not serious in his attempts to portray real grief. Is the scene therefore comic? Again the answer is not clear. However, it is perhaps a fair, although extreme, example of some confusion even in Shakespeare's mind about what the play should be.

QUESTIONS

After reading the scene described above, do you find the emotions to be aroused are pathetic or tragic, or is there an attempt to provide "comic relief"? How does this scene fit into the atmosphere of the play at this particular moment?

Perhaps our attempts to categorize the play as tragedy or comedy place an unnecessary strain on it. Perhaps the "tragedy" of Romeo and Juliet is something different from tragedy, a kind of rhythm that can be analyzed and appraised. It has been mentioned that Shakespeare wrote this play during the period in which he was writing his two great lyrical poems, and quite possibly his sonnets. His interest was divided at this point in his career between the lyrical and the dramatic. As dramatic as it is, this play is even more strongly marked by the lyrical sweep in the movement of the plot. In his compression of his source from a time span of several months to a period of five days, Shakespeare creates a dramatic movement with a speed and haste equivalent to the impetuous, spontaneous quality of the quick love of the hero and heroine. Juliet voices the fear in this haste and the audience instinctively feels it, which helps in the creation of the important sense of fatalism that accompanies this story of the "star-crossed" lovers. The very lyricism has, therefore, a dramatic effect of its own and achieves a dramatic and artistic end in our acceptance of the lovers' deaths as a natural consequence of their impetuous actions. This acceptance may be the effect of a dramatic trick but it is real nonetheless and leaves the audience breathless in the rapid fulfillment of the anticipation of doom that was early established. And if the doom is, after all, triumphant in its victory not only over the obstacles society plants in the way but over death itself, the acceptance gains even more aesthetic validity.

In one sense the idea of tragedy, or comedy, may be irrelevant. Our major interest in the drama may be in its progression, in the impetuosity of the emotions aroused, in the sense of haste and impatience with time's restrictions that suits better the lyric than the dramatic aesthetic response. Tragedy must include the elements of conflict which determine the course of events, creating a pattern complicated by the elements of the interaction of separate, special forces. The lyric is simpler in that the conflict is, if present, only an ancillary part of the work's purpose. There are the obstacles, the conflicts, but we are never aware that they are more than a matter of discretionary action on the part of the Prince, or of the two heads of the warring families, or of the various family members. The obstacles remain trivial; the triumph of their love, even over death, remains the final message. And this message may be all that we need to carry away with us at the conclusion of this most famous of all love stories.

QUESTION

Is the play's movement similar to the action of *Hamlet, Macbeth, King Lear, Othello,* or *Antony and Cleopatra?*

NOTES

CHAPTER 6

[1] Lewis, C. S. *The Allegory of Love,* New York, 1958, p. 17.

[2] Capellanus, Andreas. *The Art of Courtly Love,* trans. John Jay Parry, New York, 1941, pp. 106–107.

[3] Capellanus, p. 107.

[4] Lewis, p. 12.

[5] Capellanus, p. 185, Rule No. XIV.

[6] Ibid., Rule No. XXV.

[7] Ibid., Rule No. XXIV.

[8] Ibid.

[9] Brodwin, Leonora Lee. *Elizabethan Love Tragedy* (New York, 1971), p. 8.

[10] In *Love in the Western World,* New York, 1956.

[11] Brodwin, p. 8.

[12] Ibid., pp. 8–9.

[13] Ibid., p. 44.

CHAPTER 7

[1] Bullough, Geoffrey. *Narrative and Dramatic Sources of Shakespeare,* I, New York, 1957, pp. 277–278.

[2] Ibid., p. 278.

[3] Brooke, Arthur. "The Tragicall Historye of Romeus and Juliet," in Bullough, p. 278. In this and later quoted passages, spelling and word usage have been modernized. Hereafter line numbers of the poem will follow the passages.

[4] Charlton, H. B. *Shakespearean Tragedy,* London, 1961, p. 53.

CHAPTER 8

[1] Aristotle. "Poetics," trans. S. H. Butcher in Aristotle's *Theory of Poetry and Fine Art,* London, 1911, p. 23.

[2] Bradley, A. C. *Shakespearean Tragedy* (1904), 1st ed., New York, 1958, p. 16.

[3] Ibid., p. 18.

[4] Ibid., p. 19.

[5] Ibid., p. 28.

[6] Ibid.,

[7] Ibid., p. 23.

[8] See ibid., pp. 26 *passim.*

[9] Brodwin, Leonora Leet. *Elizabethan Love Tragedy*, New York, 1971, p. 58.

[10] Ibid., p. 58.

[11] Ibid., p. 59.

[12] Bradley, p. 33.

[13] Ibid., p. 34.

[14] Ibid., p. 40.

[15] Ibid., p. 32.

[16] Langer, Susanne. *Feeling and Form*, New York, 1953, p. 94.

[17] Ibid., pp. 94–95.

[18] Ibid., p. 95.

[19] Ibid., p. 86.

[20] Ibid., pp. 87–88.

FOR DISCUSSION

CHAPTER 5

1. In I, i, 218–230, Romeo and Benvolio speak the following dialogue, Romeo alluding to the fair Rosaline:

   ROMEO: She will not stay the siege of loving terms,
   Nor bide the encounter of assailing eyes,
   Nor ope her lap to saint-seducing gold.
   Oh, she is rich in beauty, only poor
   That when she dies, with beauty dies her store.
   BENVOLIO: Then she hath sworn that she will still live chaste?
   ROMEO: She hath, and in that sparing makes huge waste;
   For beauty, starved with her severity,
   Cuts beauty off from all posterity.
   She is too fair, too wise, wisely too fair,
   To merit bliss by making me despair.
   She hath forsworn to love, and in that vow
   Do I live dead, that live to tell it now.

   Shakespeare in Sonnet 1 says the following:

   From fairest creatures we desire increase,
   That thereby beauty's rose might never die,
   But as the riper should by time decrease,
   His tender heir might bear his memory.
   But thou, contracted to thine own bright eyes,
   Feed'st thy light's flame with self-substantial fuel,
   Making a famine where abundance lies,
   Thyself thy foe, to thy sweet self too cruel.

Thou that art now the world's fresh ornament
And only herald to the gaudy spring,
Within thine own bud buriest thy content
And, tender churl, makest waste in niggarding.
   Pity the world, or else this glutton be,
    To eat the world's due, by the grave and thee.

A. Show similarities in subject matter between the dialogue and the sonnet. Show differences.
B. Show similarities in language and structure between the dialogue and the sonnet. Show differences.
C. Using the sonnet language and form as your guide, discuss the characterization of Romeo in this first scene of the play as determined by his language in the play.

  2. Shakespeare in Sonnet 138 says the following:

When my love swears that she is made of truth,
I do believe her, though I know she lies,
That she might think me some untutored youth,
Unlearned in the world's false subtleties.
Thus vainly thinking that she thinks me young,
Although she knows my days are past the best,
Simply I credit her false-speaking tongue.
On both sides thus is simple truth suppressed.
But wherefore says she not she is unjust?
And wherefore say not I that I am old?
Oh, love's best habit is in seeming trust,
And age in love loves not to have years told.
   Therefore I lie with her and she with me,
    And in our faults by lies we flattered be.

A. This sonnet and Sonnet 1 follow the sonnet convention in certain respects. In what ways do they differ?
B. Summarize the meanings in each sonnet named above. Which is more realistic in statement and why? What is your conclusion now about the sonnet convention?

  3. Shakespeare in Sonnet 130 says the following:

My mistress' eyes are nothing like the sun,
Coral is far more red than her lips' red.
If snow be white, why then her breasts are dun,
If hairs be wires, black wires grow on her head.
I have seen roses damasked, red and white,
But no such roses see I in her cheeks.
And in some perfumes is there more delight
Than in the breath that from my mistress reeks.
I love to hear her speak, yet well I know
That music hath a far more pleasing sound.

> I grant I never saw a goddess go,
> My mistress, when she walks, treads on the ground.
>   And yet, by Heaven, I think my love as rare
>   As any she belied with false compare.

A. This sonnet is Shakespeare's answer to those of his contemporaries who ful-somely praise the beauties of their mistresses in elaborate rhetoric. How is this sonnet a praise of his mistress?
B. What is Shakespeare's comment on conventions in this sonnet?

4. Scholars only conjecture that Shakespeare was writing the sonnets dur-ing the same period in which he was writing *Romeo and Juliet*. Write a paper to prove or disprove this thesis.

CHAPTER 6

Short Topics

1. What does the introduction of Romeo as a courtly lover do to your final impression of Romeo as a character? (Imagine, for instance, your impres-sion of Romeo if you first had met him on the way to the feast with his friends, without the early dialogue with Benvolio.)
2. Compare Romeo's pose with that of the Duke in *Twelfth Night*.
3. Compare the treatment of the courtly lovers in *Romeo and Juliet* and in *Much Ado About Nothing* (using Claudio and Benedict as contrasts).
4. Reconcile the pose of the courtly lover with the seriousness of the lover dedicated to the "religion of love."
5. Why can the rules of Andreas Capellanus so easily become artificial in their application? Discuss.
6. In the source, Romeo is also in love with a chaste fair maid who will not return his love. What elements of courtly love are in Brooke's version? What changes did Shakespeare make?

Long Topics

1. Discuss examples of courtly love characterizations by other contem-poraries of Shakespeare, especially those of John Lyly, Robert Greene and others. In particular consult the model of the courtier described in Lyly's *Euphues*.
2. Discuss how the courtly lover can be both a romantic and a satiric crea-tion.

CHAPTER 7

Short Topics

1. Take one excerpt from Brooke and the comparison passage from Shake-speare's play and compare the language of each.

2. Compare the characterization of Romeus in Brooke with Romeo in Shakespeare's version. Compare the character of Juliet in each. Of Nurse.
3. Show the influence of Brooke's imagery in the first meeting of Romeus and Juliet with Shakespeare's first meeting of the lovers.
4. Discuss the importance of Shakespeare's compression of time in his adaptation of his source.
5. Discuss the use of Fortune and Fate in Brooke's and Shakespeare's versions, and the effect this change had on the characters and on the play's final effect.
6. What do you consider Shakespeare's most important improvement of Brooke? Explain.

Long Topics

1. Study carefully Arthur Brooke's *The Tragicall Historye of Romeus and Juliet* and analyze his plot structure, characterization and language. Cite examples where Shakespeare was able to capitalize on what Brooke had supplied.
2. Compare the treatment of Juliet's simulated death in Brooke and in Shakespeare, showing the effects gained in each.
3. Using the book *Love in the Western World* by Denise de Rougemont as a guide, supported by ideas gained from the works of Brodwin, Valency and others cited in the bibliography, discuss the religion of love thesis as suggested by Brooke and developed by Shakespeare.

CHAPTER 8

Short Topics

1. Discuss the element of will as asserted by Romeo and Juliet and demonstrate its effect on the play's action.
2. Of the outside forces affecting the destiny of the lovers, which is the most effective as a dramatic instrument? Discuss your answer.
3. What effect do the several references to fortune have on the play?
4. What effect do the various accidents have on your conception of the play as tragedy?
5. The Nurse, like Falstaff in the Henry trilogy, serves as a comic character but serves also a more serious dramatic role. Discuss.

Long Topics

1. Using an extended definition of tragedy from a major critic (Bradley, Francis Fergusson, Northrop Frye, Paul Siegel), discuss *Romeo and Juliet* as tragedy.
2. Compare the place of comedy in *Romeo and Juliet* and in *Antony and Cleopatra*.
3. Compare dramatic structure in *Romeo and Juliet* and in any of his other major tragedies.

4. Compare the courtly love convention in *Romeo and Juliet* and in *Troilus and Cressida*. Follow this comparison with a discussion of Shakespeare's ideas of love as seen in the two plays.

SUGGESTED READING FOR THIS STUDY

Anon. "The Imagery of *Romeo and Juliet*," *English*, The Magazine of the English Association, VIII (Autumn 1950), 121–126.

Baldwin, T. W. *Shakespeare's Five-Act Structure*. Urbana, Ill.: University of Illinois Press, 1947.

Bethell, S. L. *Shakespeare and the Popular Dramatic Tradition*. New York: Octagon Books, 1970.

Bethurum, Dorothy. "The Dramatic Appropriateness of the Queen Mab Speech," *Sewanee Review*, XXXVI (Jan.–March 1928), 62–75.

Bradbrook, M. C. *Shakespeare and Elizabethan Poetry*. New York: Oxford University Press, 1952.

Bulgin, Randolph M. "Dramatic Imagery in Shakespeare: *Romeo and Juliet*," *Shenandoah*, XI (1960), 23–38.

Clemen, Wolfgang H. *The Development of Shakespeare's Imagery*. Harvard University Press, 1951.

Cutts, John P. *The Shattered Glass: A Dramatic Pattern in Shakespeare's Early Plays*. Detroit: Wayne State University Press, 1968.

Daniel, P. A. "Brooke's *Romeus and Juliet* and Painter's *Rhomeo and Julietta*," New Shakespeare Society (1875), Ser. III, Part I, 1, 144.

Evans, Ifor. *The Language of Shakespeare's Plays*. Bloomington, Ind.: Indiana University Press, 1952.

Granville-Barker, H. *On Dramatic Method*. London, 1931. Pp. 66–72.

Hill, R. F. "Shakespeare's Early Tragic Mode," *Shakespeare Quarterly*, IX (1958), 455–469.

Joseph, Sister Miriam. *Shakespeare's Use of the Arts of Language*. New York: Columbia University Press, 1947.

Law, Robert Adger. "On Shakespeare's Changes of His Source Material in *Romeo and Juliet*," *University of Texas Bulletin*, No. 2926, *Studies in English*, No. 9 (1929), 86–102.

————. "Parallels between *Romeus and Juliet* and Sonnets 18 and 33," Studies in English, No. 9, Austin, Texas (1929), 82–84.

Lever, J. W. *The Elizabethan Love Sonnet*. London: Methuen, 1966.

Levin, Henry. "Form and Formality in *Romeo and Juliet*." *Shakespeare Quarterly*, XI (1960), 3–11.

Mahood, M. M. *Shakespeare's Wordplay*. London: Methuen, 1957.

Moore, Olin H. "Shakespeare's Deviations from *Romeus and Juliet*," *PMLA*, L11 (1937), 68–74.

Muir, Kenneth. "Arthur Brooke and the Imagery of *Romeo and Juliet*," *Notes and Queries*, III (1956), 241–243.

————. *Shakespeare's Sources*. London: Methuen, 1957.

Pearson, Lu Emily. *Elizabethan Love Conventions*. Berkeley, Calif.: University of California Press, 1933.

Ribner, Irving. *Patterns in Shakespearean Tragedy*. London: Methuen, 1960.

Spurgeon, Caroline F. E. *Leading Motives in the Imagery of Shakespeare's Tragedies*. Reprinted in: Dean, Leonard F. *Shakespeare: Modern Essays in Criticism*. New York: Oxford University Press, 1957, pp. 72–78.

Vyvyan, John. *Shakespeare and the Rose of Love*. London: Chatto and Windus, 1960.

Whitaker, Virgil K. "Shakespeare's Use of His Sources," *Philological Quarterly*, XX (July 1941), 377–389.

Wilson, Harold S. *On the Design of Shakespearian Tragedy*. Toronto: University of Toronto Press, 1957.

SELECTED READING ON THEMES IN ROMEO AND JULIET OUTSIDE THIS STUDY

Barber, C. L. *Shakespeare's Festive Comedy*. Princeton: Princeton University Press, 1959.

Bowling, Lawrence Edward. "The Thematic Framework of *Romeo and Juliet*." *PMLA*, LXIV (1949), 208–220.

Bush, Douglas. " 'Hero and Leander' and *Romeo and Juliet*." *Philological Quarterly*, IX (Oct. 1930), 396–399.

Cole, Douglas, ed. *Twentieth Century Interpretations of Romeo and Juliet: A Collection of Critical Essays*. Englewood Cliffs, N.J.: Prentice-Hall, 1970.

Dickey, Franklin M. *Not Wisely But Too Well: Shakespeare's Love Tragedies*. Huntington Library, 1957, 63–117.

Fowlie, Wallace. *Love in Literature*. Bloomington, Ind.: Indiana University Press, 1948.

Granville-Barker, H. *Prefaces to Shakespeare*, II. Princeton, N.J.: Princeton University Press, 1947, 300–349.

Harbage, Alfred. *Shakespeare and the Rival Traditions*. New York: Macmillan, 1952.

Herford, C. H. *Shakespeare's Treatment of Love and Marriage*. London: Methuen, 1921.

Horne, H. H. "Tragic Love: *Romeo and Juliet*," in *Shakespeare's Philosophy of Love*. Raleigh, N.C.: Edwards and Broughton Co., 1945.

Lyons, Charles R. *Shakespeare and the Ambiguity of Love's Triumph*. The Hague: Mouton, 1971.

Mason, H. A. *Shakespeare's Tragedies of Love*. New York: Barnes & Noble, 1970.

Meader, William. *Courtship in Shakespeare*. New York: Kings Crown Press, 1954.

Pettet, E. C. *Shakespeare and the Romantic Tradition*. London: Methuen, 1949.

Richmond, Hugh. *Shakespeare's Sexual Comedy: A Mirror for Lovers*. Indianapolis: Bobbs-Merrill, 1971.

Siegel, Paul. "Christianity and the Religion in *Romeo and Juliet*," *Shakespeare Quarterly*, XII (1961), 371–392.

―――. *Shakespearean Tragedy and the Elizabethan Compromise*. New York: New York University Press, 1957.

Stauffer, Donald. *Shakespeare's World of Images: The Development of His Ideas*. Bloomington, Ind.: Indiana University Press, 1966.

Stirling, Brents. *Unity in Shakespearian Tragedy*. New York: Columbia University Press, 1956.

Stoll, E. E. *Shakespeare's Young Lovers*. New York: Oxford University Press, 1937, 1–44.

Valency, Maurice. *In Praise of Love*. New York: Macmillan, 1958.

BIBLIOGRAPHY

Bradley, A. C. *Shakespearean Tragedy*, (1904), 1st ed., New York: Meridian Books, 1958.

Brodwin, Leonora Leet. *Elizabethan Love Tragedy*, New York: New York University Press, 1971.

Bullough, Geoffrey. *Narrative and Dramatic Sources of Shakespeare*, Vol. I, New York: Columbia University Press, 1957.

Butcher, S. H. *Aristotle's Theory of Poetry and Fine Art* (with text and translation of the "Poetics"), London, 1911.

Capellanus, Andreas. *The Art of Courtly Love*, trans. John Jay Parry, New York: Columbia University Press, 1941.

Charleton, H. B. *Shakespearean Tragedy*, London: Cambridge University Press, 1961.

Frye, Northrup. *The Anatomy of Criticism*, Princeton: Princeton University Press, 1957.

Langer, Susanne. *Feeling and Form: A Theory of Art Developed From Philosopsy in a New Key*, New York: Charles Scribner's Sons, 1953.

Lewis, C. S. *The Allegory of Love*. New York: Oxford University Press, Galaxy, 1958 (first published 1936).

Rougemont, Denis de. *Love in the Western World*. trans. by Montgomery Belgion. New York: Pantheon, 1956.

PART THREE

READING HAMLET: TEXT, CONTEXT, AND SUBTEXT

MAURICE CHARNEY

INTRODUCTION

There is no way of deciding which is Shakespeare's best play, but judging from the volume of criticism and the number of performances, *Hamlet* seems to be the play that has most fascinated readers, writers, and actors. Despite all the interpretation, we are still not able, with any certainty, to pluck out the heart of *Hamlet's* mystery, and the play remains as open and lively as it must have seemed to its original audiences around the year 1600. One of my aims in this brief approach to the play is to try to reconstruct a sense of *Hamlet* "when new," or at least to make an effort to see the play freshly and in its own terms, rather than in the light of all the commentary that has accumulated since Shakespeare's time.

I offer the reader ten significant passages for interpretation (or re-interpretation), and I try to raise questions about these passages. Not all the questions have definite answers; the series of passages is meant to stimulate a questioning spirit rather than a set of conclusions about the play. That would be approaching the texts in the wrong spirit, because it is not answers that we want but a certain way of reasoning about the play. The readers should come to the passages with open minds and with willingness to respond imaginatively and histrionically to the words on the printed page. They should honestly ask themselves how they would act or stage the words that they read.

It is well to remember that the play as performed is a temporal unit; it unfolds and develops over a period of two or three hours. The acted play must be completely intelligible to its audience, which cannot, like readers, go back over something that was missed. That puts a heavy burden on the playwright not only to make sense, but also to be able to communicate his meanings. If *Hamlet* is subtle and puzzling in some of its aspects, it is also extremely lucid in its basic plot: to discover what is "rotten in the state of Denmark" and to rectify it. The play moves with the swiftness of a mystery story, in which the murderer is revealed and a suitable revenge is set in motion. Conflicts are generated between the murderer and all his allies and the victim's son and his few friends and supporters. As Hamlet puts it, "O, 'tis most sweet/ When in one line two crafts directly meet." (III, iv, 210–211.)

If we agree that a play develops in a fixed time sequence, then it is always crucial to know at what point in the action we are at any particular moment. Context is especially important in plays. Thus, we need to know both the immediate context—who is speaking, to whom, why he is speaking in this style, whether he is giving or concealing information, and so forth—and the larger context—what preceded this speech, how this speech fits into the evolving action, whether the characterization of the speaker is consistent with the rest of the play, what the main thrust of the passage is, and so forth. The number of questions we can ask about context is almost unlimited, but the purpose of the questions is to orient ourselves in the unfolding dramatic action. We also need to know whether we are being deliberately thrown off the scent or offered "red herrings," as so often happens in plots involving crime and detection. In the discussion of the sample passages, we will constantly be coming back to the idea of context, because the passages are part of a meaningful pattern. They are not by any means independent, autonomous, self-contained units that can be taken out of context.

The word "subtext" is being more and more frequently used in dramatic criticism, especially among directors and actors, to describe the implications of the action. By the workings of Shakespeare's ever-present irony, the implications of the action are sometimes the opposite of what the characters are saying. Thus Claudius, at the beginning of I, ii, makes a smooth and oratorical speech to his court, but there are hints in this speech of an iron will and a ruthless determination to conceal the hidden murder of old King Hamlet. It is up to the actor to convey a subtext of implied significances. These are usually expressed by gesture and tone rather than by the words of the text. The subtext might also suggest associations between words and images and gestures in widely scattered contexts. The word "shuffling," for example, is particularly linked with Claudius, who knows that there is no "shuffling" (III, iii, 61) in heaven, but that on earth "a little shuffling" (IV, vii, 137) can easily trick and destroy Hamlet. Or throughout the play there is an important subtext of spying and eavesdropping and variations on poisoning the ear, as in the murder of old Hamlet through "the porches" (I, v, 63) of his ears. In the comments that follow, I will try to suggest ways of using context and subtext to interpret our ten sample texts.

9

"STAND AND UNFOLD YOURSELF" (I, i, 1—21)

Enter Barnardo *and* Francisco, *two sentinels.*

BARNARDO: Who's there?

FRANCISCO: Nay, answer me. Stand and unfold yourself.

BARNARDO: Long live the King!

FRANCISCO: Barnardo?

BARNARDO: He.

FRANCISCO: You come most carefully upon your hour.

BARNARDO: 'Tis now struck twelve. Get thee to bed, Francisco.

FRANCISCO: For this relief much thanks. 'Tis bitter cold,
　　And I am sick at heart.

BARNARDO: Have you had quiet guard?

FRANCISCO: 　　　　　　　　　　Not a mouse stirring.

BARNARDO: Well, good night.
　　If you do meet Horatio and Marcellus,
　　The rivals of my watch, bid them make haste.

Enter Horatio *and* Marcellus.

FRANCISCO: I think I hear them. Stand, ho! Who is there?

HORATIO: Friends to this ground.

MARCELLUS: 　　　　　　　　And liegemen to the Dane.

FRANCISCO: Give you good night.

MARCELLUS: 　　　　　　　　O, farewell, honest soldier.
　　Who hath relieved you?

FRANCISCO: Barnardo hath my place.
Give you good night.

Exit Francisco.

MARCELLUS: Holla, Barnardo!
BARNARDO: Say—
What, is Horatio there?
HORATIO: A piece of him.
BARNARDO: Welcome, Horatio. Welcome, good Marcellus.
MARCELLUS: What, has this thing appeared again tonight?

The beginning of a play is of special significance. We start at "point zero" and are eager to know where we are at. This is a moment of high receptivity in both audience and reader alike, because our natural curiosity is waiting to be aroused. Let us try to consider *Hamlet* freshly as a new play being staged for the first time. We have no preconceptions at all, and everything we learn must come directly from the passage before us.

Before we get to the spoken words, notice the opening stage direction: *"Enter* Barnardo *and* Francisco, *two sentinels."* (I am deliberately ignoring the scene location: *"A guard platform of the castle,"* because this is not Shakespeare's but has been supplied by later editors, as indicated by the square brackets enclosing it.) The stage direction is not part of the spoken play, so that we do not know their names are Barnardo and Francisco until they actually speak these names to each other. All we see are two soldiers in uniform, heavily armed. We know at once that this is a military play, and the dialogue that follows conveys a strong sense of national emergency.

Barnardo and Francisco do not enter together, but separately from opposite sides of the stage. Barnardo is coming on guard duty, and it is odd that he should be the one to ask the conventional question: "Who's there?" (Or, "Who goes there?") Some critics, especially Harry Levin, make much of the fact that *Hamlet* begins with a question and puts such strong emphasis throughout on the interrogative mood. Francisco is on guard duty at the moment and Barnardo enters to relieve him, so that when Barnardo asks his question, we can share Francisco's surprise: "Nay, answer *me* [that is, I'm the one who should be putting the questions]. Stand and unfold yourself [stand still and let me know who you are]." Barnardo's "Long live the King!" may be the password, but Francisco recognizes his voice and the minor crisis with which the play begins is over.

We know that the time is midnight, because we hear the bell tolling twelve times and Barnardo makes this explicit for us with his words: " 'Tis now struck twelve." Shakespeare's characters often comment on a sound effect or on some other aspect of the nonverbal staging. In this passage the emphasis would be useful, because Shakespeare's plays were performed in the afternoon in an open-air, unroofed theater. Similarly, Francisco tells us that it is "bitter cold." This kind of atmospheric detail is only significant because it helps set a mood. The soldier Francisco, who has been on guard duty all night, couples " 'Tis bitter cold" with "I am sick at heart." The general feeling is one of anxiety, and both sentinels seem awfully jumpy in their questions and answers of the first five lines. Something is up, but we do not yet know what it is. The quoted passage ends with the question of Marcellus: "What, has this thing appeared again tonight?" "Thing" is the right technical word for a ghost, which is neuter and generally addressed as "it," but it still seems a strangely insulting word, especially because the Ghost takes the form of the late King of Denmark, Hamlet's father.

There are a number of other indications of general anxiety, meant to arouse the audience's curiosity. "Something is rotten in the state of Denmark" (I, iv, 90), but what is it? How are we to put together the hints we are receiving? As Hamlet says when he learns of the Ghost, "My father's spirit—in arms? All is not well." (I, ii, 255.) Once the first note is struck, the play then moves to reveal the hidden evil that lies behind the opening scene.

Before we leave this passage, we might ask some further questions about details used to characterize the speakers. Shakespeare is a great master of quick and unforgettable sketches and cameo appearances. Is Francisco, for example, characterized in any specific ways? He disappears from the play at this point, so we should not expect anything elaborate. What are we to make of Marcellus's "O, farewell, honest soldier"? "Honest" probably means "blunt and plain-spoken," as Elizabethan soldiers were supposed to be, rather than the more general, modern sense of "truthful." What is so "honest" about Francisco? We do not learn much about him personally, but we do hear that he is "sick at heart," just as Hamlet, later, wonders whether it is worth it "by a sleep to say we end/ The heartache, and the thousand natural shocks/ That flesh is heir to." (III, i, 61–63.) At the very end of the play, just before the fatal fencing match, Hamlet tells Horatio with a sense of tragic foreboding: "But thou wouldst not think how ill all's here about my heart." (V, ii, 213–214.) Is it legitimate and helpful to make these links and analogies in the play, especially between one of the most minor characters and the hero himself, who dominates the action at almost every point? In other words, can we understand the play as a series of intricate parallels and mirroring effects?

10

"WITH MIRTH IN FUNERAL, AND WITH DIRGE IN MARRIAGE"
(I, ii, 1–39)

King: Though yet of Hamlet our dear brother's death
The memory be green, and that it us befitted
To bear our hearts in grief, and our whole kingdom
To be contracted in one brow of woe,
Yet so far hath discretion fought with nature
That we with wisest sorrow think on him
Together with remembrance of ourselves.
Therefore our sometime sister, now our Queen,
Th' imperial jointress to this warlike state,
Have we, as 'twere, with a defeated joy,
With an auspicious and a dropping eye,
With mirth in funeral, and with dirge in marriage,
In equal scale weighing delight and dole,
Taken to wife. Nor have we herein barred
Your better wisdoms, which have freely gone
With this affair along. For all, our thanks.
Now follows that you know young Fortinbras,
Holding a weak supposal of our worth,
Or thinking by our late dear brother's death
Our state to be disjoint and out of frame,   *he thinks it is weak*
Colleaguèd with this dream of his advantage,
He hath not failed to pester us with message,

97

Importing the surrender of those lands
Lost by his father, with all bands of law,
To our most valiant brother. (So much for him.)
Now for ourself and for this time of meeting.
Thus much the business is: we have here writ
To Norway, uncle of young Fortinbras—
Who, impotent and bedrid, scarcely hears
Of this his nephew's purpose—to suppress
His further gait herein, in that the levies,
The lists, and full proportions are all made
Out of his subject; and we here dispatch
You, good Cornelius, and you, Voltemand,
For bearers of this greeting to old Norway,
Giving to you no further personal power
To business with the King, more than the scope
Of these delated articles allow.
Farewell, and let your haste commend your duty.

Almost immediately after the first appearance of the Ghost, who "was about to speak when the cock crew" (I, i, 147) at daybreak, we move quickly and without any transition to the first appearance of King Claudius, Hamlet's uncle and the new husband of Hamlet's mother, Gertrude. Shakespeare likes abrupt contrasts, and it may be that the drama depends more than other literary forms on strong, unshaded, and unmodulated shifts. We are forced almost automatically to set I, i, against I, ii. There is no longer the anxiety and jumpiness of the first nocturnal scene. We are now in the Danish court, and the King enters to the sound of a trumpet fanfare, in a formal procession with his Queen, with his chief counselor Polonius, with courtiers, advisers, friends—all glittering except Hamlet, who enters last in black, a sign of mourning for his recently deceased father and also a conventional sign of melancholy. Hamlet's mourning suit is different from everyone else's clothes, and he strikes a discordant note on this otherwide happy occasion. The almost mute Hamlet is part of the on-stage audience for Claudius's speech.

The King delivers a formal oration, with elaborate grammatical constructions and complex syntax. He strives for the polished antitheses of epigrammatic wit, and in this respect his style resembles the studied artfulness of Polonius. The "equal scale weighing delight [for his marriage to Gertrude] and dole [for his dead brother, Hamlet]" is illustrated by cleverly matched pairs of opposites: "With an auspicious and a dropping eye,/ With mirth in funeral, and with dirge in marriage." The two eyes, each assigned a separate symbolic function—"auspicious" and "dropping" (presumably "dropping tears")—make a strained and farfetched image usually called a "conceit," which is like some of the grotesquely literal images in Donne and the Metaphysical Poets of the seventeenth century.

But Claudius can also speak with an alarming directness very different from his formal, rhetorical periods. "So much for him" in line 25 is menacing and not in the same tone at all as the rest of the speech: Claudius will make short work of young Fortinbras. The new King of Denmark has the power of command usually associated with Shakespeare's most effective rulers, like Henry IV and Henry V; Claudius is a man to be reckoned with. The question of whether he is a good king is closely related to his style in this speech, which is our first glimpse of him in action. He does not seem to have any of the doubts and hesitations and irritating expressions of vanity and self-concern that undermine kings like Richard II and Henry VI. But, we are soon to find out, Claudius is also a murderer, so that his first speech is also an extended act of concealment, and the play is much concerned with images like that of the "imposthume," or boil, "That inward breaks, and shows no cause without/ Why the man dies" (IV, iv, 28–29), or the deceptive salve for a skin disease, that "will but skin and film the ulcerous place/ Whiles rank corruption, mining all within,/ Infects unseen" (III, iv, 148–150). It is curious that skin disease should provide one of the dominant images of *Hamlet,* where the inner sore or evil is masked by a fair outward show. This contrast between appearance and reality is the source of Claudius's ever-present dilemma and torment.

I have already suggested some of the political implications of this speech, but we may also ask: Whom is the King speaking to, and what is the significance of the speech for his audience? More specifically, what does he mean by the insinuating statement: "Nor have we herein barred/ Your better wisdoms, which have freely gone/ With this affair along"? Does "this affair" suggest something more than the marriage to Gertrude? Doesn't it hint at a well-organized conspiracy, to which the King's audience (excluding, of course, Hamlet) have given their consent—perhaps only tacitly, but surely "freely"? Claudius does offer them his formal acknowledgment: "For all, our thanks," and he seems to be a clever manipulator, very conscious of his power. Notice that he does not appoint Cornelius and Voltemand as his plenipotentiary ambassadors to Norway, but only gives them "no further personal power/ To business with the King, more than the scope/ Of these delated articles allow." The "articles" are written down in a legal document, which he presents to Cornelius and Voltemand at this point, so we can plainly see that Claudius has thought about everything in advance and that he is leaving nothing to chance.

He powerfully refutes young Fortinbras's idea that Denmark, after the sudden death of old Hamlet, is now "disjoint and out of frame."

These are images from carpentry, with the implied extension that the human body and the earth itself—"this goodly frame" (II, ii, 306), as Hamlet calls it—may be put out of their natural, working order. It is curious that Hamlet conceives his own mission in Claudius's image: "The time is out of joint. O cursèd spite,/ That ever I was born to set it right!" (I, v, 188–189.) I have been suggesting links and analogies throughout this discussion, and it is up to the reader to evaluate these connections—either to dispute their relevance or to provide additional, corroborating ties.

11

"BY INDIRECTIONS FIND DIRECTIONS OUT"
(II, i, 37—68)

POLONIUS: Marry, sir, here's my drift,
   And I believe it is a fetch of warrant.
   You laying these slight sullies on my son
   As 'twere a thing a little soiled i' th' working,
   Mark you,
   Your party in converse, him you would sound,
   Having ever seen in the prenominate crimes
   The youth you breathe of guilty, be assured
   He closes with you in this consequence:
   "Good sir," or so, "friend," or "gentleman"—
   According to the phrase or the addition
   Of man and country—
REYNALDO: Very good, my lord.
POLONIUS: And then, sir, does 'a this—'a does—
   What was I about to say? By the mass, I was about to say something!
   Where did I leave?
REYNALDO: At "closes in the consequence," at "friend or so," and "gentle-
   man."
POLONIUS: At "closes in the consequence"—Ay, marry!
   He closes thus: "I know the gentleman;
   I saw him yesterday, or t'other day,
   Or then, or then, with such or such, and, as you say,

101

> There was 'a gaming, there o'ertook in's rouse,
> There falling out at tennis"; or perchance,
> "I saw him enter such a house of sale,"
> Videlicet, a brothel, or so forth.
> See you now—
> Your bait of falsehood take this carp of truth,
> And thus do we of wisdom and of reach,
> With windlasses and with assays of bias,
> By indirections find directions out.
> So, by my former lecture and advice,
> Shall you my son. You have me, have you not?

Polonius is the King's chief counselor—something like the prime minister of Denmark—and there is a strong feeling in the play that Claudius could never have become King without the help of Polonius, who is never directly implicated in the murder, but who, nevertheless, plays a very active role in the King's attempt to keep an eye on Hamlet —if not actually to hunt him down. Polonius is usually conceived as a foolish old man, garrulous, meandering, and verging on senility. He is all these things, but they only serve to emphasize his menacing power. He tyrannizes his daughter Ophelia and is willing to use her as a pawn in the King's game against Hamlet. Remember how he agrees to "loose" (II, ii, 162) Ophelia to Hamlet, while the prince is walking in the lobby, in order to set up an eavesdropping plot. And with Laertes in this passage Polonius is not above sending Reynaldo to Paris not only to spy on him, but also to worm out damaging information about his son by a classic device that can only be regarded as entrapment.

The speech quoted above is certainly wandering and aimless in its details. Polonius loses track of his discourse—"What was I about to say? By the mass, I was about to say something! Where did I leave?"— which is a sure sign of senility, or incipient senility, but he still knows exactly what he is doing, and his bumbling hesitations may only be a clever way of softening the repulsiveness of this spying on his son. Reynaldo neither agrees nor disagrees, but merely plays along with his master, although there are hints that he is also mercilessly ridiculing the old dodderer. Polonius explains things that need no explanation— " 'I saw him enter such a house of sale,' Videlicet, a brothel, or so forth"—and he specifies every possibility with the tediousness of a legal document—"I saw him yesterday, or t'other day,/ Or then, or then, with such or such." This is not exactly court eloquence, but the tedious repetition has a certain insidious and menacing quality. Polonius is persistent, full, explicit, sure of himself, and he has all the time in the world. Despite the fidgeting boredom of Reynaldo and the audience, he is entirely at his ease.

Some readers may be surprised that a speech so insignificant as this one between Polonius and Reynaldo has been included, while so many more important and more poetic speeches have been ruthlessly omitted. Although I know that the point is highly arguable, I believe that this dialogue contributes importantly to the dramatic design of *Hamlet*. The devious methods of Polonius reflect the moral tone of Denmark, and the use Claudius makes of Rosencrantz and Guildenstern to spy on Hamlet is analogous to Polonius's designs on Laertes. Both Polonius and Claudius are rotten to the core. Neither knows the meaning of openness, directness, fair-dealing, or honesty in any sense. Truth is not naked for them, as it is for Renaissance artists, but, rather, truth is a wily carp that can only be caught by baiting the hook with falsehood. Everything is indirect, twisted, distorted, if not actually crooked. Polonius's image of "assays of bias" comes from the game of bowls, in which the alley was deliberately curved so that the ball had to be rolled "on the bias," or in a circuitous path. Thus, directions are found out not directly, but by indirections. To discover the truth becomes a roundabout game of cunning, bluffing, and pretense, in which spying and eavesdropping are essential for success. It is quite evident that Polonius is an expert in perverting the truth. He is a politician in a Machiavellian sense that has a very modern ring to it, and he is eminently suited to be prime minister in the new regime of Claudius. The two are made for each other.

Even if I think Polonius a bit sinister, that does not mean that he is not also the object of a good deal of ridicule in the play. But he acts the clown with wonderful mastery of the arts of rhetoric. He is not only formal and elaborate and inclined to orate at the slightest provocation, but he can also express himself in a lively and colorful colloquial style. He dramatizes the answer of Reynaldo's imaginary informant in Paris with a good deal of skill: "and, as you say,/ There was 'a gaming, there o'ertook in's rouse,/ There falling out at tennis." Notice how many contractions there are to make the speech smoothly conversational, including the regular Elizabethan form " 'a" for "he." Nothing is said in the play about Claudius as a tennis player, but we often hear about his "rouse": "The King doth wake tonight and takes his rouse,/ Keeps wassail, and the swagg'ring upspring reels" (I, iv, 8–9), and Hamlet imagines killing Claudius while he is "At game a-swearing" (III, iii, 91). Again, relations between words and between characters are suggested, and the reader may wish to pursue them further. Drinking and gambling are vices connected with the central evil in the play, or at least the evil Hamlet imagines as central.

Polonius's phrase, "a thing a little soiled i' th' working," that is, in "working" or fashioning it, also offers some insight into what tragedy means, because it may serve as a metaphor for what Aristotle in the *Poetics* calls the "tragic flaw." In other words, the tragic protagonist is a man like us, neither all good nor all bad, but in a middle state between virtue and vice, who has one proclivity or inclination that, followed through, brings him to his doom. "A thing a little soiled i' th' working" means something that inevitably becomes sullied or tarnished by use; that is, it receives a taint, or "is subdued/ To what it works in, like the dyer's hand." (Sonnet 3.) Earlier in the play, Hamlet is much concerned with the "dram of evil" (I, iv, 36)—if that is what the line actually says—"the stamp of one defect" (I, iv, 31) that can destroy an otherwise virtuous man. One may ask why Shakespeare would want to include suggestions for a theory of tragedy by which to interpret the play. Is it possible to understand the tragedy of both Laertes and Hamlet by using only criteria that are already in the play? In what sense can we claim that the play is "self-interpreting"?

12

"MUST, LIKE A WHORE, UNPACK MY HEART WITH WORDS" (II, ii, 559—617)

Hamlet: Now I am alone.
O, what a rogue and peasant slave am I!
Is it not monstrous that this player here,
But in a fiction, in a dream of passion,
Could force his soul so to his own conceit
That from her working all his visage wanned,
Tears in his eyes, distraction in his aspect,
A broken voice, and his whole function suiting
With forms to his conceit? And all for nothing!
For Hecuba!
What's Hecuba to him, or he to Hecuba,
That he should weep for her? What would he do
Had he the motive and the cue for passion
That I have? He would drown the stage with tears
And cleave the general ear with horrid speech,
Make mad the guilty and appall the free,
Confound the ignorant, and amaze indeed
The very faculties of eyes and ears.
Yet I,
A dull and muddy-mettled rascal, peak
Like John-a-dreams, unpregnant of my cause,
And can say nothing. No, not for a king,

Upon whose property and most dear life
A damned defeat was made. Am I a coward?
Who calls me villain? Breaks my pate across?
Plucks off my beard and blows it in my face?
Tweaks me by the nose? Gives me the lie i' th' throat
As deep as to the lungs? Who does me this?
Ha, 'swounds, I should take it, for it cannot be
But I am pigeon-livered and lack gall
To make oppression bitter, or ere this
I should ha' fatted all the region kites
With this slave's offal. Bloody, bawdy villain!
Remorseless, treacherous, lecherous, kindless villain!
O, vengeance!
Why, what an ass am I! This is most brave,
That I, the son of a dear father murdered,
Prompted to my revenge by heaven and hell,
Must, like a whore, unpack my heart with words
And fall a-cursing like a very drab,
A scullion! Fie upon't, foh! About, my brains.
Hum—
I have heard that guilty creatures sitting at a play
Have by the very cunning of the scene
Been struck so to the soul that presently
They have proclaimed their malefactions.
For murder, though it have no tongue, will speak
With most miraculous organ. I'll have these players
Play something like the murder of my father
Before my uncle. I'll observe his looks,
I'll tent him to the quick. If 'a do blench,
I know my course. The spirit that I have seen
May be a devil, and the devil hath power
T' assume a pleasing shape, yea, and perhaps
Out of my weakness and my melancholy,
As he is very potent with such spirits,
Abuses me to damn me. I'll have grounds
More relative than this. The play's the thing
Wherein I'll catch the conscience of the King.

I give this long soliloquy in its entirety, because it is worth considering how much happens in these 59 lines and how varied are Hamlet's tones and moods. This is a more characteristic soliloquy than "To be, or not to be" (III, i, 56ff.), which is unusually meditative and philosophical. Most soliloquies have a more expository and a more practical function. When Hamlet says "Now I am alone," he means it literally, because this is the first time in this long scene that he is alone. He enters at line 167 and is on stage and actively participating in the action for almost 400 lines before he can find emotional relief in the soliloquy. This is why his speech begins so strongly, since it serves as a safety-valve for pressures that have been building up over the course of II, ii. Shakespeare's soliloquies tend to function more as an outlet for pent-up emotions than as a vehicle for reflection and speculation, although they are often used for purposes of straight exposition, especially of plots and future plans. Most of the speculation in this soliloquy is devoted to Hamlet's chagrin at his own sluggishness ("A dull and muddy-mettled rascal"), which will be corrected by his new, intensely vigorous plan to "catch the conscience of the King" with a play of his own choice and partly of his own devising. He begins his speech full of self-reproach, but ends with animated self-confidence in the success of his new plot.

See the change in him in the speech

Between these two points, a great deal seems to happen, and it is especially notable how quickly Hamlet moves between moods of dejection and exhilaration. Hamlet is always aware of being an actor himself. We hear him working up to a grand, denunciatory climax against his enemy Claudius: "Remorseless, treacherous, lecherous, kindless villain!/ O, vengeance!" This is a mannered and affected style, not unlike that of Richard II, in which the inner pair of adjectives ("treacherous-lecherous") and the outer pair ("Remorseless-kindless") are matched as part-rhymes. But there is a sudden break in the discourse, and Hamlet pauses to ridicule his own ranting style, which is "most brave," or insincerely showy and ostentatious: "brave" was used most often to describe the effect of flashy clothes. Hamlet mocks his own whorish fondness for fine words, because he takes pleasure in unpacking his heart with swaggering speeches while forgetting about the murder of his father and the incestuous whoredom of his own mother and the revenge he has promised to take. Hamlet is more self-conscious of his own style than any other protagonist of Shakespeare, and we may pair this passage with Hamlet's more extended ranting contest with Laertes at the burial of Ophelia. Hamlet is fully aware of what he is doing, although he is not particularly proud of his rhetorical agility. As he tells Laertes with contempt: "Nay, an [= if] thou'lt mouth,/ I'll rant as well as thou." (V, i, 285–286.)

Hamlet's "rogue and peasant slave" soliloquy is completely histrionic, and the illusions of acting and the theater inform his acute sense that, in the words of Jaques in As You Like It, "All the world's stage" (II, vii, 138). This is supposed to have been the motto of Shakespeare's own Globe theater (Totus mundus agit histrionem). Hamlet's soliloquy was prompted by the First Player's "passion" in delivering the antiquated speech about Pyrrhus's murder of old Priam at the end of the Trojan War, and Hecuba's intense grief—so unlike Gertrude's superficial sorrow for her own dead husband. "Passion" means both strong emotion and intense sorrow, and the word combines the fictive and the actual suffering of Hamlet, Hecuba, the First Player, and, by extension, old Priam and old Hamlet. Pyrrhus's "passion" as the relent-

107

less and bloody revenger is also relevant, since revenge is the thera-peutic opposite of a maudlin and ranting sorrow. "Passion" also, in its Latin sense, means the suffering itself, as in Christ's "passion" on the cross. The complexity of the word "passion" helps to define various meanings (some contradictory) that are relevant to Hamlet's situation.

Hamlet ends the soliloquy with the folk belief, well documented in Shakespeare's time, that a successful play could, by its powers of em-pathy, cause guilty persons in the audience to suddenly confess their crimes. "Murder will out," as the proverb says, but a powerful reenact-ment on stage is one of the most efficacious means for drawing it out. Suddenly, Hamlet knows clearly what he has to do. It is worth remark-ing that no matter how powerful and how effective the sense of psychological truth is at this point, the actual psychological processes are extremely simplified. Hamlet hits upon the device of a play to catch the conscience of the King with a hot flash like those in comic strips: "About, my brains./ Hum—." A modern playwright would certainly feel the need to make this sudden discovery more complex, although the effect as Shakespeare has it gains both strength and surprise from its very abruptness and lack of development. This is a point with wide implications for Shakespeare's method of characterization. He often wants an absolute character or situation, as in folktales: good or evil, virtuous or vicious.

One other point worth noting is Hamlet's conception of the Ghost at the end of this soliloquy: "The spirit that I have seen/ May be a devil, and the devil hath power/ T' assume a pleasing shape." Students usually take it as a sign of hopeless vacillation in Hamlet that he can't make up his mind about the Ghost, who clearly tells him: "I am thy father's spirit,/ Doomed for a certain term to walk the night." (I, v, 9–10.) But most of Shakespeare's good Protestant contemporaries gen-erally were afraid of ghosts and thought they were creatures of the devil. Hamlet is genuinely worried that he has been so quickly per-suaded by the Ghost, and he even attributes his credulousness to his ill-health and melancholy following the death of his father. Remember, when the Ghost first appears to Hamlet, his good friends Horatio and Marcellus try to stop him by force from following it, for fear that it might "deprive your sovereignty of reason/ And draw you into mad-ness." (I, iv, 73–74.) Hamlet's desire to test the truth of the Ghost's frightening narration is, then, perfectly natural and fits the complex ghost-lore of Shakespeare's time. The status of the Ghost is perhaps the single most puzzling feature in this play, and Shakespeare seems to have combined, syncretistically, Protestant, Catholic, and skeptical ideas. We might well ask why Shakespeare wants to make the Ghost so comprehensive rather than clearly and narrowly defining its nature. Is this a characteristic approach to other issues in the play?

13

"MAY ONE BE PARDONED AND RETAIN TH' OFFENSE?" (III, iii, 36—72)

King: O, my offense is rank, it smells to heaven;
It hath the primal eldest curse upon't,
A brother's murder. Pray can I not,
Though inclination be as sharp as will.
My stronger guilt defeats my strong intent,
And like a man to double business bound
I stand in pause where I shall first begin,
And both neglect. What if this cursèd hand
Were thicker than itself with brother's blood,
Is there not rain enough in the sweet heavens
To wash it white as snow? Whereto serves mercy
But to confront the visage of offense?
And what's in prayer but this twofold force,
To be forestallèd ere we come to fall,
Or pardoned being down? Then I'll look up.
My fault is past. But, O, what form of prayer
Can serve my turn? "Forgive me my foul murder"?
That cannot be, since I am still possessed
Of those effects for which I did the murder,
My crown, mine own ambition, and my queen.
May one be pardoned and retain th' offense?
In the corrupted currents of this world

> Offense's gilded hand may shove by justice,
> And oft 'tis seen the wicked prize itself
> Buys out the law. But 'tis not so above.
> There is no shuffling; there the action lies
> In his true nature, and we ourselves compelled,
> Even to the teeth and forehead of our faults,
> To give in evidence. What then? What rests?
> Try what repentance can. What can it not?
> Yet what can it when one cannot repent?
> O wretched state! O bosom black as death!
> O limèd soul, that struggling to be free
> Art more engaged! Help, angels! Make assay.
> Bow, stubborn knees, and, heart with strings of steel,
> Be soft as sinews of the newborn babe.
> All may be well.

One of the functions of this surprising, confessional soliloquy of Claudius is to confirm the authenticity of the Ghost and the truth of its murderous tale: "O, horrible! O, horrible! Most horrible!" (I, v, 80.) This sets up a dramatic irony between what the audience knows and what the characters on stage do not know. But Hamlet's fears and hesitations about the Ghost, as expressed in his soliloquy at the end of II, ii, have already evaporated. *The Mousetrap* play has been a great success, and it has accomplished all that was expected of it to "catch the conscience of the King." (II, ii, 617.)

Between this point and Claudius's attempt to pray in the passage above, there is also the King's strange and unanticipated aside in III, i. Polonius is busy "loosing" his daughter as a bait for Hamlet, and even the callous old counselor seems to be aware of some nagging moral scruple about setting up Ophelia as if she were reading in a prayer-book: "with devotion's visage/ And pious action we do sugar o'er/ The devil himself." (47–49.) Claudius is much struck by these conventional sentiments of Polonius: "O, 'tis too true./ How smart a lash that speech doth give my conscience!" (49–50.) He then draws on the familiar Renaissance image of cosmetics as the whore's way of making a fair outward show although rotten within: "The harlot's cheek, beautied with plast'ring art,/ Is not more ugly to the thing that helps it/ Than is my deed to my most painted word. O heavy burden!" (51–54.) Hamlet too is perturbed by the feminine arts of creating false illusions, as he berates Ophelia, the representative woman: "I have heard of your paintings, well enough. God hath given you one face, and you make yourselves another." (III, i, 144–146.) Claudius's aside seems to be inserted artificially as a comment on Polonius's platitude, and we may well ask whether it is effectively used for its intended purpose. Because the aside is a kind of warm-up for the King's soliloquy in III, iii, we may also question the relation between the two speeches.

Claudius's highly developed soliloquy comes almost at the very middle of the play, and it marks a high point for the King in winning over the audience's sympathies (just as Hamlet's soliloquy that follows, back to back, marks a low point for Hamlet in alienating the audience's sympathies). The King's desire to pray and to repent is sincere and even moving, but it is also shallow and pointless, as Claudius so well understands. The pressures of Christianity have taught us to admire any signs at all of confession and repentance, and to detest with unrelieved loathing hard-heartedness and obduracy, and even more than these vices, we shrink from the smiling hypocrite, who pretends to a virtue that is forever lost to him. In this context, we are positively relieved to learn that Claudius is, at least, not a hypocrite.

He begins his soliloquy extremely well, with a frank acknowledgment that his "offense is rank," a word that connotes bad smells, and especially the strong odor of an animal in heat, as in Shylock's meandering tale: the "ewes being rank/ In end of autumn turnèd to the rams." (*Merchant of Venice*, I, iii, 77–78.) The "primal eldest curse" on Claudius is for the murder of his brother, just as God cursed Cain for the murder of Abel. Claudius's questions are extremely clever and they show that he understands the paradoxes of theology: of course there is enough rain (and mercy) in the sweet heavens to wash any sinner's offense "white as snow." Claudius also understands that no form of prayer can serve his turn, because it is not a matter of proper forms and rituals. The central question is: "May one be pardoned and retain th' offense?" Claudius knows that he has no contrition, no true repentance for his crime, "since I am still possessed/ Of those effects for which I did the murder,/ My crown, mine own ambition, and my queen." That is the heart of the matter. The King's moral lucidity makes him appealing, but he is also powerfully self-condemned and self-castigated. In heaven there is no "shuffling"—no bribery, no influence-peddling, no packing a crooked deck—and "there the action lies/ In his true nature." "Action" is a legal word, and Claudius understands with a chilling clarity, like that of Dr. Faustus in Marlowe's play, that he cannot pray and that he is damned by his own unrepentant spirit. The final comment is the jingling couplet tacked on after Hamlet's soliloquy: "My words fly up, my thoughts remain below,/ Words without thoughts never to heaven go." (III, iii, 97–98.) Claudius rises from his futile praying, and we never hear anything further about the King's guilt. He has decided to tough it out.

We may question the structural purpose of this soliloquy. The King has by no means been destroyed by Hamlet's powerful reenactment of the murder of his father in his *Mousetrap* play of the previous scene.

(III, ii.) Claudius has been visibly shaken, but that is all, and he is now stronger than ever and beginning to move directly against Hamlet. The murder of Polonius in the next scene (III, iv) gives Claudius a perfect pretext for shipping Hamlet out of the country and presumably to his death in England. Once the King's confession is over and done with, he emerges with an iron will, determined like Macbeth to grapple with his destiny "In the corrupted currents of this world." By formally abandoning any possible comfort or help from heaven, Claudius commits himself to an utterly ruthless and unscrupulous counteraction against Hamlet.

14

"UP, SWORD, AND KNOW THOU A MORE HORRID HENT" (III, iii, 73—96)

Hamlet: Now might I do it pat, now 'a is a-praying,
And now I'll do't. And so 'a goes to heaven,
And so am I revenged. That would be scanned.
A villain kills my father, and for that
I, his sole son, do this same villain send
To heaven.
Why, this is hire and salary, not revenge.
'A took my father grossly, full of bread,
With all his crimes broad blown, as flush as May;
And how his audit stands, who knows save heaven?
But in our circumstance and course of thought,
'Tis heavy with him; and am I then revenged,
To take him in the purging of his soul,
When he is fit and seasoned for his passage?
No.
Up, sword, and know thou a more horrid hent.
When he is drunk asleep, or in his rage,
Or in th' incestuous pleasure of his bed,
At game a-swearing, or about some act
That has no relish of salvation in't—
Then trip him, that his heels may kick at heaven,

> And that his soul may be as damned and black
> As hell, whereto it goes. My mother stays.
> This physic but prolongs thy sickly days.

Hamlet suddenly enters with his sword drawn. He is on his way to his mother's "closet," or private room (definitely not a bedroom, which is a "chamber" in Elizabethan English), and the fearful mood of Hamlet's soliloquy at the end of III, ii, carries over into this chance encounter with the King. In that brief soliloquy, Hamlet vaunted: "Now could I drink hot blood/ And do such business as the bitter day/ Would quake to look on" (III, ii, 398–400)—note that I read "bitter day" (or Judgment Day) as in Quarto 2 rather than "bitter business" as in Folio. Hamlet steels himself not to commit the crime of Nero (matricide), as he goes to his mother to "speak daggers" but use none, and to be "cruel, not unnatural." This cruelty is plainly evident in the bridge scene with Claudius before Hamlet reaches his mother (III, iii), and his soliloquy there prepares us for his harsh and ·biting dialogue with Gertrude in the next scene (III, iv).

Why does Hamlet enter with his sword drawn if he is not in some way struggling with the idea of matricide? The sword itself as a stage property gives a special emphasis to Hamlet's swaggering, colloquial style: "Now might I do it pat, now 'a is a-praying,/ And now I'll do't." " 'A" is the familiar contraction for "he," and "pat" is a contemptuous word for "opportunely, just in the nick of time." Edmund, the Bastard, speaks disdainfully of his foolish brother Edgar, about to be tricked: "and pat he comes, like the catastrophe of the old comedy." (*King Lear,* I, ii, 137–138.) This is an unusual style for Hamlet, who does not seem comfortable with the words and postures of the traditional stage revenger. But he takes on the role with his usual vigor and full participation, despite the fact that he sounds like the swordsman Tybalt, "King of Cats," in *Romeo and Juliet.* (III, i, 78.) The culmination of this machismo style and mood comes in Hamlet's casual murder of Polonius in the next scene: "How now? A rat? Dead for a ducat, dead!" (III, iv, 25.) This sounds like a phrase from gambling, as we might say: "Dead for two bits (or half a crown), dead!"

Students, taking advantage of the fact that this is a play and not real life, generally cheer Hamlet on to commit murder and are genuinely disappointed that he does not run Claudius through "pat" and without any long speeches and Hamlet-like hesitations. But it is quite plain why Hamlet does not kill Claudius, even though he is standing right next to him and Claudius is on his knees, with his back turned. Hamlet does not want to murder a man who is praying not because he has any scruple about the deed—he is certainly not a moping intellectual at this moment—but because he is afraid that the soul of Claudius will go straight to heaven if he is killed "in the purging of his soul,/ When he is fit and seasoned for his passage." Hamlet wants to wait for a better opportunity for his revenge, so he puts his sword back in its scabbard ("Up, sword") until it will have a "more horrid hent." "Horrid" was a very strong word in Shakespeare's time, with a close relation to its Latin meaning—something "horrid" causes "horror"—and "hent" is the Anglo-Saxon word for grasping something. In other words, Hamlet will not draw his sword until he has an almost perfect setting for his revenge, and he can be sure of damning Claudius's soul as well as killing his body. Samuel Johnson, who was no namby-pamby and not easily shocked, thought Hamlet's sentiments in this speech "too horrible to be read or to be uttered."

I am inclined to agree with him, mostly because, as a matter of principle, I believe what Hamlet is telling us in this soliloquy. I reject any overly subtle interpretation which insists that Hamlet really does not mean what he says, because he is merely procrastinating and making up all sorts of wild excuses to keep himself from getting on with his task—in other words, murdering Claudius. I believe that Hamlet, like all other revengers (at least in Elizabethan plays), gets so caught up in his revenge at this point that he overreaches himself and longs for a perfect, poetic justice that is almost impossible for him to attain. He conjures up a whole set of revenge scenarios that are better than Claudius praying: "When he is drunk asleep, or in his rage,/ Or in th' incestuous pleasure of his bed,/ At game a-swearing." Notice that all of these scenes seem to have a double aspect: not only gaming, but also swearing; not only making love with Gertrude, but also polluting the marriage bed of his former sister-in-law; not only sleeping, but in a drunken sleep. Hamlet's imagination is exceedingly vivid, and he moves far beyond the warrant of being heaven's "scourge and minister" (III, iv, 176) in his inflamed desire to trip Claudius up so that "his soul may be as damned and black/ As hell, whereto it goes." Here, Hamlet as revenger seems to be acting as an agent of hell rather than heaven. This is a serious theological confusion, and it may partly account for the low point in Hamlet's fortunes at this moment. He is too actively pursuing his own "deep plots" (V, ii, 9), without any of his later wisdom that "The readiness is all" (V, ii, 223–224).

The Claudius we see through Hamlet's imagination is very different from the Claudius we see on stage, whose moving and lucid soliloquy we have just listened to. Hamlet is constantly speaking of his uncle-father as a drunkard, a swaggerer, and a disgusting satyr, obscene and never satisfied sexually, pinching "wanton" on Gertrude's cheek or "paddling" in her "neck with his damned fingers." (II, iv, 186.) In short, a "paddock" (= toad), a "bat," a "gib" (= tomcat) (III, iv, 191). How do these details affect the characterization of Claudius? Can we say, simply, that Hamlet is wrong, or must we consider what he says as an essential aspect of Claudius that he struggles to hide? Claudius is, after all, a murderer who is trying to keep up respectable appearances at all costs. How do these considerations affect the acting of Claudius and, more basically, the casting of the part? The questions should suggest that Shakespeare's characterization is more complex than a mere inventory of attributes.

15

"YOUNG MEN WILL DO'T IF THEY COME TO'T"
(IV, v, 41—73)

KING: How do you, pretty lady?

OPHELIA: Well, God dild you! They say the owl was a baker's daughter. Lord, we know what we are, but know not what we may be. God be at your table!

KING: Conceit upon her father.

OPHELIA: Pray let's have no words of this, but when they ask you what it means, say you this:

> [*Sings.*] Tomorrow is Saint Valentine's day.
> All in the morning betime,
> And I a maid at your window,
> To be your Valentine.

> Then up he rose and donned his clothes
> And dupped the chamber door,
> Let in the maid, that out a maid
> Never departed more.

KING: Pretty Ophelia.

OPHELIA: Indeed, la, without an oath, I'll make an end on't:

> [*Sings.*] By Gis and by Saint Charity,
> Alack, and fie for shame!
> Young men will do't if they come to't,
> By Cock, they are to blame.

117

> Quoth she, "Before you tumbled me,
>   You promised me to wed."
> He answers:
> "So would I 'a done, by yonder sun,
>   An thou hadst not come to my bed."

KING: How long hath she been thus?

OPHELIA: I hope all will be well. We must be patient, but I cannot choose
but weep to think they would lay him i' th' cold ground. My brother shall
know of it; and so I thank you for your good counsel. Come, my coach!
Good night, ladies, good night. Sweet ladies, good night, good night.

Exit.

The mad Ophelia introduces a new element into the action of
Hamlet, one that moves us closer to the tragic end. Her madness is
tragic and pathetic and intensely lyrical, because she is an innocent
victim without any complicity. By no stretch of the imagination can
we say that Ophelia has a "tragic flaw" that causes her undoing. She
is the mere unwitting tool of her father, who has already met his accidental death while eavesdropping on Hamlet and his mother in III, iv.
Ophelia's doom is like that of Cordelia in *King Lear,* and Cordelia's
eloquent words while she is being led away to prison with her father
also apply to Ophelia: "We are not the first/ Who with best meaning
have incurred the worst." (V, iii, 3–4.) Ophelia and Cordelia are tragic
not because they are punished for their sins or even for their weakness
of character, but rather because there is no reason at all for their suffering except their association with those whose tragic doom is more
predictable—Lear, Hamlet, Polonius, Laertes. In Ophelia and Cordelia
we feel profoundly the idea of tragic waste, of characters caught up
by circumstances in which they are not direct participants. "Best meaning" is not enough to save you.

Shakespeare was very interested in showing madness on stage, in
all of its degrees from Hamlet's "wild and whirling words" (I, v, 133)
after his scene with the Ghost to Ophelia's pitiful state. The First
Quarto of *Hamlet,* which may represent some sort of road-show version of the play, has Ophelia enter here *"with her hair down singing."*
Since Elizabethan ladies wore their hair in elaborate, emblematic designs, supported by "tires," or wire frames—we know that Shakespeare
boarded with a Huguenot tire-maker in London for a brief period—
to let your hair down represented a loss of control (as in the case of
the raving Cassandra in *Troilus and Cressida*) that could only be at-
tributed to distraction.

Madness in Shakespeare (and in other Elizabethan dramatists) has its
own set of conventions. It allows for a freer, more personal, more
emotional kind of expression, and it makes much use of free association, stream of consciousness, broken syntax, random and disconnected

thoughts, and sudden snatches of song, especially old ballads. Ophelia is suddenly freed from the unbearable pressures of propriety and parental authority, but she cracks under the strain of her new freedom and new grief. On the one side, her thoughts are colored by the sexuality she was forced to repress—her mind plays on what Blake calls "the lineaments of gratified desire." At the opposite side is her overwhelming sorrow for her father, whose death now seems touching and poignant. Like Juliet, torn between Romeo and her dead kinsman Tybalt, Ophelia cannot solve the paradox of her lover killing her father. It is too much for her to bear, just as the tough and high-minded Portia, the wife of Brutus in *Julius Caesar,* unable to cope with her husband's defeat, falls "distract" (IV, iii, 152), swallows live coals, and dies.

The speech of mad people in Shakespeare is also a kind of dark discourse, full of hints and implications and innuendos that relate to the main themes of the play. How are we to understand Ophelia's "Lord, we know what we are, but know not what we may be"? This seems to connect with the familiar theme of Fortune: we do not control our own destinies, but are the playthings of Fortune, and we cannot therefore predict what may happen to us or how our plans will succeed. In tragedy, fate is ironic, and things turn out just the opposite from what is intended and the "enginer," or deviser, is "hoist," or blown into the air," "with his own petard," or bomb. (III, iv, 208.) Because Ophelia is speaking to Claudius, we may also understand her to be probing his secret guilt: "we know what we are" and we know what you are, but do not count on your continued success, because we "know not what we may be."

Ophelia worries Claudius, and we can imagine that his first concern after she exits—"Follow her close; give her good watch, I pray you" (IV, v, 74)—does not seem to be for Ophelia's health and well being. Ophelia is much disturbed by her father's questionable death and his hasty burial "in hugger-mugger" (IV, v, 84), and she threatens to reveal all to her brother in France. With typical dramatic economy, Laertes enters within 40 lines, at the head of a successful rebellion against Claudius. Ophelia seems to worry Gertrude, too, who at first refuses to see her, but then consents because of Horatio's essentially political argument: " 'Twere good she were spoken with, for she may strew/ Dangerous conjectures in ill-breeding minds." (IV, v, 14–15.) Ophelia's first words when she enters are the supremely ironic question: "Where is the beauteous majesty of Denmark?" (IV, v, 21.) Because Ophelia sees the Queen right before her, what can this question mean? Has Gertrude lost the beauty and majesty she once had as the wife of old Hamlet? The question insinuates: What has happened to the once-beauteous majesty of Denmark?

Ophelia seems to know a lot of dirty songs, and students, working backwards, are tempted to reconstruct a racy past for Ophelia that is not so maidenly as she makes out. But this is to fall into the fallacy of Mary Cowden Clarke's three-volume work of fiction, *The Girlhood of Shakespeare's Heroines* (1850–1852). Madness releases Ophelia's hidden sexuality, but she is no less innocent than Juliet or Desdemona, neither of whom want to be deprived of the pleasures of the wedding night. In her madness, Ophelia is now free to sing songs of the loss of virginity and to swear "by Cock" and celebrate the traditional rites of Saint Valentine's day. Madness extends Ophelia's part and endows her with more intense emotions and a wider range of expression than she had earlier in the play. But her new scope is wasted and misdirected and can only arouse feelings of tragic pity. Being a minor character, Ophelia defines our sense of tragedy in a more limited and therefore more lucid way than the major characters. In what sense can we say that Ophelia is "caught up" in the tragic action that transforms and destroys her?

16

"TO CUT HIS THROAT I' TH' CHURCH"
(IV, vii, 107—139)

KING: Laertes, was your father dear to you?
   Or are you like the painting of a sorrow,
   A face without a heart?
LAERTES: Why ask you this?
KING: Not that I think you did not love your father,
   But that I know love is begun by time,
   And that I see, in passages of proof,
   Time qualifies the spark and fire of it.
   There lives within the very flame of love,
   A kind of wick or snuff that will abate it,
   And nothing is at a like goodness still,
   For goodness, growing to a plurisy,
   Dies in his own too-much. That we would do
   We should do when we would, for this "would" changes,
   And hath abatements and delays as many
   As there are tongues, are hands, are accidents,
   And then this "should" is like a spendthrift sigh,
   That hurts by easing. But to the quick of th' ulcer—
   Hamlet comes back; what would you undertake
   To show yourself in deed your father's son   ——
   More than in words?
LAERTES: To cut his throat i' th' church!

121

KING: No place indeed should murder sanctuarize;
   Revenge should have no bounds. But, good Laertes,
   Will you do this? Keep close within your chamber.
   Hamlet returned shall know you are come home.
   We'll put on those shall praise your excellence
   And set a double varnish on the fame
   The Frenchman gave you, bring you in fine together
   And wager on your heads. He, being remiss,
   Most generous, and free from all contriving,
   Will not peruse the foils, so that with ease,
   Or with a little shuffling, you may choose
   A sword unbated, and, in a pass of practice,
   Requite him for your father.

In a different sense from his sister, Laertes too is pathetic, especially as we see Claudius leading him on with questions and ensnaring him in a web of subtle innuendo, so that Laertes's manly resolution is completely sapped and he becomes a willing tool in the King's plot to kill Hamlet. Laertes is all bluster and swagger—no match for the wily Claudius, who wilts Laertes's already successful palace revolution by old-fashioned appeals to divine right. In this context, Gertrude's physical intervention to restrain Laertes is the wrong tactic: "Let him go, Gertrude. Do not fear our person./ There's such divinity doth hedge a king/ That treason can but peep to what it would,/ Acts little of his will." (IV, v, 122–125.) Laertes is rendered impotent by the King's cajolery.

One implication of the passage above is that Laertes is pathetic because he is so imperceptive and so easily led by the nose. Claudius manipulates his questions as if he were dealing with a schoolboy: "Laertes, was your father dear to you?" This is essentially a rhetorical question, but Claudius insists on beginning the game at square one, and he treats Laertes throughout like a headstrong adolescent, who needs direction and encouragement. When Laertes replies that, to show himself in deed (with wordplay on "indeed") a loyal son he will cut Hamlet's "throat i' th' church," even Claudius seems to be shocked, and he feels the need to restrain this impetuous youth who may spoil everything by his ardor. It is not very satisfying to be told, at the height of your heroic endeavor: "Keep close within your chamber." Why doesn't Laertes have the sense to see that he is merely Claudius's tool?

By the workings of analogy, Laertes, Hamlet, Fortinbras, and Pyrrhus (in the First Player and Hamlet's narration) are all pursuing revenges for dead fathers (or against father surrogates, as in Pyrrhus's murder of old Priam). Of these four Laertes is clearly the least heroic, and his eventual revenge against Hamlet is executed by fraud and trickery (as is Achilles's revenge against Hector in *Troilus and Cressida*). Yet in the moral balance, Laertes is in some way absolved—"The King, the King's to blame" (V, ii, 321)—and his final act before he dies is to "exchange forgiveness" (V, ii, 330) with Hamlet. He even has an aside, deliberately thrust into the fencing match, in which he tempers his desire to "hit" Hamlet with the unbated and poisoned rapier: "And yet it is almost against my conscience." (V, ii, 297.) All in all, Laertes is a puzzling character, and Shakespeare's intentions for him do not all seem to have been successfully realized.

Claudius dominates the scenes with Laertes in Act IV. Once we get past the soul-searching of the prayer scene (III, iii), Claudius becomes more and more assured of himself and more formidable as Hamlet's antagonist; in fact, he becomes more and more like Macbeth. Is Claudius, too, becoming a man of sorrows, and his life now "fall'n into the sear, the yellow leaf"? (Macbeth, V, iii, 23.) The passage above suggests strains in his relations with Gertrude, because "the very flame of love" is fueled by what will eventually destroy it—compare Macbeth's "Out, out, brief candle" (V, v, 23)—and time "qualifies the spark and fire" of love's candle. The only reality, then, lies in strength of will, and Claudius enunciates the villain's creed: "That we would do/ We should do when we would." Again, Macbeth almost exactly echoes these sentiments in his quick determination to annihilate Macduff and his family: "From this moment/ The very firstlings of my heart shall be/ The firstlings of my hand." (IV, i, 146–148.) It is in this damnable, voluntaristic belief that Laertes is being nurtured by Claudius, who experiences a degree of success with Laertes that he surely never anticipated.

Another consistent aspect of Shakespeare's villains is to have contempt for their victims, or at least for those qualities of openness, candor, and largeness of spirit which make the victims vulnerable and which eventually lead to their destruction. Hamlet can be easily duped because, with aristocratic nonchalance, he is "remiss/ Most generous, and free from all contriving." He believes in the honorableness of other men, and he will not, therefore, stoop so low as to "peruse the foils," or examine them closely to see whether there is one whose end has not been blunted. Compare Iago's even more facile assault on Othello, who "is of a free and open nature/ That thinks men honest that but seem to be so." (Othello, I, iii, 388–389.) Hamlet and Othello are both easy marks, and the key word of Claudius is "shuffling," which we remember vividly from the prayer scene: "But 'tis not so above./ There is no shuffling." (III, iii, 60–61.) Can we consider the play as a self-enclosed world, in which key words and key images echo each other in different contexts?

One of the questions raised by Hamlet is whether indeed "Revenge should have no bounds." Laertes means to speak boldly and blasphemously when he says he is ready to cut Hamlet's throat "i' th' church." This is like the strangely distorted and slow-motion type of revenge that Pyrrhus executes on old Priam in the narration begun by Hamlet and continued by the First Player. The "rugged Pyrrhus" (II, ii, 461) is so overdrawn that he seems to be a parody of a revenger as he stalks his victim: "roasted in wrath and fire [= the flames of burning Troy]/ And thus o'ersized with coagulate gore,/ With eyes like carbuncles." (II, ii, 472–474.) "Size" is a kind of glue used as a stiffening material, but there is significant wordplay on Pyrrhus's being "oversized." So is Laertes, at least in his new-found role of revenger, and it is worth questioning the more ruthless and hard-boiled critics of the play whether they want Hamlet to take his revenge in the overblown style of Pyrrhus and Laertes. If "Revenge should have no bounds"— and Claudius prepares a triple plot of unbated rapier, envenomed tip, and poisoned chalice of wine—then what is the point of justice and Christianity? And how can you distinguish morally between the revenger and his victim?

17

"ALAS, POOR YORICK! I KNEW HIM, HORATIO" (V, i, 165—214)

HAMLET: How long will a man lie i' th' earth ere he rot?

CLOWN: Faith, if 'a be not rotten before 'a die (as we have many pocky corses nowadays that will scarce hold the laying in), 'a will last you some eight year or nine year. A tanner will last you nine year.

HAMLET: Why he, more than another?

CLOWN: Why, sir, his hide is so tanned with his trade that 'a will keep out water a great while, and your water is a sore decayer of your whoreson dead body. Here's a skull now hath lien you i' th' earth three and twenty years.

HAMLET: Whose was it?

CLOWN: A whoreson mad fellow's it was. Whose do you think it was?

HAMLET: Nay, I know not.

CLOWN: A pestilence on him for a mad rogue! 'A poured a flagon of Rhenish on my head once. This same skull, sir, was, sir, Yorick's skull the King's jester.

HAMLET: This?

CLOWN: E'en that.

HAMLET: Let me see. [*Takes the skull.*] Alas, poor Yorick! I knew him, Horatio, a fellow of infinite jest, of most excellent fancy. He hath borne me on his back a thousand times. And now how abhorred in my imagination it is! My gorge rises at it. Here hung those lips that I have kissed I know not how oft. Where be your gibes now? Your gambols, your songs, your flashes

of merriment that were wont to set the table on a roar? Not one now to mock your own grinning? Quite chapfall'n? Now get you to my lady's chamber, and tell her, let her paint an inch thick, to this favor she must come. Make her laugh at that. Prithee, Horatio, tell me one thing.
HORATIO: What's that, my lord?
HAMLET: Dost thou think Alexander looked o' this fashion i' th' earth?
HORATIO: E'en so.
HAMLET: And smelt so? Pah! [*Puts down the skull.*]
HORATIO: E'en so, my lord.
HAMLET: To what base uses we may return, Horatio! Why may not imagination trace the noble dust of Alexander till 'a find it stopping a bunghole?
HORATIO: 'Twere to consider too curiously, to consider so.
HAMLET: No, faith, not a jot, but to follow him thither with modesty enough, and likelihood to lead it; as thus: Alexander died, Alexander was buried, Alexander returneth to dust; the dust is earth; of earth we make loam; and why of that loam whereto he was converted might they not stop a beer barrel?

The graveyard scene, with its irreverent Clown-gravedigger and with its grotesque mixture of jokes, conundrums, and meditations on mortality, was particularly offensive to French neoclassical critics, who thought it pointless, in bad taste, and merely put in to entertain the "groundlings" in Shakespeare's audience. The scene is characteristic of Shakespeare's method of constructing a play, which never moves linearly and purposively from beginning to end, but keeps moving from side to side and generally puts scenes together by the principle of abrupt contrast. Right before the catastrophe in *Hamlet*, we are suddenly treated to a clown show, with random reflections on death, burial, and preservation of corpses. A skull is turned up and identified as that of Yorick, the King's jester, and the plot seems to stand still at a moment of great excitement, when Hamlet has just miraculously returned from his fated voyage to England. Those much-needed explanations are put off until the beginning of the next scene, while the gravedigger and his assistant, Hamlet, and Horatio engage in witty repartee and philosophical speculation.

This kind of encounter is usually called a "choral scene," and there are a great many like it in Shakespeare, when the plot of the play seems to stop, and characters we have never seen before (and will most probably never see again), often anonymous and always outside the action, comment in their own idiomatic way on some larger issue of the play's meaning. Thus in *Coriolanus*, II, ii, "*Enter two* Officers, *to lay cushions, as it were in the Capitol,*" but they are really brought on to have an extremely lucid conversation about the strengths and weaknesses of Caius Marcius. Or in *Macbeth* after the murder of King Duncan, an Old Man more than threescore and ten reports the horrors of the night, including that fact that Duncan's horses ate each other.

(II, iv.) In *Hamlet*, then, the choral scene in the graveyard tries to establish larger meanings of life and death and man's mortality before the many deaths that conclude the action in the next scene. In V, i, there is a meditation on death, with a wide range of dramatic effects and moods that make some comment on the theme. Hamlet's curiosity about how long a corpse may last before it rots suggests that he is trying to find out what it must feel like to be dead, because he senses his doom inevitably closing in on him. He is no longer fighting his own death, which he now accepts as imminent, and this, in some important way, frees him to take his revenge. There is not much direct statement on the *memento mori* theme, but a good deal of physical evocation of death. Hamlet's disgust at the stink of the skull is plainly evident, even if it is the skull of Alexander the Great: "And smelt so? Pah!" "Pah" is one of those vague Shakespearean words that can only be rendered by a gesture. Earlier, Yorick's skull is "abhorred" in Hamlet's imagination; his "gorge rises at it." The "gorge" is the mass of food being digested in the stomach, and the rising gorge is a sign of vomiting. It is worth noting how directly physical Hamlet's imagery often is.

The larger theme of this passage is, of course, that of earthly vanity. Both Yorick and Alexander have had their moment of greatness, which is now irrevocably past, and all that remains is the pitiful skull to show that they once lived. This is a familiar theological subject. In Hamlet's "curious," or fastidious, reasoning, Alexander is progressively transformed from the great king of Macedonia to a lump of clay used to stop up the bunghole on a beer barrel. Like a good Christian, Hamlet is learning how to die, as in the devotional manual of Jeremy Taylor, *Holy Dying* (1651). Death is, above all, a process of transformation. Hamlet meditating on the skull of Yorick, which he holds in his hand, provided an unforgettable image for playgoers and playwrights alike, and it was much repeated in subsequent literature. The theme of vanity also includes the satirical notion of cosmetics as a mockery of the skull beneath the skin. Once more, as with Ophelia, Hamlet taunts the painted woman who tries to defy death: "Now get you to my lady's chamber, and tell her, let her paint an inch thick, to this favor she must come." This is what a preacher would call a moralization of the theme.

The jester Yorick, who died 23 years before, is vividly invoked by Hamlet. Along with old Hamlet, Horatio, and the First Player, Yorick is one of the few figures in the play for whom Hamlet feels strong and spontaneous affection. Hamlet, too, aspires to be "a fellow of infinite jest, of most excellent fancy"—all terms of aesthetic achievement. We see him in this role of jester and master of ceremonies during the scene of the *Mousetrap* play, where he tries, sardonically, to put everyone at his ease. "You are merry, my lord," says Ophelia, and Hamlet answers: "O God, your only jig-maker!/ What should a man do but be merry?" (III, ii, 125, 128–129.) But Yorick was a professional entertainer, whose "flashes of merriment" were "wont to set the table on a roar." Besides being an idealized figure from the past, Yorick also reminds Hamlet of a different world with different values. Then, Hamlet was the courtier, soldier, scholar, whom Ophelia remembers with so much poignant regret, "Th' expectancy and rose of the fair state,/ The glass of fashion, and the mold of form,/ Th' observed of all observers." (III, i, 155–157.) Just before Hamlet's own impending death, the "remembrance of things past" (Sonnet 30) is reinvoked for one beautiful moment by the skull of Yorick.

18

"WHY, EVEN IN THAT WAS HEAVEN ORDINANT"
(V, ii, 47—74)

HORATIO: How was this sealed?
HAMLET: Why, even in that was heaven ordinant.
  I had my father's signet in my purse,
  Which was the model of that Danish seal,
  Folded the writ up in the form of th' other,
  Subscribed it, gave't th' impression, placed it safely,
  The changeling never known. Now, the next day
  Was our sea fight, and what to this was sequent
  Thou knowest already.
HORATIO: So Guildenstern and Rosencrantz go to't.
HAMLET: Why, man, they did make love to this employment.
  They are not near my conscience; their defeat
  Does by their own insinuation grow.
  'Tis dangerous when the baser nature comes
  Between the pass and fell incensed points
  Of mighty opposites.
HORATIO: Why, what a king is this!
HAMLET: Does it not, think thee, stand me now upon—
  He that hath killed my king, and whored my mother,
  Popped in between th' election and my hopes,
  Thrown out his angle for my proper life,
  And with such coz'nage—is't not perfect conscience

> To quit him with this arm? And is't not to be damned
> To let this canker of our nature come
> In further evil?
> HORATIO: It must be shortly known to him from England
>   What is the issue of the business there.
> HAMLET: It will be short; the interim's mine,
>   And a man's life's no more than to say "one."

This passage starts *in medias res* ("in the midst of things"), as does Hamlet's whole account of his escape from certain death in England that begins the final scene of the play. His stealing, from Rosencrantz and Guildenstern, of Claudius's "grand commission" to have him executed by the King of England, his forging of a new document, his escape to the pirate ship—all these details of swashbuckling adventure make for an exciting narrative set into the dialogue form of drama. Hamlet's resourcefulness, boldness, and cunning in his escape show a figure entirely different from the brooding intellectual incapable of action much cherished by Romantic criticism. Hamlet seems to know exactly what to do, and he does not hesitate at all in pursuing his advantage.

Everything falls exactly right for him. It is "happy," in the Elizabethan sense of "good hap" or good fortune—what we might call a "stroke of luck," but in context it is clearly meant to be providential. It proves, for Hamlet at least, that "There's a divinity that shapes our ends,/ Rough-hew them how we will." (V, ii, 10–11.) This is a theological image from woodworking: man can only "Rough-hew" or crudely shape out his intentions; it is left to God the carpenter to "finish" them and bring them to perfection. The deliberateness of "deep plots" is only an illusion of free will, because "deep plots do pall" (V, ii, 9), as was amply demonstrated by the futility of Hamlet's plotting against Claudius earlier in the play. Before the sea voyage Hamlet was at a standstill in his revenge; now he moves with a new sureness. He has finally abandoned all plotting and placed himself in the hands of Providence. He has learned how to be spontaneous again, and that is why he praises his own "rashness" and "indiscretion." (V, ii, 7, 8.)

All of this is probably a way of explaining what Hamlet means by his mysterious pronouncement, "The readiness is all" (V, ii, 223–224), which is analogous to Edgar's words of comfort for his old father: "Men must endure/ Their going hence, even as their coming hither:/ Ripeness is all." (*King Lear*, V, ii, 9–11.) The image in *Lear* is from fruit ripening on a tree, which knows its own moment to fall, but Hamlet, too, is ripe as well as ready—the words are synonyms for a spiritual condition—and he is prepared to endure his destiny. He is no longer struggling against his own death, and his own readiness to die makes him, in some paradoxical sense, also ripe to execute his revenge. As Hamlet says in the passage above, "the interim's mine," as if nothing could any longer stand in his way, as if he were not only filled with confidence in himself, but also charmed and lucky. The meaning of a man's life may be "no more than to say 'one,' " as a person might say "one" in a fencing match. (Cf. V, ii, 281.) Only one moment is needed to prove oneself. Hamlet's narrative is meant to show that heaven is "ordinant"—ordering, ruling things—and even such a tiny detail as his father's "signet," or seal, which Hamlet just happens to have in his purse, proves that Hamlet is favored by the gods and that nothing can impede him. We can, of course, ask: Why, if Hamlet feels himself the minion or darling of the gods, does he also feel doomed: "But thou wouldst not think how ill all's here about my heart"? (V, ii, 213–214.)

There has been much sentimentalizing of Rosencrantz and Guildenstern, and students sometimes speak of Hamlet's callousness and cruelty in sending them to their death without a qualm. But it is merely tit for tat in the struggle for survival. They are not near Hamlet's conscience, because their doom is sealed by their own attempt to insinuate themselves into the King's favor by spying on Hamlet. They are, like Oswald in *King Lear*, "serviceable" (IV, vi, 253) villains, and they made love to the base employment in which they died. In Tom Stoppard's play, *Rosencrantz and Guildenstern Are Dead* (1967), the two factotums are comic and scared onlookers of a play by Shakespeare in which they happen unwittingly to be involved. In Stoppard's version, *Hamlet* becomes the play within the play.

Hamlet talks much about "conscience" in this passage, which makes a final moral inventory of the reasons for killing Claudius (and Rosencrantz and Guildenstern). No longer does conscience "make cowards of us all" (III, i, 83), as in the "To be, or not to be" soliloquy. Just the reverse, since conscience now provides the justification for Hamlet's revenge: "is't not perfect conscience/ To quit him with this arm?" "Quit" or "requite" also recalls the "quietus" (of the earlier soliloquy) that one might make "With a bare bodkin." (III, i, 76.) The legal and commercial meaning of being quit or discharged of a debt is again reversed in the later passage, where Hamlet will take revenge on Claudius rather than kill himself. Notice the hard monosyllabic verbs by which Claudius is judged: "killed," "whored," "Popped in," "Thrown out." There are no qualifications or extenuating circumstances for Claudius's crimes, and Hamlet speaks more strongly than he has ever done before. All his doubts and hesitations are gone. In fact, he sees himself as being "damned" if he allows this diseased growth of human nature to continue to live and commit "further evil." Hamlet has transformed his own conception of revenge from a personal nightmare to a public act of justice and the purgation of evil.

The role of Horatio in this scene is crucial for understanding Hamlet.

He is Hamlet's confidant, but not his straight man. He listens carefully and sympathetically to what the prince is saying, but he also leads the conversation. Horatio, for example, begins the judgments of both Rosencrantz and Guildenstern and Claudius with a brief but significant statement. "So Guildenstern and Rosencrantz go to't": they actively and vigorously pursue the mission which will, ironically, end in their deaths. Hamlet continues from Horatio's opening gambit, as he does with Horatio's exclamation: "Why, what a king is this!" Horatio mostly plays the role of a creative listener, but he can also try to curb Hamlet's extravagant imagination, as in his reply to Hamlet's fanciful account of the noble dust of Alexander now "stopping a bunghole": " 'Twere to consider too curiously, to consider so." (V, i, 206–208.) For Hamlet, Horatio is a model of a man in perfect equilibrium, "one, in suff'ring all, that suffers nothing." (III, ii, 68.) He is kind of stoic "that Fortune's buffets and rewards/ Hast ta'en with equal thanks." (III, ii, 69–70.) But the theatrical tradition has not been kind to Horatio. It is regrettable that he is usually played by a minor and nearly anonymous actor, because there is such a rich duet between Hamlet and Horatio, with many overtones, implications, and possibilities of development. Horatio is the perfect unheroic counterweight to Hamlet's impetuous and ever-changing nature. Can we honestly, without distorting the play, see the prince through the eyes of his loyal, trusting, admiring, and rational friend?

FOR FURTHER READING

There is a vast critical literature on *Hamlet,* part of which is accounted for in Anton Raven's bibliography, which stops at the year 1935. There is an annual bibliography of *Hamlet* studies in *Shakespeare Quarterly, Publications of the Modern Language Association, Shakespeare Survey,* and *Studies in English Literature.* The last two are selective and in the form of a running commentary. Claude C. H. Williamson has compiled a large volume called *Readings on the Character of Hamlet, 1661–1947* (New York: Macmillan, 1951).

Shakespeare's *Hamlet* exists in three different versions: the First Quarto (1603), which is an extremely garbled text probably used by a touring company; the Second Quarto (1604–1605), which is the basis for most modern editions of the play; and the Folio (1623), which is in the collection of Shakespeare's plays published seven years after his death and with a certain amount of revision and modernization. The two quartos are available in the Shakespeare Quarto Facsimiles series, edited by W. W. Greg and Charlton Hinman (Oxford: Clarendon Press, nos. 4 and 7), and the Folio text is best represented in Charlton Hinman's edition, published by Norton in 1968. G. I. Duthie has a book trying to explain the mysteries of the First Quarto: *The Bad Quarto of Hamlet: A Critical Study* (Cambridge University Press, 1941), and the Second Quarto is well edited, with notes, by Thomas Marc Parrott and Hardin Craig (Princeton University Press, 1938).

Students should begin their study of *Hamlet* with a careful reading of an annotated edition of the play, so that problems of text and interpretation are immediately evident. George Lyman Kittredge's single-volume edition of the play is especially useful for its elaborate paraphrases of difficult passages (Boston: Ginn, 1939). John Dover Wilson's New Cambridge edition (Cambridge University Press, 1934) is also valuable for its lively notes. The older Variorum edition, published by Horace Howard Furness in 1877, is obviously out of date, but it is a mine of helpful and curious information (New York: Dover reprint, 2 vols., 1963). For a cheap, readily available, paperback edition with notes, I suggest the Signet *Hamlet,* edited by Edward Hubler (New York: New American Library, 1963), from which the play is quoted in the present essay. The new Parallel Text series published by Simon & Schuster has a volume on *Hamlet* by John Richetti, with a valuable line-for-line "translation" of the play into modern English (New York, 1975).

Of general criticism on *Hamlet,* I would particularly recommend a few books that are likely to stimulate readers to further exploration of specific topics. A. C. Bradley's chapters on *Hamlet* in *Shakespearean Tragedy* (London: Macmillan, 1904) are powerfully argued, and Harley Granville-Barker's long essay in *Prefaces to Shakespeare,* vol. I (Princeton University Press, 1946) is especially persuasive on matters of acting, staging, and theatrical presentation. *The Question of Hamlet,* by Harry Levin (New York: Oxford University Press, 1959), raises exciting questions of its own and offers new perspectives in interpretation. J. Dover Wilson's fascinating book, *What Happens in "Hamlet"* (Cambridge University Press, 1935) concentrates on interpreting the action, with ingenious and often far-fetched suggestions. My own book, *Style in Hamlet* (Princeton University Press, 1969), focuses on problems of imagery, character, and staging, as these are related to stylistic expression. The best psychoanalytic study is Ernest Jones's *Hamlet and Oedipus* (Garden City, N. Y.: Doubleday-Anchor, 1954), which is based on theories of Sigmund Freud. Further account of the extensive psychoanalytic literature on *Hamlet* may be found in Norman N. Holland, *Psychoanalysis and Shakespeare* (New York: McGraw-Hill, 1966). The religious background of the play and its relation to Greek drama are intelligently discussed in a long chapter in H. D. F. Kitto's *Form and Meaning in Drama* (London: Methuen, 1956). A fine introductory essay on the play is Maynard Mack's "The World of 'Hamlet' " (*Yale Review*, XLI [1952], 502–523), which is reprinted in the Signet edition and in Leonard F. Dean's anthology, *Shakespeare: Modern Essays in Criticism* (New York: Oxford University Press, 1967). Volume IX of *Shakespeare Survey* (1956) is devoted entirely to *Hamlet*.

The theatrical history of *Hamlet* is compiled, with many illustrations, in Raymond Mander and Joe Mitchenson, *Hamlet Through the Ages: A Pictorial Record from 1709* (London: Rockliff, 1952). Additional information may be found in standard theatrical histories such as Arthur Colby Sprague, *Shakespeare and the Actors* (Harvard University Press, 1944) and George C. D. Odell, *Shakespeare from Betterton to Irving* (New York: Dover reprint, 2 vols. 1966). There is an excellent account of John Gielgud's Hamlet, perhaps the most acclaimed version of our time, in Rosamond Gilder's book, *John Gielgud's Hamlet: A Record of Performance* (New York: Oxford University Press, 1937).

PART FOUR

OTHELLO AND THE WAYS OF THINKING

STEPHEN ROGERS

19
QUESTIONS AND OBSERVATIONS

1

A soldier—a man of great talent and personal power and charm—has been married. His wife is innocent, brave, clear-headed; she has rank and beauty: she is "the cunning'st pattern of excelling nature" and might "lie by an emperor's side and command him tasks." In the world where they are supposed to live they "have it made": they ought to be very happy. They are not, however, at least not for long. Why not? What reason can there be why they should fail? Why should he kill her, though she is innocent, and then kill himself? The reason is no accident of fate or act of God. It is his choice—and perhaps her naïveté—but above all, it is Othello's choice that draws his ruin on him. This sketch of the play's premises leads us naturally to state a critical principle: tragedies are about choices.

It is at bottom our choices that make us happy or wretched. The actions that really matter take place in our mind: "reason also is choice."[1] How we think, how we judge, how we imagine are all ingredients of our choice, so that reason and will must be inseparable powers.

137

To quote the devil himself, or one of his tribe: "If the balance of our lives had not one scale of reason to poise another of sensuality, the blood and baseness of our natures would conduct us to most preposterous conclusions" (I, iii, 330–334), always or most of the time. But on the contrary, Iago implies, we avoid these preposterous conclusions fairly regularly. Therefore, the "power and corrigible authority of this lies in our wills." (I, iii, 328–329.) That is not a bad proof of sorts for our freedom, for *librum arbitrium* or free judgment, as a Renaissance philosopher might say.

Like one of Dante's devils (*Inferno*, 27) Iago is a logician, whatever else we may find him to be. In the passage quoted he neatly sums up not only a Renaissance doctrine of moral freedom, but also what seems to be an assumption of the tragic poets: Men, or at least heroic examples of men, are responsible for what they do, because they can choose, even though their choices are bound up with knowledge, which may be mistaken. Indeed, the famous "tragic flaw," mistranslated from Aristotle, is really a sort of sin which the hero commits as much through misunderstanding as through pride or violence. The hero may be hard-pressed; he may be deceived; but he is responsible because he can think and choose, because he is a man. "The devil made me do it" is no excuse; it was not an excuse for Eve in the Garden of Eden. The hero must answer, the tragic poets seem to say, even if, as may sometimes happen, there apparently is no possible action that is absolutely right.

A favorite tragic situation is the dilemma. This is a fork in the road, a logical disjunction, an alternative. The hero must go one way, or he must go the other. Each course leads to some good; but each is a way to some bad consequence as well: to some loss or injury or violence that will cost the hero dearly.

Among the Greeks the typical dilemma was a choice between personal roles. Agamemnon, for instance, must choose whether to behave as a king, sacrificing his daughter so that the fleet might sail to war, or whether he shall act as a father, keeping his daughter alive but breaking his word to lead the other generals in a righteous campaign. Whichever way he goes, he both gains and loses. He acts in accord with one of his identities, develops it, but neglects or injures the other. And there is no third way out. Whatever he does is an answer to this problem. He cannot escape or change it in any way. It is what is given, and the emphasis naturally falls upon his decision—upon the one thing that lies in his power—and on what follows from his act of making up his mind.

The tragic poets are fond of showing choice on a global scale. When Milton retold the story of Adam's fall in "tragic" notes, he carefully set up the crisis in such a way that Adam would see his problem as a dilemma. Eve, his "second self," is at the end of one branch; God, his creator and friend, is at the end of the other. The rest of human history, "a world of woe," was the consequence that followed that decision.

But what of Othello, then? What is his dilemma? Though the natural world is not changed, his action does not lack moral significance. When he has done his dreadful work, before he fully understands it, he thinks that "it should be now a huge eclipse/ Of sun and moon, and that the affrighted globe/ Should yawn at alteration" (V, ii, 99–101), to show how nature groans at his enormous mistake. In fact, there is no such thing, there is only the rhetoric of his misery, a change of command, a slight adjustment in the social patchwork. Still, could it be that his dilemma is like Adam's, though turned all askew? Then Desdemona would be on the side of God, a good angel (she will judge Othello at "compt"); Iago would be the devil, and Othello would seem to be choosing. But where is the second good? A dilemma is a choice between two goods. The devil is not a representative of anything valuable, is he?

Let's go back to the givens, to the premises of the story, as we stated them at the beginning. Maybe Othello is like Agamemnon. Maybe he, too, is put in a conflict of roles, a cleavage between identities which pull him in opposite directions. At the literal center of the play we watch him oscillate between his belief in his wife's fidelity (this is a poor, pale word to describe Desdemona's loyalty, but it will do) and his belief in Iago's honesty.

We have it: We can say what Othello's dilemma is. He is divided between loyalties to important persons in his life. He is under enormous strain—the sort of strain the tragic hero must endure—because his loves, if you will, are absolutely split. At the very center of the play we see him on a moral rack: "I think my wife be honest, and think she is not. I think that thou art just, and think thou art not." (III, iii, 384–385.) The branches of his dilemma lead to the two persons who represent to him the two goods or highest values in his life. If we can say what these values are, we may convince ourselves that this play does fit our general description of tragedy.

It is easy to see how Desdemona is a locus of values. Othello himself tells us plainly enough. "Excellent wretch," he calls her. The term is a fragment of love language, like a hundred private expressions that grow up within a family. But this oxymoron reverberates with ironic foreshadowings of Desdemona's final condition. The whole speech is full of foreboding which Othello himself could not have grasped on any level of his consciousness: "Perdition catch my soul/ But I do love thee/ And when I love thee not,/ Chaos is come again." (III, iii, 90–92.) The speech looks ahead to the dissolution that is to come, to the disorder brewing within him. But the lines look backward, too. The marriage is not just a social triumph. It is an intimate satisfaction of deep needs: "She loved me for the dangers I had passed,/ And I loved her that she did pity them." (I, iii, 167–168.) Othello's "free, unhoused condition," his life in the "tented field," which he so greatly prizes, was somehow incomplete. Under the splendid shell of masterful hardness Othello must have felt an inner loneliness. Desdemona made up this deficiency. "I saw Othello's visage in his mind," she says. (I, iii, 253.) The literal obscurity of this line is all the more effective because it suggests that the new wife looked past color and even past physical beauty, to greet the spirit behind these things. "My heart's subdued/ Even to the very quality of my lord" (I, iii, 251–252), she says, meaning that she has submitted to her vision of his inmost character ("quality" seems to mean more than just profession), perhaps even that she has been stamped with it, become one with it, by virtue of that strange capability which women and poets have of becoming profoundly at one with what they intuitively know.

We may wonder how far Desdemona's psychological insight is supposed to go. She is surprised by Othello's jealousy; who is not? But we have no warrant for doubting either the fullness or the firmness of her love. It does not change, even after he strikes and bewhores her: For example: "his unkindness may defeat my life,/ But never taint my love." (IV, ii, 160–161.) And: "My love doth so approve him/ That even his stubbornness, his checks, his frowns— . . . have grace and favor in them." (IV, iii, 19–21.) It does not change even after he strangles her: "Commend me to my kind lord." (V, ii, 125.) We may question the melodramatics of such lines. But the play leaves no room to doubt the fixity of Desdemona's love; it "looks on tempest and is never shaken." Nor can we doubt the intensity with which Othello returns it. She is the storehouse of his joy: "where I have garnered up my heart,/ Where either I must live or bear no life,/ The fountain from the which my current runs/ Or else dries up." (IV, ii, 57–60.) She is, at the very least, his spirit's refuge from the chaos of his isolation. Even his greeting to her, early in Act II, is expressed as a flight from natural tempest to an intimate bliss.

The other side of the dilemma where Iago stands is clearer now, as well. That life of military hardness was not pure chaos; neither was the prestige Othello had won. There were the shared risks and achievements in "the imminent deadly breach," the excellence among peers and subordinates, the joy of striving and surviving together. There was company, if not intimacy, perhaps the shared rudeness of male speech and male knowledge: We have hints of something like this between Othello and Iago, though we also, unaccountably, have a sense of something almost approaching prudishness: "Let me not name it to you, you chaste stars." (V, ii, 2.)

In this rough, companionable former life, there was a code of friend-ship, loyalty, manliness: a code of honor, really. That word seems to sum up the moral idea. At this point we do not know what to make of Iago's suspicions about Othello and Emilia, or how to interpret Othello's declaration that Emilia is a bawd (as if he knew something). We do know, however, that whatever licenses the soldier's life may have allowed, it also had a set of standards, which Othello preemi-nently met. Measured by these, he had earned universal esteem. He was the general, the bulwark, the worthy Moor who had proved him-self to have the heart that "passion could not shake." By his calm superiority he quells riots in the streets: "Keep up your bright swords, for the dew will rust them." (I, ii, 59.) These eleven words display a power to impose his will through an aura of manly authority. He never altogether loses that aura.

Nevertheless, it is closely bound up with his honor. Honor for a man is the public acknowledgment of his power; it is conspicuous prestige. For a woman it means chastity mainly, but also the social perquisites of her relations and connections. It is, in either case, a function of one's roles, the public acknowledgment of what one is.

Othello knows himself mainly by his public reflection. His habitual personality, as we may call it, is his public one. His mind is like a huge hand, strong and skillful in managing large matters, but inept at sub-tleties: they escape its notice. His imagination is vivid, but it tends to hyperbole: "I had been happy if the general camp,/ Pioners and all, had tasted her sweet body,/ So I had nothing known." (III, iii, 345–347.) It is his public personality which is threatened by the suspicion of Desdemona's disloyalty: "Othello's occupation's gone." (III, iii, 357.) He even speaks of himself in the third person, as the whole army, for instance, might speak of him if they had this knowledge of his dis-grace. It is the public hero who appears self-sufficient, even a law unto himself. The man who marries needing intimacy confesses that he is incomplete.

The dilemma, then, is a conflict of roles. It arises from the premise of the play, that the soldier becomes a husband. Its terms are apparent goods. No one would ever choose evil if it did not appear to be good. But the roles are associated with persons: soldier with Iago, husband with Desdemona. Iago's semblance of virtue, his "heart that passion cannot rule," makes him an image of Othello's self. If, on the side of the angels, Desdemona stands for intimacy and surrender of self, Iago, on the devil's side, represents Othello's public personality, its aura and its code. In choosing to side with Iago, Othello chooses himself, perverted and disguised: this is the mechanism of his sin and the form of his tragedy.

So much for the dilemma then. The next question is, how does it come to be?

2

In the ancient tragedies some external circumstance drives a wedge between the hero's important roles. A goddess set the problem for Agamemnon. But for Othello there seems to be no extrinsic necessity that his identity as a soldier should clash with his identity as a married man: "The Moor, howbeit that I endure him not,/ Is of a constant, loving, noble nature,/ And I dare think he'll prove to Desdemona/ A most dear husband." (II, i, 297–300.) Iago can tell the truth sometimes.

But clearly the dilemma is produced by a falsehood. It is itself a sort of fiction. The question really becomes: Whose fiction is this tragedy? Is it Iago's or Othello's or a chemical effect resulting from the combination of the two?

Our likeliest candidate as maker of fictions is Iago, of course. If he is not the father of lies, he is surely one of that character's tribe, by his own admission. He works "by wit, and not by witchcraft" (II, iii, 379), but lying is a form of wit, as Hazlitt tells us. False claims of love and service, false protestations of friendship and loyalty are Iago's most casual performances. He tosses off plain slanders on the spur of the moment, just glancing around to be sure no one is listening who knows the truth. His more interesting inventions are interpretations of fact or approximations and simulations of the truth. These prodigious feats of mind hold us spellbound while they appall us.

The whole play is concerned with interpreting facts and establishing likelihoods. Roderigo and Iago come on stage reacting to the new marriage. It has raised a difficulty between them which Iago is trying to smooth over. They awaken Brabantio with the news: "An old black ram/ Is tupping your white ewe." (I, i, 88–89.) They "are making the beast with two backs." (I, i, 117.) The rhetoric is calculated to arouse prejudice and kindle fears and disgusts which the old father might have suppressed had he received a letter, say, from the Duke, congratulating him on his daughter's fortunate marriage with the most remarkable man in Venice. The same beastly turn of phrase, of course, will infect Othello's mind: he will mutter about "goats and monkeys," whine about "toads in a cistern," rumble about "flies in the shambles." Brabantio's mental flurry, a scattering of orders and self-pity, prefigures Othello's disintegration of mind in Act IV.

Iago obviously uses facts to generate fictions; he also uses fictions to create facts. He is a creator of uproars in the night, for instance. The play has five or six of them at least, depending on how you count them: the clamor under Brabantio's window; the near riot when Othello's men and Brabantio's meet; the outbreak of wrath on the battlements in Cyprus, when Cassio beats Roderigo and wounds Montano; the domestic uproar in Act IV when Othello bewhores his wife;

the skirmish not far from Bianca's house, in which Cassio is wounded and Roderigo killed; and finally the tumult in the bedroom. The murder is sickeningly quiet. We need some shouting, and it comes after Emilia finds Desdemona dead. Iago causes all these disturbances in one way or another, though in the latter half of the play Othello takes over the directorship.

Uproars, we notice, are one constant feature in Iago's work, but only one. There is a whole set of typical events, a scenario we might call it, which he creates in diverse ways for each of his victims. He baptizes them in sexual obscenity; he induces a mental confusion; he gets them to accept some falsehood; he leads them to perform an act of violence. It is easy to see how uproar, especially if it happens at night, is to be naturally associated with such a set of events. It is a symptom, a trace of Iago's touch upon circumstances, answering to his effect upon souls. Lewdness, confusion, deception, and violence are only the elements he works with. They are possibilities, raw materials in the abstract. The main thing is not their sequence but rather their combination. Like notes in a musical theme, they may be rearranged. They may be repeated in different tones by different instruments. The whole combination may even be transposed from one key into another. The uproars are like cymbal clashes: they orchestrate diverse versions of the theme and underscore its variations.

3

The stories that are produced by variation and permutation of these elements (lewdness, confusion, deception, violence) are unfolded at different paces throughout the play, their results being woven intricately together. Brabantio's version happens quickly and contributes several things to the main plot. We have already noticed how Brabantio is doused with lewdness in the middle of the night, and we have seen his confusion as a reaction to that shock. He must find an explanation that will suit his awakened wrath and his fears: "Are there not charms/ By which the property of youth and maidhood/ May be abused?" (I, ii, 172–174.) But he practices his "probable and palpable" reasoning on Othello: "O thou foul thief [the robbery metaphor is Iago's suggestion] . . . I'll refer me to all things of sense/ If she in chains of magic were not bound,/ Whether a maid so tender, fair, and happy,/ So opposite to marriage that she shunned/ The wealthy curlèd darlings of our nation,/ Would ever have, to incur a general mock,/ Run from her guardage to the sooty bosom/ Of such a thing as thou, to fear, not to delight." (I, ii, 62–71.) In the senate chamber Brabantio rests his case on the belief that such a mating is unnatural. (Iago's animal language implies that idea, too.)

He believes it is unnatural for his white daughter to marry a black man. What is unnatural is what is contrary to expectation, apparently. To suppose that his daughter chose such a marriage with all its connotations is unacceptable. But if Desdemona was drugged, the unnaturalness was imposed on her, perhaps by the devil himself in the form of this black husband. Whether true or not, the drug theory is a fine explanation.

The motif of drugs and charms, and for that matter of magic too, first appears, then, as Brabantio's theory, his hypothesis for interpreting a fact. The same motif legitimately describes the power of Othello's personality; it becomes a metaphor for the charming story of his life: "This only is the witchcraft I have used." (I, iii, 169.) Beyond this rhetorical flourish, however, magic turns up among Othello's stock of beliefs: "there's magic in the web" of his fatal handkerchief.

Brabantio's prejudice has more important after-effects. Perhaps that is why it is repeated so often, and why it is given so much attention. Brabantio's charges are so important that a whole scene is devoted to their statement, to Othello's answer, and to establishing the integrity and even the mental competence of the judges. The Duke and senators are engaged in interpreting facts (like everyone else in the play). There is a question of war. They are figuring out what the enemy is up to, interpreting the sailors' reports as they filter in. The focus suddenly shifts from military to domestic matters, but the new question requires essentially the same kind of discrimination. These clearheaded judges hear and dismiss the charge of witchcraft. Othello's "round, unvarnished tale" would "win my daughter too," the Duke says. Brabantio's notion of nature is not nature at all: it is nothing but "thin habits and poor likelihoods/ Of modern seeming." The splendor of Othello's person sweeps the old man's premise away. The clear reasonableness of Desdemona's passion discredits her father's theory that she was drugged. The luminousness of her speech makes his suspicion of enchantment seem absurd, even to him apparently, because he abandons the hypothesis at once.

This scene in the senate chamber is, among other things, a trial. It is constructed as a complete and decisive refutation of a false theory. It is an example of how moral assessments can be made. This scene might have proved a model for all such judgments throughout the play. All Othello ever had to do is "send for the lady" and listen to her. But of course this scene is a model against which we may measure the growing falsehood. It furnishes a standard of truth, which Shakespeare worked into his expository design.

Brabantio's prejudice does not disappear from the play just because it is refuted. It becomes an instrument in Iago's major fiction. Othello, too, is susceptible of the fear or the suspicion that there is something unnatural in his marriage. Does Othello really believe Brabantio's premise? Does he really think that Desdemona has violated the order of nature in marrying a black man? If he does, his soul must be harboring a profound self-hatred.

The Cassio variation is more interesting, its result more essential: It is a slightly shifted image of the main event. The sequence for Cassio is exposure to obscenity, befuddlement, rage, and deception. His self-description names the two central elements: "To be now a sensible man, by and by a fool, and presently a beast!" (II, iii, 308–310.) He is befuddled by wine of course. Perhaps the one simply funny episode in the whole play is Cassio's sobriety test: "This is my Ancient, this is my right hand and this is my left. I am not drunk now, I can stand well enough and speak well enough." (II, iii, 117–120.)

Iago has an artistic sense of economy: His use of ideas is marvelously elastic. He also knows his victims, "knows all qualities, with a learned spirit,/ of human dealings." (III, iii, 259–260.) His psychology and his esthetics come together in his choice of wine as the means to bring Cassio under his spell. Drink is a form of drug, a magical instrument in the service of devilish wit. Iago has heard this cluster of ideas before. Or was he the one who planted them?

And once the Circean cup has been fastened upon him, Cassio is turned to a beast. Beast is one of the ideas in Iago's stock, one of the favorite guises in which he likes to see human beings; and he combines that identity with the phases of his scenario to produce variety, as well as permutation. Cassio's beastliness is a simple, clear, classical kind, as if the devil had unlaced his humanity momentarily: "It has pleased the devil drunkenness to give place to the devil wrath." (II, iii, 297.) The devil deception comes in afterwards, when Cassio accepts the plausible notion, false in this case, that Desdemona is the way to win the Moor again. This deception is an important part of the fabric, the "net" that will enmesh them all.

But what of the immersion in lewdness?

We cannot entertain the slightest suspicion that Cassio has any sexual designs on Desdemona. His formal baptism in obscenity is the test on this very point. Iago tries to engage him in a discussion of her sexiness: "And, I'll warrant her, full of game. . . . And when she speaks, is it not an alarum to love?" (II, iii, 19–26.) Cassio is plainly not interested: "She is indeed perfection." A soldier who speaks like that obviously feels nothing more intense than courteous esteem for his general's wife. Maybe experience with the likes of Bianca has immunized him against Iago's kind of sexual temptation. But we are going outside the play for that conclusion. All we know is that lewdness does not perplex or even move him, and this fact makes him different from the rest of Iago's victims.

Violence is one of the forms which beastliness assumes under Iago's influence. For Roderigo, the beast phase comes at the very beginning, as a precondition of his being fooled. He is already a beast by virtue of his lust, his lack of self-control. The idea of beastliness is very clearly defined in Iago's speech to Roderigo about the one scale of reason to balance another of sensuality. On the other hand, in the Othello sequence, beastliness is associated with the stages of confusion and deception, when the falsehood has been imposed and Othello thinks he is a cuckold: "A horned man's a monster and a beast." (IV, i, 63.) And of course Iago works on Othello, not with wine or through a presupposed lust, but with the far headier enchantments of wit operating directly. In Othello's case the whole scenario is played out on a higher psychological level among richer moral nuances. I suppose, to complete the picture, we should say that Brabantio is reduced to a beast by association, through Iago's conception of his daughter and his kin: "you'll have your daughter covered with a Barbary horse; you'll have your nephews neigh to you."

But what is important to realize now is that the same notes recur throughout the play, on various levels, in different sequences, and in different combinations. The scenario is not any actual story, but only a potential multitude of stories made up by the permutation and variation of certain essential ingredients. Its range, though limited, is considerable: there are 24 permutations, not to mention the indefinite number of substitutions that can be made for each of these elements.

4

Iago is a creator of stories about lewdness, confusion, deception, and violence. He is like some "ethereal chemical" which, when compounded with certain human substances, produces a horrible reaction: intoxication, dissolution. Wit is the instrument of his venom. Wine is only one of its symbols. His is a super witchcraft, stronger than all drugs; it outdoes all other poisons. (IV, i, 45–48.) His scenario is the formula: Deception plus lewdness plus confusion plus violence. This is the order of the main event.

He is a creature of his own scenario too, or should we call him one of its victims? Though he gets others to do his dirty work at first, he is finally driven to murder twice. He is bathed in obscenity—from within, if we suppose him to have a psyche. The seamier side of his wit is what judges women. He even hints at some feeble sexual inclination toward Desdemona: "Now, I do love her too,/ Not out of absolute lust, though peradventure/ I stand accountant for as great a sin,/ But partly led to diet my revenge." (II, i, 300–303.) This is equivocal language of what is and is not: it gives and takes away. It sounds like a special kind of story which Iago tells himself.

Periodically, moreover, he lapses into his own kind of confusion. It seems to go along with invention and improvisation. In the first soliloquy his whole scheme is "here but confused." Sometimes he changes direction in midplot, as when he switches from moralist to panderer for Roderigo. Or else we may hear his mind spinning its wheels, as he temporizes before bringing forth some creative detail:

It were a tedious difficulty, I think,
To bring them to that prospect. Damn them then,
If ever mortal eyes do see them bolster
More than their own! What then? How then?
What shall I say? Where's satisfaction?
It is impossible you should see this,
Were they as prime as goats, as hot as monkeys,
As salt as wolves in pride, and fools as gross
As ignorance made drunk. But yet I say
If imputation and strong circumstances,
Which lead directly to the door of truth,
Will give you satisfaction, you may have it.   (III, iii, 397–408)

And having stalled thus, he comes up with the story of Cassio's dream.

Admittedly, the confusion Iago feels is not the same as that which he produces. It is his response under a pressure he creates for himself. But it conforms structurally to his scenario. It makes his case analogous to that of his victims. The same might be said about deception.

Critics have long speculated about Iago's motives. In the next section the reader will be asked to consider some of their hypotheses. But for now let us follow out the line of reasoning begun here. It runs like this: If Iago is above all a maker of fictions, then his motives may be fictions too. "It is thought abroad that 'twixt my sheets" the Moor "has done my office. I know not if't be true,/ But I for mere suspicion in that kind/ Will do as if for surety." (I, iii, 393–396.) The whole action is thus founded on a mere supposition, on an "as-if." The cornerstone of Iago's main plan is a hypothesis. It may be either true or false; it is a deception and it is not. Iago himself admits that he does not know its truth. Its value may lie precisely in his not knowing. He repeats the point, as one is likely to repeat the basis of a serious action: "I do suspect the lusty Moor/ Hath leaped into my seat." (II, i, 304–305.) He seems to relish the suspicion, as if by entertaining it, he set himself up for action. Iago's hypothesis that he is a cuckold may have no more truth than Brabantio's hypothesis that his daughter was drugged. This hypothesizing of a moral position is a form of self-deception, at least in a loose sense, for once the assumption is made, it rules out other possible ideas. In assuming that he is a cuckold, without any test, Iago behaves exactly like his victim. By thinking himself a cuckold, he puts on a mask, adopts a role; he finds a purpose and a set of feelings to go with it; he assumes, as it were, a moral costume, which is "to plume up" his will, by taking on himself a definite story.

147

The supposed past implies an actual future: vengeance. Once it is believed in, the moral fiction creates facts.

The idea of feigned or fictional motives is not so farfetched, though most of us tend to take behavior as a sign of true feeling. We know that people who "play games" adopt certain standard roles—tough guy, damsel in distress—and let their behavior, feelings and all, follow from that stereotype. Actors, too, control their behavior to fit some preconceived idea. Some actors study themselves in a mirror to be sure that every gesture implies the feeling they intend. Some actors testify that they become so wrapped up in their parts that they forget who they are in real life. Others say they put roles on and take them off with ease, slipping in and out of a set of motives as they might change costumes. The actor who gets lost in his role might say "I don't know who I am." What might the more calculating kind of actor say? Might he not say, "I am not what I am"?

"I am not what I am" (I, i, 65) is the figure for the hypocrite and the actor alike. It is the trope of all disguises. Shakespeare's Viola utters exactly this sentence (a man playing a woman playing a man). This rhetorical figure is called *diaphora,* from a Greek word meaning "difference." Ordinarily it employs one term in opposite senses at the same time. Here, where people and situations are not what they are, this trope is a sign of Iago's effect on the whole play. Desdemona uses it to register her astonishment at the change in her husband: "My lord is not my lord." (III, iv, 124.) Iago uses it to point to ambiguities in the word "honor": "They have it very oft that have it not." (IV, i, 17.) One even sees a trace of it in Othello's mistake: "My wife! What wife? I have no wife" (V, ii, 97), though this is not strictly speaking an example.[2]

Above all, diaphora is the trope of Iago, in whom hypocrite and actor seem inseparable. Iago is the moral magician: He shows you what happens behind the scenes while he performs his tricks; then he tries to deceive you in spite of your understanding. Perhaps he almost tricks himself. His soliloquies are his moral tiring rooms, where he tries out his parts before the mirror of his critical thought. "That Cassio loves her, I do well believe it" (II, i, 295)—is he really fooled by his own contriving, by all those asides about Cassio's courtesy? Or is he only half-fooled, drawn under the spell of a plausible fiction? "That she loves him, 'tis apt and of great credit." (II, i, 296.) Here he is clearly speaking of what others believe—Roderigo for instance—though again we may justly feel that Iago is partly taken in by his own invention. He half believes his reiteration of Brabantio's premise about the unnaturalness of love for the Moor. He is almost carried away by the dirty joke about the "incorporate conclusion." "And what's he then that says I play the villain?/ When this advice is free I give and honest,/ Probal to thinking, and indeed the course/ To win the Moor again?'' (II, iii, 342–345.) Is he simply reviewing his own performance, checking to be sure the victim will really accept the suggestion and the appearance of friendship? Surely Iago does not surprise himself (maybe he is only amused), when he pulls off this mask of friendship and exclaims: "Divinity of Hell!/ When devils will the blackest sins put on,/ They do suggest at first with heavenly shows,/ As I do now." (II, iii, 356–359.) He has associated himself with the devil too many times already for us to suppose that the idea is new to him here in the fourth soliloquy. He is by turns the friend, the soldier, the philosopher, the devil, the hypocrite-actor, and he is flourishing each of these parts one after another. We have no guarantee that any of them is his "real self." If we can believe Beatrice in *Much Ado,* the devil is an old cuckold, wearing horns. Iago is a cuckold by hypothesis. His association with the devil may be one of his fictions, too.

On the Elizabethan stage, which jutted out among the standing groundlings, the actor might come very close to some of the spectators while he recited his soliloquies.[3] Only the imaginary walls of theatrical convention surrounded him. He was both overheard and all alone, as he exploited the duplicity in the actor's situation, the fundamental diaphora of the theater. Iago's soliloquies must have produced a frightening intimacy with evil: Not with its manifestations merely, but with the slime of equivocation out of which it is created, with the thing itself, which is nothing. Iago embodies equivocation. "I am not what I am" is an ultimate mask. Like the statement, "this statement is false," it has no truth value; it is and is not, like the vanishing image in opposing mirrors. To this extent Iago's self-representation is also his deception. He is a victim of his own scenario.

He is the playmaker on stage, a producer of grim farces as well as an actor in them. His fictions are all representations of himself; he costumes his victims in aspects of himself. Subtle knave and disloyal friend are guises from his moral wardrobe. Even Desdemona the adulteress coincides with one of his fantasies about himself, as we shall see. And Othello's roles—supposed cuckold, devil, coward—all have their analogues in him.

The great soldier and his vile tempter turn out to be structural look-alikes: They do the same deeds with personal differences (variations). Both kill their wives, Iago to silence the truth, Othello to perform a sacred murder (his mind vibrates with this ambiguity) in accord with a false system: if she is untrue, she must die; otherwise she will betray more men. This is not only an echo of Desdemona's song; it is also a pitiable reminder of the masculine code. Othello's reason for murder is but a version of Iago's stale joke about womankind. Othello's acknowledged cowardice in the aftermath of murder is only an obvious sign of moral collapse, which he shares with Iago by becoming one of his likenesses.

Othello looks for Iago's cloven hooves: "I look down toward his feet, but that's a fable." (V, ii, 286.) But Amelia has already had cause to call Othello a devil himself. Some readers are unwilling to accept this peculiar effect. But Othello does become all the things that Brabantio said he was. Claims that were preposterous come true. We catch our breath realizing what has happened. Black—under a pall of prejudice at first—is shown to be beautiful in the person of Othello; then that person is caused to be morally black as hell. This is the "Iago effect." He is the one who kept the "tribe of Hell" before our attention. The two hypothetical cuckolds become two agents of the devil, and they resemble him.

5

Still we have not answered our question: Whose fiction is Othello's dilemma? We must go back to the heart and actual center of the play, where the deception begins, to the temptation scene itself. How can a sensible and heroic figure be induced to accept a false supposition about himself and then to act out a story based on Iago's scenario? Iago can create a false identity, make the mask stick, in the mind of some onlooker, but can he actually make the victim see himself under the aspect of some such guise, unless the victim consents? Roderigo and Cassio partly choose what happens to them. Desdemona, on the other hand, remains absolutely innocent. Is there something in Othello which Iago brings out and gives dramatic form to? Does Othello somehow deceive himself? The answer must lie in III, iii.

We read the great scene again, for the tenth, perhaps for the hundredth time. It works as it always has before (this is, after all, the fourth variation of Iago's plot). Recurrence puts the whole theme into esthetic time, like music, rather than into a flat imitation of real time. In a few pages, a couple of hundred lines, a beloved hero reaches a most preposterous conclusion, which he holds as if it were a fact of holy writ.

We notice that by turning a select fact into an object of attention— "Ha, I like not that!" (III, iii, 34)—Iago turns up some deep portion of the Moor's nature. Othello shows his wife a flash of sudden and extraordinary anger, which stings and puts her a little out of countenance. We have already cited Othello's reaction to this brief encounter. It includes the oxymoron of love; it balances love against chaos. Iago keeps the question alive, which could be dropped and perhaps forgotten forever. He picks up an idea from Desdemona about Cassio the go-between. His hint of suspicion seems not to be creative in itself; it only reinforces something in Othello's mind. There must be some potentiality, though it literally has no form. It has never before been put into a conscious thought; it has certainly never been given words, never fully imagined. Iago suggests, encourages, but Othello asks the question: is Cassio "not honest"?

Iago's first trick is to amplify the question. He frowns and echoes Othello's words. The echo effect is an enlargement. It tantalizes with the suggestion of a further meaning. Thus Iago creates a duplicate of some idea and Othello tries to guess what it is: "By Heaven, he echoes me/ As if there were some monster in his thought/ Too hideous to be shown . . ./ . . . thou cries't 'Indeed!'/ And did's't contract and purse thy brow together/ As if thou then hadst shut up in thy brain/ Some horrible conceit." (III, iii, 106–115.) *As if! As if!* Othello is using hypothesis to bring the hidden thought into his ken. His commitment to supposition is one stage in his transformation. He is being turned into the hypothetical man. By cutting him loose from certainty, Iago is inducing the state of mind he has fabricated in himself.

The hypothesis is first about Iago's thought: what is he thinking? They wrestle over that thought, Othello guessing, Iago holding back, so that more and more energy is invested in it. The struggle makes it seem larger, more terrible. Iago comes close to giving it utterance: "I do beseech you—/ Though I perchance am vicious in my guess." (III, iii, 144–145.) But he draws it back at the last moment, changes his intent in midsentence, perhaps seeing some hint that delay is to his advantage.

Iago temporizes, this time with general sentences about "good name" (he is a nominalist of the spirit, a moral nominalist). Later he will temporize pretending to show concern about Othello's state of mind. At each stage he leaves time for the idea to sink in. He moves fast, yet not too fast, for if he did, he would lose the quarry, and he would lose the audience, too.

If the first stage is to let conjecture shape itself around an unsubstantial thought, the second is to give the hypothesis a name. The giving of names has much to do with the birth of the unspeakable thought. Iago talks about good name, and Othello mentally gives a bad name to his wife and Cassio. Iago talks of jealousy, and Othello applies that idea to himself, negatively, by way of protest, but still to himself; "Think'st thou I'd make a life of jealousy? . . ." (III, iii, 177.) The pangs of birth into a new identity give the emotional pain to this passage. An animal emblem lends a special cast to the new mask: "Exchange me for a goat/ When I shall turn the business of my soul/ To such exsufflicate and blown surmises,/ Matching thy inference." (III, iii, 180–183.) The mask has not quite stuck; the birth is not quite complete; it is all still merely supposititious. But Othello will grow into this identity. The headache, which causes him to need and spurn Desdemona's handkerchief in the next episode, is one of the growing pains: "A hornèd man's a monster and a beast." (IV, i, 63.) The monster in Iago's thought is, at least in part, Othello's creation.

The third stage is the crucial one; it is the essence of the deception. Though Iago speaks "not yet of proof," it entails a specious sort of proof and a test to see how strong the fiction is. Iago finally hands over the thought: "Look to your wife. Observe her well with Cassio." (III, iii, 197.) This is not much really, but in Othello's mind it becomes the conclusion of an intricate syllogism. The major premise, which Iago supplies, is that Venetian women are hypocrites: "In Venice they do let Heaven see the pranks/ They dare not show their husbands." (III, iii, 202–203.) The minor premise, the connection with Desdemona, is Brabantio's warning revived: "She did deceive her father, marrying you." (III, iii, 206.) Her one important act, the proof of her courageous love, is suddenly the sign of her falseness. The trick is dazzling: "Why, go to, then./ She that so young could give out such a seeming/ To seel her father's eyes up close as oak—/ He thought 'twas witchcraft." (III, iii, 208–211.) Iago has to be laughing here, as if he made Othello his accomplice in drawing the veil from a dirty, but not unexpected, joke.

Anyhow, once accepted, the fallacy, or lie, becomes like a fact itself: It requires interpretation. Othello muses on it: "And yet, how nature erring from itself." (III, iii, 227.) There must be some prodigious discrepancy between what appears and what is. Othello will come back to this perplexity.

Iago pounces on the idea of nature. He amplifies what is already implicit in it: There must have been something wrong with Desdemona from the beginning. The love for Othello must have been a perversion. What other explanation could there be, after all?

> Aye, there's the point. As—to be bold with you—
> Not to affect many proposed matches
> Of her own clime, complexion, and degree,
> Whereto we see in all things nature tends—
> Foh! One may smell in such a will most rank,
> Foul disproportion, thoughts unnatural. (III, iii, 228–233)

Iago has pulled back the veil all the way. What he discloses is his own dirty joke, expressed here in the timid, but no less corrupt, language of philosophy. (Philosopher is one of his masks.) In philosophical terms, Othello and Desdemona are said to be crossing links in the great chain of being. They are violating a natural classification. In plainer language, Desdemona must have been lusting after a beast, Iago suggests. "But pardon me. I do not in position/ Distinctly speak of her, though I may fear/ Her will, recoiling to her better judgment,/ May fall to match you with her country forms,/ And happily repent." (III, iii, 236–238.)

This is an unspeakable insult. It should touch Othello where he lives. Why doesn't he beat Iago, kill him on the spot? Anyone who sympathizes and understands what he just heard must want such a reaction. "And happily repent," Iago says, as if Desdemona's supposed adulteries with one of her own kind were a correction of her unnaturalness, and almost to be preferred.

But Othello accepts it all. He is docile and obedient under Iago's suggestions. And we know the reason. It is the paradox of the great inferior. He both denies and accepts his inferiority. He both accepts and denies his greatness. His idea of being a great man includes being unmanned and made a beast: " 'tis the plague of great ones,/ Prerogatived are they less than the base./ 'Tis destiny unshunnable, like death./ Even then this forkéd plague is fated to us/ When we do quicken." (III, iii, 273–277.) Answering to Iago's "I am not what I am," there is a fundamental equivocation in Othello, too.

Jealousy, then, is potentially his life story, as he conceives it. Iago's hypothesis externalizes it: Iago recreates its image in himself. His insinuations bring it to consciousness. The verbal dance around his thought endows it with energy, and the scenario gives it direction and shape. But it is still Othello's fiction. It is based on an opposition deep in his mind. According to Othello's notion of the great soldier, the beloved—any woman who loves him—must be a whore.

We suddenly glimpse the tragic dilemma in a duplicity within Othello's soul. There, in his very most basic conception of himself, the soldier is opposed to the husband. The chaos of the "free, unhoused condition" has passed unconscious judgment on domestic intimacy. It is from a lack of self-worth that Othello takes the spur to greatness. His bravery and promptness to war are sublimated desperation. He foreknows that he cannot be loved, though he may seem quite loveable. It may be true that he would "prove to Desdemona a most kind husband," but it is also true that in order to be deceived, he had to have the seeds of deception in himself.

It is plain that the rest of Iago's scenario takes root in this deception. Lewdness, confusion, and finally violence follow like a chain reaction.

Few passages in world literature could rival Cassio's supposed dream (III, iii, 421–425) for obscenity:

And then, sir, would he gripe and wring my hand,
Cry "O sweet creature!" and then kiss me hard,
As if he plucked up kisses by the roots
That grew upon my lips. Then laid his leg
Over my thigh, and sighed, and kissed . . .

Iago substitutes himself for Desdemona. There can be no doubt of the intent. Cruelty and emotional muddlement tumble together promiscuously. The confusion over the handkerchief, for instance (III, iv), ends in a threat; Desdemona reacts to it as violence. After the lie has been clamped on the truth in Act IV, moral and physical violence are paired. In the "bewhoring" scene falsehood reaches its logical extreme. Values are inverted. Innocence is cast as treachery and lust. Marriage appears in the likeness of prostitution; the marriage chamber in the manner of a brothel; the servant in the guise of a procuress; and the whole episode is conceived under the aspect of hell.

To dwell further on these elements here would be to labor the obvious. Besides, the evidence will really be the material for the final chapter, where we will develop it in a subtler, more comprehensive context.

20

INFERENCES:
A DO-IT-YOURSELF
SECTION

1

Are there fixed, everlasting truths which may serve as principles? Or must we make do with fictions to think and even to act by?

This question divided the mind of Shakespeare's age. It was the formula for the intellectual scenario. Like some persistent lump beneath the skin, it strays and shifts and is not easily traced, but it is there. Poet, philosopher, critic confess its presence; science, ethics, politics betray its effects. And surprisingly enough, (1.0—1) Othello reflects this split in a number of ways.

The section that follows will track this split; or rather, we will set up a framework within which the reader can efficiently track it for himself.

We also want to provide exercises and recapitulate in a small space some of the scholarly findings and critical opinions about our play. Some of the numbered propositions represent conclusions which scholars and critics have reached. Other numbered statements indicate new territory for the reader to explore. Taken together with the framing discussion, they might be thought of as materials for a large number of lectures or essays. Taken in sets of one or two or three, these propositions generate hundreds of topics or arguments that make sense References should show the reader where to look if he wants to see how established writers have handled some of these points.

The reader's imagination may be whetted, too, if he realizes that he is not bound to accept other people's findings as the last word on any subject. He can entertain any proposition about Shakespeare as a question, then as a hypothesis to be tested, and finally he can hold it with some degree of certainty, or he can disprove it.[1]

The propositions for discussion here have been classified. Each category represents a critical point of view. The propositions in it all derive from the same fundamental premises about literature. The reader with a taste for logic will want to test our classification.

The categories are numbered as if they were theorems in a mathematics textbook. The system is simple enough. The number to the left of the decimal refers to the class. The number to the right of the decimal identifies the proposition further within its class. For the sake of brevity, authors are identified by name, and where appropriate, page numbers are given. Works are identified fully in the bibliography.

Class One assumes: that (1.0—2) art is mimetic; that (1.0—3) drama copies or imitates some truth (1.0—4) about individual men; (1.0—5) about human types, which are taken to have a reality; (1.0—6) about mankind in general; or (1.0—7) about the working-out of immutable laws which are found in nature or grounded in the will of God.

PRELIMINARY EXAMPLES

(1.0—8) Characters have psyches that can be analyzed.
(1.1—1) Othello is the great, simple-minded soldier, a man of power and integrity, who is deceived. Bradley.
(1.1—2) Othello is the Elizabethan equivalent of the *macho*.
(1.1—3) Othello ends up as a user of empty words and a maker of mere false gestures. Eliot.

(1.1—4) Othello shows all the stress of the great outsider.

(1.1—5) Othello's self-image is like that of a member of any minority who distinguishes himself in a way that society can accept.

(1.1—6) Othello's self-image is like that of any handicapped person who distinguishes himself in spite of great odds.

(1.2—1) Iago is the loyal soldier, who is justly angered when a less able man is advanced ahead of him; his anger goes too far, however. Kittredge.

(1.2—2) Iago is the *macho*.[2]

(1.2—3) Iago is an incomplete man, an emotional eunuch. Coleridge, Spencer.

(1.2—4) Iago is a "motiveless malignity next to the devil." Coleridge.

(1.2—5) Iago is casting about for a personality because he does not want to be a mere function—a slave. Stewart.

(1.2—6) Iago is the artist; he is like the actor, the comic improviser, the playwright on the stage. Bradley. (See Chapter 19).

(1.3—1) Desdemona is more intelligent in the ways of love than Othello is.

(1.3—2) Desdemona really is the "cunning'st pattern of excelling nature," which means that she represents a real truth. Bush.

(1.3—3) Desdemona is Othello's good angel, though he does not know it.

(1.4—1) Othello and Iago are doubles or decomposed parts of a single self divided by internal conflict, and Cassio is Othello's psychic twin, at least with respect to their attitudes toward women. Robert Rogers, Kenneth Burke. (Compare this point with the remarks about scenario and permutations of a single formula in Chapter 19.)

(1.4—2) Iago and Othello are related by latent homosexual feelings.

Class Two considers: that (2.0—1) the work of art is a complex symbol which (2.0—2) calls on our private emotions and (2.0—3) on our public or collective habits, in order (2.0—4) that we might discover humane meanings, or even (2.0—5) that we might create such meanings for ourselves.

PRELIMINARY EXAMPLES

(2.0—6) The play is like a public dream.

(2.0—7) The play provides blank forms into which we pour our spirit.

(2.1—1) Othello is the comic type of the abused husband.

(2.1—2) Othello is the comic type of the braggart soldier or *miles gloriosus*.

(2.1—3) Othello is a stand-in for Everyman.

(2.2—1) Iago is the Vice of the Morality play. Ribner, Stoll, Bush.

(2.2—2) Iago is the *fallax servus* or "false deceiving slave" of comedy. Stoll.

(2.2—3) Iago is the *miles* in fact. S. Rogers.

(2.2—4) Iago is the Machiavel. Stoll.

(2.3—1) Desdemona is the "good angel." Coleridge, Bush.

(2.3—2) Desdemona is the "sexy meretrix" of Roman comedy. Stewart.

(2.4—1) *Othello* is like a morality play. Ribner, Bush, McGuire, Spivack.

(2.4—2) *Othello* is a tragedy made from comic symbolic forms; it is a comedy in reverse. S. Rogers.

(2.4—3)   The design of *Othello* is even more elegant than the design of *Hamlet,* since, besides plots that mesh and image one another, we have constant play within a play, with the difference that Iago is continually the artist and playmaker.

(2.4—4)   *Othello* takes place in double-quick or esthetic time. (See *Othello,* New Variorum, pp. 358ff.)

Class Three reflects a biographical bias. It supposes (3.0—1) that a work of great art expresses a great mind, and (3.0—2) that this mind should become the object of primary interest.

PRELIMINARY EXAMPLES

(3.1—1)   Shakespeare's life is, like Scripture, allegorical, and his works are the commentary on that life. Keats.

(3.1—2)   Shakespeare puts himself into his characters; he "conceives them out of his own intellectual and moral faculties, by conceiving any one intellectual or moral faculty in morbid excess and then placing himself, thus mutilated and diseased, under given circumstances." Coleridge.

The reader is urged to develop any one or any set of these propositions by using the hypothetical-deductive method outlined above (see also note 1). In the pages that follow other more subtle theses will be partially developed.

2

The reader will quickly notice that these categories seem somehow to be mutually inclusive. They are like magical boxes contrived so that each one contains the other two; and we can step between them almost within a single sentence. The reason is that they are nothing but distinct intellectual lenses for perceiving and sorting the same set of facts. Though we consider them separately, they may all be used in combination to get at the truth.

We will elaborate an example of Class Three in the next chapter. Class Two will be under consideration in various ways hereafter. Let us now illustrate some consequences of the mimetic theory, Class One, for the interpretation of *Othello.*

We might be tempted to call this theory naive, except that it has been held by some of the world's greatest poets and critics who have been naive in nothing else, and most playgoers are likely to concur with them in it. The principle of the mimetic theory means that characters are like real people. They are usually treated as if they had a psychology of their own. They are imitations of nature in some sense of that manifold term.

The purpose of playing, according to this theory, is "to hold as 'twere the mirror up to Nature." The office of poet is next to that of the pulpit, Milton said. The truth to be shown might therefore be everlasting. Dramatized stories, tragedies especially, are moral examples, more philosophical than history and more compelling than ethical precept. The effect of such poetic teaching would be, in Sidney's wonderful phrase, a "heart-ravishing knowledge."

Those who subscribe to this classic view sometimes glean trivial or obvious lessons: "We learn from *Othello* this very useful moral, not to make an unequal match; in the second place, we learn not to yield too readily to suspicion." (Samuel Johnson; see also Rymer.) Our own age might invert this lesson and conclude (1.5—1) that, because the white man is the devil, as Malcolm X supposed, he will easily corrupt the noble black, who is inevitably an outsider in white society.

If we notice how Othello thinks, he may teach us a lesson in logic as well as in morals. Then let us set his way of thinking beside some interpretations of Iago.

Othello reasons thus: if Iago were a villain, his insinuations would be false shows put on by malice. But Iago is of "exceding honesty." Othello holds onto this proposition as to a principle. It is a belief from which it follows that there must be truth in what Iago is hinting. Further, on the strength of this principle, he builds a crucial action, so that in his own judgment the truth of his principle makes him an executioner of justice in Act V. It takes a mighty clamor of fact to undermine his principle, and Othello finally questions it tentatively, by hypothesis, to see the consequence of denying it: if Iago is not honest, then Othello is a murderer.

Considered merely as logic, Othello's reasoning is perfectly valid. Logicians tell us that from an if-statement that is true we can validly infer only a truth; but from a false if-statement we can validly infer a conclusion that is either true or false. The invalid "if-then" reasoning is the kind where the "if" is true, but the "then" is false. If we have a truth, we cannot validly infer an error. But if we believe an error, we can validly infer either a truth or a lie.

This is a mysterious fact about our thinking. Its consequences have become enormously important and problematic since the Renaissance. *Othello* is a remarkably subtle example of these problems. Othello takes Iago's honesty for truth and thinks he has concluded rightly when he has not. He judges the idea of Iago's villainy to be false, and validly infers a truth which he disregards. (2.4—5) The design of this play tortures the audience by exploiting the possibility of valid falseness. Or (1.5—1) the play imitates the moral "action of knowing and judging," and "that imitation is itself an assay of the limits of intelligent and rational cognition" under trial. (McGuire.) (1.5—2) The moral lesson seems to be that if false beliefs were a significant excuse for immoral actions, most of us would have to be found innocent most of the time; but life requires us to act while it makes no guarantee that the grounds of our action will be either right or clear.

Some writers, indeed, have concluded (1.5—3) that Othello is a reworking or reembodiment of what one of them calls the "allegory of evil." (Spivack.) It follows that Iago stands for the devil; Desdemona is the good angel; Othello is a particular case of Everyman, or even of Adam, who must choose between good and evil in spite of deceiving appearances. (This view further supposes that good, evil, God, angels, devil are all realities to be represented, and man's relations with them are "real.")

Others say either (1.2—7) that Iago is Machiavellian or (2.2—4) that Iago is a Machiavel. A Machiavel is a standard villain type, a symbol. A Machiavellian is one who adopts the doctrine of *The Prince*. (3.1—3) Shakespeare had been preoccupied with the Machiavellian position in several of his earlier plays and was to concern himself with it again in *King Lear* (Danby). It is altogether possible that he was exploring some of its ramifications in *Othello*.

The main difference between the Machiavellian and the devil is in the attitude toward the truth. The devil is a liar, but he knows the truth. The Machiavellian denies that there is any fixed moral truth at all. He thinks there is no ultimate court of appeal; his own purposes consequently determine what is right and wrong; ends justify means. Such a person regards this life, cut off as it is from the will of God, as a free-for-all where power prevails. Thomas McFarland, stressing this last point about power, judges (2.1—4) that Othello, not Iago, is the Machiavel.

3

What Machiavelli was in politics, Montaigne and the sceptics, or Pyrrhonists, were in the domain of knowledge. In the *Apology for Raymond Sebond*, by Montaigne, Shakespeare surely read that the sceptic, not wishing to believe in anything, seeks suspension of judgment, a state of mind denoted by the formula, "no more this than that." Imperturbability is the sceptic's goal. But to an emotional nature like Othello's, indeed to a believer in principles, doubt is torture.

Montaigne could also have shown Shakespeare the five ways by which the Pyrrhonist thought he could reduce a mind to suspension. He would do it by showing: (1) that there are discrepancies in the perception of an object; (2) that the judgments we make are relative and depend on our own point of view; (3) that all thinking is hypothetical, and one assumption is as good, or as unreliable, as another which contradicts it; (4) that in the search for certainty the mind is lost in infinite regress, since there are no firm principles to base our thinking on; and (5) that many a piece of reasoning is really circular after all.

(1.2—8) At least the first three of these argumentative modes, and possibly all five, are among the tools Iago uses to tempt and deceive Othello. (1.2—9) In other words, Iago acts like a sceptic. The sceptics were fond of self-destruct statements: "All things are false"; "nothing is true." Such formulas "are virtually cancelled out by themselves." (*Outlines of Pyrrhonism,* I, 14–15.) They resemble Iago's "I am not what I am" and the equivocal nature of the theater.

Scepticism and belief dwelt side by side in Shakespeare's age. Doubt touched every branch of knowledge with ambiguity.

> Our law hath, as some say, certain lawfull fictions, on which it groundeth the truth of justice, [Montaigne said, and] as in all things else, Philosophy presenteth unto us, not that which is, or she beleeveth, but what she inventeth, as having most apparance, likelyhood, or comelinesse.
>
> (Florio, II, 249–250)

For the scientist truth itself might be "twofold." Francis Bacon thought it was. If the scientist was a man of religion, he believed in the reality of certain spiritual facts beyond the reach of sense. In his scientific research, on the other hand, he might be a nominalist, and believe that sensible things are the only realities; that intangible ideas are mere names, mere breath. He might satisfy himself with explanations by connecting facts to strong presuppositions or axioms. Bacon went this far. (Willey, p. 2 and p. 27. Boase, p. 17.)

Some scientists in our time claim that their theories are merely symbolic systems which lead to truth. Their suppositions, they say, need not be true; they need not contain or copy real entities. Instead, their predictions must approximate truth (Duhem).

This modern view is more flexible than Bacon's. Because of its basis in fiction, he would probably indict it along with the other "idols of the theatre" that he knew: "in my judgment all the received systems are but so many stage plays, representing worlds of their own creation after unreal and scenic fashion." (*New Organon,* I, xliv.) But the notion that truth may be founded on symbolic fiction would not be foreign to the men of Shakespeare's age. They had felt the topsy-turvydom of premise shift. They had seen how a single hypothesis could move the earth, as it were; could carry it from the center of the universe to set it in a wandering course among the heavens. Hypothesis was like

Archimedes' point, on which, with a leaver long enough, he said he could lift the world. "Whosoever is believed in his presuppositions," Montaigne said, "he is our master, and our God." (Florio, II, 253.)

If (1.1—7) Othello thinks like a believer in principles and if (1.2—10) Iago is a nominalist (II, iii, 270–71; III, iii, 154ff), (1.2—11) a hypothetical man, then (1.0—8) this play transposes the ambiguity of the "twofold truth" into a moral mode.

Or shall we rather say (3.1—4) that this play expresses Shakespeare's intellectual and emotional apprehension of the "twofold truth" and his ambivalence toward it.

4

This line of thinking prompts a further conjecture, which may be more interesting than all the rest: (3.0—3) What if the playwright were like one kind of scientist, not the recorder of facts, but a user of symbolic constructs, and false ones at that? What if he exploited the remarkable human condition that if we do not possess the truth, we are allowed the freedom of fiction in order to find it? Without fiction our thought could not advance, unless we were sure of the truth to start with.

This freedom has been realized by many for whom imagination was truer than fact. But it seems the special province of the creative scientist and the poet. And no poet has been more self-conscious than Shakespeare about the truth in falsity upon the stage.

He knew—archnominalist—that the poet "gives to airy nothings a local habitation and a name." He insisted, even in a history, that the stage is a "wooden O." He called attention to the falsity of art; he underscored theatrical illusion.

A playwright, then, is a scientist, as it were, of moral action, of *praxis*. His play is a laboratory or substitute world, which is to say it is a symbolic world; and as such it is a translation, always a metaphor, and not the thing itself. Therefore it is always somewhat false. There is a gap between original and translation.

At a performance of *Othello* in a small mining town, one spectator was so taken in that he forgot this difference. In the midst of a climactic scene he leaped to his feet and shouted: "Why you black bastard! Can't you see?" (Muir.)

If there were not some falseness, if the symbol of the theater coincided exactly with some truth of history or philosophy, a small number of conclusions could be validly drawn. But if the play is a falsehood, then many conclusions, true or false, can validly be drawn; not just any conclusion, surely, the play's inner logic, its structure, sets some limits—but many conclusions all the same, most of which the playwright never foresaw.

From a few simple premises, pure suppositions, the playwright deduces what human actions might follow. He conjectures, he constructs, he infers, partly by logic and partly by association. He demonstrates, makes plausible, persuades. If the playwright has done his work well, we enter into his substitute world. We grant him one esthetic idea after another. We step smoothly from implication to implication, swiftly looking behind and ahead, sensing intuitively how the many events have bearing on the main action.

In *Hamlet* Shakespeare had already explored the difficulty a sensitive man has in finding a solid basis for acting justly. The play within a play is a sort of experiment, consciously designed by Hamlet and therefore by Shakespeare, to test a set of hypotheses about innocence or guilt, about the "undiscovered country," about the justice of certain projected acts. (2.4—6) *Othello* is a variant of this process and this problem.

If the playwright is the scientist of the heart, he is equally the Machiavel by virtue of his art. In the making of his substitute world, ends not only justify means; they prescribe them. He is a maker of scenarios, a manipulator of masks, a teller of plausible lies, all for the sake of the "heart-ravishing knowledge" he aims at. (2.4—7) *Othello* is an ultimate proof of these claims, since the evil art of the Machiavel who is contained reflects the containing art of the innocent playwright.

In the next chapter we will first let the reader judge whether we can draw any useful conclusions from an outrageous hypothesis. The practice will be fun and pertinent to our study. Then we will develop the idea of the substitute world under the specific (and literally false) theory that the play is a public dream.

21

A DREAM OF PASSION

A play, like a dream, is a complex symbol. It expresses, usually in disguised form, some important events in the playwright's psyche. We propose to uncover this kind of hidden meaning in *Othello* by following lines which psychologists have laid down for the interpretation of dreams. (The reader might wish to consult Freud's *General Introduction to Psychoanalysis.*)

Our thesis is that *Othello* is Shakespeare's waking dream and that dream has been preserved for us by his art.

Our first step is to pick out important elements of the play and treat them as associative symbols. If we were really analyzing a dream, we would ask the dreamer to tell us what each of these elements brought to his mind when he let his thought go wherever it would. Of course, we can not do that with Shakespeare: very little is actually known about his life. We must ask ourselves instead: What do we find in Shakespeare's personal history that we can associate with the symbols from the play?

This process of association, along with some careful conjecture, should conduct us to a story, just as a dream brings the interpreter to personal memories from the dreamer's unconscious. The outlines of the story should be a simple discovery, just waiting for us. But it may be partly the result of conjecture—of a crucial "abduction"—by which we make sense of facts that do not quite jell until the theory is added.

If this method works, we should see what *Othello* meant to Shakespeare himself. The play will image a portion of his life. It will not be as an exact copy—a dream is rarely a copy of what it expresses—but as a transformation which varies some facts, providing, we suppose, a profound emotional release for the writer. The argument becomes a two-way street, from literature to life by way of association, and from life to literature again by way of interpretive explanation. Armed with the elements of our personal story, we will turn back again to *Othello*, and we will be able to give a plausible account of how the play was constructed from materials in the playwright's mind.

Before we go further, we should also be conscious that our thesis is metaphorical: to call a play a dream is to use a metaphor, and that can be dangerous. But metaphors become untrustworthy only when we forget that they have built-in limitations: They include a certain deliberate inaccuracy. They are bad when they replace genuine thinking with borrowed enthusiasm. But the conscious transfer of method from one discipline to another has often generated sound ideas; it may be the most fruitful course of new thought there is. We intend to treat our analogy with rigor. We will carefully adjust terms to their new context, and we will make our terms bear the weight of thought in their own right. Our metaphor shows us a way to go. We shall see how useful the journey is.

First, then, what are the pieces of the play? What is this dream about?

It is about love; about jealousy; about imaginary love triangles, lots of them. It is about blackness in at least two senses, one physical, the other moral. It is about whiteness or fairness, too. It is about the outsider who is a big social success and a terrible emotional failure. These, then, are our categories, the basic kinds of symbol which may have meanings of the sort we are looking for.

Biographical facts that connect Shakespeare with the play are scanty. We know that he was an outsider, a country fellow come to London; an actor-writer who found considerable success by virtue of talent. Perhaps he had social pretensions too: He became a gentleman officially and was self-conscious about it. Once in his life he performed one of Cassio's functions. In 1604 he acted in his landlord's behalf as a go-between to negotiate the terms on which a fellow lodger would marry the landlord's daughter. Eight years later he was called to testify in a lawsuit over the dowry. (See Bellott-Mountjoy, p. 23.) But all this is very little, though we may sense some thin ties.

The obvious place to turn is not to biography but to the sonnets. There we find love and jealousy and triangles and all the rest. The sonnets are a record of personal torment, great emotional investment, high hopes, heavy risks, and terrible self-disparagement amounting to seeming depression. In spite of all that can be said about convention and cliché in this most frequented poetic form, Shakespeare's sonnets are a testament of anguish. They disclose more real feeling than any other sonnet sequence we know.

Triangles? We look at the sonnets and behold, sure enough, there it is! In Sonnet 41, for instance, it is all there. Shakespeare suspects his handsome young friend "hath leaped into my seat": "thou mightst my seat forbear,/ And chide thy beauty and thy straying youth,/ Who lead thee in their riot even there/ Where thou art forced to break a two-fold truth—/ Hers, by thy beauty tempting her to thee,/ Thine, by thy beauty being false to me." The form is only a container for the gentle pleading of the friend who feels rejected where he had "garnered up his heart."

The Shakespeare of the sonnets had both Iago's motives and Othello's feelings. There was a woman, the famous "dark lady," and he "loved her dearly." There was a young man, whom Shakespeare made his friend and whom he praised so extravagantly in the early sonnets, bidding him beget children in order to leave copies of his beauty in the world. In some ways this friend is a perfect analogue to Cassio, "framed to make women false," "A man in hue, all hues in his controlling,/ Which steals men's eyes and women's souls amazeth." (Sonnet 20.) The young man and the woman met. Perhaps he pleaded Shakespeare's case with her; perhaps he went between them "very oft." The sonnets give the impression that some uncertainty developed among the three: "Thou mayst be false, and yet I know it not," says Sonnet 92; and the first lines of the poem immediately following are even more tantalizing: "So shall I live, *supposing* thou art true,/ Like a deceivèd husband."

In the sonnets Shakespeare tries to put the best face on things. He rationalizes what has been done to him. (Sonnet 42.) He plays word games by way of emotional self-defense. (Sonnet 95.) He can scarcely bring himself to reproach his friend. It is easier to be openly angry with the woman. All his tricks are thin disguises, however. He is tortured in spite of them, and if we allow for natural differences between drama and personal narrative, or simply take into account different emotional economies, it becomes clear that the same psychic material, one single story, is present in both the sonnets and the play.

When we read the later poems in this group, our theory grows to conviction. In a score of them, starting with Sonnet 127, the anger against the "dark lady" becomes full-throated. There she is black in deed as well as look. (Sonnet 131.) She is a seductress, a tormentress, a devil; her bed is a hell. She is a bad angel in a struggle for souls. The handsome young man is the good angel. Shakespeare's soul is caught between their contrary *suggestions* or temptations, and at the same time the good angel himself is caught and at least suspected of being dragged into hell. (Sonnet 144.)

Love, jealousy, triangles, black, white, the "allegory of evil"—it is all here, "yet confused." Some of the elements are distributed differently; there is a different emotional economy. Relationships are turned askew. But the elements are here. Of that there can be no mistake.

We could identify a large number of analogues which we discover from reading the sonnets with Othello in mind as an overarching model. There are analogies of meaning. There are mere verbal analogies, where the meanings, at least on the surface we can see, are merely accidental. It is as though these phrases represented some deep preoccupations; if we could unlock them, we might find riches of explanation we have not imagined. But we leave the reader to go through the sonnets for himself and make his own associations with the play. We must concentrate on what is abundantly clear. We must describe how the play transforms the fragments of personal meaning. Now the life story which we have reconstructed becomes our instrument of comparison.

We learn that in order to explain the transformation we have only to apply our theory of dreams. It will predict, or at least account for, all the results by means of "condensation" and "displacement," which are two standard devices of dream interpretation. They seem invented to suit our purposes.

The condensation in this case is rather simple. In the sonnet story there is a rival poet, who apparently bested Shakespeare in competition for patronage or appreciation from the fair young friend. We can link the envy of the rival with Iago's scheme against Cassio through the use of "ship" language in both cases. Sonnet 80 compares the rival poet's great ship with Shakespeare's little bark. Iago not only treats the Moor's success as boarding a "land carrack" (I, ii, 50), he also conceives his own scheme as a prospering ship (II, iii, 65). This connection is one of those attenuated verbal analogies which we have mentioned above. The Othello story enabled Shakespeare to combine or telescope his jealousy and his envy so as to find one object for both kinds of hostility. The rival and patron of the sonnet story are reduced to one in the play. Both become entrapped in a vengeful net. But that is what condensation is: The compressing of several emotional objects into one portmanteau symbol.

The displacements, on the other hand, are much more interesting because more varied and elegant. In fact, displacements in this play occur in three ways: By doubling or multiplication, by mirror inversion, and by a process of skewing or permutation.

Shakespeare is the prototype for all the male victims in the play. That is to say, he doubled or multiplied himself in the creation of these characters. An odd bit of fact ties him to Cassio, as we have noted. In

Roderigo he is the fooled victim, the "gull," the dullard. We can imagine him regarding himself with unbelief. Sonnet 129, a sermon inspired by self-disgust, might be a practice run for Iago's preachment to Roderigo.

More importantly, Othello and Iago are opposite sides of the same coin, for which Shakespeare's life supplied both the metal and the configuration. The sonnets unmistakably testify that he knew the irresolution and the suppositiousness of jealousy and that he battled against them with his art. But Othello represents that inner lining of the writer's soul that felt the jealousy directly and could not protect itself with postures and rationalizing. Othello's motives, once they exist, are like the sea currents he compares them to. They cannot be repressed; they cannot be "sublimated" through artifice. Iago's can. He is the protean soul, that artistic part, which tried in the sonnets to rationalize and wear the mask of the self-deceiving lover. The action of the play translates Iago's motives into Othello's feelings, thus expressing Shakespeare as man of both power and sensibility.

Displacement by doubling aims at resonance and clarity for the emotions. Doubling isolates and emphasizes for the emotions certain features which life and psychic economy would blur. This kind of displacement is a form of intuitive analysis, common alike to poetry and dreams. Shakespeare divided himself up, the better to contemplate what had happened, the better to feel what it meant.

He likewise reduplicated and varied the expression of his own situation. The one triangle in the sonnet story is multiplied many fold in the play. The triangle, after all, is the inseparable form of jealousy: what would jealousy be without it? The dream-play says: "Let's see what this essence is; let's look at its various species." And that is exactly what happens. Given the five main characters—Othello, Desdemona, Iago, Emilia, Cassio—there are ten distinct triangles that they can possibly get into. We list them below, using the characters' initials for the sake of brevity.

ODI ODE ODC OIE OIC OEC

DIE DIC DEC

IEC

Most of these are Iago's inventions. For instance, he supposes the Othello/Iago/Emilia triangle (OIE). That is the one he first plumes up his will with. He desires the Othello/Desdemona/Iago triangle (ODI). "Now I do love her too." He pretends to perceive the Othello/Desdemona/Cassio triangle (ODC), and his main action is to persuade

Othello that it exists. To get himself into the mood for the main event, he suspects Cassio "with my nightcap too" (which brings in IEC).

Other triangles are present by implication. For example, OIE implies ODE, and ODI implies DIE. We will leave the reader to check these implications for fun.

There is a still more interesting collection which is swept up into Iago's fantasy about Cassio's dream. Iago insinuates himself into the make-believe affair between Cassio and Desdemona, when he pretends to have been Cassio's bedfellow (DIC). But as his representation of the dream comes across to Othello, Iago is substituted for Desdemona in Cassio's supposed imagination (it is almost too complicated to say). We have the homosexual triangle (OIC). If we take seriously the antimarriage at the end of the same scene, then Iago is perhaps supposed to be imagining a homosexual relationship between himself and Othello, into which Cassio intrudes. This fantasy about sexual relations copies the military relationship in which Cassio was also the intruder.

All the triangles in the figure on p. 168 are present implicitly or explicitly, except the two (OEC and DEC) which involve the hero and the heroine respectively with the Emilia/Cassio combination. But the absence of these two remote possibilities is made up for by the inclusion of two combinations that are far more dramatically signicant. One of these is Othello/Desdemona/Roderigo (ODR), which Iago pretends to further, producing one of the subplots. The other—Desdemona/Cassio/Bianca (DCB)—is the most fantastic of all, the archmock, which Iago contrives: "Yours [the handkerchief], by this hand. And to see how he prizes the foolish woman your wife! She gave it him, and he hath given it his whore." (IV, i, 185–187.)

Through these triangles, then, and by means of the divided self, Shakespeare unfolded his own story. The technique of doubling makes this clear. But the basis of such reduplication is analogy, and straightforward analogy alone does not explain enough.

Some strong personal feeling must have exploded into *Othello*. Shakespeare must have felt some huge but thwarted fury. Emotions, which the writer of the sonnets disguised and which the living man probably suppressed, receive their satisfaction in the play. They achieve a fierce release there. If the play is Shakespeare's dream—his psychic drama—then it must fulfill some wishes; there must be some gratification which he got from reconceiving a novella and working out his own poem.

But if Shakespeare was discharging some enormous anger, whom is he angry with? In the sonnet story, both the dark lady and the fair young man get off scot free. They inflict great suffering; but they receive no punishment. The young man is especially exempt. Shakespeare can scold the woman and call her devil and even threaten her but he excuses his friend.

We notice that the play turns all that inside out. It inverts some values and redistributes some characteristics. It exacts punishments all around.

Thus, it is that Shakespeare the dreamer has a twofold satisfaction: he sees the equivalent for the young friend suffer and be punished; he also sees that figure's innocence vindicated. Incidentally, in the play as in life, Shakespeare seems to inflict less gratuitous suffering on the man than on the woman. But by the trick of thought that enables him to confound himself with Othello and the dark lady, Shakespeare punishes himself.

When we try to see all these transformations at once, we discover that there is a mirror inversion. The life story (sonnets) is a box; and the play, with all its variations, is another box, which contains the first. When we move from the life-box to the play-box and look back, we look at the same set of facts from another direction. What happens is that the basic shape of those facts remains the same, but left becomes right and right becomes left. Or, in this kind of mirroring, good can become bad and vice versa. The play in this sense is a mirror indeed— a mirror which both copies and distorts life, for the sake of psychic relief.

In the dream or psychodrama, there is a kind of terrible esthetic justice. Characters who stand in for Shakespeare's tormentors, including Shakespeare himself, since he must have contributed to his own pain and guilt, are punished. And if this justice goes beyond the justice of the philosopher, it is a corrective to the injustice of life. It is the justice of the imagination, at once poetic justice in a true sense of that misunderstood cliché and the justice of the injured ego.

As Iago, Shakespeare can look upon the symbols of his friends with cynicism and contempt. He can enjoy their suffering. He can take a subtle, exquisite pleasure in the artfulness of their torture. After all, it is only esthetic pleasure; it is only a dream.

As Othello he can revel in self-pity. He "dotes, yet doubts, suspects, yet strongly loves." (III, iii, 170.) He can glorify his sufferings. He can transform them into the illusion of justice, and then he can have the moral and intellectual satisfaction of correcting that illusion. Finally, he can die (in imagination, that is).

What a splendid, what a godlike dream!

There is only one more point. I can hear someone stand up and say: "All this is very well, except that the dream, if that is what it is, is not original. Shakespeare did not invent the *Moor of Venice*. He read it. It is the nth novella in the collection by Giraldi Cinthio. It is mentioned in every introduction to the play, and one can read it in the *New*

Variorum Othello, in Italian or in a translation. How can it be Shakespeare's dream if he did not even make it up?"

To be sure, Shakespeare read or remembered the novella as he prepared *Othello.* It is a dull, flat, moralizing tale at that, which, incidentally, would in its moral respect have satisfied Thomas Rymer and Dr. Johnson better than Shakespeare's play did, since the tale includes Desdemona's fear "that I shall become a warning to young girls not to marry against the wishes of their parents, and that the Italian ladies may learn from me not to wed a man whom nature and habitude of life estrange from us."

But what we have shown is how such a story, uninspired as it is in its original form, answered to Shakespeare's heart's desire. There were immediate channels between himself and the chief male characters. There were analogies with the remaining characters, as well. His unconscious mind must have been deeply touched. The tale must have stirred, must have enticed him to rouse his inventive powers.

And he did invent. Aside from the wondrous music of Othello's speech and Desdemona's pathos and most of Iago's craft—aside, that is, from all the poetic realizations—he invented all but the merest skeleton of the story. The moral ambiguity is his idea. The permutations and mirrorings are his. The art bears the imprint of his singular mind.

Of the triangles, Cinthio gave him only two. All the rest, including the crucial supposition of Iago (OIE), are Shakespeare's creations. It is as though Beethoven were touched to the heart by the sudden recollection of some peasant tune, upon which he then composed a flood of variations for full symphonic orchestra.

Or to put it another way, in keeping with the thesis of this section, Cinthio's story is what the interpreter of dreams would call the "event of the day before." It is scarcely more than a matter of chance. It crossed the path of Shakespeare's life—and mated with his inner life— almost by accident, and then it had the good fortune to lend its shape to the profound self-expression of genius.

But *Othello* is not just Shakespeare's dream. The artist produces a symbol for others to contemplate, and audiences variously endow that symbol with meanings. We must therefore step into a more public domain. We need not on this account, abandon our analogy with dreams, however. A play in this present view may be a communal dream, like a liturgy, even when it is only read. Art is a public dream, a dream for those who are awake as Plato thought.

The analogy with dreams suggests a method of interpretation, and this method can be transposed with remarkable ease into the public domain. We have only to turn our procedure inside out. What before we called "elements" (those pieces of the dream which had private meanings) are to be thought of now as public symbols. Soldier, abused husband, bride, deceiving servant, dupe, gull: such symbols are types. They imply potential stories. They are very well known to everyone who shares the culture they belong to, and they are rich in connotations, which are public meanings.

The place occupied by the artist's unconscious (or by Shakespeare's personal life) in our previous analysis is taken now by a public memory, that is, by tradition. It is there that we now must hope to find a coherent pattern which will hold the symbols together and explain the play.

The process of association leads us this time, not to guess about Shakespeare, but to search the collective memory as scholars habitually do when they look for sources or prototypes.

We let the obvious symbols float in our mind so that hookups with cultural materials may begin to form. Is there some single body of tradition where all these types play together, tangled perhaps at cross-purposes in their own machinations? Of course there is. These types all belong to comedy.

For a long time scholars have flirted with this idea. Thomas Rymer knew that if the great temptation scene had been played in old Rome as it was played in the seventeenth century, the actors would have to leave off their boots of tragedy and go barefoot as the Roman comedians did. What is that scene about, if not the abusing of a simple-minded husband by a crafty servant? The paradox of a tragedy made from comic elements may have blocked the full development of this idea. Let us pursue it.

There are actually two main stories in the comic tradition. In one version an old man is keeping a young girl under his thumb. The old man may take many forms: crotchety father, cruel master, ruthless pander; he may even be a soldier as we shall see. He need not be very old, just a little "declined into the vale of years." The main thing is that he is a tyrant. He keeps the charming young girl away from the charming young man who would carry her off to love, fruitfulness, prosperity, respectability—to whatever may be the opposite of her oppressed condition.

But though the young girl is resourceful enough, the young man is not. The function of love in young heroes of this type is divided from the function of brains. The masculine brains are given to a servant, who takes his whole delight in conniving, manipulating, arranging disguises, and contriving deceptions, perhaps because sex for him is out of the question. It is the servant's function to remove all obstacles and bring the lovers together while securing the downfall and discomfort of the tyrannical old one.

The ending, of course, is the public union (usually though not always in marriage) between the lusty, youthful perpetuators of the race. Let us call this first version the spring plot. If we think of the episode in the senate chamber not merely as a trial but as a triumph of new love, then Othello and his bride appear to have passed already through this spring version of the comic plot.

The second version, which we will call the autumnal plot, is really a permutation and variation of the first. Here two lovers are publicly yoked already. They may be married, but remember, we are dealing with basics, and betrothal will do, and so will a simple liaison. This union is then threatened: some third party is lusting after one member of the pair, usually, though not always, a youth after the woman. And this time the servant is in the outsider's camp, conniving to bring him satisfaction. The couple must fight for its life. It must drive the enemy off. Then there is a reunion, in which the participants, though touched with melancholy, are wiser in their love.

The tradition of such plots is unspeakably large, probably because puzzles of sexuality recur for every generation on the earth. Both plots clearly treat love in its elemental form, reducing it to a pattern of frustration followed by gratification or to a pattern of gratification, threat, and triumphant gratification again. In the two plots taken together there is symmetry; there is completeness. They complement each other, as Shakespeare showed in *Much Ado about Nothing*, where he hooked and wove them together in an intricate, dance-like design, but as separate stories. The coming to love of Beatrice and Benedick is a spring plot. The tale of Hero and Claudio is autumnal, of course, with its betrothal broken by slanders, its heroine's apparent death, its sudden leap into life as she emerges from her disguise and the marriage takes place.

Both plots are evident in Othello (the spring plot being implied in the beginning). But the autumnal plot corresponds more closely to what actually happens. The union of lovers is scarcely formed when it is threatened from outside. Iago pretends to be furthering Roderigo's lust; he pretends that Cassio's lust has already intruded; and using these pretenses, he serves himself. It is really Iago's passion that is the threat, and whatever its true nature may be, it is directed toward Othello. By means of the antimarriage Iago comes between Othello and Desdemona and achieves in his perverted way what he pretends that others are trying to achieve.

The comic analogies are compelling indeed. If we believed that characters had a life outside their plays, we might think that Iago had read the Roman comic playwright, Plautus, for himself. Shakespeare certainly did: Plautus was probably one of his Latin chores in school. Iago patterns several of his tricks on the chicaneries of Palaestrio, the cozening servant, in Plautus's play, the *Miles Gloriosus*. The improvisation of Cassio's dream is a steal directly from that play. So is the substance of Iago's conversation with Cassio (IV, i), that conversation about Bianca which Othello misconstrues. But the really big theft is not a matter of specific lines. The big theft is the idea of a storied type, the whole idea of the *miles gloriosus* himself.

The *miles* is the boastful, arrogant soldier who goes chasing women. (You can still see his type in *A Funny Thing Happened on the Way to the Forum*.) The Latins call him a great adulterer. In fact, he struts and parades before any woman he meets, "bragging and telling her fantastical lies." He pretends to be from here and everywhere, with a string of ponderful victories far and wide.

At heart, of course, the *miles* is a coward. The great, hilarious, but perhaps finally bitter joke in Plautus' play is the exposing of this coward for what he is. Stealing his girl away is part of the joke. Accompanying the dispossession of the *miles*—perhaps as a symbolic equivalent—is the taking away of his occupation, along with the threat of a literal unmanning. These three ideas—losing the woman, losing the soldiership, and losing virility—are all associated in the ancient play, as they are in *Othello*.

Doesn't this explain how Iago acts? He treats Othello as a kind of joke. While all the world believes that Othello is the truly great soldier (and they are undoubtedly right in this belief), Iago tries to think of him as the *miles*. He supposes the great soldier to be a fake. He adopts the hypothesis that Othello is the cowardly soldier of the comic type, that all his exploits are a mere facade; and he makes this supposition stick.

If we look to the literary source from which Iago came—the place where this character had his life before Shakespeare found him—we discover these remarkable words: "Now amongst the soldiery there was an Ensign, a man of handsome figure, but of the most depraved nature in the world. This man was in great favor with the Moor, who had not the slightest idea of his wickedness; for, despite the malice lurking in his heart, he cloaked with proud and valorous speech and with a specious presence the villainy of his soul with such art that he was to all outward show another Hector or Achilles." (Cinthio.) The reason why the idea of the false soldier occurred so naturally to the false servant is that Iago, in his origin, was a *miles*.

Iago's huge joke, then, is a projection of himself. And the form of the projection, the *Miles* plot, seems even to have suggested the elements of all Iago's mischief. Confuse the old soldier; deceive him; get the girl away for the purposes of sex (there is something of lewdness in that); punish him with the threat of a supreme violence. The *Miles* plot is an instance, perhaps a prototype, of that scenario by means of which Iago both conceives himself and victimizes others. All the pieces are here waiting in the tradition. All the implications are here, too. Shakespeare saw them, with instant clarity, as one imagines; but however it actually was, he saw them and worked them out for himself (the scenario is Shakespeare's emotional instrument, too) but also for us, for audiences in unknown generations who would bring their own feelings and their own meanings to bear.

It is time now to separate Shakespeare and his villainous creation without any damage to the analogy between them. Iago imposes the joke, but Shakespeare's art controls how we perceive it. That art, as a public fact, is the containing circle which defines how we conceive everything that happens.

Comic wit, on which Iago draws, is subtle but abstract. It may be ultimately malicious too. Its victims rarely engage our sympathy. They are mere types, mere ideas, appropriate victims. Braggart soldiers, for instance, have no life that we really sense. Their vitality is shut away by thicknesses of stereotype, by layers of habitual abstraction. They behave like automata. Mechanism, in Henri Bergson's suggestive metaphor, has been "encrusted" upon their life. Bergson says that the reducing of a person to a machine is what turns him into a joke; and laughter is the cure for mechanical men.

Though *Othello* is no laughing matter, Bergson's thesis fits it exactly. Othello adopts a false and ridiculous idea; and once he takes it fully into his head, it turns him into an image of himself, into a caricature. He begins to repeat himself. He draws out the consequences and acts upon them without referring them to life—to Desdemona—as he has ample opportunity to do. That murder is justice becomes his *idée fixe*, another form of mechanism, as Bergson says. "It is the cause, it is the cause, my soul." (V, ii, 1.)

It is the encavement scene (IV, i) that fixes the falsehood like cement in Othello's mind. A lid is clamped on his thought. He works out his folly in the dark and does not emerge into the truth until his mistake has run its terrible course.

But all the while, Shakespeare makes us sit like gods, knowing everything. We watch the events on stage with perfect clarity. We watch a terrible evil taking shape. We have a full knowledge of all Iago's tricks, and we see deep into his character, though not to the bottom of it. We know the precise moral valuation of every character on the stage; how they are valued, truly or falsely, by each other; how they are valued in Iago's hypotheses.

We also know how it feels to be Othello. That is one of the crucial differences between this play and comedies. We watch the mechanism of his mistake take its inevitable form, as we might were this a comedy; but we also feel the lid come down on his understanding. We feel his love, his loyalty, being stifled. We share his divided consciousness.

Now this tension, the tension of God's elect, mirrors in a way the tension on the stage. For us that tension is a question of knowledge: When will the truth be revealed? The truth is the jack-in-the-box. In the comedies it comes in time. Sebastian appears, and the lid comes off the mistakes, just in time to prevent some serious trouble. Dogberry finally gets through with the truth about the conspiracy against Hero. Dogberry, mechanical man *par excellence*, has been waiting in the wings all the while, like the winter ground with a little seed of truth planted in it. But in *Othello* there is no such safety factor. The winter prevails. The truth does not come forth, until the person who might embody it is no longer there.

Instead of springtime rejoicing there is lamentation: eyes that "drop tears as fast as the Arabian trees their medicinal gum." And in this phrase the complex alcohol comes back—the play of magic and wit, the course of falsehood and truth, the clash of hardness and tender intimacy—the fabric of an inexhaustible dream.

NOTES

CHAPTER 19

[1] *Paradise Lost,* III, 108.

[2] Sister Miriam Joseph Rauh, C.S.C., *Shakespeare's Use of the Arts of Language* (New York, 1947), p. 84: "Diaphora is the repetition of a common name so as to perform two logical functions: to designate an individual and to signify the qualities connoted by the common name, as when Desdemona remarks to Cassio of Othello's manner: 'My advocation is not now in tune,/ My lord is not my lord; . . .' (III, iv, 123–124)."

[3] G. E. Bentley, *Shakespeare: A Biographical Handbook* (New Haven, 1961). See Chapter V, "The Playwright."

CHAPTER 20

[1] The process of forming such a proposition has been called "abduction" by the great American philosopher Charles Sanders Peirce. (See Peirce's essay, "Abduction and Induction.") It is the beginning of all new and original thinking, the beginning really of all thinking we have not yet done for ourselves. Any proposition that connects one fact with other facts or with ideas is an abductive proposition, Peirce says, and it may be treated as a hypothesis.

[2] I owe this idea to Mr. Lionel Munoz.

BIBLIOGRAPHY

Bacon, Francis. *The New Organon.*

Bentley, G. E. *Shakespeare: A Biographical Handbook.* New Haven, 1961.

Boase, Alan M. *The Fortunes of Montaigne: A History of the Essays in France, 1580–1669.* New York, 1970.

Bradley, A. C. *Shakespearean Tragedy.* New York, 1949.

Burke, Kenneth. "*Othello:* An Essay to Illustrate a Method," *Hudson Review,* IV (1951), 165–203.

Bush, Geoffrey. *Shakespeare and the Natural Condition.* Cambridge, Mass., 1956.

Coleridge, Samuel Taylor. *Shakespeare and the Elizabethan Dramatists.* Edinburgh, 1905.

Coleridge's Shakespearean Criticism, ed. Thomas Raysor. 2 vols. Cambridge, Mass., 1930. (See "The Character of Hamlet.")

Danby, John F. *Shakespeare's Doctrine of Nature: A Study of King Lear.* London, 1949.

Dowden, Edward. *Shakespeare: A Critical Study of His Mind and Art.* New York, 1967.

Duhem, Pierre. *The Aim and Structure of Physical Theory,* trans. Philip Wiener. New York, 1974.

Eliot, T. S. *Selected Essays, 1917–1932.* New York, 1932. (See "Shakespeare and the Stoicism of Seneca.")

Florio, John, trans. *The Essays of Montaigne,* ed. W. E. Henley. Vol. 2. New York, 1967.

Homan, Sidney R. "Iago's Aesthetics: *Othello* and Shakespeare's Portrait of an Artist," *Shakespeare Studies,* V (1969), 141–148.

Johnson, Samuel. *On Shakespeare,* ed. W. K. Wimsatt, Jr. New York, 1960.

Kittredge, George Lyman, ed. *The Complete Works of Shakespeare.* Chicago, 1936.

McFarland, Thomas. *Tragic Meanings in Shakespeare.* New York, 1966.

McGuire, Philip C. "*Othello* as an 'Assay of Reason,'" *Shakespeare Quarterly,* XXIV (1973), 198–209.

Muir, Kenneth. *Shakespeare's Sources.* London, 1957.

Norwood, Gilbert. *Plautus and Terence.* New York, 1932.

Othello, New Variorum Edition, ed. Horace Howard Furness. New York.

Rauh, Sister Miriam Joseph, C.S.C. *Shakespeare's Use of the Arts of Language.* New York, 1947.

Ribner, Irving. "*Othello* and the Pattern of Shakespearean Tragedy," *Tulane Studies in English,* V (1955), 69–82.

Rogers, Robert. "Endopsychic Drama in *Othello,*" *Shakespeare Quarterly,* XX (1969), 205–215.

Rogers, Stephen. "*Othello:* Comedy in Reverse," *Shakespeare Quarterly,* XXIV (1973), 210–220.

Rymer, Thomas. *Critical Works,* ed. Curt A. Zimansky. New Haven, 1956.

Sextus Empiricus. *Outlines of Pyrrhonism,* trans. the Rev. R. G. Bury. Loeb Classical Library, vol. 1. Cambridge, Mass., 1933.

Spencer, Theodore. *Shakespeare and the Nature of Man.* New York, 1949.

Spivack, Bernard. *Shakespeare and the Allegory of Evil.* New York, 1958.

Stewart, Douglas. "*Othello:* Roman Comedy as Nightmare," *Emory University Quarterly,* XXII (1966), 252–276.

Stoll, E. E. *Shakespeare and Other Masters.* Cambridge, Mass., 1940.

Wieand, Helen E. *Deception in Plautus: A Study in the Technique of Roman Comedy.* Boston, 1920.

Willey, Basil. *The Seventeenth-Century Background: Studies in the Thought of the Age in Relation to Poetry and Religion.* London, 1934.

PART FIVE

LOVE AND DEATH IN KING LEAR

J. W. HOUPPERT

INTRODUCTION

"NO MAN WILL EVER WRITE
A BETTER TRAGEDY THAN *LEAR*."[1]

Few critics have shared George Bernard Shaw's unqualified endorsement of *Lear*. Samuel Johnson, upset particularly at Cordelia's death, gave *Lear* mixed reviews; and even Coleridge, the greatest of the bardolators, felt that the sufferings of Gloucester urged the tragic "beyond the outermost mark and *ne plus ultra* of the dramatic."[2] Whole generations, in fact, rejected Shakespeare's play out of hand. From 1681, when Nahum Tate's romanticized version took to the boards, until 1838, when William Macready virtually restored the original, no one saw Shakespeare's play. And those who did see a version of *Lear*—or who read Shakespeare's version—did not feel compelled to write about their experiences. Until the Romantics, there is little criticism of *Lear*. But even in the hands of Lamb, Coleridge, and Hazlitt, *Lear* was never quite able to catch up with *Hamlet, Othello,* or *Macbeth*. In the twentieth century, however, the play is making up for lost time. After Auschwitz and Hiroshima we are not easily reduced to nausea by the spectacle of a public blinding or a daughter hanged. Death no longer appalls us as it appalled Johnson: "Death is neither punishment nor reward: it is simply in the nature of things."[3]

Since we have become reconciled to death, our present concern with *Lear* is aesthetic, an examination of form and of the power of

181

words. We have become accustomed to looking at the play from different perspectives, not simply from a tragic one. We have only recently remembered that in the quarto edition the play is described, not as a tragedy, but as the *True Chronicle Historie of the life and death of King Lear and his three Daughters,* a curious title, because the play is not true, not even in terms of the legendary history from which it derives. It is, in fact, the only version of the Lear story which deliberately distorts legendary history.

"True chronicle history" or not, no other play evokes divided responses as successfully as *Lear.* We move with ease from the world of medieval tournaments, where we champion the disguised Edgar vanquishing the Black Knight, to the world of street singers and balladeers, captured in spirit at least in the Fool's songs and verses.[4] We turn from the world of Christian morality drama, where we reap what we sow, to the world of pastoral romance, with its disappearances, disguisings, and renewals. No English Renaissance drama violates Sir Philip Sidney's dicta on tragedy with such enthusiasm as *Lear.* Violations of time, place, and action are accompanied by violation of decorum, as Fools mingle with Kings. Close to melodrama with its sharp distinction between the good and evil children, *Lear* nevertheless remains hard as adamant.[5] Unlike Nahum Tate after him, Shakespeare will not permit the spectacle of a Cordelia saved, a Lear returned to pomp and splendor. Lear must lose everything—only then will he learn that something can come from nothing. Lear is not for the sentimental. "What a world's *convention* of agonies," Coleridge was moved to write.[6] If *Lear* teaches us anything, it is that "the way to the best is through the worst."[7]

Whatever else *Lear* is, it is not a typical Elizabethan tragedy (whatever that is). Tragedy usually combines violent death with treachery, but in *Lear* both of the protagonists die a natural death. There is treachery a-plenty in the Gloucester story, but little in the Lear story. Edmund is a practicer who lies to his father (and everyone else) to further his own selfish ends. But Goneril and Regan do not lie to their father.[8] They tell him to his face that he is an old fool:

> O, Sir! you are old;
> Nature in you stands on the very verge
> Of her confine: you should be rul'd and led
> By some discretion that discerns your state
> Better than you yourself.
> (II, iv, 147–151)[9]

Gloucester is driven from his castle by the lies of Edmund; Lear drives himself from the castles of Goneril and Regan, because he cannot tolerate the truth.

In tragedy, also, we are meant to feel the loss occasioned by the death of an energetic personality, either good or evil, either a Hamlet or a Macbeth. But Lear is an octogenarian who is so totally exhausted by his experiences that he has virtually no life left to lose. In fact, Kent would not revive his dead master even if he could:

> Vex not his ghost: O! let him pass; he hates him
> That would upon the rack of this tough world
> Stretch him out longer. (V, iii, 313–315)

King Lear is not even a tragedy in the Shakespearean sense of the word. Shakespeare's plays, both comedies and tragedies, are usually rich in dramatic irony. We usually know much more than the actors, thus becoming, as it were, almost copartners in the act of creation. In this respect, the Gloucester story is typical. Edmund is a conventional practicer, like Iago, who operates through deceit and treachery. Neither Gloucester nor Edgar has any idea of the practice that Edmund is working on them. The audience, on the other hand, knows everything about Edmund's plan because he tells us what he is going to do. Soliloquies, therefore, are essential to the subplot for exchange of information between playwright and audience. The Lear story is virtually devoid of dramatic irony. In fact, instead of sharing important information with us, Shakespeare deliberately withholds it from us. We do not know, for example, that Lear has already decided to leave the most opulent share of the kingdom to Cordelia. Kent and Albany, in the opening scene, cannot decide whether Albany or Cornwall will be favored, when Lear has already decided upon Cordelia as the favorite. After the division of the kingdom, Goneril and Regan do not practice upon their father (they do practice upon each other!), so Lear's perspective is not obscured. Finally, Shakespeare even withholds from us the ending, which is contrary to anything a familiarity with the Lear story would prepare us for.[10]

King Lear not only departs from Shakespeare's usual methods of construction but also marks a departure from his usual subject matter. *King Lear* explores intense, soul-searing parental love. Other tragedies, of course, touch on this: Capulet is quite interested in securing a good match for Juliet; Hamlet's mother is mildly interested in her son's curious behavior; Desdemona's father is justly upset over her disaffection; Donalbain and Malcolm are distraught over Duncan's death, and Macduff even more distraught over the death of his children. But none of these approach the quality of love which ultimately unites Cordelia and Lear:

> O my dear father! Restoration hang
> Thy medicine on my lips, and let this kiss
> Repair those violent harms that my two sisters
> Have in thy reverence made! (IV, vii, 26–29)

> Upon such sacrifices, my Cordelia,
> The Gods themselves throw incense. Have I caught thee?

> He that parts us shall bring a brand from heaven,
> And fire us hence like foxes. Wipe thine eyes;
> The good years shall devour them, flesh and fell,
> Ere they shall make us weep: we'll see 'em starv'd first. (V, iii, 20–25)

In placing such a heavy emphasis on parental love, *King Lear* marks a general departure from Elizabethan values in general. There is much in Elizabethan literature about Eros, but little about Agape, the all yea-saying love of creation that is reflected in Cordelia's love for Lear. There is little in Elizabethan literature generally about childrens' love for their parents. No Elizabethan poet sings the praises of his dear old mother, and mothers and fathers were chary when praising their progeny. Perhaps because infant mortality was so high, parents were reluctant to place their hopes in barks so frail. Whatever the reason, parental love was not a theme often adapted to tragedy, and never before or again would Shakespeare so use it.

Because *King Lear* defies the usual categories, into which Shakespeare's other tragedies fit more comfortably, critics have turned to other forms of literature in an attempt to describe more accurately the kind of drama that *Lear* is. The play has, accordingly, been described as pastoral romance and morality play.

22

KING LEAR AS PASTORAL ROMANCE

> "WHO'S THERE, BESIDES FOUL WEATHER?"
> *(III, i, 1)*

Shakespeare's major additions to the old Lear story are the Fool and the Gloucester subplot, the latter proving an obstacle over which many a critic has tripped. Is it there, as some claim, to make the Lear story more credible?[11] According to this interpretation, two foolish fathers are more believable than one. Perhaps, but if *Lear* is a pastoral romance —or an antipastoral, as Maynard Mack argues[12]—then the Gloucester story can be accounted for on different grounds. According to the tradition of pastoral romance, the sojourner in Arcadia must see his situation reflected in that of others. Gloucester, then, may be present to reflect Lear's roughly parallel situation, a condition requisite for the healing of the pastoral invalid. It is not accidental that Shakespeare discovered the Gloucester story in Sidney's *Arcadia*, the greatest pastoral the age produced. The elements of the pastoral romance are generally present in *Lear*: disappearance, disguise, reintegration.[13]

The action of a pastoral is from the outside to the inside, from the turbulent outer world to the refined pastoral world, reaching finally the pure center of the world, which is always supernatural.[14] The pastoral action is the action of purification, or reunification—the pastoral sojourner is driven to Arcadia by an unhappy love affair. In Arcadia, the sojourner is sensitive to his reflection in others, and treats their griefs as his own. This sympathetic identification indicates that the sojourner is becoming aware of himself; he is approaching self-knowledge. Finally, the pastoral hero is always a visitor in Arcadia, never a citizen.

This brief sketch of pastoral literature suggests a wealth of parallels with *Lear*. Lear leaves the outer world, the world of Court, to find support in Nature:

> I tax you not, you elements, with unkindness;
> I never gave you kingdom, call'd you children,
> You owe me no subscription: then let fall
> Your horrible pleasure. . . . (III, ii, 16–19)

He is driven onto the heath (hardly Arcadian, though) by an unhappy series of disaffections, imaginary and real; first, Cordelia, and then Goneril and Regan. Finally, Lear's disavowal of his fatherhood will separate him from his daughters. The relationships with Goneril and Regan will not prove worth healing—that with Cordelia will require a miracle to heal. But Arcadia (and the heath) is the place where miracles occur.

On the heath Lear becomes aware for the first time in his life of the sufferings of others:

> Come on, my boy. How dost, my boy? Art cold? (III, ii, 68)

And as he does so he becomes aware for the first time in his life of his own common humanity. When Lear admits, "I am cold myself" (III, ii, 69), he has taken his first tentative step toward reintegration. Before Lear can become a saved man, he must first become a man. His earlier question, "Who is it that can tell me who I am" (I, iv, 238), is now answered, "a Man." Here is where Gloucester's importance is most obvious. In Arcadia a pastoral visitor must find his situation reflected in others, a matter of relative ease in pastorals such as *Arcadia*, where unrequited love between healthy, nubile men and women is at issue. But Lear's unhappy love affair is unusual. Where other pastoral visitors are seeking an erotic partner, Lear is seeking a daughter. What better for Shakespeare's purposes, therefore, than the story of Gloucester who is seeking a son?

The point of the parallel situations is clear. When Edgar appears disguised as Poor Tom, Lear asks:

> Didst thou give all to thy daughters?
> And art thou come to this? (III, iv, 48–49)

> What! has his daughters brought him to this pass?
> Couldst thou save nothing? Would'st thou give 'em all? (III, iv, 63–64)

Although Lear notes many of the obvious parallels between his situation and that of others, he fails, because of his growing madness, to note the differences in the situations. When Shakespeare directs our attention to the parallels, he also directs our attention to the differences. And because the parallels are so exact, they accentuate the differences. Both Lear and Gloucester, for example, begin their misfortunes with the identical word "nothing." But, when Cordelia says "nothing," she means nothing and is speaking the truth; when Edmund says "nothing," he means something, the forged letter, and is speaking a lie.[15] Lear, however, takes the truth for selfishness, whereas Gloucester takes the lie for selflessness. And this antithetical pattern is generally observed throughout the remainder of the parallels in the play.

Lear has no real difficulty in recognizing the false. He knows, for example, that Goneril and Regan flatter him in the opening scene (witness his later reference to Cordelia as that "little-seeming substance" [I, i, 198], in contrast to her "seeming" sisters). Lear's problem is in recognizing the true. He banishes Cordelia and fails to recognize her when reunited; he banishes Kent and barely recognizes him at the end. Gloucester, on the other hand, must learn to recognize both the true and the false. He accepts false coin for true, and trades away Edgar's inheritance for a mess of pottage.

The end of the Arcadian journey is to the pure center of the world, which is always supernatural. Geographically speaking, the journey in *Lear* is to Dover, hardly the center of the world. Why the journey ends at Dover is not clear. A. C. Bradley was disturbed at Gloucester painfully journeying all the way to Dover just to destroy himself.[16] The answer may be found in Shakespeare's source. In Sidney's *Arcadia* the Prince of Paphlagonia, who like Gloucester has been tricked by his evil son into driving away his good son, asks to be taken to a high rock in order to commit suicide. Now where in England would a higher place suggest itself than the cliffs of Dover? Whatever the reason Shakespeare takes Lear and Gloucester to Dover, the fact remains that there they reach their own true centers. Both are driven toward death. Gloucester attempts suicide, and Lear offers to drink poison. Both, however, are led from the brink of despair by the supernatural agency of love. "Thy life's a miracle" (IV, vi, 55), Edgar tells Gloucester. And Lear protests to Cordelia, "you do me wrong to take me out o' th' grave." (IV, vii, 45.) Again, though, the similarity accentuates the difference. Gloucester is "saved" by Edgar and dies, secure in the knowledge that his beloved son lives; Lear is "saved" by Cordelia, who dies before her father's very eyes.

No Shakespearean tragedy ends so perplexingly as *Lear*. No tragedy comes to point so sharply. When Lear says, "look there, look there" (V, iii, 311), he dies and his tragedy is finished. But what does Lear mean? Does he mean that Cordelia lives? Perhaps, but the odds are even that he means just the opposite. How, then, does Lear die? In joy, as Bradley and others would have it:

> Though he is killed by an agony of pain, the agony in which he actually dies is one not of pain but of ecstasy.[17]

Or in despair, as Judah Stampfer would have it:

> The final, penultimate tragedy of Lear, then, is not the tragedy of *hubris*, but the tragedy of penance. . . . the fear that penance is impossible, that the covenant, once broken, can never be re-established, because its partner has no charity, resilience, or harmony—the fear, in other words, that we inhabit an imbecile universe.[18]

The answer may lie with Gloucester. The lives of Gloucester and Lear have been paralleled through life, why not also in death?[19] And since we learn that Gloucester dies "twixt two extremes of passion, joy and grief" (V, iii, 198–199), why not Lear, as well? Such an interpretation fits the facts and is emotionally sound, as well as aesthetically consistent.

King Lear, with its heath in place of Arcadia, with its fools and madmen in place of shepherds and nymphs, is certainly something of an antipastoral. Yet the journey is consistent in terms of form, from outside to inside, from outer appearance to inner reality, from chaos to reintegration. But the end is not revitalization, but exhaustion and death. Pastoral elements are undeniably present in *Lear,* but *Lear* is not a pastoral.

23

KING LEAR AS MORALITY DRAMA

"WHAT! HATH YOUR GRACE
NO BETTER COMPANY?"
(III, iv, 146)

This question was asked in one morality play after another, Harley Granville-Barker notes, as he goes on to suggest that in *Lear* Shakespeare "metamorphosed the didactics of those old Moralities which were the infancy of his art."[20] The insistence in *Lear* on contraries—speech opposed to silence, blindness opposed to sight, true service opposed to false—encourages a psychomachian interpretation. Jan Kott, for example, describes the characters thusly:

> Of the twelve major characters half are just and good, the other half, unjust and bad. It is a division as consistent and abstract as in a morality play.[21]

Such division, however, obfuscates rather than illuminates the characterization in *Lear*. To which category does Lear belong, this man of unbridled wrath? Presumably to the former, but how can Lear be called just and good? And what of the lecherous Gloucester, who fails to choose sides until Lear is driven to the heath? And what of Edmund, whose deathbed reprieve spares the life of Lear? To label these characters, and most of the others, as either good or bad, just or unjust, merely confuses, because none is all the one or the other. Even the most extreme examples must give us pause. The angelic Cordelia could have spared her father his agonizing pilgrimage by playing his game.

The loving Edgar could have spared Gloucester his "suicidal" leap by revealing his identity earlier. In fact, of the 12 major characters, only Goneril and Regan yield to Kott's categorization. But Coleridge had these two typed:

> Regan and Goneril are the only pictures of the unnatural in Shakespeare—the pure unnatural; and you will observe that Shakespeare has left their hideousness unsoftened or diversified by a single line of goodness or common human frailty.[22]

He could have also included Cornwall. These three are as efficient as bayonets, and just as human.

As a genre, the morality drama has only recently earned literary respectability. The Protestant bias of the English-speaking intelligentsia effectively suppressed it until our own century. But now that it has reemerged, critics have found much that is illuminating. Maynard Mack sums up the contemporary attitude:

> Lear himself, as Professor Harbage among others has pointed out—flanked in that opening scene by "vices of flatterers on the one hand, virtues or truth-speakers on the other"—stirs memories of a far more ancient dramatic hero, variously called Mankind, Everyman, Genus Humanum, Rex Vivus, Rex Humanitas, Magnificence, etc. He is about to endure an *agon* that, while infinitely more poignant and complex than theirs, has its roots in the same medieval conception of psychomachia, interpreting man's life as "the arena of a Holy War between the contending forces of his own nature."[23]

Reading *Lear* as a morality play is illuminating, but reading it as an antimorality play is also illuminating. It may be the greatest antimorality ever penned.

Most English morality plays turn on the struggle between the Virtues and the Vices, and feature a youthful protagonist who is about to face the blandishments of the World for the first time. But King Lear is an old man who is well acquainted with the blandishments of the world, not a callow young bumpkin easily led astray. If anyone stands in the position of the morality protagonist, it is Cordelia. Lear more closely resembles the World. After all, he is about to distribute his kingdom. What more can the World offer? Cordelia, on the other hand, is the one exposed to the temptations of the World. The nice irony, though, is that Cordelia can have the world without falling out of grace. All Cordelia has to do is to tell the truth, to tell her father how much she loves him. Ironically, Cordelia falls out of Lear's grace by refusing to tell the truth. She will simply answer "nothing." Lear has, of course, made her situation untenable. If she answers Lear as her sisters do, she will stand accused of flattery. If she says "nothing," she is ungrateful. Cordelia finds it impossible, in short, to articulate her love.

Before Lear can become a saved man, he must first become a man, must divest himself of his royal robes and worldly trappings, must echo Mankind's lament:

> I am naked of limb and lend,
> As Mankind is shapen and shorn.[24]

The World is present in *Lear;* so too is the Flesh. Gloucester brags about Edmund's conception:

> Though this knave came something saucily to the world before he was sent for, yet was his mother fair; there was good sport at his making.   (I, i, 21–24)

And Goneril and Regan are led to a common death by their shared lust for Edmund who, by comparison with Lear's two daughters, seems almost innocent. No wonder Lear can say, though he forgets for a moment that Cordelia is a woman:

> Down from the waist they are Centaurs,
> Though women all above:
> But to the girdle do the Gods inherit,
> Beneath is all the fiend's: there's hell, there's darkness,
> There is the sulphurous pit—burning, scalding,
> Stench, consumption; fie, fie, fie! pah, pah!   (IV, vi, 126–131)

The Flesh and the World are present in *Lear;* so too is the Devil.

The scenes on the heath symbolically reenact a journey through the Underworld, where "sheets of fire" accompany the "Prince of Darkness," where "red burning spits" torment, and where the "foul fiend/ bites." In *Lear,* as in Dante's *Inferno,* Hell is not so much a place *where* we are; Hell is *what* we are. Because on the heath Lear is Hell, Shakespeare renders Hell dramatic through Lear. A landscape of Hell is created which functions symbolically. The frequent references to Underworld figures, especially demons, by Edgar and Lear create setting for Lear's journey. When Lear tells Cordelia, "You do me wrong to take me out o' th' grave" (IV, vii, 45), we know what he means. Lear has completed his pilgrimage through the Underworld, Lear has died to his old life and has been born into a new.

It is appropriate, therefore, that when Gloucester makes his life-saving plunge into the abyss, Edgar reports that his father's companion was "some fiend":

> As I stood here below methought his eyes
> Were two full moons; he and a thousand noses,
> Horns whelk'd and wav'd like the enridged sea. . . .   (IV, vi, 69–71)

Along with the World, the Flesh, and the Devil, *Lear* might also be said to incorporate the Four Daughters of God, a morality motif derived from *The Castle of Perseverance* (c. 1385). In the *Castle of Perseverance* Truth and Justice argue for Mankind's damnation, but Mercy pleads for his salvation. Peace finally refers the dispute to God, who decides in favor of Mankind. Like Truth and Justice, Goneril and Regan are quick to point to Lear's human failings:

GONERIL: You see how full of changes his age is; the observation we have made of it hath not been little: he always lov'd our sister most; and with what poor judgment he hath now cast her off appears too grossly.
REGAN: 'Tis the infirmity of his age; yet he hath ever but slenderly known himself.
GONERIL: The best and soundest of his time hath been but rash; then must we look from his age, to receive not alone the imperfections of long-engraffed condition, but therewithal the unruly waywardness that infirm and choleric years bring with them.   (I, i, 288–299)

Lear can no more withstand the attack of Truth and Justice than Mankind can. He also needs Mercy to plead his case:

CORDELIA: All bless'd secrets,
          All you unpublish'd virtues of the earth,
          Spring with my tears! be aident and remediate
          In the good man's distress!   (IV, iv, 15–18)

But in *Lear* there is no Peace to present the case to God, and no God to extend His hand in benediction. There is, however, again Cordelia, who from time to time assumes a Christ-like posture:

                    O dear father!
          It is thy business that I go about. . . .   (IV, iv, 23–24)

But ultimately it is Lear, not Cordelia, who becomes divine as he becomes human. As Cordelia asks her father,

                    O! look upon me, Sir,
          And hold your hand in benediction o'er me.   (IV, vii, 57–58)

Lear kneels before his daughter confessing that he is "a very foolish fond old man," and with that recognition Lear's spiritual pilgrimage is almost complete. Divinity is at hand, as Cordelia replies to Lear's claim that she has cause to hate him, "No cause, no cause." (IV, vii, 75.)

Lear is still trying to reason his way through life. He still believes that cause precedes effect, and that the two are inextricably linked. But Cordelia's reply raises us to a level of existence above reason and causality. To say "no cause" when there is cause is more divine than human. "Final grace will reason nothing and say merely, " 'No cause, no cause.' "[25]

The basic metaphor of the morality drama—the pilgrimage—also operates in *Lear*. Lear moves literally and figuratively in time and space. In time, Lear moves to the very farthest limits of human endurance, to a point when life's substance cries out to its spirit, "stop." In time,

Lear moves from a consideration of his own kingly nature ("we shall retain/ The name and all th' addition to a king" [I, i, 135–136]) to a consideration of eternity ("Why should a dog, a horse, a rat, have life,/ And thou no breath at all? Thou'lt come no more,/ Never, never, never, never, never!" [V, iii, 306–308]). With this question, Shakespeare unites the pastoral journey and the morality pilgrimage. Why should the victim die, and not someone else?

In space, Lear moves from castle to heath, coming to rest finally in Cordelia's arms at Dover. The physical distance can be measured in miles, but the spiritual distance is infinite. A confirmed materialist at the start, Lear knew only that a half did not equal a whole, and that from nothing, nothing comes. Lear's pilgrimage is torturous, from his opening imperious command, "Attend the Lords of France and Burgundy, Gloucester" (I, i, 34), to his final, humble request, "Pray you, undo this button: thank you, Sir" (V, iii, 309). The pilgrimage has taken Lear through the Underworld, through death to life, from negation to affirmation.

Is *King Lear*, then, a morality drama, or an antimorality drama? Neither, really. Although it integrates moral elements, it presents legendary historical characters, not personified abstractions. Furthermore, it leads not to ethical guidance but to spiritual integration. Although Arthur Sewell argues that Shakespeare has created supreme drama out of the question, "What shall we do to be saved,"[26] *King Lear's* concern is not with how we should live but with what makes life worth living in the first place.

Although it combines the pastoral journey with the morality pilgrimage, *King Lear* is neither morality play nor pastoral romance. It is not even tragedy in the usual Shakespearean sense. It is, rather, a drama partaking of the natures of all three. If *Lear* belongs to a genre, then it is a genre with a total membership of one.

24

FROM CASTLE TO HEATH

> "CAN YOU MAKE NO USE OF
> NOTHING, NUNCLE?"
>
> (I, iv, 136–137)

Shakespeare's usual method of construction is to share with his audi-ence important information which he withholds from his actors. We know, for example, how Cassius practices on Brutus, but Brutus does not; we know of the assassination plot on Caesar, Caesar does not. In *Hamlet* only the audience shares in the private conversation between Hamlet and the ghost of his father, as we share also in the private conversation between Iago and Roderigo in *Othello*. We know what Macbeth and his wife plan for Duncan, he does not. We are not shocked by subsequent events, because we have been encouraged to anticipate them, however terrible. But in *Lear*, Shakespeare departs from his usual methods in so far as the main story is concerned.

Lear is more secretive than most of Shakespeare's protagonists. No one knows about his proposed division of the kingdom—not Kent or Gloucester, and certainly not us. Neither Kent nor Gloucester can decide whether Lear favors Albany or Cornwall the most, when in fact he favors neither. Lear favors Cordelia's husband-to-be, a fact that only Lear possesses. Since almost everyone's perspective is near zero, the opening of *Lear* appears ambiguous or confused. Jan Kott, for example, finds the opening beyond the limits of psychological credibility:

The exposition of *King Lear* seems preposterous if one is to look for psychological verisimilitude in it. A great and powerful king holds a competition of rhetoric among his daughters, as to which one of them will best express her love for him, and makes the division of his kingdom depend on its outcome. He does not see or understand anything: Regan's and Goneril's hypocrisy is all too evident. Regarded as a person, a character, Lear is ridiculous, naive and stupid.

Kott, unfortunately, is not alone in this interpretation. More critics than not share Kott's view of an idiotic old man so dependent upon flattery that he will trade his kingdom for it.[27]

But is this, in fact, what really happens in *Lear?* If Lear intends to divide his kingdom on the basis of a flattery contest, why does he award to Goneril and Regan their shares before Cordelia speaks? If the contest is fair, how can the result be determined beforehand? But this is exactly what happens in *Lear.* How else does Lear know that Goneril's or Regan's protestations of love will not win for them the most "opulent" share of the kingdom? The answer is, of course, that he does not know. But, that does not matter in the least, for there is really no contest at all.

Lear does not, as many have argued, intend to divide his kingdom equally among his three daughters. He intends to leave the most opulent part to Cordelia. This is a point overlooked by critics who see *Lear,* like *Gorboduc,* arguing against a divided kingdom. The comparison is superficially attractive, but ultimately misleading because *Gorboduc,* against the advice of his good advisor, Eubulus, divides his kingdom equally between his two sons, Ferrex and Porrex. On the folly of equal division, *Gorboduc* is blatantly clear.[28] Notice, though, that in *Lear* no one warns Lear about division. Kent, who is quick to call Lear to account on every other issue, says absolutely nothing about the dangers of division. Besides, equal division is precisely what Lear wants to prevent. Lear wants to oversee the peaceful transference of power while he lives, an eminently reasonable political action. And since there was no rule in the Renaissance against abdication, Lear violates no Law of Nations.[29]

The problem which Lear faces is one of decorum: How can the King leave the most opulent share of the kingdom to his youngest daughter without insulting his older daughters? Legally, according to Tudor law, the daughters would share equally if Lear were to die intestate.[30] How, then, can Lear arrange for his youngest, his "least," to inherit the best part of his kingdom? Why, by conducting a contest, with the winner taking the choicest part but with the losers also sharing in the prizes. This is why the contest is rigged, why Goneril's and Regan's prizes are awarded to them before Cordelia even has a chance to speak. What enkindles Lear's wrath, then, is not Cordelia's refusal to declare her love for him, but rather her refusal to play his game. Failure to recognize Lear's "game" leads to the creation of problems where none exist:

> The relation of the rhetorical contest among the daughters, then, to the original political division remains, like so much else in the play, mysterious and irrational.[31]

If Lear's "game" is not clear, then the "coronet" should be. When Lear enters the action in I, 1, he is accompanied by a coronet. Now, a coronet is not a king's crown, at least not in Shakespeare's plays.[32] It is a small crown, fit, in this case, for Cordelia's head, and to be awarded to her upon the finish of the "game." No wonder Lear is upset at her refusal to play. Only if she plays, and wins, can he award her the coronet. Lear has arranged for the peaceful transference of power. He has arranged for the security of his own future as Cordelia's perpetual guest, free from responsibility and cares; but Cordelia will not play, will not speak the meaningless words that will insure her fortune and Lear's dream. A few words, that is all Lear asks. A small price for a large reward. No wonder Lear explodes!

Lear's folly is no folly at all. Quite the contrary, Lear has worked out a plan that would benefit the kingdom, his daughters, and Lear, himself.[33] Perhaps the plan explains Lear's secrecy, for Albany and Cornwall, both natives to Britain, are to be subordinate to a Frenchman, either Burgundy or the king of France. Shakespeare is here faced with an uncomfortable fact of history. How can he, writing at a time when France and England were continually at odds, sympathize with a foreign invasion? Actually, Shakespeare evades the problem, since France departs from Britain immediately after the invasion, and Cordelia is left alone to be reunited with her father. In Shakespeare's *King Lear* France never sits on England's throne, as he always does in Shakespeare's sources. The invasion in *King Lear* is, contrary to the sources, unsuccessful.

Lear is not, then, a fool who fails to "see or understand anything." Lear sees and understands much. He knows that Goneril and Regan do not measure up to Cordelia. He knows that words are cheap and that power is attractive. What he does not know, however, is what he is. The inciting incident in *Lear*, Cordelia's "nothing," is like the tip of the iceberg, one-tenth above and nine-tenths below. What lies beneath is ignorance, mostly ignorance of self. We have the valuable endorsement of Goneril and Regan that Lear "hath ever but slenderly known himself." (I, i, 293–294.) When Lear asks, "Who is it that can tell me who I am?" (I, iv, 238), he does not expect the Fool's reply, "Lear's shadow," and does not understand it. Lear must ultimately answer the question for himself, no one else can do it for him. But for Lear, the answer lies at the bottom of the world, and the only route is through suffering and death.

This is not to say that knowledge is at the heart of *Lear*, for it is not. If we sympathize with Lear it is not because of what he knows but because of what he suffers. If we compare Lear with *Othello*, the difference becomes clear. Othello *knows* finally of Iago's practice, but his suffering did not begin until the middle of the play (III, iii), and throughout his self-righteousness sustains him. Only in the last scene, when the dumb monosyllables, "O! O! O!," replace the old formal rhetoric, does Othello stand self-condemned. But has there been any significant change in character? Othello has made a mistake, and he will pay dearly for it. But, if Desdemona had been false, then her execution would have been justified. That he has taken upon himself the roles of judge, jury, and executioner, does not disturb Othello.

Lear, at the end of his tragedy, does not know what has happened to him. His suffering begins in I, i, and grows more intense throughout the play, culminating in Cordelia's death. But at the end Lear is barely cognizant of his situation. He fails to recognize his old associates, his mind continually clouds over, and only the fact of Cordelia registers. Lear has endured more than any of us will ever endure. Lear has suffered more than any of us will ever suffer. We can say to Lear, as Edgar said to Gloucester, "Thy life's a miracle." (IV, vi, 55.)

At the beginning of his tragedy, Lear is characterized by the imperative voice:

Attend the Lords of France and Burgundy, Gloucester.	(I, i, 34)
Give me the map there.	(I, i, 37)
Goneril,/ Our eldest-born, speak first.	(I, i, 53–54)

Lear does not make requests; he gives orders. He knows neither "please" nor "thank you," unlike the Lear of the last scene, who says, "Pray you, undo this button: thank you, Sir." (V, iii, 309.) One road Lear travels is from arrogance to humility.

But it is not arrogance that will overthrow Lear. When Lear tells Cordelia, "Nothing will come of nothing" (I, i, 90), he articulates the classical doctrine of materialism. And this materialism explains the false premise upon which Lear bases the love contest. The idea of a contest is excellent, but its subject, love, is not suitable to a game. Lear is often accused of bartering love, but why shouldn't he? To the materialist love is, like everything else, something that can be measured. And things can be traded and sold, as well as given away. Lear puts love on the auction block, certainly, but so do Goneril, Regan, and Edmund. These three use love to achieve ends quite divorced from love—property, power, and prestige. Goneril and Regan mask contempt with love, Edmund masks ambition. Only those who, like

Lear and Cordelia "take upon's the mystery of things" (V, iii, 16) will ever get beyond things.

Although writing in quite a different context, the modern writer, Flannery O'Connor, sounds a note that reverberates throughout Shakespeare's *King Lear:*

> if the writer believes that our life is and will remain essentially mysterious, if he looks upon us as beings existing in a created order to whose laws we freely respond, then what he sees on the surface will be of interest to him only as he can go through it into an experience of mystery itself. . . . He will be interested in characters who are forced out to meet evil and grace and who act on a trust beyond themselves—whether they know very clearly what it is they act upon or not.[34]

At the start of his tragedy Lear recognizes only one absolute:

> 'tis our fast intent
> To shake all cares and business from our age,
> Conferring them on younger strengths, while we
> Unburthen'd crawl toward death. (I, i, 38–41)

To Lear, only death has an absolute claim upon us. Death, that can make nothing out of something. Later, Lear calls upon Nature to make nothing out of something:

> Hear, Nature, hear! dear Goddess, hear!
> Suspend thy purpose, if thou didst intend
> To make this creature fruitful!
> Into her womb convey sterility!
> Dry up in her the organs of increase,
> And from her derogate body never spring
> A babe to honor her! (I, iv, 284–290)

In the pastoral tradition Nature is a beneficent goddess with the power to heal the wounded soul of the pastoral sojourner. She has something of the same power in *Lear:*

> Our foster-nurse of nature is repose,
> The which he lacks; that to provoke in him,
> Ar many simple operatives, whose power
> Will close the eye of anguish. (IV, iv, 12–15)

But in *Lear* this is the best that Nature can do; at her worst, however, she does make nothing out of something:

> Bids the wind blow the earth into the sea,
> Or swell the curled waters 'bove the main,
> That things might change or cease; tears his white hair,
> Which the impetuous blasts, with eyeless rage,
> Catch in their fury, and make nothing of; (III, i, 5–9)

What Lear must learn is that there is another absolute with the power to make something out of nothing. Until Lear learns about love his pilgrimage will not be complete. For it is love which is above cause, which can say with Cordelia, "No cause, no cause." Love transcends reason and causality, and though Lear pauses at reason midway through his journey, his destination is love. Only when Lear discovers love does he discover what makes life worth living at all.

In the first act Lear is a mathematician who reckons that a half does not equal a whole. When Cordelia tells him, "that Lord whose hand must take my plight shall carry/ Half my love with him" (I, i, 101–102), Lear is aware that she is only matching half of her sisters' love. Lear measures Cordelia's love, as he measures everything (prestige, for example, consists of having a hundred knights rather than fifty), and finds it wanting. Lear has yet to learn that love cannot be measured, because it is infinite. It is, in fact, the only "thing" that increases when it is shared.

Lear will learn; so will Gloucester. Although he does not share Lear's mathematical bent, Gloucester also places a premium on causality in the world. He finds causes in different places from Lear, however: "These late eclipses in the sun and moon" are Gloucester's sources, and his explanation for familial discord. Like Lear, Gloucester fails to see the mystery of life above causes. Like Lear, Gloucester tries to reason the effect. Like Lear, Gloucester will go through Hell and will pay with his life to discover what makes life worth living.

Shakespeare returns to his usual methods of construction in the Gloucester subplot. Set in dramatic irony, and complete with practicers, the Gloucester story is far more direct. We share in all of the important information. We know, for example, about Edmund's plan to rid himself of his brother and father, and about Edgar's practice on Gloucester. Because he uses dramatic irony throughout the subplot, Shakespeare is faced with the problem of getting information to the audience. Because neither Edgar nor Edmund has a confidant, the soliloquy becomes Shakespeare's device for communicating with us. Of the play's eleven soliloquies, Edmund has six and Edgar has three. (The remaining two are assigned to Kent, whose role also depends upon dramatic irony.) Lear is thus the only one of Shakespeare's major tragedies in which the central figure does not have a single soliloquy.

Although Gloucester's "nothing" comes after Lear's, the basis for his tragedy comes before. The staging of the beginning of I, i, is thoroughly conjectural. Does Edmund hear his father, this "rib-digging clubman with a fat chuckle,"[35] jest over the fact of his conception?

> though this knave came something saucily to the world before he was sent for, yet was his mother fair; there was good sport at his making, and the whoreson must be acknowledged. (I, i, 21–24)

If the "whoreson" hears, we need look no further for Edmund's motivation. And if this is, in fact, what happens, then Gloucester's tragedy, like Lear's, begins with an abuse of love. By jesting at the expense of Edmund and his sportive mother, Gloucester insures that his "sin" will come home to roost.

If, however, Edmund does not hear this part of the conversation between Gloucester and Kent (if he does hear, he never takes his father to task for it), sufficient motivation for Edmund's treachery is still provided by Gloucester when he tells Kent that Edmund "hath been out nine years, and away he shall again." (I, i, 32–33.) With these words Gloucester seals his own death warrant. If Edmund is to claim a share of his father's estate, he must act quickly and decisively. Because he cannot inherit by law, he must pursue extralegal means.[36] First, he will arrange for Edgar to be disinherited; later, he will arrange for Gloucester's death. Finally, Edgar will take aim at the throne, so that Lear, Cordelia, and Albany will have to die, Cornwall having conveniently expired earlier. One act of betrayal leads to another and, where ambition and greed reign, love must be suppressed, for it thrives on giving rather than taking. Edgar's banishment, therefore, results from Edmund's ambition and hatred.

Kent's banishment, on the other hand, as well as Cordelia's, is occasioned by love. "Kent is continually getting himself into trouble in trying to get others out."[37] Like Cordelia, Kent loves and speaks the truth. But in a world regulated by self-interest, love and truth "must to the kennel." Like the Good Angel in *The Castle of Perseverance*, Kent does more than merely chide Lear for his folly. Kent's "truth" strikes deep:

> Kill thy physician, and thy fee bestow
> Upon the foul disease. Revoke thy gift;
> Or, whilst I can vent clamour from my throat,
> I'll tell thee thou dost evil.   (I, i, 163–166)

Evil, Kent says, *evil!* Not folly, not rashness, but *evil*. Kent leaves no doubt as to the consequences of Lear's actions. And, unwittingly, perhaps, Kent also indicates the problem with the king. Lear needs a physician to cure his materialism, but when he banishes Cordelia he banishes his physician. Later Cordelia will say:

> O my dear father! Restoration hang
> Thy medicine on my lips, and let this kiss
> Repair those violent harms that my two sisters
> Have in thy reverence made!   (IV, vii, 26–29)

The entrance of France and Burgundy reinforces the dual value system at work in *King Lear*. Like Lear, Burgundy articulates the doctrine of materialism:

> Give but that portion which yourself propos'd,
> And here I take Cordelia by the hand,
> Duchess of Burgundy.   (I, i, 242–244)

Without a dowry, says Burgundy, Cordelia is nothing. But France paradoxically replies,

> Fairest Cordelia, that art most rich, being poor;
> Most choice, forsaken; and most lov'd, despis'd!
>
> . . .
>
> Not all the dukes of wat'rish Burgundy
> Can buy this unpriz'd precious maid of me.   (I, i, 250–251, 258–259)

Like Lear, Burgundy will put love on the auction block, but France sees through the paradoxical nature of love to its true character, its "unpriz'd" preciousness. Love, in short, has no value, at least not in the sense "value" is taken in this scene. Love is valueless because it only lives by being given away. But, as St. Francis reminds us, it is in giving that we receive.

As far as Edmund is concerned, it is in taking that we receive: "Well then,/ Legitimate Edgar, I must have your land." (I, ii, 15–16.) When Gloucester insists that Edmund show him what he is reading, Edmund replies that he is reading "nothing." (I, ii, 31.) But Edmund's "nothing," unlike Cordelia's, is actually something (a letter), and is false (that is, forged), whereas Cordelia's "nothing" was nothing and was true. Lear, then, is overthrown by what is true, Gloucester by what is false.[38] So even though the same word, "nothing," precipitates both tragedies, the word means something different in each case, and each must seek a different resolution.

The resolution to Lear's tragedy begins with Goneril and Regan who, now that they have everything, give their father nothing in return. Goneril's judgment on Lear indicates the course that Lear's pilgrimage will take:

> Idle old man,
> That still would manage those authorities
> That he hath given away! Now, by my life,
> Old fools are babes again, and must be us'd
> With checks as flatteries, when they are seen abus'd.   (I, iii, 17–21)

The wheel begins to turn. He who had everything will soon have nothing. "The Lear who had disinherited Cordelia and banished Kent retains a power of banishment, but only over himself."[39]

In a world where "everything" responds with "nothing," true loyalty must travel in disguise. Kent, having been banished on pain of death, returns disguised as Caius, a servant seeking a master. Interestingly, in the topsy-turvy world of King Lear those who change shapes most often (Kent and Edgar) remain the most constant. Constancy is not a matter of appearance, but of reality. And in a world where might makes right, true loyalty must travel in disguise when its object is good.

Oswald, however, needs no disguise, even though he is loyal to Goneril. Yet we love Kent, and we despise Oswald. Loyalty is not enough! The value of loyalty, Shakespeare suggests, is inextricably tied to the object of loyalty. True loyalty to a false object is self-defeating. To serve another well is to will what is good for another. Loyal service must be based on truth. A servant who sees no distinction between a good and evil master, but serves blindly merely for the sake of serving, is disloyal rather than loyal. To serve blindly is to serve selfishly, because the goal of such service is not the real advantage of the person served but only the exercise of the server. True service respects the truth, and the welfare of the person served.[40] Oswald will serve Goneril to her destruction; Kent will serve Lear to his forgiveness. Oswald never risks rebuke at the hands of his mistress; Kent is ever-ready to speak the truth to Lear.

In the world of *King Lear* "only a Fool dare say the king's a fool."[41] The Fool is everything to everybody, from the conscience and tutor of Lear to the intellectual master of the universe. But, however much he is, he is not enough. The Fool is a critic whose satire holds Lear's folly up to ridicule and scorn. But, the laughter will not purge Lear. "In tragedy, it takes a bloody awareness to dissolve man's folly; in comedy, awareness and contrition come without blood. The line between comedy and tragedy is red."[42] Something of a materialist himself, the Fool is highly qualified to subject Lear's value system to close scrutiny. The Fool also knows that from nothing, nothing comes. But in the context of the Fool's remarks, it is Lear, not Cordelia, who offers nothing. "Thou hast pared thy wit o' both sides, and left nothing i' th' middle" (I, iv, 194–195), the Fool tells Lear, and adds a moment later, in reply to Goneril's criticism,

> The hedge-sparrow fed the cuckoo so long,
> That it's had it head bit off by it young.   (I, iv, 224–225)

thus introducing a sordid note of cannibalism. Goneril is more than merely ungrateful; she is figuratively devouring her father alive. If Goneril has become a moral monster, what does that make of Lear, her father?[43] No wonder Lear asks: "Does any here know me?" (I, iv, 234.) "Who is it that can tell me who I am?" (238.) Ironically, as Goneril's identity begins to clarify for Lear, his own begins to fade.

Lear's world is beginning to collapse around his ears. The corollary of "from nothing, nothing comes," surely must be "from something, something comes." But Lear gave Goneril something, half, in fact, of all he owned, yet she gives him nothing in return. Is it possible, then, that since nothing comes from something, that something can come from nothing? Unfortunately, the Fool can hold Lear's actions up to ridicule and scorn, but he cannot lead Lear to the truth. The force of the Fool is negative, purgative; the greater force of Cordelia will be positive, restorative. The Fool can detect disease but he cannot heal.

The answer to Lear's question, "Who is it that can tell me who I am," must come from within. The answer itself is simple—Lear is a man—but the process of arriving at it is complex. So complex, in fact, that before he is through Lear will, like Dante before him, come to understand fully what it means to be a man. Lear will become aware of the potentiality for evil within the self. Lear will become aware not only of the evil of Goneril and Regan but also of the universal evil of mankind. Lear will have to journey through his own personal Hell before the simplicity of "I am a man" can be realized.

In I, i, Lear banishes Cordelia and Kent for the wrong reasons; in I, iv, he banishes himself and curses Goneril for the right reasons. Lear can now recognize the difference between Cordelia's "small fault" and Goneril's monstrous ingratitude. Lear's evil daughter, Goneril, thus ironically becomes the occasion of Lear's initial remorse over his unjust treatment of his good daughter, Cordelia. This is not to say, however, that Lear now sees clearly. He does not. Lear says, near the end of this scene,

> Thou shalt find
> That I'll resume the shape which thou dost think
> I have cast off for ever. (I, iv, 317–319)

In this, we see that what he wants is exactly what he must not have if his transformation is to be complete. He must not resume his old shape, he must assume a new. The old Lear will die in the storm, the new Lear will be born in the arms of Cordelia.

Once satire uncovers what tries to remain hidden, its work is done. Once Lear becomes aware of his folly in giving everything to Goneril and Regan, the Fool has little more to do. Neither the Fool's satire nor Albany's moralizing can restore Lear in a world governed by Goneril and Regan.[44] These two do not care what the world thinks of them, they are a law unto themselves. The Fool shows us what is, Albany what might be, but both are ineffectual against evil. "The laws are mine, not thine," says Goneril to Albany (V, iii, 158), but ironically it is Albany's law that finally convicts her, and precipitates the murder of Regan and the subsequent suicide of Goneril. The lawless are judged by the law and found guilty. But justice in King Lear is too late. Justice can prosecute the evil, but it cannot save the good.

The first two acts of Lear shock the king out of his old world view; the last three acts lead him to a new. The new can only be reached, however, by throwing off the old. And the old will be discarded only when it becomes unbearable. Although he has been "disinherited" by Goneril, Lear still believes that his future is secure with Regan. His eyes remain partly closed, even though the Fool keeps prying open Lear's lids:

> Shalt see thy other daughter will use thee kindly; for though she's as like
> this as a crab's like an apple, yet I can tell what I can tell.   (I, v, 14–16)

Although he fails to heed the Fool's warning, Lear is learning something about the quixotic nature of the Fool's universe. Having attended the Fool's school, Lear is now able to answer his questions:

FOOL: The reason why the seven stars are no mo than seven is a pretty reason.
LEAR: Because they are not eight?   (I, v, 35–38)

The final word, however, remains with the Fool. Lear's anticipation of comfort from Regan is unfounded, and the Fool's act-concluding rhyme points to the bleak reception in store for Lear:

> She that's a maid now, and laughs at my departure,
> Shall not be a maid long, unless things be cut shorter.   (I, v, 52–53)

Any girl, that is, who sees only the humor in the Fool's jests is so stupid that her virginity is in danger.

Bit by bit, Shakespeare takes from Lear those things which made life livable: first, Cordelia and Kent; then the sway, revenue, and execution of rule; and now Goneril. The first act ends with Lear's fear reverberating throughout the audience:

> O! let me not be mad, not mad, sweet heaven;
> Keep me in temper; I would not be mad!   (I, v, 46–47)

"Lear is caught in the vise that can kill a man": being cruel to Cordelia and suffering cruelty at the hands of Goneril.[45] But this is only the beginning of Lear's purgation. All the dross must be burned away, Lear must be stripped, scourged, and deprived of everything so that he will come to realize the unprized preciousness of nothing. Lear's materialistic, rationalistic value system must undergo total change if Lear is to stand in awe at the mystery of life. At the end of the first act Lear fears for his reason: "O! let me not be mad, not mad, sweet heaven." (I, v, 46.) By the end of the second act Lear will no longer place a premium on reason at all: "O! reason not the need." (II, iv, 266.) But Lear's disaffection from reason will require still another sacrifice. By the end of Act I Cordelia and Goneril have been disowned; by the end of Act II Regan will have joined them.

As Lear prepares to visit Regan, the action temporarily focuses on Gloucester who is also banishing a child. Convincing his father that Edgar is false, convincing Edgar that Gloucester is false, Edmund catches them both in his trap. "The scene is painfully ironic in that the evil ones righteously appear virtuous in their slander of the truly good ones. Anarchy is glazed with morality."[46] When Edmund stabs himself in II, i, a note of mutilation is added to the earlier note of cannibalism. And both will touch Gloucester, who will be mutilated by Cornwall and Regan and cannibalized by Edmund. Edmund is no stranger to the corridors of mendacity.

The theme of false service rewarded is thus repeated in the first two scenes of Act II. Gloucester tells Edmund,

> Loyal and natural boy, I'll work the means
> To make thee capable. (II, i, 84–85)

In other words, he will see that the bastard has his reward. And when Kent is stocked in II, ii, Oswald receives his reward. This scene approaches pure allegory, as true service finds false service offensive, and labels it filth:

> My Lord, if you will give me leave, I will tread this unbolted villain into
> mortar, and daub the wall of a jakes with him. (II, ii, 65–67)

Oswald takes Vanity the puppet's part, Kent claims, but in a world governed by Cornwall and Regan Vanity wins and Truth loses. Lies go unquestioned while the truth remains suspect. Cornwall cannot recognize the truth for what it is, so he assumes that it is falsehood and puts it into the stocks until noon. Regan, however, doubles and then triples the punishment, just as later she will demand both of Gloucester's eyes. "Truth's a dog must to kennel," or to the stocks, "when the Lady Brach may stand by th' fire and stink." (I, iv, 117–119.)

A line from Kent's closing soliloquy in II, ii, might serve as the motto of *King Lear:* "Nothing almost sees miracles,/ But misery." (165–166.) The words "nothing," "sees," "miracles," "misery" reverberate through the play. The tragedies of both Lear and Gloucester begin with nothing. Kent says, "See better, Lear." (I, i, 158.) And Gloucester "sees" clearly only after he has lost his eyes. Both Lear and Gloucester are subdued by *misery.* Gloucester's heart, we are told, burst " 'Twixt two extremes of passion, joy and grief." (V, iii, 198.) And Lear is exhausted by having been stretched out "upon the rack of this tough world." (V, iii, 314.) "Thy life's a *miracle,*" Edgar tells Gloucester. (IV, vi, 55, italics mine.) And Lear's miracle occurs in the following scene: "You do me wrong to take me out o' th' grave." (IV, vii, 45.) Both Lear and Gloucester travel through misery; both learn to "see better"; both come to experience the miracle that from nothing something comes.

25

ON THE HEATH

In a world where falsehood is rewarded, goodness must wear a disguise. As "Poor Turlygod! poor Tom!" (II, iii, 20), Edgar returns in disguise, as Kent had earlier returned as Caius. (In *King Lear* those who change appearance the most are the most constant.) The concluding words of Tom's soliloquy—"Edgar I nothing am" (II, iii, 21)—return us to the opening scene of the play. As Edgar, Gloucester's legitimate son is nothing, since he has been disinherited by his father, just as Cordelia has been disinherited by Lear. But, as Poor Tom, Edgar is something, the something that will restore Gloucester and lead him to Dover and, in still another disguise, away from Dover. Poor Tom will lead his father from the grave, just as Cordelia will redeem Lear.[47]

Shakespeare is also preparing Edgar to become Lear's successor. Disguised as an abject creature, Edgar says:

> To take the basest and most poorest shape,
> That ever penury, in contempt of man,
> Brought near to beast; my face I'll grime with filth,
> Blanket my loins, elf all my hairs in knots,
> And with presented nakedness outface
> The winds and persecutions of the sky.   *(II, iii, 7–12)*

He becomes Lear's "unaccommodated man" (III, iv, 109), a "poor, bare, forked animal," a Bedlam beggar who will accompany Gloucester through Hell, and thereby earn his right to the crown.

Early in the play Lear shows a willingness to trade words for reality. He offers Cordelia an opportunity to mend her speech a little lest it mar her fortunes. (I, i, 94–95.) What Cordelia means is less important than what she says. That willingness reappears when Lear refuses to accept the reality of Kent in the stocks. "No," Lear says, but four times Kent replies with the bleak, intolerable "yes." (II, iv, 15–22.) "Yes" quadrupled finally forces itself upon Lear, as reality will continue to force itself upon Lear until it cracks his mind.

When he discovers Kent in the stocks, Lear is no longer the king he was at the start. When Cordelia persisted in her "nothing," Lear exploded and exiled her upon the spot. Now, however, as Kent persists in saying "yes," Lear asks the reason:

> Resolve me, with all modest haste, which may
> Thou might'st deserve, or they impose, this usage,
> Coming from us. (II, v, 25–27)

Lear wants to know why. If the world is reasonable, Lear implies, then effects follow from causes. It is all very logical. Kent in the stocks (the effect) must have a reasonable explanation (the cause).

Logically speaking, Lear is admirably correct: Causes do precede effects. There is a cause for Kent in the stocks, but it is a cause reasonable only to the perverted souls of Cornwall and Regan. What is reasonable to the vicious, therefore, is unreasonable to the helpless. Lear's belief in materialism has begun to shatter; his dependence upon reason must experience a similar shock. Later, Lear will say "reason not the need" (II, iv, 266), indicating his growing disenchantment with rationalism, but old habits die hard. As late as the fourth act Lear will tell Cordelia that he will drink poison because, he says,

> I know you do not love me; for your sisters
> Have, as I do remember, done me wrong:
> You have some cause, they have not. (IV, vii, 73–75)

Lear has been unkind to Cordelia (cause), therefore it follows that she will be unkind to him (effect). But Cordelia's reply, "No cause, no cause" (75), suggests a world at odds with Lear's world of causes. In Cordelia's world the really important matters are without cause, because they are fraught with mystery. Cordelia stands above causes; Lear must join her there.

Lear's companions on the heath, the Fool and Kent, cannot, unfortunately, guide Lear in his journey. The Fool is basically a forerunner of the philosopher Hobbes, who sees others as self-seeking. Lear and the Fool live in the same world, but the Fool understands it much better than does his master. The Fool is never shocked at the conduct of Goneril and Regan, because he knows that when a father has nothing left to give he becomes nothing. The Fool is actually more firmly rooted in Lear's world than is Lear. Lear is passing through the world of materialism and rationalism, but the Fool will never leave it. Perhaps that is why he is a Fool.

Kent, on the other hand, is simply unable to grasp the premises of the Fool's world. When Kent asks, "How chance the King comes with so small a number" (II, iv, 63), he betrays an ignorance of the principles of materialism. Already Lear's followers have begun to flee, an action which makes perfect sense to the Fool. Since Lear has nothing left to give, only a Fool will remain:

> That sir which serves and seeks for gain,
>   And follows but for form,
> Will pack when it begins to rain,
>   And leave thee in the storm.
> But I will tarry; the Fool will stay,
>   And let the wise man fly:
> The knave turns Fool that runs away;
>   The Fool no knave, perdy. (II, iv, 78–85)

But Kent's world of determinism ("It is the stars,/ The stars above us, govern our conditions" [IV, iii, 33–34]) is as firmly rooted in cause and effect as the Fool's. The difference, of course, is that in Kent's world the causes are cosmic, not petty, as in the Fool's world.

The confrontation between Lear and his daughters toward which II, iv, has been leading is nicely prepared for by Gloucester's announcement that Cornwall and Regan will not meet with Lear. Again, Lear tries to reason the cause: "may be he is not well." (II, iv, 105.) But Lear now faces a successor who echos his predecessor:

> You know the fiery quality of the Duke;
> How unremovable and fix'd he is
> In his own course. (II, iv, 92–94)

Lear obviously has no monopoly on choler and stubbornness. Change "duke" for "king" and the description of Cornwall could be applied to the early Lear. But, Lear changes and Cornwall does not. And the point is clear. Cornwall dies "unremovable," with the words of the Second Servant sounding in the background:

> I'll never care what wickedness I do
> If this man come to good. (III, vii, 98–99)

Cornwall dies mourned by none, as Regan immediately sets about filling her empty bed. When Lear dies he is mourned by all who are still able to speak.

When Goneril arrives in support of Regan the daughters put their father into a vice and they squeeze and squeeze: dismiss half your train, Regan tells Lear; what need has Lear for a hundred knights? Then Goneril halves the fifty: "What need you five-and-twenty," she asks her father, and then proceeds to reduce the number even further, to ten, to five, before Regan closes the vise: "What need one?" (II, iv, 265.) But Lear, still clinging to his materialism, can only complain, "I gave you all," and yet not draw the obvious conclusion that he now has nothing left to give. And what comes from nothing? Lear's original argument with Cordelia comes home to roost. He told her that from nothing nothing comes. Now Goneril and Regan tell Lear the same thing. Lear's two daughters live the materialistic life to the hilt, and by so doing ironically prepare Lear for his disaffection with materialism. Lear recognizes the monstrous characters of Goneril and Regan and is repulsed by them. And when their characters sicken their father, so does their philosophy. When Lear says,

O! reason not the need; our basest beggars
Are in the poorest thing superfluous . . .   (II, iv, 266–267)

the great change begins. Lear's disappointment with Goneril and Regan signals his entrance into a new world. Reason, cause and effect, are not enough, Lear realizes; there must be more. What constitutes the "more" Lear cannot say, but it is clear that it must come from Cordelia. The "more" will come from "less," from the "nothing" of Cordelia rather than the "everything" of Goneril and Regan.

Although Lear says, "reason not the need," the scene ends with Lear's two daughters adducing reasons for banishing Lear to the heath: (1) Gloucester's house is too little, (2) Lear can stay but his followers must leave, (3) when Lear gets into a mood there is nothing they can do with him, (4) his followers may incite Lear to rebellion, and (5) Lear has brought it all on himself. The only contrast to the daughters' reasons, the only support for Lear's "reason not the need" is Gloucester's impotent plea for help:

Alack! the night comes on, and the bleak winds
Do sorely ruffle; for many miles about
There's scarce a bush.   (II, iv, 302–304)

"Truth's a dog must to kennel," the Fool said; "he must be whipp'd out when the Lady Brach may stand by th' fire and stink." (I, iv, 117–119.) Now Lear, Kent, and the Fool make their way into the night's bleak exposure, while Goneril, Regan, Cornwall, and Oswald retire to the warmth of Gloucester's fire. But, in the paradoxical universe of *King Lear,* in is out and out is in. Lear, who is out, will discover what lies beyond reason, and will ultimately be in; those who are now in will discover nothing and will ultimately be out. The second act, then, has virtually reversed the action of the first act.

What Lear does to others in Act I is done to him in Act II. In Act I Lear banished Cordelia; in Act II Lear is banished by Goneril and Regan. The tables are turned, not only around but also upside down. In Act I, Lear banished Cordelia and gave all he owned to Goneril and Regan. In Act II, Goneril and Regan give nothing to Lear, not even one knight, and banish their father.[48]

The first two acts bring Lear to the brink. In the third act he will fall. But, in falling Lear will rise.

Lear's *agon* is prepared for by the anonymous Gentleman who serves as chorus to Lear's present condition. The fury of the storm, Lear's increasing madness, the Fool's unsuccessful attempts to relieve Lear's "heart-strook injuries" are all conveyed by the Gentlemen. He also tells us that Nature can make nothing out of something:

> [Lear] tears his white hair,
> Which the impetuous blasts, with eyeless rage,
> Catch in their fury, and make nothing of. . . . (III, i, 7–9)

Lear, of course, must learn to make something out of nothing. As a force, Nature cannot be denied. What else is death but Nature finalized? Lear must learn not to be defeated by death, which is the lot of all men, kings and beggars, but to overcome death. And the only force that can overcome death, is love.

Shakespeare reminds us here of the political problems posed by the play's action. Kent announces that Albany and Cornwall are secretly plotting against each other, and that France has invaded the kingdom. A Britain united under Cordelia wearing the "coronet" would be strong; a Britain under divided rule is weak, an invitation to foreign invasion. When Kent sends his ring to Cordelia (III, i, 47), he is technically guilty of treason, just as Cordelia herself will be. Although his sources are clear about the success of France's invasion, Shakespeare arranges that Albany will emerge victorious. Only in Shakespeare's version of the Lear story does France lose.

Lear's *agon* begins with universal hatred. Lear has been betrayed by Goneril and Regan; now Lear will betray the world.

> And thou, all-shaking thunder,
> Strike flat the thick rotundity o' th' world!
> Crack Nature's moulds, all germens spill at once,
> That makes ingrateful man! (III, ii, 6–9)

Lear will have revenge, not only on his ingrateful daughters, but on all humanity, forgetting momentarily that Cordelia is part of that humanity. At this point, as William Main points out, "our sympathies conflict without judgments."[49] Our sense of justice may be against Lear, but our pity is for him. Lear may be his own worst enemy, but the fury of the storm is more than any man should have to bear, a point stressed by the Fool's insistence that Lear take shelter, and by Kent's reminder that "man's nature cannot carry/ Th' affliction nor the fear." (III, ii, 48–49.) Lear condemned Cordelia for saying nothing. Now he echoes her when he proclaims, "I will be the pattern of all patience;/ I will say nothing." (III, ii, 37–38.) But patience will not answer to Lear's needs. Purgation presumes suffering. Love comes only after contrition and sacrifice. Expiation, not patience, is what Lear needs.

Although materialism and rationalism are gradually losing their hold on Lear, no compensating positive values are taking their place. Spiritual negation now assumes a different mask as Lear cries for vengeance. But neither the lust for vengeance nor an appeal for pity— "I am a man/ More sinn'd against than sinning" (III, ii, 58–59)—will lead to expiation. Kent's two speeches in III, ii clarify Lear's situation. The first emphasizes the extreme nature of the storm:

> Since I was man
> Such sheets of fire, such bursts of horrid thunder,
> Such groans of roaring wind and rain, I never
> Remember to have heard; man's nature cannot carry
> Th' affliction nor the fear.   (III, ii, 45–49)

And the second translates the first into action. The storm is so terrible that Kent, in spite of having just come from the stocks, will return again to Gloucester's house to "force/ Their scanted courtesy." (66–67.) Shakespeare's point is clear. As long as there are men like Kent in the world, there can be no argument for universal pessimism.

In portraying Lear mad, Shakespeare does not ask the impossible from his audience. He never gives us more than we can bear. In their entirety, the three mad scenes run to about 400 lines, which would require about 25 minutes of playing time. But this is too long for emotion to remain taut, so Shakespeare breaks the madness into three manageable scenes, none of which exceeds 200 lines. The two interrupting scenes (III, iii and III, v) do more than merely break the action. The former brings Gloucester squarely into Lear's camp, and the latter shows how Gloucester is rewarded for joining Lear. Gloucester's situation has become increasingly like Lear's. "They took from me the use of mine own house," Gloucester says (III, iii, 3–4), as a nice irony attends his words. Edmund's comment, "The younger rises when the old doth fall" (27) has more application than he realizes. He imagines that his words apply to himself; as we see, his words will apply to the brother he is intent upon overthrowing. Edmund expects to rise as Gloucester falls. Edgar will actually rise, but his rise will not be at the expense of anyone's fall. Edmund inhabits a morally pernicious universe where the success of one man must be accompanied by the failure of another. Edmund's expectations will be frustrated, because Gloucester does not fall. Gloucester leaps up, and his ascent begins here as he declares his willingness to die for Lear:

If I die for it, as no less is threatened me, the King, my old master, must be
reliev'd.   (III, iii, 18–19)

Gloucester's resolve is additional evidence that Shakespeare did not
intend for *King Lear* to be a play about the decline and fall of the
world.[50]

In the first mad scene Lear recognized that the Fool was cold. In the
second he comes to recognize universal need:

Poor naked wretches, whereso'er you are,
That bide the pelting of this pitiless storm,
How shall your houseless heads and unfed sides,
Your loop'd and window'd raggedness, defend you
From seasons such as these?   (III, iv, 28–32)

More important still, Lear acknowledges his own negligence when he
occupied the throne:

O! I have ta'en
Too little care of this. Take physic, Pomp;
Expose thyself to feel what wretches feel,
That thou mayst shake the superflux to them,
And show the Heavens more just.   (III, iv, 32–36)

Although Lear is now at the nadir of his fortunes, he at last realizes
his own guilt, the first necessary step in expiation. Cast out into the
storm like an animal, Lear learns that man is more than an animal.[51]
And because he is more, more is demanded of him. Earlier, Lear knelt
in mockery before Regan (II, iv, 156); now Lear kneels in repentance
before his subjects. Later, Lear will kneel before Cordelia. Lear's
repentance has begun.

26

THROUGH THE UNDERWORLD

"TAKE HEED O' TH' FOUL FIEND"

(III, iv, 80)

When Edgar appears in III, iv, the stage is peopled with madmen. One is born mad (the Fool), one achieves madness (Edgar), and one has madness thrust upon him (Lear). Edgar serves both as a foil to Lear (false madness opposed to real) and as a way to introduce a demonic atmosphere on the heath. Lear's purgation now assumes the form of the Underworld journey. From Virgil through Dante and Conrad, writers have found in the Underworld journey the most poignant form of man's realization of himself. Some of the journeys are fictionally real (*The Aeneid*), some visionary (*The Inferno*), some suggestive (*Heart of Darkness*); Shakespeare's will be symbolical. And the symbolism of Hell will be provided by Edgar, whose first words to Lear— "Away! the foul fiend follows me!" (III, iv, 45)—set the tone for the remainder of the action on the heath. As Edgar adds that he has been led through fire and flame by the foul fiend, his feigned madness highlights Lear's real madness. As far as Lear is concerned, only one cause could have produced this misfit. "Didst thou give all to thy daughters?/ And art thou come to this?" (III, iv, 48–49), Lear asks, as he senses a kinship with this miserable social reject. Edgar must be a sobering sight, for he moves Lear to his most perceptive observation about the miserable condition of man:

> thou art the thing itself; unaccommodated man is no more but such a poor,
> bare, forked animal as thou art. (III, iv, 109–111)

What makes this moment especially significant is that the sight of
Edgar moves Lear to do something about the poor and the needy.
Words are cheap, actions are dear. When Lear places his robe on
Edgar's shoulders, Lear has done "an act of redemption. When one
man will make himself a "poor, bare, forked animal" to save another,
then man reveals his divinity. Lear has now shattered his old belief in
materialism. Lear now gives something and asks nothing in return.
Furthermore, because Edgar is to succeed Lear, it is fitting that the
mantle of authority now pass from king to successor. If kingship is
divine, Edgar earns his divinity because he suffers with Lear and Gloucester, and with them journeys through the Underworld.[53]

The materialistic Fool enjoys his creature comforts, and now interrupts this scene with an appeal to his master to come in out of the
rain:

> Prithee, Nuncle, he contented; 'tis a naughty night to swim in. Now a little
> fire in a wild field were like an old lecher's heart; a small spark, all the
> rest on's body cold. (III, iv, 113–116)

"Look," the Fool concludes, "here comes a walking fire" (116–117),
and who should enter carrying a torch ("walking fire") but the old
lecher, Gloucester, who risks his life to see that Lear is accommodated.
But for this act of kindness Gloucester will pay dearly. In the world of
Goneril and Regan charity is punished and self-interest rewarded.

With the entrance of Edgar and Gloucester the two stories become
virtually one. As Lear, now all calmness, walks up and down with his
philosopher, his "learned Theban," Gloucester unifies the two stories:

> Thou say'st the king grows mad; I'll tell thee friend,
> I am almost mad myself. I had a son,
> Now outlaw'd from my blood; he sought my life,
> But lately, very late; I lov'd him, friend,
> No father his son dearer; true to tell thee,
> The grief hath craz'd my wits. (III, iv, 169–174)

But the similarity again serves to emphasize the difference. Lear, at
least, knows who his true and false children are; Gloucester has yet to
find out. "Although Gloucester brings light, he is still in the dark."[54]

At the beginning of *King Lear* Cordelia's silence provoked Lear's
wrath; now silence promises to ease Lear's tortured mind. "No words,
no words," Gloucester urges, "hush." (III, iv, 185.) The wheel turns.
What before was reprehensible is now praiseworthy.

With Gloucester's "no words" echoing in our ears, we turn from
the heath to the castle where Edmund, the purveyor of words, takes
advantage of Gloucester's selflessness to satisfy his own selfishness.

Edmund uses words as a magician uses props: to mislead. His *modus operandi* is, of course, the word on paper, the forged letter. But Edmund's end proves to be in his beginning. As he used a forged letter to overthrow Edgar, he will himself be overthrown by a true letter. (V, ii, 40.) The wheel will come full circle, Edmund will be hoist on his own petard.

Edmund has never experienced a real father. We know that he was out of the kingdom for nine years, and that Gloucester intended to send him out again. (I, i, 32.) Now Cornwall becomes a surrogate father to Edmund: "I will lay trust upon thee; and thou shalt find a dearer father in my love." (III, v, 24–25.) Here language is used without deception. Cornwall trusts Edmund and does, as it were, take him into his family. But, if Cornwall becomes Edmund's father, what does Regan become? Edmund's mother? And his lover? When trust is misdirected, perversion follows. This scene, then, which involves Edmund's treachery and Cornwall's trust in a false object provides a sleazy contrast to the scenes on the heath. Lear and his company journey through a fictional Hell complete with demons; Cornwall and Edmund inhabit a real Hell of self.

In Hell Lear tries Goneril and Regan and finds them guilty. The third, and last, of the mad scenes intensifies the demonic imagery, including even three dogs with heads (not exactly Cerberus, the three-headed dog, but close). Edgar enters speaking of Frateretto, the Lake of Darkness, and the foul fiend. Lear envisions "a thousand with red burning spits/ Come hissing in upon 'em," and Edgar replies that "the foul fiend bites my back." (III, vi, 15–17.) Hellish justice is a fearful thing, and Shakespeare arranges the details in this scene to stretch our emotions to the breaking point. The theme of reversal of values has been advanced throughout the play: Cordelia, a dispossessed princess, has become a queen; Lear, sometime king, has become his daughter's subject; Gloucester, sometime duke, has been dispossessed by his "unpossessing" son; Edgar and Kent, to the manner born, masquerade as beggar and servant. That reversal now intensifies as Lear appoints a madman (Edgar), a fool (the Fool), and a lowly servitor (Kent), to sit in judgment on the rulers of the realm.

The daughters, whose performance in the first act won them a kingdom, are to be judged again. And again the trial is fixed. If Cordelia had played, neither Goneril nor Regan would have won the realm. Now, even though others judge in Lear's place, neither Goneril nor Regan can be acquitted. Both stand self-confessed before their father. They must be found guilty! But, before they can be sentenced, they must be present. And they are not. Not, that is, unless we perceive them, as Lear does, in the form of joint stools. But we see joint stools, not Lear's daughters. Sane men see joint stools; only madmen can see daughters. But that is as it should be, for only madmen can execute justice in the world of Goneril and Regan. So long as these women rule, justice, like truth, "must to kennel."

A grim irony pervades this scene: As Lear conducts a mock trial of Goneril and Regan, he is himself undergoing a real trial imposed by them. They have driven him to the Underworld, and the voyage, like that of Aeneas or Christ, is not without drama. But, anyone can descend to the Underworld; only a very few have ever returned. And the price for a passage is dear: A life for a life. Palinurus, the helmsman, dies so that Aeneas can return; Christ the man dies so that Christ the god-man can arise; Kurtz dies so that Marlowe can return. Lear's return passage also demands a life. Is it any wonder that Cordelia must die?

Lear now needs a savior; he no longer needs a fool. It is, therefore, appropriate and necessary that the Fool disappear before Lear's recovery in love. When Dante moves from Hell and Purgatory to Heaven his guide changes from Virgil to Beatrice. As Lear moves from the heath to Dover his guide changes from the Fool, with his biting jabs, to Cordelia, with her loving kindness. The Fool is a satirist who holds human folly up to ridicule and scorn, but like all satirists he is basically negative. The Fool knows what is wrong with the worldly Lear, but he does not know what will be right for the spiritual Lear. Like the early Lear the Fool is essentially a rationalist who places his faith in cause and effect. With a mad Lear the Fool is at a loss for words. In the last two mad scenes the usually voluble Fool has little to say. A mad Lear upstages the Fool because cause and effect are no longer operative. What can a satirist say to a madman?

In III, vi, Lear tries Goneril and Regan and finds them guilty; in III, vii, Cornwall and Regan try Gloucester and find him guilty. But where the vicious sisters escape without punishment, the faithful Gloucester will pay with his eyes. Gloucester is technically guilty of treason, but Shakespeare seems intent upon muting the political complications in the action. Cordelia, for example, herself guilty of treason, tells us that her invasion has not been motivated by political considerations:

> No blown ambition doth our arms incite,
> But love, dear love, and our ag'd father's right. (IV, iv, 27–28)

But love and right will not take Cordelia very far in a world governed by might. The old codes, similarly, no longer function in this new world. Vainly, Gloucester invokes the hospitality code:

> Good my friends, consider
> You are my guests; do me no foul play, friends. (III, vii, 30–31)

> I am your host:
> With robber's hands my hospitable favours
> You should not ruffle thus. (III, vii, 39–41)

But what force can the hospitality code have with men and women who have already violated the kinship code?

We might ask why Shakespeare removes Edmund from the scene of Gloucester's blinding. Cornwall's answer is that Edmund's sensitivities will be wounded:

Edmund, keep you our sister company: the revenges we are bound to take upon your traitorous father are not fit for your beholding.   (III, vii, 6–9)

But in Shakespeare's source the king of Paphlagonia is blinded by his illegitimate son. Besides, Cornwall does not elsewhere evince much concern for the sensitivities of others.

The real answer lies in the manner in which Edmund's death contrasts with the deaths of Goneril and Regan. In spite of his selfish ambition, Edmund is not without a conscience, as his deathbed reprieve of Lear indicates. But it would be extremely difficult for us to pity Edmund if we had watched him watching his father blinded. If the manner of a man's death is in some way a measure of his life, then Shakespeare mitigates Edmund's life with the combative nature of his death. Edmund dies a heroic, public death, surrounded by decent human beings. Goneril and Regan die in isolation, by murder and suicide.

Gloucester's blinding is horrible, but the horror is made bearable by the anonymous Servant who stops Cornwall's attempt to put out the second eye. How characteristic of anonymous mankind to react to the putting out of Gloucester's second eye. We will stand by while the first eye is blinded, but we will take action when the second is threatened. How much savagery must we experience before we will act? Late though he may be, the Servant does act. And his action, along with the concluding conversation between the two remaining servants, is of crucial importance. Even in a world where might makes right, atrocities do not go unnoticed:

SECOND SERVANT: I'll never care what wickedness I do
    If this man come to good.
THIRD SERVANT: If she live long,
    And in the end meet the old course of death,
    Women will all turn monsters.
SECOND SERVANT: Let's follow the old Earl, and get the Bedlam
    To lead him where he would: his roguish madness
    Allows itself to any thing.
THIRD SERVANT: Go thou; I'll fetch some flax and whites of eggs
    To apply to his bleeding face. Now, heaven help him!   (III, vii, 98–107)

As long as there are servants like these who will risk everything for someone who has nothing left, then the cause for universal pessimism is weak. *King Lear* is not a play about the decline and fall of the world.

Lear has gone through Hell; now Gloucester must follow. And as

Lear changes guides, so will Gloucester. "When Gloucester had eyes, he followed the treacherous Edmund; now that he is blind, he follows the loving Edgar."[56] And now that he is blind, Gloucester begins to see. He sees, for example, that he is a danger to anyone who would help him, and urges his companion to flee. He sees, too, that Edmund is false and that Edgar is true. He refuses, however, to condemn Edmund. After the blinding, Gloucester never utters a word of reproach against Edmund. Instead, he settles for the poignant wish that he might be reunited with Edgar. Unlike Lear, Gloucester will not be sidelined by a desire for revenge. Gloucester will go more directly to love, but not until he has wrestled with the demon of despair.

> As flies to wanton boys, are we to th' Gods;
> They kill us for their sport. (IV, i, 36–37)

These, Gloucester's most famous, lines articulate the case for universal pessimism. But we must remember that the lines are spoken by a man just blinded. His despair is understandable, but it is not necessarily correct. In *King Lear* the gods do not kill us for their sport; they simply do not intervene to keep us from killing each other.

Edgar, by maintaining his disguise, actually contributes to his father's despair. He knows that Gloucester wants nothing more than to be reunited with his loyal son, and by revealing himself Edgar can ease Gloucester's tortured soul, if not his body. Yet he persists in his disguise, an action which he later regrets. Why, then, does Edgar continue to pose as Poor Tom?[57] It may be that artistic symmetry guided Shakespeare here. Throughout the first three acts Gloucester was led by the false Edmund pretending to be the true son, so in the last two acts he will be led by the true Edgar pretending to be the false Tom. Furthermore, if Gloucester's pilgrimage is to parallel Lear's, it is fitting that his Underworld journey end with a death wish. Later, Lear will say to Cordelia, "If you have poison for me, I will drink it." (IV, vii, 72.) And Lear will experience a symbolic death and resurrection. "You do me wrong," Lear says, "to take me out o' th' grave." (IV, vii, 45.)

Gloucester will also experience a symbolic death and resurrection. This would not occur, however, if Edgar were to reveal his true identity to his father, for then the cause for despair would disappear. But, the way to death and resurrection is through despair, not around it. Edgar's refusal is, therefore, required by overriding thematic considerations, but it does do violence to his character, which is why he later admits,

> Never—O fault!—reveal'd myself unto him,
> Until some half-hour past. . . . (V, iii, 192–193)

Additional motivation for Edgar's refusal to identify himself to Gloucester is indicated by his aside, "Why I do trifle thus with his despair/

Is done to cure it." (IV, vi, 34.) And Edgar proves to be more successful than he imagines.

> The problem in this complete scene [IV, vi] is how to save a despairing man from death. Gloucester must somehow get to the other side of despair, so that he is reconciled to life. . . . Gloucester must psychologically and symbolically go through despair and death, not circumvent it. Before one can authentically take on the burden of life, he must shoulder the burden of death.[58]

And Gloucester, with Edgar's help, comes through despair to shoulder the burden of life. After his plunge into the abyss, Gloucester, like Lear, will endure:

> henceforth I'll bear
> Afliction till it do cry out itself
> "Enough, enough," and die.   (IV, vi, 75–77)

The miracle occurs! Gloucester is brought past death to life, from negation to affirmation. And the pilgrimage, as Edgar tells us, has been through Hell. Gloucester's companion is as hellish as anything we encounter on the heath:

> methought his eyes
> Were two full moons; he had a thousand noses,
> Horns whelk'd and wav'd like the enridged sea:
> It was some fiend. . . .   (IV, vi, 69–72)

And Edgar's "eye-witness" testimony convinces Gloucester, who replies,

> That thing you speak of
> I took it for a man; often 'twould say
> "The Fiend, the Fiend": he led me to that place.   (IV, vi, 77–79)

There now follows one of the truly great moments in drama as the mad Lear, the light of his mind extinguished, meets the blinded Gloucester, the light of his eyes put out. The "sight" of Lear is almost enough to destroy Gloucester's newly acquired moral toughness. If the king can be brought to such a pass, what hope is there for the rest of mankind? Well, the hope is represented by Gloucester, himself, even though he does not know it. When Gloucester calls Lear "O ruin'd piece of Nature!" (IV, vi, 136), his description may be accurate, but what is more important is that Gloucester weeps for Lear. Throughout the play calamity to the good occasions shock in the merciful. When Cordelia is exiled, Kent comes to her defense; when Gloucester is blinded, Edgar grieves for him; and when Lear goes mad, Gloucester weeps. As long as there are men like Kent and Edgar and Gloucester, we can hold no brief for universal pessimism.

Although Lear has eyes, he fails to recognize Gloucester; although

Gloucester is blind, he recognizes Lear. The point is clear: Gloucester's pilgrimage is virtually over. All that remains for Gloucester is to savor the reunion with Edgar, the rest is silence. When he retires from this scene, he will appear only one more time (V, ii) and will deliver only three more lines. Gloucester will die offstage, secure in the knowledge that his loving son is safe. But in tragedy, knowledge is not enough. Conflict will reign over Gloucester's death just as it reigned over his life:

> but his flaw'd heart,
> Alack, too weak the conflict to support!
> 'Twixt two extremes of passion, joy and grief,
> Burst smilingly.   (V, iii, 196–199)

But his heart "burst smilingly," his pilgrimage has not been in vain. Although he has been the victim of unspeakable acts, Gloucester's death mingles joy and grief. And because it does, his death occasions our divided response. We also receive his death with mingled joy and grief, grief at the horrors he experienced, joy that he found happiness before he died. None of Shakespeare's other tragedies evoke a similar response. There is no cause for joy when the "star-cross'd lovers . . . bury their parent's strife" or when that fell sergeant, Death, arrests Hamlet; or when Othello dies upon a kiss; and certainly not when the "dead butcher," Macbeth, and "his fiend-like queen" make their exit.

Although Gloucester's pilgrimage is virtually over, Lear still has some distance to travel. He has got beyond his original materialism, but not beyond negation. Lear sees what the world lacks:

> Through tatter'd clothes small vices do appear;
> Robes and furr'd gowns hide all. Plate sin with gold,
> And the strong lance of justice hurtless breaks;
> Arm it in rags, a pigmy's straw does pierce it,
> None does offend, none, I say, none. . . .   (IV, vi, 166–170)

Since justice is helpless, what is left but savage revenge?

> And when I have stol'n upon these son-in-laws,
> Then kill, kill, kill, kill, kill, kill!   (IV, vi, 188–189)

Lear must be brought from negation to affirmation, from hatred to love, from causality to mystery. Lear still clings to his world of causes: When we are betrayed (cause), we strike back in revenge (effect). It is all very logical; it is all very reasonable. It is also very self-defeating.

27

DEATH AND RESURRECTION

> "YOU DO ME WRONG
> TO TAKE ME OUT O' TH' GRAVE"
> *(IV, vii, 45)*

To get beyond the world of causes Lear will require a new guide, one who has embraced the mystery of existence as that which makes life worth the living. Shakespeare clears the stage for Lear's encounter with Cordelia. The Fool departs, Edgar and Gloucester, although still present, comfort each other, and Kent somewhat awkwardly disappears. Some "dear cause," he says, will wrap him in concealment awhile (IV, iii, 52–53), but the cause is never revealed. But even though Kent may be, as Coleridge claims, "the greatest to perfect goodness of all Shakespeare's characters,"[59] he cannot proceed farther with Lear. Kent is an astrological determinist: "It is the stars,/ The stars above us, govern our conditions." (IV, iii, 33–34.) Lear, however, does not need an astrologer; Lear needs a miracle, a redeemer. And the miracle happens! Cordelia returns, Lear's daughter who, Lear is told, "redeems nature from the general curse/ Which twain have brought her to." (IV, vi, 207–208.)

Cordelia's role as Lear's redeemer has been prepared for earlier (IV, iii), with imagery conveying her mercy and love. Her tears, especially, suggest the new life into which Lear will be born:

And now and then an ample tear trill'd down
Her delicate cheek; it seem'd she was a queen

> Over her passion; who, most rebel-like,
> Sought to be king o'er her. (IV, iii, 13–16)

>   You have seen
> Sunshine and rain at once; her smile and tears
> Were like, a better way; those happy smilets
> That play'd on her ripe lip seem'd not to know
> What guests were in her eyes; which parted thence,
> As pearls from diamonds dropp'd. (IV, iii, 18–22)

>   There she shook
> The holy water from her heavenly eyes,
> And clamour moisten'd, then away she started
> To deal with grief alone. (IV, iii, 30–33)

Water, which earlier threatened to drown Lear, now promises to save him.

Even more important than her tears, however, is Cordelia's paraphrase of St. Luke's *Gospel* (2:49):[60]

>   O dear father!
> It is thy business that I go about. . . . (IV, iv, 23–24)

It is therefore fitting that when Lear recognizes Cordelia he kneels before her, before his savior. The reversal of roles is now complete, as Lear, who had banished Cordelia, kneels before her asking her forgiveness. The king becomes the divine Cordelia's subject. "Nothing almost sees miracles," Kent said, "But misery." (II, ii, 165–166.) Lear now experiences his miracle, and the miserable king is at last able to answer his own question, "Who is it that can tell me who I am?" At last Lear knows who he is: "I am a very foolish fond old man," he tells us. (IV, vii, 60–61.) And a moment later he repeats. "I am old and foolish." (84.) Lear now knows who he is, but he does not yet know what he must become.

We may be tempted to feel that Lear's pilgrimage has ended. That Lear, like Gloucester, has come to rest in the arms of his loving child. The truth is, however, that Lear's greatest test has yet to come. Lear must be stripped of everything before he realizes that something can come from nothing. Furthermore, there has been rebirth: "You do me wrong," Lear says, "to take me o' th' grave." (IV, vii, 45.)[61] But rebirth demands a death. Christ the man dies so that Christ the God-man can arise. The Savior dies to save Mankind. Now Cordelia is Lear's savior ("O dear father!/ It is thy business that I go about"), and as such she must pay with her life.

As Lear savors reunion with Cordelia, the political action eddies about them. Goneril and Regan are divided by their mutual lust for Edmund, who is himself undone by an incriminating letter, but not before he orders the execution of Lear and Cordelia. With a forged letter Edgar's rise began, with a true letter his fall is assured, the wheel comes full circle. As Lear and Cordelia are taken to prison, Lear's greatest temptation is at hand. He has all but passed beyond materialism and rationalism, beyond causality and desire for revenge. Now prison promises release:

> Come, let's away to prison;
> We two alone will sing like birds i' th' cage:
> When thou dost ask me blessing, I'll kneel down,
> And ask of thee forgiveness: so we'll live,
> And pray, and sing, and tell old tales, and laugh
> At gilded butterflies, and hear poor rogues
> Talk of court news; and we'll talk with them too,
> Who loses and who wins; who's in, who's out;
> And take upon's *the mystery of things,*
> As if we were God's spies. . . . [*Italics mine*]   (V, iii, 8–17)

Lear believes that he now embraces the "mystery of things," the "what" that makes life worth the living. Is his pilgrimage now at its end? What more can be asked of this old man? Why, the "mystery of things," that is what. Lear thinks he has arrived, but in reality he is barely getting close. Lear loves Cordelia, but a note of materialism still attends. When Lear says, "Have I caught thee?" an aura of possessiveness clings to his words. Lear thinks he *has* Cordelia, as one might possess a thing. Lear has not yet learned that "love is not a thing one possesses; love is a spirit that possesses one."[62]

As Albany asserts himself politically and morally, Edmund is defeated in combat by Edgar, yet dies in harmony with him after revealing the plot on the lives of Lear and Cordelia. Goneril poisons Regan, and commits suicide. The point is clear: the truly evil destroy themselves. But, they also destroy the good, as Edmund's reprieve arrives too late to save Cordelia. What Lear has come to value most is now taken from him. But only in this way can Lear come to truly experience the "mystery of things."

Cordelia's death has sickened many, including Dr. Johnson, but it is necessitated by a number of considerations. First, the Lear story demands it. In all of Shakespeare's sources Cordelia dies by her own hand, either by rope or knife. Shakespeare at least spares his Cordelia a suicidal death. Second, the Underworld journey requires a death for a life. Third, Lear's pilgrimage will not be complete while Cordelia lives. Lear knows now what it means to love something; what he must experience is what it means to love no thing. Only then will his pilgrimage be complete. Only then will we all know that from nothing something comes.

"Look there, look there," Lear says, and dies. (V, iii, 311.) But where are we to look, or at what? These four words, present in the Folio but not in the Quarto, make the ending of *King Lear* more problematical than that of any other tragedy. The words may mean, as many have argued, that Lear detects some movement of Cordelia, her lips, perhaps, that leads him to believe that she lives, and leads us to the melodramatic conclusion that Lear dies in bliss. Or they may mean that Lear sees no movement at all, thus leading to the bleak, albeit equally melodramatic, conclusion that Lear dies in absolute despair.[63] The answer is that we simply do not know what Lear means. Shakespeare's actors undoubtedly knew, but we do not, and additional argument is futile.

To assume that Lear dies in either bliss or despair is to do an injustice to Lear and violence to the play. At the end of the play, Lear's mind is so clouded that he is well beyond what we ordinarily call "tragic recognition." Edgar and Albany tell us what Lear's mind is like:

ALBANY: He knows not what he says, and vain is it
   That we present us to him.
EDGAR: Very bootless.   (V, iii, 292–294)

The truth is, of course, that *King Lear* was not written for King Lear; it was written for Shakespeare's audience. It is not important, therefore, that Lear derive meaning from his tragic pilgrimage; what is important is that the audience derive meaning from it. If we sympathize with Lear it is not because of what he learns but because of what he suffers. But we learn. We learn for example that, when Lear comes on stage carrying the body of Cordelia in his arms, Death is not the final arbitrator. So long as there is a Lear to weep for a Cordelia, Death may be inevitable but is not supreme. So long as someone cares, love will overcome death:

> Certainly death has power over everything, but love is stronger, the only indestructible power in existence: it comes from "Nothing"; therefore no-thing can destroy it.[64]

King Lear does not end with the death of King Lear. From the man who undoes Lear's button, to Albany, who arranges for a peaceful transference of authority, *King Lear* ends with a display of love for a man who truly has nothing left to give. It ends with the brokenhearted Kent, whom Lear does not even recognize, urging the others not to stretch Lear out longer "upon the rack of this tough world" (V, iii, 314), and promising to join his master soon:

> I have a journey, sir, shortly to go;
> My master calls me, I must not say no.   (V, iii, 321–322)

It ends with the compassionate Edgar poignantly aware of the miracle which has occurred:

> The weight of this sad time we must obey;
> Speak what we feel, not what we ought to say.

> The oldest hath borne most: we that are young
> Shall never see so much, nor live so long. (V, iii, 323–326)

The earth may claim Lear's body but not his spirit. As long as there are men like these to remember, Lear will live on. For what else is the memory but the living grave of the present which holds the treasured remains of the past?

King Lear does not end on a note of bliss. There are two many bodies littering the stage for that. But neither does it end on a note of despair. There is too much love for that. *King Lear* ends on a note of affirmation, but it is muted. The play may be, as R. W. Chambers claims, "a vast poem on the victory of true love";[65] but it is also a sad poem. We may have to be content with the thought that "after life's fitful fever," Lear "sleeps well."[66]

NOTES

[1] Edwin Wilson, ed., *Shaw on Shakespeare* (New York, 1961), p. 117.

[2] Terence Hawkes, ed., *Coleridge's Writings on Shakespeare* (New York, 1959), p. 180.

[3] Evelyn G. Hooven, an unpublished paper, quoted by Maynard Mack, *King Lear in Our Time* (Berkeley, 1972), p. 85.

[4] On the Fool's songs and verses, see John Danby, *Shakespeare's Doctrine of Nature* (London, 1949), pp. 102–113.

[5] On the melodrama inherent in Lear, see Mack, pp. 11ff.

[6] Hawkes, p. 187.

[7] William Main, ed., *The Tragedy of King Lear* (New York, 1962), p. 135.

[8] Their declarations of love in I, 1, are not lies so much as set speeches in a game (see above, pp. 206–208).

[9] All citations are from the Arden edition of *King Lear,* ed. Kenneth Muir (Cambridge, Mass., 1952).

[10] See F. T. Flahiff, "Edgar: Once and Future King," in *Some Facets of King Lear,* ed. Rosalie Colie and F. T. Flahiff (Toronto, 1974), pp. 221–237.

[11] See, for example, H. N. Hudson, *Lectures on Shakespeare,* vol. II (New York, 1848), p. 226. (Quoted in Helmut Bonheim's *The King Lear Perplex* [Belmont, Calif., 1960], p. 27.)

[12] Mack, p. 65.

[13] On pastoral elements in *Lear,* see David Young, *The Heart's Forest* (New Haven, 1972), pp. 73–103, and Nancy R. Lindheim, "King Lear as Pastoral Tragedy," in *Some Facets of King Lear.*

[14] Walter Davis, *A Map of Arcadia* (New Haven, 1965), charts the pastoral journey.

[15] Main, p. 23.

[16] A. C. Bradley, *Shakespearean Tragedy* (London, 1904), p. 257.

[17] Ibid., p. 291. See also Harold Wilson, *On the Design of Shakespearean Tragedy* (Toronto, 1957), p. 204, and Geoffrey Bush, *Shakespeare and the Natural Condition* (Cambridge, Mass., 1956), p. 128.

[18] J. Stampfer, "The Catharsis of *King Lear,*" in *Shakespeare: Modern Essays in Criticism,* ed. Leonard Dean, rev. ed. (New York, 1967), p. 375.

[19] See Bridget Lyons, "The Subplot as Simplification in *King Lear,*" in *Some Facets of King Lear,* pp. 23–38.

[20] Harley Granville-Barker, *Prefaces to Shakespeare,* vol. I (Princeton, N.J., 1946), p. 293.

[21] Jan Kott, *Shakespeare Our Contemporary* (New York, 1964), p. 152.

[22] Hawkes, p. 177.

[23] Mack, pp. 57–58.

[24] *The Castle of Perseverance*, lines 279–280, in *English Morality Plays and Moral Interludes*, ed. Edgar Schell and J. D. Shuchter (New York, 1969), p. 13.

[25] Main, p. 177.

[26] Arthur Sewell, *Character and Society in Shakespeare* (Oxford, 1951), p. 121.

[27] Kott, p. 130. For a popular view, see John Wain, *The Living World of Shakespeare* (Middlesex, 1966), p. 183:

> His [Lear'] personal folly is matched only by his political naïveté, since he intends to split England into three and divide it among the husbands of his three daughters.

Robert Ornstein, *The Moral Vision of Jacobean Tragedy* (Madison, Wisc., 1960), argues, conversely, that Lear's "division of the kingdom to 'prevent future strife' seems eminently sensible" (p. 264). See also Harold E. Tolliver, "Shakespeare's Kingship," in *Essays in Shakespearean Criticism*, ed. James L. Calderwood and Harold E. Tolliver (Englewood Cliffs, N.J., 1970), p. 75.

[28] Sackville and Norton compose an 89 line speech by Eubulus on the dangers of division *before* Gorboduc divides his kingdom. (I, ii, 247–336.) No one in *Lear* mentions the dangers of division until *after* Lear divides his kingdom.

[29] Rosalie Colie, "*King Lear* and the 'Crisis' of the Aristocracy," *Some Facets of King Lear*, p. 197, notes that Charles V voluntarily gave up his empire.

[30] Paul S. Clarkson and Clyde Warren, *The Law of Property in Shakespeare and the Elizabethan Drama* (Baltimore, 1942), p. 218.

[31] Colie, p. 218, n. 31.

[32] The *O.E.D.* defines a coronet as "a small or inferior crown, *spec.* a crown denoting a dignity inferior to that of the sovereign, worn by the nobility, and varying in form according to rank." In the seven times that he employs the word in his plays, Shakespeare never varies from this definition. (*TMP*, I, ii, JC 114; *MND*, IV, i, 52; *IH6*, III, iii, 89, V, iv, 134; *H5*, 2 pr. 10; *H8*, IV, i, 54; *JC*, I, ii, 238.)

[33] Harry V. Jaffa "The Limits of Politics: An Interpretation of *King Lear*, Act I, Scene I," *American Political Science Review*, LI (1957), 405–427, argues convincingly for Lear's political wisdom in his projected division of the kingdom.

[34] Flannery O'Connor, *Mystery and Manners*, ed, Sally and Robert Fitzgerald (New York, 1969), pp. 41–42.

[35] Wain, p. 183.

[36] Clarkson and Warren, p. 225.

[37] Hudson, *Lear Perplex*, p. 31.

[38] Main, p. 23.

[39] W. Frost, "Shakespeare's Rituals and the Opening of *King Lear*," *Hudson Review*, X (1958), p. 583. (Quoted by Edward G. Quinn, ed., *William Shakespeare: King Lear* [New York, 1970], p. 19.)

[40] This paragraph is a paraphrase, with interpolations, of a passage from Thomas Merton's *No Man Is an Island* (New York, 1955), p. 5.

[41] Main, p. 37.

[42] Ibid.

[43] Ibid., pp. 41–42.

[44] Ibid., p. 44.

[45] Ibid., p. 49.

[46] Ibid., p. 57.

[47] Edgar's disguise also permits Shakespeare to explore "the theme of the good and the wise deliberately teaching the weaker through painful experience." (Donald A. Stauffer, *Shakespeare's World of Images* [Bloomington and London, 1949], p. 197.)

[48] Main, p. 85.

[49] Main, p. 91.

[50] Kott, p. 152.

[51] Main, p. 101.

[52] R. W. Chambers, "King Lear," *Glascow University Publications*, LIX (1940), 20–52, offers a rough sketch of Shakespeare's Underworld in terms of Dante's division in *The Inferno*.

[53] Main, p. 107.

[54] Ibid., p. 110.

[55] Joseph Satin, *Shakespeare and His Sources* (Boston, 1966), p. 529.

[56] Main, p. 140.

[57] Edward Young wrestles with this problem in *The Heart's Forest*, pp. 101–102.

[58] Main, pp. 155–156.

[59] Hawkes, p. 183.

[60] For an argument about Lear as Christ, see Main, pp. 125–127.

[61] Ornstein, p. 272, notes that "Almost literally born again, [Lear] is child-like in his weakness and unable to organize his thoughts."

[62] Main, p. 191.

[63] For two contrasting views, see Bradley, p. 291, and Stampfer, pp. 366–367.

[64] Main, p. 212.

[65] Chambers, p. 49.

[66] *Macbeth*, III, ii, 22.

PART SIX

THE WORLD
OF MACBETH

WILLIAM G. LEARY

INTRODUCTION

Although Hamlet defied Guildenstern to pluck out the heart of his "mystery," I do not believe that Shakespeare ever intended to issue a similar defiance to the reader or playgoer who seeks to understand his plays. Put another way, Shakespeare's plays are susceptible of an orderly and systematic analysis. And if this analysis will not quite yield up Shakespeare's "mystery" (the indefinable quality of his genius), it will reveal the workings of his plays in a manner that should both inform and please the previously uninstructed reader and playgoer.

If we should liken a dramatic masterpiece to an intricate carpet, we would discover that the play's fabric, like the carpet's, has both a warp and a weft. We may compare the *structural* elements of any drama—character, world, and plot—with the warp; the *textural* elements—all the aspects of language including diction, syntax, and imagery—with the weft. And then, to borrow a famous metaphor from Henry James, we may describe the play's theme as "the figure in the carpet."

A clear examination of the workings of a play will expose the directions of these "threads" and the patterns they make. This is what all successful drama critics must do, either explicitly, if systematically analyzing a play, or implicitly, if passing judgment on it—judgments which, to be sound, must be predicated on such an analysis.

Brilliant critics often stun us with the apparent swiftness and ease with which they reach their flashing judgments. But they are only doing what the playwright did before them—concealing the workings of their looms while dazzling us with a fabric so cunningly woven as to appear seamless. Nonetheless, we need not let the art blind us to the artifice. If sound, their judgments will be rooted in the workings of the play they are judging. In short, these critics must undertake the analytical process without which their brilliant syntheses cannot stand. It is just that they do it so much more swiftly and elegantly than most of us can hope to do: they foot it featly.

One explanation for their sureness and swiftness afoot is their skill at determining which element most directly leads to the heart of a play and their incisiveness in following this thread to the center. Years of experience permit them the luxury of this economy of effort. Students learning the process of literary analysis do not yet have this experience. They cannot, therefore, confidently determine which of the play's threads will lead most certainly to the heart of its mystery. Like all beginners, they must laboriously work their way along the lengthwise warp and the crosswise weft until they have enough threads in their hands to discern the pattern that runs through the entire fabric.

One of the assumptions underlying this approach to *Macbeth* is that students must learn by doing, not just by being told or being shown. Still the two processes are not and cannot be divorced. One who learns by doing must first learn what to do. And for this, more frequently than not, he needs a model. With a model, he then may be given an opportunity to do for himself—at first on a small scale, and then many times over—what he has witnessed. Finally, his skills of analysis sharpened and honed by many opportunities to study limited problems and present solutions to them orally, he is ready to compose in writing a more complex answer to a more complex problem. He is, in short, ready to essay a modest piece of literary criticism.

With such a threefold purpose in mind, this treatment of *Macbeth* has been divided into three chapters. The first exhibits how the close analysis of a single element of a play—here the *world* of *Macbeth*—can be made to yield a rich harvest of insights into the workings of the play in the directest possible way. Since this method is new to the reader, Chapter 28 is given over entirely to straightforward exposition buttressed by constant documentation from the play. This chapter may serve as a model for the kinds of inquiries students should be encouraged to make.

With this single method made clear, Chapter 29 examines *all* the elements of drama and their interrelationships. Assisted by its brief commentaries and guided by its extensive sets of questions, you can conduct your own inquiries and come up with your own answers. At the outset, since skill in oral composition is not automatic, many of the answers probably should be written out prior to being delivered orally.

Chapter 30 provides the student with seven possible opportunities to engage in a full-fledged written composition that rests on the insights acquired from studying the material in the first two chapters. One or more of these compositions may be viewed as the culminating activity in which you seek to demonstrate not only your understanding of the play, but also your grasp of the process of analytical thinking and critical writing. If the result of this three-step process is a clear understanding of *how Macbeth* means, and some fairly good notion of how one goes about compelling any play to yield its fullest meaning, then this approach to *Macbeth* will have fulfilled the brightest hopes of its author.

28

THE WORLD
OF MACBETH

Although the term *"world,"* as used here, is gaining common currency, it is still new enough to require careful definition.

All playwrights, from the Greeks to the moderns, have had to work with two indispensable elements: actors and a stage. For his actors, Shakespeare created roles that symbolize particular aspects of human behavior. He also had to create for these actors some space in which to breathe and move and have their being. For this space around the actor, and the feel of it, the customary descriptive terms have been, variously, *"setting," "mood,"* and *"atmosphere."* These terms, however, do not work well with a Shakespearean play. *Setting,* for instance, suggests something fixed in place; but Shakespeare's strategy calls more often than not for a placeless stage, an unlocalized scene which permits him the fluidity he needs to move his characters freely in time and space. *Mood* seems better because it suggests attitude and feeling, and it is the attitudes and feelings of the characters and then our own attitudes and feelings in response to them that are probably the most appealing components of drama. But mood denotes more of what is "in here" and less of what is "out there." It is a word that attaches more to the character than to the space around him. *Atmosphere* seems better still: it suggests something surrounding, enveloping, even pervading the environment of the characters. But atmosphere suggests something immobile, and we need a term that will convey the notion of an active force.

Clearly what is wanted is a word that embraces all of these meanings and more: that suggests place and feeling and envelopment, but also size and weight and pressure. In short, force. Contemporary criticism has come up with such a word. To designate the space around the actor, to refer to the total environment that at once surrounds, impels, conditions, and reflects the actions of dramatic characters, we speak of the *world* of the play. Like Shakespeare's metaphor of the world as a stage, this, too, is metaphorical. But it alludes only to the special "world" of each play, not to the great outside world in its entirety. Just as stage characters are not complete human beings but only carefully selected representatives of those human attributes and attitudes the playwright wishes to dramatize in a given play, so stage "worlds" represent not the total world of mankind but only those selected aspects of the human environment the playwright wishes to focus on.

We must not confuse the creation of Shakespeare's unique worlds with mere scene painting, as our easy response to visual imagery might invite us to do. The world of a play has far more than just a physical dimension. In any play by Shakespeare it will have a moral dimension, as well. And it may also have a psychological and social and even a political dimension. Moreover, with Shakespeare, the world of a play is never photographic. Its fidelity is to the spirit of life, not to the letter. A Shakespearean world will always show us something true *about* life without necessarily being true *to* life. This is still another way of reminding ourselves—and we cannot be reminded too often—that Shakespearean drama is symbolic, not representational. Shakespeare's worlds, like his characters, reveal the principle of radical selection at work: in each instance he gives us a sharply defined essence, not a total existence. That George Bernard Shaw understood this fully is revealed by his remark on the famous passage from *Hamlet* that declares "the purpose of playing . . . was, and is, to hold as t'were, the mirror up to nature." "This," said Shaw, "is playwriting's *purpose,* but it is certainly not its *method.*" (Italics supplied.)

All of the foregoing becomes clearer when we turn to an examination of the particular world of a particular play: *Macbeth.* The world of *Macbeth* may be epitomized searingly: it is a hell on earth. The play is a harrowing dramatization of crime and punishment; and the greater part of it is given over to the punishment. After Macbeth's initial murder of Duncan, we witness the relentless charting of the progress of his damned soul on its way to perdition. Macbeth is a man who wittingly commits a brutal murder for gain. The man he kills is at once his guest, his kinsman, his benefactor, and his king. The fearfulness of the crime is exceeded only by the horror of its retribution.

Before he commits this fatal crime, we catch a glimpse of the man Macbeth outwardly appears to be: a fearless warrior, a great military captain, an admired patriot. We learn, in addition, that he is endowed with a powerful imagination and that he is possessed of a clear-eyed moral sense. In short, he is that most puzzling of killers, the kind who could not possibly commit a murder. Shakespeare never attempts to answer our question: How could such a man commit such a crime? Instead, he creates a world that envelopes Macbeth from the moment he recognizes his own moral contamination until he reaches the end of "the way to dusty death."

Brief as it is—and the brevity of *Macbeth* is one of its significant structural features—the play is almost a textbook of the resources available to the playwright as he sets about to create the *world* of a play. Shakespeare's task is this: By all the means at his disposal, but chiefly by means of language, to create a world that both illuminates the progress of a sick soul on its way to damnation, and transmits the terrible effects of that progress when this soul is the possession of a powerful, courageous, imaginative, and suffering man. Shakespeare, realizing that prose with all of its explicitness will sharply limit the range of this dramatic world, turns to poetry which, with metaphor as its principal agent, not only permits the creation of a larger world but—because of its compression—does so with greater economy. This compression conveys, in turn, a feeling of greater density: poetic words are susceptible of multiple meanings. A single word like "strange" may, like a stone dropped in the waters of a still pond, send out semantic shock waves that on examination turn out to have physical, psychological, political, and moral significance.

The rest of this chapter will demonstrate, with copious quotations from Shakespeare, how the playwright can create a world made up of physical, psychological, social and political, and moral dimensions, and at the same time fuse them so as to achieve a *tour de force* of artistic unity. Although treated serially, it should be evident from the outset that these dimensions are intertwined and that our separation of each strand is a necessary convenience for the purposes of clear analysis. At the end we shall be at pains to reunite them.

THE PHYSICAL WORLD OF <u>MACBETH</u>

From the play's opening moment, when we dimly see three witches hovering "through the fog and filthy air," the physical world of *Macbeth* is one of almost unrelieved darkness. Although the witches—

appropriately referred to as "instruments of darkness"—make their several appearances in the daytime, there is no wholesome light there: they are inevitably accompanied by rain, thunder, and lightning, and enveloped in curtains of foul fog.

The principal human characters move in darkness, too. The killing of King Duncan takes place in the blackest night. Even the stars are hidden ("Their candles are all out"). And on the day after Duncan's murder, the sun is eclipsed ("dark night strangles the travelling lamp"). Dark murder leads to dark murder. The good man of the play, Banquo, rides too late, fatally becoming a "borrower of the night," and is extinguished by three hired assassins just as certainly as is the torch he is carrying. The guilt-ridden Lady Macbeth sleepwalks at night; but Macbeth, on his own testimony, seems scarcely to sleep at all. Finally, having lost all—his honor, his reputation, his wife, his very soul—Macbeth welcomes the ultimate darkness of death ("I 'gin to be aweary of the sun") and would, if he could, return the very universe to chaos and old night ("And wish th'estate of the world were now undone").

If this is a dark world, it is also, as all the commentators on the play have observed, a bloody one. "What bloody man is that?" are the unconsciously ironic first words uttered by King Duncan immediately following the opening scene with the three witches. This "bloody man" is an honorable officer who reports on the "bloody execution" with which Macbeth has stamped out rebellion. And from that moment on we are never far removed from either the sight or the stench of blood. Indeed, further report of the battle against the rebels describes the great generals, Macbeth and Banquo, as men intent "to bathe in reeking wounds."

Such bloodshed, it may be argued, flows from honorable actions. If so, it is nearly the last instance of its kind. For Macbeth, blood—whether imaginary or real—will hereafter be associated with murder. On occasion, blood may be hallucinatory ("Is this a dagger that I see before me . . . on thy blade and dudgeon gouts of blood?"). But too often it is real, and when it is he looks with horror on his "hangman's hands" and gives near-hysterical expression to his terror (not "all great Neptune's ocean" can "wash the blood clean from my hand").

So pervasive is the blood imagery in "Macbeth" that on one occasion Shakespeare employs it to glorify the noble Duncan ("His silver skin laced with his golden blood"). But its normal use is to invoke fear. Ross, who serves as a commentator, employs both blood imagery and the metaphor of world-as-stage to describe the cosmic effects of Macbeth's heinous crime ("Thou seest the heavens, as troubled with man's act,/ Threatens his bloody stage").

Unable to screw his own courage to the sticking place a second time, Macbeth strikes at Banquo through hired assassins. But this murder by agency relieves neither his conscience nor his imagination: he alone sees Banquo's bloody ghost ("Never shake thy gory locks at me"). And, alas, in his progress toward damnation, there is no turning back ("I am in blood/ Stepped in so far that, should I wade no more,/ Returning were as tedious as go o'er"). If his decision to press on is fatal for Macbeth, it is very nearly so for Scotland, as well. In far-off England, the legitimate heir to the throne, Malcolm, hears reports from his despairing country ("it weeps, it bleeds, and each day a new gash/ Is added to her wounds").

While Macbeth rages like a pathological monster, his wife, who once boasted that she was made of sterner stuff than he, is reduced to madness. Walking in her sleep, she is observed vainly trying to rub the fancied "spot" of Duncan's blood from her "little hand" and uttering words her lady-in-waiting and her physician are afraid to repeat ("Yet who would have thought the old man to have had so much blood in him?"). Just once, nearly at the play's end, the seemingly irredeemable Macbeth displays something like contrition. To Macduff he says, "But get thee back! My soul is too much charged/ With blood of thine already." But it is too late, and the play's last image of blood is visual rather than verbal—Macbeth's head (presumably on a pike) displayed before the restored king, Malcolm, by the triumphant Macduff.

THE PSYCHOLOGICAL WORLD OF <u>MACBETH</u>

A masterpiece of literary art seems as wonderfully organic as that miracle of organization, the human body. And, just as modern medicine has discovered no clear-cut division between the soma and the psyche, so in examining *Macbeth,* we find no clean distinction between those dimensions of its world we have denominated *physical* and those we can label *psychological.* For example, several of the images of darkness and of blood convey another closely related aspect of this world that is as much psychological as physical—its congested, thickened, congealed quality. The following images all have an undeniable viscous quality, but the play of metaphor transforms than instantly from the material to the mental plane.

At her first appearance, because she would feel no compunction for the act of murder, Lady Macbeth invokes the spirits of evil to "make thick my blood." And, a moment later, she appeals to "thick night" to hide from heaven the fearful deed she and her husband will commit. That deed committed, we are told on the authority of Ross, serving as a chorus, that displeased heaven "strangles" the sun so that "darkness does the face of the earth entomb." Later, setting the stage for the murder of Banquo, Macbeth echoes his wife in both word and image when he declares, "light thickens," although this time he does not elect to tell even her what he proposes to do under the cover of "seel-ing night," that eloquent metaphor borrowed from the falconer's prac-tice of sewing closed the eyes of a falcon.

From congestion it is only a step to claustrophobia. Deluded into thinking that the death of Banquo will give him room to move and breathe freely, "as broad and general as the casing air," Macbeth dis-covers in the escape of Banquo's son, Fleance, matter that leaves him instead "cabined, cribbed, confined, bound in/ To saucy doubts and fears." And his lady, whom he once called his "dearest partner of greatness," is reduced to entertaining "thick-coming fancies . . . perilous stuff/ Which weighs upon the heart." When we recall that Shakespeare opens his play in an atmosphere of "fog and filthy air," that the very first metaphor used to describe the struggle between the loyalists and the rebels is "two spent swimmers that do cling together/ And choke their art," and that Macbeth's own point of no return is likened to the lot of one who has waded in blood so far that "return-ing were as tedious as go o'er," we are compelled to conclude that Shakespeare wants us to feel something of the physical, psychological, and even moral weight of the world that is slowly suffocating his strug-gling hero-villain.

If, like our own frontier Kentucky, fabled Scotland is a dark and bloody ground, it is also a bleak and barren one. Not for nothing are we told that Macbeth first meets the witches on a "blasted heath." It is no accident that the terrible words "unsex me here" spring to the lips of Lady Macbeth as she apostrophizes the spirits of darkness. It is more than coincidence that Macbeth learns that, whereas he shall become a king, he shall beget none, but wear "a fruitless crown" and hold "a barren sceptre" in his hand. This turns out to be the awful story of a once-great warrior who becomes a butcher of women and children! Of a man at the peak of his powers whose way of life falls "into the sear, the yellow leaf." Of a noble thane to whom his loving king could say, "I have begun to plant thee and will labor/ To make thee full of growing," but whose avenging enemy will later say, with an irony richer than he knows, "He hath no children."

As Freud repeatedly reminded us, the older poets (notably Shake-speare and the Greek dramatists) explored the inner recesses of the human mind long before modern psychology set out to survey that dark terrain. If Shakespeare did not know the term *psychosomatic*, he was fully aware of the interrelationship of mind and body. Mac-beth's burly physique can be pitifully shaken by the workings of his mind. To Banquo's ghost, visible only to his mind's eye, he shouts in terror:

> Take any shape but that, and my firm nerves
> Shall never tremble. Or be alive again
> And dare me to the desert with thy sword.

> If trembling I inhabit then, protest me
> The baby of a girl. Hence, horrible shadow!

Nor is his suffering all hallucinatory. Both sometime before he commits his crimes and forever after he suffers in his mind ("why do I yield to that suggestion/ Whose horrid image doth unfix my hair . . ." and, later, "O full of scorpions is my mind, dear wife"). His mind becomes as dark, bloody, and blasted as the world he stumbles through.

This close parallel between "inner and outer weather," as Robert Frost once called it, is in keeping with the Elizabethan notion of the individual man as a kind of microcosm reflecting in little the elements of the macrocosm he occupies. Shakespeare persistently follows this pattern. Perhaps nothing will advance the reader's and playgoer's grasp of the worlds of various Shakespearean tragedies more swiftly than a clear recognition of this principle. (One recalls the parallel between the to-and-fro conflicting elements in Lear's mind and the great storm that serves as the background for the expression of these terrible thoughts, or the "little insurrection" that takes place in the mind of Brutus as he attempts to find the straight course of justice in the crookedly divided state of Rome.) So Macbeth's Scotland and his mind mirror each other, but with this difference: Scotland lives in fear of Macbeth; Macbeth lives in fear of his own fancies ("the affliction of these terrible dreams/ That shake us nightly").

All this is terrible. But there is worse to come. Shakespeare is relentless in charting every step on Macbeth's path to perdition. As those "terrible dreams" signify, Macbeth, after the first murder, never again "sleeps well." Shakespeare makes his suffering explicit ("Methought I heard a voice cry, 'Sleep no more!/ Macbeth does murder sleep'"). Anyone tempted to play the dangerous game of guessing what Shakespeare the man was like from the evidence of his plays might easily conclude that he was an insomniac, so eloquent are his characters in praise of sleep, and so wretched appear those to whom "great nature's second course" is denied. Without speculating about Shakespeare, one may be certain that Macbeth's sleeplessness was both real and horrible, as these words wrung from the suffering man testify:

> Better be with the dead
> Whom we, to gain our peace, have sent to peace,
> Than on the torture of the mind to lie
> In restless ecstasy.

A man who could utter such words is desperate. Can he experience any worse mental state? The horrifying answer is "yes." Nearly 400 years before modern technology taught an audience of millions of television viewers that a daily diet of horror can be cloying rather than galvanizing, Shakespeare gave us the portrait of a man for whom evil has become a banality.

I have almost forgot the taste of fears . . .
                    I have supped full with horrors,
Direness, familiar to my slaughterhouse thoughts,
Cannot once start me.

Little wonder, then, that such a man—now become a kind of moral zombie—could greet the news that his once-beloved queen was dead, with the words, "She should have died hereafter;/ There would have been a time for such a word." Or that, to him, life itself becomes reduced to ". . . a tale/ Told by an idiot, full of sound and fury,/ Signifying nothing."

THE POLITICAL WORLD OF <u>MACBETH</u>

What is true of the man is true of the state. In Shakespeare's plays we see this equation spelled out again and again. It was an assumption stemming from an old and widely held tradition that the physical, mental, and moral health of the ruler had a direct effect on the health of the state over which he presided as God's steward on earth. This legacy of medieval thought that Shakespeare the dramatist shared with his audiences is peculiarly congenial to the artist since it both suggests and promotes unity. Thus, if man is viewed as the microcosmic counterpart of the macrocosm he occupies, so the political state is seen as the mirror of its ruler, and vice versa. It is as though individual man, society, the physical world, the political state, the ruler, and even the cosmos, are all reflectors—greater or lesser—of some universal truth that unites them all and which they in turn mirror. It is easy to understand how such a concept can serve a dramatic artist whose task is to create a set of immediate particulars that will powerfully suggest a set of ultimate universals—that will make the current and present emblemize the forever and always.

The political and social dimensions of the world of *Macbeth* evince a striking unity with its physical and psychological dimensions. Nor do we need many words to exhibit this unity. The play begins with Scotland threatened by invaders from without and rebels from within. Both threats appear to be warded off by the valiant Macbeth. But, alas, the sickness from within is catching: Macbeth will inherit the treacherous heart of the Thane of Cawdor along with his title. And so from overt rebellion we progress to covert regicide. But murder will out. Since Duncan's death casts suspicion on Macbeth, despite his efforts to divert that suspicion elsewhere, and since his succession is contested by the sons of Duncan, albeit they are in exile, Scotland is reduced to a kind of police state. Beginning with the murder of Banquo, his chief rival for fame, Macbeth is driven to acts of ever-increasing frenzy. He establishes a sort of Gestapo ("There's not a one of them but in his house/ I keep a servant fee'd"). He exacts a fearful revenge on Macduff when the latter flees to England ("The castle of Macduff I will surprise,/ Seize upon Fife, give to the edge 'o th' sword/ His wife, his babes, and all unfortunate souls/ That trace him in his line"). He practices a policy of ruthless repression calculated to abort rebellion ("Each new morn/ New widows bowl, new orphans cry, new sorrows/ Strike heaven on the face"). In short, he instigates a blood bath ("Bleed, bleed, poor country! . . . It weeps, it bleeds, and each day a new gash/ Is added to her wounds").

But Shakespeare is not content to give us just a picture of cruel violence. He knows that a garrison state signifies a divided state, and, more subtly, that a divided state promotes irrational fears among its citizens ("But cruel are the times when we are traitors/ And do not know ourselves; when we hold rumor/ From what we fear, yet know not what we fear/ But float upon a wild and violent sea/ Each way and none"). Worse yet, a poisoned society can produce a poisoned morality ("But I remember now/ I am in this earthly world, where to do harm/ Is often laudable, to do good sometime/ Accounted dangerous folly"). Worst of all is the solitariness that infects such a society. Everyone is fearful of everyone else. Every man's hand is turned against his brother.

It is, of course, fitting that the most solitary man in Scotland should be Macbeth himself. His drift into isolation begins fairly early. When he is planning Banquo's death, Lady Macbeth speaks of the change that has come over him ("How now, my lord? Why do you keep alone?"). Observe that in his reply she is for the first time excluded from his counsels. When she asks, "What's to be done?" she is told "Be innocent of the knowledge, dearest chuck,/ Till thou applaud the deed." It is significant that Macbeth's first turning away from his wife is expressed in an utterance that includes the last term of endearment he ever will use to her. From that time on we witness the alienation of Macbeth from all mankind. As usual, this damned soul describes his own pitiable condition with remarkable eloquence:

> And that which should accompany old age,
> As honor, love, obedience, troops of friends,
> I must not look to have; but in their stead,
> Curses, not loud but deep, mouth-honor, breath,
> Which the poor heart would fain deny, and dare not.

As is his way, Shakespeare follows this soliloquy with the entrance of a paid hireling, the physical embodiment of the only kind of automaton fit to associate with Macbeth. Ironically, his name is Seyton. This isolation of a ruler from a society fractured by fear and atomized by suspicion is one more instance of the artistic unit that fuses the several aspects of the world of this play into one compelling force, and then directs that force against a powerful protagonist whose savage strength cannot withstand its relentless pressure.

THE MORAL WORLD OF <u>MACBETH</u>

All these manifestations of the world of *Macbeth*—the physical, the psychological, the social and political—are essentially a metaphoric prelude to its moral condition. And, as our previous consideration of artistic unity would lead us to expect, the moral attributes of this fearful world are all of a piece with its physical, psychological, and political-social attributes. The moral attributes, however, do have their unique imagery and vocabulary, and we single out two for special comment. One is rooted in traditional thought and has a religious cast; the other has a universal stamp but is rinsed in the irony that characterizes so much of modern thought. The world of *Macbeth* is discovered to be both morally abnormal (the more traditional concept) and morally ambiguous (the universal concept).

Shakespeare employs two words (and by implication their antonyms) with great deliberateness to underline the moral abnormality of Macbeth's world—*strange* and *nature*. These words crop up like discordant notes in a musical composition to assert their importance by jarring on our ear. And it is their literalness that causes us to single them out for special mention. Arguably, everything in this play—every character, every action, every image cluster, every irony, every spectacle, every gesture—is levied on to support the great moral judgment that the play trumpets: Thou shalt not kill! The work of a great moral artist (by no means the same thing as a moralist) none of whose plays is devoid of moral concerns, *Macbeth* is the play wherein moral concerns are most focal. They constitute both the means and the ends of this play, which helps to explain why Shakespeare who, as a supreme dramatist, is normally content to *show* and not to *tell*, here does both. And the words *"strange"* and *"nature"* dong through the play like an iron-tongued bell tolling its fearful message with a terrible insistence.

The word *"strange"* appears several times in *Macbeth*, twice in clusters—relatively brief passages in which the insistent repetition of the word compels us to pay attention to it and to come to terms with its significance. Near the outset, Ross, the choral bearer of what should be hailed as glad tidings—further news of Macbeth's victories over the combined forces of the invaders and the rebels—is curiously described as he approaches King Duncan and his retinue ("What a haste looks through his eyes! So should he look/ That seems to speak things *strange*"). A little while later, Ross's remarks will seem as curiously cryptic as the descriptive passage used previously to introduce him.

This same word, *strange,* issues from his mouth as he summons Macbeth to appear before King Duncan to receive his reward ("The King hath happily received, Macbeth,/ The news of thy success . . . In viewing o'er the rest o' th' self-same day,/ He finds thee . . ./ Nothing afeard of what thyself didst make,/ *Strange* images of death"). It should be readily acknowledged that the reader (or spectator) probably will not plumb the full meaning of the word this early in the play, but he surely will find it an odd and unpleasant way to characterize the military exploits of a conquering hero.

However, even if only subliminally affected by these appearances of the word, he cannot remain innocent of its dark meaning when he hears it from the lips of Macbeth and Banquo. Macbeth uses it first when he attempts to compel the witches to remain and tell him more ("Stay, you imperfect speakers, tell me more! . . . Say from whence/ You owe this *strange* intelligence . . ."). But Macbeth is bemused and morally cloudy. Not so is Banquo, who warns Macbeth against the three witches and their all-too-attractive prophecies ("But 'tis *strange:*/ And oftentimes, to win us to our harm,/ The instruments of darkness tell us truths,/ Win us with honest trifles, to betray's/ In deepest consequence"). A moment later he follows this warning with a metaphor that contains a serious play on the word *strange* ("New honors come upon him,/ Like our *strange* garments, cleave not to their mould/ But with the aid of use"). Here, of course, *strange* has the denotative meaning of *new.* In its syntactical context, and in the larger context of the scene in which it is used, the word's connotation is clear: The grim implication is laid down that the new honors predicted for Macbeth—like his prior feats of arms—are somehow abnormal. (This interpretation is reinforced by other clothing images that appear later in the play, all with the same import: a true monarch's robes do not fit the man who has stolen his crown. "Now does he feel his title/ Hang loose about him, like a giant's robe/ Upon a dwarfish thief.") Abnormal conduct breeds abnormal behavior, so we are not surprised a short time later to hear Lady Macbeth on her first appearance warn her husband, "Your face, my Thane, is as a book where men/ May read *strange* matters."

The face of a potential murderer might well look strange to normal men, and this might be true of the world of men anywhere and at any time. But the world of *Macbeth,* as has been suggested, takes on huge proportions: what is reflected in the face of its protagonist is likewise mirrored in the "outer weather" ("The night has been unruly," one of the choral characters tell us. "Where we lay,/ Our chimneys were blown down; and, as they say,/ Lamentings heard i' th' air, *strange* screams of death,/ And prophesying, with accents terrible,/ Of dire combustion and confused events/ New hatched to th' woeful time").

Abnormality follows abnormality. In a world where a great general can treacherously slay his king, we are not altogether surprised that ghosts walk, and not at all surprised that their visitations are reserved for the eyes of the guilty murderer. If this eye-filling spectacle does not obliterate thought, we will be aware of the grim irony that invests these lines of Macbeth who, although himself guilty of the most abnormal behavior, protests this particular manifestation of abnormality:

> Blood hath been shed ere now, i' th' olden time,
> Ere humane statute purged the gentle weal;
> Aye, and since too, murders have been performed
> Too terrible for the ear. The time has been
> That, when the brains were out, the man would die,
> And there an end. But now they rise again,
> With twenty mortal murders on their crowns,
> And push us from our stools. This is more *strange*
> Than such a murder is.

Then this unconsciously ironic expostulation is followed by the even more ironic "explanation" to his startled guests ("I have a fretful *strange* infirmity, which is nothing/ To those that know me"), by the complaint to his wife, who does not see the ghost ("You make me *strange* even to the disposition that I owe"), and finally by the grim resolve to keep steadfastly on his murderous course ("*Strange* things I have in head, that will to hand"). It comes almost as an anticlimax when we hear a little later from still another of the choral characters, "Things have been *strangely* borne."

If the word *strange* serves to make the "point" of abnormality, the word *nature* (or variations on it) serves the office of "counterpoint." Before he commits in fact the first murder that irretrievably damns him, Macbeth commits it in imagination ("why do I yield to that suggestion/ Whose horrid image doth unfix my hair/ And make my seated heart knock at my ribs/ *Against the use of nature?*"). Preparing to commit the actual murder, he speaks of night, which to a good man might connote a time for "innocent sleep," in these revealing images: "Now o'er the one-half world/ *Nature seems dead,* and wicked dreams abuse/ The curtained sleep." And, even though later he summons the courage to look upon the dead body of the king when, to conceal his own guilt, he pretends to discover for the first time the murdered Duncan, the imagery of his report to the shocked noblemen betrays him ("Here lay Duncan,/ His silver skin laced with his golden blood;/ And his gashed stabs looked like a *breach in nature*"). We are ready, then, for the quietly ominous words of the old man, still another of those minor Shakespearean characters commandeered to serve the office of a chorus, when he says, referring to both the murder and the "things strange" that characterized the night of the murder: " 'Tis *unnatural,*/ Even like the deed's that done." And we fully comprehend Lady Macbeth's doctor when, late in the play, he characterizes her sleepwalking as "*A great perturbation in nature,* to receive at once the benefits of sleep and do the effects of watching." His final remarks have the quality of the conscious redundancy we associate with a sentence of death: "*Unnatural deeds/* Do breed *unnatural* troubles."

If at this point the reader feels like crying out, "Hold, enough!" we are constrained to reply that we are being no more relentless than Shakespeare. If this torrent of evidence seems overwhelming, so is the avalanche of guilty suffering with which Shakespeare buries Macbeth. It is difficult to examine painful matters without experiencing some pain. But, of course, the marvel of artistic tragedy is that it subtly modulates this pain. Aristotle pointed out long ago that it is the peculiar office of tragedy to present the spectacle of great suffering in a manner calculated to engender deep pleasure. How this paradoxical feat is accomplished is not always easy to say. In *Macbeth,* a good part of this accomplishment is achieved by means of one of the most primitive appeals of drama—sheer spectacle.

We have seen how Shakespeare tells us about (as well as shows up) the moral abnormality of the world of *Macbeth.* But when he wishes to suggest something as subtle and ironic as moral ambiguity, he wisely eliminates the commentator's "tell" in favor of the dramatizer's "show." It says something very revealing of Shakespeare the dramatist that he turns to extravagant spectacle to emphasize the moral ambiguity that is so significant a part of the world of this play.

Surely the most spectacular figures in the play are the three witches. That Shakespeare seems to have thought so is arguable from the amount of attention he devotes to them and the very full array of stage machines, properties, and "special effects" which accompany their appearance on the stage. Tellingly, they are the first figures to appear, rising, in all probability in a cloud of artificially induced smoky fog, from the "cellerage" beneath the great platform stage by means of one of the trap doors cut into it. In their first appearance, they are given only eleven lines comprising 61 words, but even in that tiny compass they firmly establish the world of moral ambiguity with which they will be associated throughout and which will become one of the principal ingredients of the world of the play. Line 4 contains their first equivocation: "When the battle's lost *and* won." This plants the question: Who is the real winner, who the real loser? Line 10 announces in the most explicit manner the kind of moral ambiguity that will invest the greater part of the play: "Fair is foul, and foul is fair." (I cannot resist pointing out two relatively obscure marks of inversion as well. In this passage, the normal iambic meter with its unaccented beat followed by an accented stress is reversed, and we have in its place the trochaic measure with heavy stress first followed by light. Again, the witches' "pets" [Graymalkin, Paddock] summon the witches, instead of being called by them—another reversal of expectation. The uninitiated reader is not accustomed to recognizing the refined means that an artist frequently employs, in combination with more obvious means, to achieve his desired effects. But an occasional reminder like this one may whet his appetite for further such discoveries on his own.)

No commentators—and few readers—have missed the significant fact that the very first words uttered by Macbeth, "So foul and fair a day I have not seen," are an unconscious echo of the witches' equivocation. This, of course, has a literal explanation: Macbeth has won a "fair" victory on a day when the weather is "foul." But it is an obtuse reader or playgoer who does not attach a much more sinister significance to this "Freudian echo," the more especially since its occasion is Macbeth's first meeting with the witches—who, note, speak at first only to him. They speak in cryptic Delphic utterances, hailing him as "Thane of Cawdor" and "King hereafter" as well as by his proper title of Thane of Glamis. It is significant that all of the critical remarks about the witches, including a pretty clear perception of their ambiguous status and their equally ambiguous prophecies, come from the lips of the good man, Banquo. Macbeth, if not already tainted, then ripe for moral corruption, "seems rapt withal," dangerously beguiled by the "things that do sound so fair." And, after the witches disappear (doubtless through the selfsame trapdoor by which they entered), Macbeth is content to repeat and paraphrase their dubious promises, leaving to Banquo the expressions of dubiety and warning ("Were such things here as we do speak about?/ Or have we eaten on the insane root/ That takes the reason prisoner?").

Macbeth not only echoes the witches' words; he begins to mirror their equivocal morality ("This supernatural soliciting/ Cannot be ill, cannot be good"). Alas, the order of his sentence betrays the disorder of his soul: He wants to believe the witches because they are giving expression to the murderous ambition that is corroding his sense of rectitude. From this time forward, despite some momentary hesitation and one severe twinge of moral scruple, Macbeth is irredeemably lost.

It is, of course, most fitting that a man who equivocates so nicely between ill and good should himself be the easy victim of equivocation. Macbeth's relationship with the witches throughout the play makes this painfully clear: He hears from them only what he wants to hear and interprets their deliberately ambiguous prophecies the way he wants to interpret them.

Thus, on the occasion of his second meeting with the sinister sisters, he will confront three apparitions and misread them all: He will not foresee that the "armed head" foretells the loss of his own; he will not grasp the fact that a babe "untimely ripped" from his mother's bomb is, in that technical sense, not of "woman born" and so will misconstrue the meaning of the "Bloody Child"; and he will not guess the means by which Birnam Wood might indeed "march to Dunsinane," and so will not rightly riddle the apparition of the "Child Crowned, with a tree in his hand."

All of this riddling stuff is great theater; it provides Shakespeare with spectacle that entertains and at the same time gives him the stuff of a world he relentlessly hurls at his hapless hero. Then, at the end, having *shown* his protagonist hopelessly enmeshed in the snares and traps of moral ambiguity, Shakespeare twice permits him to *tell* of his tardy awareness of the relentless workings of a moral universe. ("I pull in resolution, and begin/ To doubt the equivocation of the fiend,/ That lies like the truth." And again, "And be these juggling fiends no more believed,/ That palter with us in a double sense,/ That keep the word of promise to our ear/ And break it to our hope.")

If he permits his hero's evil will to capture his reason and to blind him to moral truth, Shakespeare is, as always, solicitous of his audience's understanding. Dramatic irony operates throughout this play, and the reader and spectator are never permitted to share the moral confusion of the play's suffering protagonist. We always have our moral bearings and we are never in any doubt as to when and how Macbeth has lost his. Shakespeare's regular practice of letting his comic scenes parallel and illuminate his tragic scenes is interestingly employed in this connection. Immediately after Macbeth has irretrievably lost his soul by murdering his king, the drunken porter of the castle pretends to be the porter of hell gate, admitting lost souls. Of the three sinners he conjures up—a farmer, a tailor, and an equivocator— he lavishes the greatest attention on the equivocator. ("Faith, here's an equivocator, that could swear in both scales against either scale; who committed treason enough for God's sake, yet could not equivocate to heaven. O come in, equivocator.") The parallel between the porter's imaginary sinner and Macbeth is startling. Behind the slurred speech of the drunken porter we hear with terrifying clarity the unmistakable invitation issued to Macbeth by Satan: "O come in, equivocator."

If Shakespeare is solicitous of his audience's understanding, he is equally solicitous of their well-being. He may, for a brief time, have invited them to view a hell on earth, but he is at pains to restore a sense of moral order. If Macbeth lives in a world of moral ambiguities and equivocations, young Malcolm does not. Beginning as early as IV, iii, we see the gradual preparation of the forces of moral law and order, and we witness the conduct of an untainted prince who will come to his country's rescue and be appropriately awarded the kingship which is his by legal right and moral fitness. Mark Van Doren has given a particularly apposite description of the way in which Shakespeare has kept this picture of hell tightly controlled by a framework of moral order: "The circle of safety which Shakespeare has drawn around his central horror is thinly drawn, but it is finely drawn and it holds."

THE FOUR-DIMENSIONAL WORLD OF <u>MACBETH</u>

We said at the outset that we would discuss serially four dimensions of the word of *Macbeth*—the physical, the psychological, the social and political, and the moral. We also said that these dimensions were not separate but were all parts of a unified whole. A moment's reflection will disclose the truth of this assertion. This physically dark and bloody world is made so by the fact that its most powerful occupant is morally corrupt. Once embarked on his career of crime, he discovers there is no turning back: one crime begets another as he vainly seeks security by ridding himself of all possible threats to his safety. This, in turn, creates a divided society which must be ruled as a police state. A police state can only operate by means of terror. When terror is sufficiently widespread there is insurrection. The threat of insurrection breeds fear in the tyrant, who thereupon becomes even more vicious and always more alienated from everyone. A despot grown odious in the eyes of all becomes odious in his own eyes. And so at last the man who made life a hell for all those around him discovers the worst form of hell within his own soul. He despairs, grows reckless, and is finally brought down, really indifferent to the prospect of losing his life since he has already lost everything that might make life worth living.

29

ANALYZING THE DRAMATIC ELEMENTS IN MACBETH

PRELIMINARY REMARKS

Falstaff somewhere says, "I am not only witty in myself, but the cause that wit is in other men." The same claim can be made for a literary masterpiece: it is not only the work of an inspired author, it can inspire "other men" to display depths of insight they do not even suspect they are capable of.

Macbeth is such a literary masterpiece. And it is the premise of this chapter that this play can be made to yield up to students insights that they are scarcely aware they possess.

How is this to be accomplished? By suggestion. And how are these suggestions to appear? In the twofold form of brief commentary and extensive questions. Some of these suggestions, therefore, will be explicit (the commentary) and some implicit (the questions), which is to say that some of the suggestions will be mine, and some will be yours. Because the greatest pleasure of literature is discovery, most of the suggestions, finally, should be yours. This is possible because the suggestions emerging implicitly from the questions will everywhere and always outnumber those made explicitly in the commentary. What you will take away from this study, then, will be essentially your own thoughts. But, whereas at this moment these thoughts are subconscious and unsystematic, they will in good time become conscious and systematic. You not only will have had an experience, but you also will have achieved an understanding of that experience.

The commentary and questions will be geared to the way a play unfolds itself before the spectator in a theater, and a playscript unfolds itself before a reader in his armchair—scene by scene. Because *Macbeth* is usually divided by editors into 28 scenes, this chapter will have 28 parts. Each part will have its own integrity and may be studied by itself. But, because all 28 are parts of a larger artistic whole, some of the comments and some of the questions will point to linkages between one part of the play and another, thus inviting you to discover larger patterns, as well as smaller ones.

This method of scene-by-scene analysis is especially fitting for a Shakespearean play because, contrary to popular opinion, Shakespeare did not conceive of or write his plays in acts. However, starting as early as the First Folio, editors divided his playscripts into five acts. This is not the place to discuss why they did this; it is sufficient to note that all later editors followed suit and that still later reference books—indispensable for the serious student—have been compiled on the basis of the act-scene-line system of notations. For this reason, we will place the conventional act-and-scene notation in parentheses after the number of each part. But, in keeping with what appears to have been Shakespeare's own practice, we will think of the scenes as running consecutively from first to last, and will, therefore, number our parts from 1 to 28. This is not a fussy display of pedantry. Quite the contrary, it is an organizational device designed to assist you to think of the structure of *Macbeth* as Shakespeare presumably did, and thus be able to discover the unfolding patterns in the order in which he established them.

There are many reputable editions of *Macbeth,* some of them inexpensive paperbacks. Any of these standard editions may be used with this chapter. The occasional slight deviations in line numbering, especially among the prose passages, that distinguish one edition from another will not handicap the student. The deviation is so slight that he is in no danger of losing his way. The edition I have used is *The Pelican Shakespeare,* edited by Alfred Harbage, and published by Penguin Books. Besides its other virtues, it has the additional merit of signaling by means of a printer's device the correct scene-by-scene divisions of the playscript, in addition to reproducing marginally the act-scene division established by an older editorial tradition.

SCENE-BY-SCENE ANALYSIS

Part 1 (I, i)

COMMENTARY

All playwrights must be masters of *literary economy:* they must tell their entire story in about two hours. Although good at this, Shakespeare was nowhere better than in the first scene of *Macbeth,* which has only 11 lines and 61 words, exclusive of the stage directions, but which can be made to yield an impressive number of meanings and suggestions.

QUESTIONS

Which of the following tasks of a dramatist does Shakespeare accomplish in this 11-line scene? Does he identify important characters? Contribute a feeling of suspense? Establish a unique atmosphere? Explain events that preceded the actions of this play? Foreshadow things to come? Combine language with theatrical spectacle to convey a tone and a mood? Plant the seed of some significant idea that may flower in the mind of the reader or playgoer? Use language in a way that seems peculiarly suitable to the speakers?

COMMENTARY

Everywhere and always the *language* is the richest and the most suggestive element in Shakespeare's plays. Totally devoid of stage scenery as we know it, and relatively free from stage properties, Shakespeare's platform stage and the plays performed there were designed to afford essentially an *auditory* experience (as opposed, say, to our movies that afford essentially a *visual* experience). Therefore, one cannot study Shakespeare's language too closely.

QUESTIONS

How many principal stresses (accents) appear in each of these 11 lines? What is the pattern of these stresses? Is this the common or expected pattern in a verse play of Shakespeare's? Is the reversal of expectation in the metrical pattern the only reversal that can be found in these lines? Are there, for instance, any reversals of meaning? Do the witches appear to be calling their pets, or do their pets call them? Is this a reversal of sorts? What do these several reversals insinuate about the speakers and the world of the play they introduce?

What part does *rhyme* play in these speeches? Why is it appropriate for three witches to speak in rhyme? How does the sound effect produced by the rhyme support the sound effect produced by the metrical pattern? What tonal effect do these sound patterns give to the witches' talk?

What are the principal *images* found in the 11 lines? The final line is a separate sentence: What is the predicate of that sentence? Who or what is the subject? What picture of things to come is conjured up by your answers to these two questions?

Which lines are *deliberately ambiguous?* What does this deliberate ambiguity suggest about the speakers? About the moral dimension of the world they are associated with?

COMMENTARY

In this discussion the term *"world"* embraces what is ordinarily meant by the words *"setting," "mood,"* and *"atmosphere."* It is a more all-inclusive and useful word than any of these, because it takes account of the moral and psychological, as well as the physical and political, dimensions of the characters' environment and because it suggests force and pressure, as well as background.

QUESTIONS

What are the principal *physical* components of the world of the play that we discover in this first scene? Are there *moral* components suggested here? *Political* components? If so, what are they? Does this world seem claustrophobic? Would you designate this attribute as *physical* or *psychological* or both?

COMMENTARY

In a *filmed version of Macbeth* (issued in 1963, starring Maurice Evans and Judith Anderson), the witches are shown in the opening scene as three disembodied faces arranged on the screen like the sides of a triangle—two faces on each side, and one at the base of the screen. They are given the same speeches you have read in Scene i.

QUESTIONS

Do you find justification in the text for this departure from "realism"? In your opinion, did Shakespeare intend his witches to be "real"? Regardless of your answer to the previous question, what do you mean by "real" in this context?

Part 2 (I, ii)

COMMENTARY

The play's second scene adds physical, political, and moral dimensions to the *world* of the play. It does so by means of two successive reports —one by a nameless "sergeant," the other by a Scots nobleman named Ross—and King Duncan's reactions to these reports.

QUESTIONS

What is the principal color image that dominates the sergeant's account? What does this suggest concerning Macbeth? What is the key word uttered by Lennox, just before Ross reports, that best designates the substance of that report? Shakespeare sometimes assigns the meaning "unnatural" to the word *"strange."* What event reported by Ross might be termed unnatural? What kind of *political* world have we been introduced to in these reports? What kind of *moral* world? Who is the present hero of this world? What attributes does he display that equip him to survive in such a world? What is suggested by the fact that Macbeth is rewarded for his heroism by being given the title of the deposed traitor, Cawdor? By the fact that in lines 64–65, Macbeth's very name is rhymed with death?

Part 3 (I, iii)

COMMENTARY

Shakespeare seldom wastes a word. Thus the words used in scenes that appear to emphasize spectacle, like this one involving the three witches, are just as fraught with meaning as are the soliloquies of a principal character. Here the reader has an advantage over the player: he may slow the pace and scrutinize the special significance of words whose deeper meanings may elude the spectator in the theater.

QUESTIONS

One of the witches' images looks backward: What does "killing swine" echo in the mind of a reader or playgoer who has been hearing of Macbeth's savage fight with the armies of the rebels and invaders? One of the images looks forward: How does the sleeplessness of the sailor victim of the First Witch foreshadow the later condition of Macbeth? Of this sailor the First Witch declares, "Though his bark cannot be lost,/ Yet it shall be tempest-tost." How does this image foreshadow the role of the witches vis-a-vis Macbeth? Finally, why is it significant that the witches in winding up their "charm" make absolutely no mention of Banquo, or of anyone save Macbeth?

COMMENTARY

Film directors often *cut, or modify, the text* of Shakespearean plays for various reasons.

QUESTIONS

In the Maurice Evans film, all of the lines (1–37) which depict the preparation of the three witches for meeting Macbeth are omitted. What is the possible justification for this cut? What is gained and what is lost by it?

COMMENTARY

One of the most economical means at the disposal of a dramatist is *characterization by contrast:* two characters confront the same event and react differently to it.

QUESTIONS

Why is it significant that, whereas Banquo first *sees* the witches, they *speak* first to Macbeth? Why is it equally significant that it is Banquo who is able to reply to them first? What does his reply tell us about Banquo? About Macbeth? Do you see any significance in the fact that the witches refuse to speak again to Macbeth when, at last, he finds words to speak to them? Which of the two generals seems more willing to believe that the witches are real and their prophecies should be taken as "truths"? What does this willingness to believe suggest?

COMMENTARY

Like all good dramatists, Shakespeare is the master of *juxtaposition:* the placing of words or actions in cunning relationship to other words or actions to produce a startling and revealing effect.

QUESTIONS

The first words we hear Macbeth utter (and the first words in this scene) are "So foul and fair a day I have not seen." What similar words does this unusual expression immediately put us in mind of? Halfway through the scene, Ross and Angus enter. What news do they bring to

Macbeth? Why does this news startle Macbeth, Banquo, and the reader or playgoer?

COMMENTARY

A *dramatic convention* may be defined as "a departure from reality which an audience unquestioningly accepts." Today we accept the convention of the movie close-up, in which we view an impossibly gigantic face on a screen so as to better understand a character. Shakespeare's audience accepted the convention of the *soliloquy* and the *aside,* in which a character speaks words that only the audience hears; and by this means they learn his inner thoughts.

QUESTIONS

What do Macbeth's series of *asides,* in the latter part of this scene, tell us of his ambition? Of his attitude toward "supernatural soliciting"? Of his imagination? Of his loyalty to his king? Of his resoluteness in making a decision once and for all? Of his morality?

COMMENTARY

Concerning the *moral state of* his *principal characters,* Shakespeare is never evasive and never purposely vague.

QUESTIONS

What is the evidence *in this scene* to support the conclusion that Macbeth was morally contaminated before he met the witches, and that their "prophecies" trigger responses in him that do not appear there for the first time?

COMMENTARY

A characteristic way in which Shakespeare depicts the falling into error and sin of his tragic heroes is to show them unconsciously acquiring some of the mental and verbal patterns of the evil persons in the play. (For example, you may recall how Othello takes on some of the patterns of lewd thought and foul language of Iago.)

QUESTIONS

What patterns of thought and language which we have come to associate with the three witches (those "instruments of darkness") does Macbeth reveal in this scene?

Part 4 (I, iv)

COMMENTARY

We spoke in Part 3 of Shakespeare's skill with *juxtaposition*. Often this device is used to emphasize *dramatic irony:* when a dramatic character acts in a manner inconsistent with his own welfare, and we in the audience know this but he does not.

QUESTIONS

What is the effect of dramatic irony achieved by Shakespeare's having Macbeth enter immediately on the heels of Duncan's puzzled remarks about the past Thane of Cawdor? How is the mystery surrounding the treason of the latter (his treachery is never explained, and he dies repentant) used to foreshadow Macbeth's subsequent treachery?

COMMENTARY

The *images* a character uses to give expression to his thoughts are often very revealing of his character.

QUESTIONS

King Duncan and Banquo make repeated use of images of planting, growth, and harvest when they speak to each other. What do these images connote about the men? By contrast, what images does Macbeth employ when responding to the king's thanks? What does this difference in imagery suggest?

COMMENTARY

Perhaps nothing so sharpens a student's awareness of the purpose or function of a Shakespearean scene than to be asked what happens to the play when the *scene is omitted,* as happens sometimes in a modern stage production, and often in a film adaptation.

QUESTIONS

The Maurice Evans film leaves out I, iv, entirely, transferring the speech where King Duncan announces his plan to establish his son, Malcolm, as his successor, and Macbeth's dark reaction to this news, to a scene (not by Shakespeare) at dinner in Macbeth's castle just before the murder. What is gained and what is lost by this omission and transfer? In your response, take into account the nature of the motion picture as a dramatic medium, and also what you may assume to be the nature of a modern cinema audience.

Part 5 (I, v)

COMMENTARY

This scene may be viewed as a little textbook of some *methods of characterization* available to a dramatist: the revelations of a private letter read aloud, the unguarded remarks of a person confronted by surprising news, the self-revealing remarks of a person talking to herself, and the confidential remarks of a loving married couple speaking privately to each other.

QUESTIONS

What does the phrase, "my dearest partner of greatness," in his letter reveal about Macbeth's intentions? Lady Macbeth blurts out an unguarded reply to the messenger's announcement, "The King comes here tonight." What does her reply disclose? Does Lady Macbeth appear to be ambitious for herself or for her husband? Do her terrible remarks addressed to "you spirits" prove that Lady Macbeth is a kind of amoral monster without feeling, or do they demonstrate the opposite? Explain your answer. Is there evidence in this scene that these potential murderers love each other? Does the coexistence in a person of two seemingly contradictory emotions—love and cruelty—make him more or less convincing as a dramatic character? Do your answers to the last questions shed light on Shakespeare's seeming treatment of the nature of evil in this play as something shrouded in mystery?

Part 6 (I, vi)

COMMENTARY

Devoid of stage settings, Shakespeare's platform stage required vivid words for *scene painting,* whenever he thought there was some good reason that the physical setting be impressed on the minds of his listeners.

QUESTIONS

Given our knowledge of the use to which Macbeth and his Lady will put their castle, with what attitude do we hear Duncan and Macbeth speak of that castle's *"pleasant"* situation and *"delicate"* air, and hear them say that "heaven's breath/ Smells wooingly here"? What is the obvious parallel between the appearance and the reality of this castle, and the appearance and reality of its principal occupants?

COMMENTARY

Because this is a poetic drama, we must constantly search the meanings of its words for suggestions that will support the more obvious elements of drama, such as the actions of the principal characters.

QUESTIONS

What is the significance of the fact that Duncan, speaking of his gratitude to Lady Macbeth for her hospitality, uses the word *"love"* four times in less than 15 lines, whereas in her reply Lady Macbeth speaks of *"service"* and uses a metaphor—*"audit"*—from bookkeeping? How does the language of her replies consort with Macbeth's language (Scene iv) when he replies to Duncan's expressions of gratitude? What does Duncan's language tell us about him? How does this affect our attitudes toward his potential murderers?

Part 7 (I, vii)

COMMENTARY

Because they are brought up chiefly on a diet of motion pictures and prose fiction—which tend to emphasize the psychology of their principal characters, and to explore fully the *motivations* of these characters—modern students often are puzzled by Shakespeare's seeming neglect of motivation, or, much worse, are willing to take at face value statements concerning motives which a little examination reveals are inadequate. Thus, when they are told that it is simplistic to view *Macbeth* as a warning against inordinate ambition, they are apt to feel puzzled or even downright resentful.

QUESTIONS

In the opening soliloquy, Macbeth gives a full and compelling inventory of all the reasons against the murder of Duncan, and, when he is through, is left with only one argument for it—his ambition to be king— which by comparison is made to look as mean and limited as indeed it is. How does this disproportionate weighing of the arguments pro and con demonstrate that Shakespeare never intended his listeners to think ambition an adequate motivation for the murder? How does the absence of any adequate motivation add another quantum to the mystery that surrounds this study of evil? How does the inexplicable quality of evil sophisticate one's approach to this subject and to any work of literary art that views evil in this way?

COMMENTARY

A cold-blooded murder is a damnable act in any culture. But to Shakespeare's essentially Christian audience the murder of a king—God's steward here on earth—was an act of irredeemable impiety, as well.

QUESTIONS

How does the foregoing explain the order of the four reasons for not committing the murder to which Macbeth gives such clear expression? How does it help to account for the seemingly extravagant figures of speech in lines 18–25? Compared to other great villains in Shakespeare —Iago, Edmund, Richard III—Macbeth is possessed of a most acute moral sense ("We still have judgment here"). Is this why Macbeth is often termed a "hero villain"? Explain.

COMMENTARY

When it suits his purpose, as when he wishes to suggest the mystery of evil, Shakespeare can *deliberately cultivate ambiguity*. But he is never vague about matters that he wishes to make clear. So there is ample evidence in this first act, some of which has been already alluded to, to indicate that Macbeth had thought about winning the crown unlawfully before he ever met the witches.

QUESTIONS

What passages spoken by Lady Macbeth in this scene give clear evidence that she and her husband had talked about the kingship and about murdering Duncan to obtain it before the action of this play began?

COMMENTARY

We already have spoken of the way in which a dramatist can sharpen *characterization by contrast:* two characters (Macbeth and Banquo) can view the same event (meeting the witches) differently. Another form of contrast is to make one character deficient in some quality with which another character is richly endowed. Thus Shakespeare confers a vivid imagination on Macbeth, but denies this quality to his wife.

QUESTIONS

How does Lady Macbeth's deficient imagination manifest itself on the practical level: her scheme to murder Duncan and to place the blame on his two drunken attendants? How does it manifest itself on the moral and psychological level: her confidence that sheer physical courage and boldness of action will suffice to insure their "desire," to attain that which they esteem the "ornament of life"?

COMMENTARY

Lady Macbeth's mention of having "given suck" and knowing "how tender 'tis to love the babe that milks me" followed by her terrible picture of plucking "my nipple from his boneless gums/ And (dashing) the brains out" gives rise to an interesting example of the difference between *poetic truth* and *literal truth*. These lines seems to suggest that Lady Macbeth has been a mother. But we never hear another reference to her children. And we have already seen and will see much more evidence in the future that the Macbeths are always associated with sterility and the death of children.

QUESTIONS

In view of the witches' prophecy that Banquo and not Macbeth shall beget future kings, and Macbeth's subsequent attempts to kill Banquo's sons, Duncan's sons, and his successful killing of Macduff's children, and in view of Shakespeare's associating the Macbeths with many images of sterility and blight, how are you inclined to respond to the question of whether or not the Macbeths are childless? How do the lines just quoted that seem to give literal support to the notion that Lady Macbeth has been a mother at the same time give poetic support to the notion that she is a death-dealing rather than a life-giving figure?

Part 8 (II, i)

COMMENTARY

The subjects of this scene are *dreams* (Banquo) and *hallucinations* (Macbeth's).

QUESTIONS

Banquo is reluctant to go to sleep because of "the cursed thoughts that nature/ Gives way to in repose." A few moments later, Macbeth says of the hallucinatory dagger, "Thou marshall'st me the way I was going." In what sense are these very different men attesting to the power of evil over the unguarded minds of men?

COMMENTARY

Once again Shakespeare achieves a fine *ironic effect* by the careful juxtaposition of words and acts.

QUESTIONS

Preparing for bed, Banquo says to his son, Fleance, who is acting as his squire, "Hold, take my sword." Seconds later, Macbeth enters, and Banquo, uncertain of who is there, exclaims, "Give my me sword!" What does Shakespeare achieve by this carefully planned bit of stage business?

COMMENTARY

It is a commonplace of criticism that Shakespeare's tragic heroes and hero-villains are endowed with great poetic powers of expression. It is less commonly observed that, like poets, these men are gifted with extraordinary imaginations, and it is their imaginations that magnify their suffering.

QUESTIONS

How many instances of a double awareness of the real and the imagined, experienced simultaneously, does close reading of lines 33–61 yield? The combination of the real dagger in Macbeth's hand and the imaginary dagger he sees before him is one such instance. What are the others?

Part 9 (II, ii)

COMMENTARY

This scene casts a searching light on the *characters* of Lady Macbeth and Macbeth seconds before and moments after the murder of Duncan.

QUESTIONS

In what specific ways has Lady Macbeth helped her husband commit the murder? Although earlier she accused her husband of cowardice when he hesitated, she now discovers the need to fortify her own courage. How? What prevents her from committing the actual murder herself? How effective have been her invocations to evil spirits to make thick her blood and render her devoid of normal human feelings? What does all this augur concerning her future state of mind?

Leaving the stage to commit the murder, Macbeth walks like a man in a trance. What is he like when he reenters, the murder done? How does this device (as well as others) serve to link these last two scenes, so that for dramatic purposes they are really one? How does the conduct of this man, who seems to be struggling to awake from a nightmare, somehow lessen the odium with which we view him? Macbeth apprehends a world of figures here: He plaintively tells his wife he "could not say 'Amen,' " reports he "heard a voice cry 'Sleep no more! Macbeth does murder sleep,' " and conjectures that "all great Neptune's ocean" cannot wash the blood from his hands. How do these unexpected responses serve to mitigate our feelings toward him? In what sense is the magnitude of his imagination equal to the magnitude of his crime? What does this suggest about the magnitude of his suffering? How are the dimensions of Macbeth's imagination increased by the language of Lady Macbeth, with her "A little water clears us of this deed," and " 'tis the eye of childhood/ That fears the painted devil"?

COMMENTARY

Readers of a playscript should be alert at all times to *sound effects.* Unlike other forms of literature, a playscript is like a musical score: We must *see* and *hear* the play performed, at least in our imaginations, before we can begin to understand and enjoy a playscript to any full degree.

QUESTIONS

What various sounds play a big part in achieving the terror of this murder scene, and the one immediately preceding it? How does the last sound effect serve to establish an important link between this scene and the next?

Part 10 (II, iii)

COMMENTARY

The scene with the drunken porter well illustrates one of the most important *structural principles* employed by Shakespeare in nearly all his plays: A seemingly irrelevant comic scene, on closer examination, turns out to be closely linked thematically to the serious scenes that flank it.

QUESTIONS

Why is it appropriate that this particular porter should pretend that he is the keeper of "hell gate"? Playing his game, he pretends that he is about to admit three different kinds of sinners to hell. Why is the second sinner, the equivocator, particularly suitable here? (In this connection, how does this matter of equivocation link with the play's opening scene?) What might be the darker undercurrent of meaning in the joking words of the porter, "But this place is too cold for hell. I'll devil-porter it no further"? Why is it ironically fitting that the first man the porter actually admits to the castle courtyard is Macduff?

COMMENTARY

In Shakespearean plays the *world* often mirrors the characters and moods of the men who make it up, and the events that take place there.

QUESTIONS

What is the significance of the "unruly" night described by Lennox? What perversions of nature are mentioned? Why is this description "fitting" here?

COMMENTARY

Shakespeare could have had Macduff announce the murder of Duncan very simply. Perhaps "The king has been murdered." This would have been in keeping with Macduff's straightforward, low-keyed style. Instead, his words are very elaborate and seem excessively artificial.

QUESTIONS

What does Macduff's elaborate metaphor describing Duncan's death disclose about the Elizabethan attitude toward the relationship of a king to God and to the universe? Why, then, would the murder of

Duncan have seemed even more horrifying to Shakespeare's Elizabethan audiences than to us?

COMMENTARY

How a man speaks is often as revealing of his character as what he says.

QUESTIONS

What are the striking differences between the utterances of Macbeth and Macduff immediately after Macbeth, Lennox, and Ross reenter the courtyard? (87–113.) What do they tell us about their respective speakers? Given what is to follow in the play, why are Macbeth's first remarks (87–92) unconsciously ironic?

COMMENTARY

Like a composer of a symphony, a playwright must frequently *orchestrate* several "instruments," so as to achieve a number of purposes and at the same time preserve unity.

QUESTIONS

How do the hurried coming and going of several characters, the fainting and removal of Lady Macbeth, and the cries of horror and sounding of alarm bells serve to counterpoint the muttered dialogue of Malcolm and Donalbain and to establish just the right note for their stealthy exit?

Part 11 (II, iv)

COMMENTARY

Shakespeare frequently presses into service a minor character or two who operates in much the way a Greek *chorus* did to comment on and moralize about the ensuing action.

QUESTIONS

What passage in the previous scene do the remarks of Ross and the Old Man echo and form a parallel to? What aspects of "nature" are again underscored? Why is Shakespeare so anxious to emphasize the abnormal? The Maurice Evans film combines the roles of the Old Man here and the Doctor in V, i and iii. What is gained by this? What is lost, if anything?

COMMENTARY

Since Shakespearean plays contain more "story stuff" than do modern plays, Shakespeare must occasionally resort to *scenes that report* some of the off-stage action, not all of which can be dramatized. He usually succeeds in combining this "reportage" with some dramatic advance.

QUESTIONS

In the final lines of Scene iv what information is supplied to the audience? How does Shakespeare introduce a new element of suspense? At the end of the scene, what does the audience look forward to finding out?

Part 12 (III, i)

COMMENTARY

The Banquo soliloquy which opens this scene is yet another example of the *economy* of a skillful dramatist: Banquo not only serves as a conscious chorus to comment on Macbeth's crime, he also unconsciously reveals much about himself.

QUESTIONS

What do you make of Banquo's seeming willingness to wait a while to see if the witches' prophecies concerning him will come true? Has the evil which oozes through this play like unstaunched blood begun to stain Banquo? How does this conform with Shakespeare's apparent way of treating evil?

COMMENTARY

Because by its very nature it involves two or more meanings operating simultaneously, *irony* is a favorite ingredient of poetry. Can you detect the example of irony in this brief exchange between Banquo and Macbeth?

BANQUO: I must become a borrower of the night
   For a dark hour or twain.
MACBETH: Fail not our feast.
BANQUO: My lord, I will not.

COMMENTARY

Shakespeare seldom wastes words in his plays. The keenest-eyed critics only rarely find a nonfunctional passage.

QUESTIONS

Shakespeare here devotes 70 lines to Macbeth's interview with the assassins, unlike his usual brief treatment of hired murderers. Why do you suppose he has lavished so much time and attention on this dialogue?

COMMENTARY

The *rhythm* or *pattern* of this scene is symmetrical: soliloquy, dialogue, soliloquy, dialogue.

QUESTIONS

Assuming that such symmetry suggests the presence of conscious art, what does Shakespeare appear to achieve by this pattern?

Part 13 (III, ii)

COMMENTARY

Irony—the reversal of expectations—may take many forms. None is more interesting than a reversal of behavior in a principal character.

QUESTIONS

How does this scene show the beginning of a reversal in the respective behaviors of Macbeth and Lady Macbeth? Who now seizes the initiative? Who now, apparently for the first time, feels the sadness of penitence?

COMMENTARY

One of the marvels of a great writer is the way he seems to anticipate contemporary concerns. Today we brood much on *alienation*. Shakespeare was there before us.

QUESTIONS

What is the evidence in this scene that his loving pair of murderers is already beginning to drift apart? What is the evidence that they are resisting this drift? What is the implied comment on the nature of evil?

COMMENTARY

A work of literary art is characterized by a nearly limitless series of *patterns*.

QUESTIONS

Macbeth's closing words in this scene suggest many remarkable parallels with his words just before the murder of Duncan. One of these is the incantatory quality of the words: Macbeth seems to be conjuring up a charm. As you have seen his character unfold, why is this appropriate?

COMMENTARY

Everywhere and always the best revealer of character is *language*—what a man says and the way he says it.

QUESTIONS

Compare Lady Macbeth's analysis of their situation (4–7) with Macbeth's (13–26). What significant differences are revealed by the language they use (the choice of words, the figures of speech, the images, the rhythms, etc.)?

Part 14 (III, iii)

COMMENTARY

Because a work of art reveals much *ingenuity*, critics sometimes are tempted to be overingenious. Such a display has attended the business of the "third murderer," one writer even proposing it was Macbeth himself. Close reading usually dispels such nonsense. Shakespeare tells us what we need to know.

QUESTIONS

How does the second murderer's first remark and that delivered by the third murderer just before Banquo and Fleance enter supply us with a completely satisfactory answer to the question: Why a third murderer?

COMMENTARY

Serious *wordplay* is a characteristic of Shakespearean language. It can appear anywhere.

QUESTIONS

What is the probable double meaning of the first murderer's exclamation following Banquo's observation about the weather:

BANQUO: It will rain tonight.
FIRST MURDERER: Let it come down!

What is the probable double meaning in the imagery of the third murderer's question:

Who did strike out the light?

Part 15 (III, iv)

COMMENTARY

In Chapter 28 we discussed one of the principal ingredients of the *physical world* of Macbeth: Nowhere is it more apparent than in this scene.

QUESTIONS

What image, evoking a vivid picture in the mind of the reader as well as shockingly confronting the playgoer, runs through this entire scene like some terrible refrain?

COMMENTARY

Playing in broad daylight, without benefit of modern lighting effects, Shakespeare's company employed a live actor to play the role of Banquo's ghost, although, following the theatrical convention of the day, only Macbeth can see him.

QUESTIONS

How has Shakespeare prepared us to accept the fact that only Macbeth will see the ghost? We know that Lady Macbeth is now guilt-ridden. Why doesn't she see the ghost? How does this singling out of Macbeth dramatize one of the most fearful results of evil?

COMMENTARY

If, unlike modern novelists, Shakespeare is not interested in depicting the complexities of *motivation* that precede an act like murder, he is very interested in depicting the complexity of the possible *effects* of his crime on the murderer.

QUESTIONS

What is the startling contrast between those qualities of character displayed by Macbeth when he plans a murder and those he displays as the observer or contemplator of these murderous acts? What is the incredible contradiction in his thinking at those moments when his conscience speaks to him and at those moments when he seeks some means to insure security? Macbeth began his career of crime by committing a murder, and his object thereafter is to avoid detection. What is the dreadful irony in the means he invariably finds to avoid detection for that initial murder?

COMMENTARY

Verbal refrain, like the deliberate repetition of visual images, may be used to help construct the unique *world* of a play. Consider the four uses of the word *"strange"* in lines 82, 86, 112, 139.

QUESTIONS

What is the common denominator of meaning that unites all four uses of the word *"strange"*? What does this suggest about the *world* of Macbeth? What are the different manifestations of abnormality that confront the reader and playgoer from the beginning of this scene to the end?

COMMENTARY

One reason Shakespeare seems as alive to audiences today as in his own time is his reference to human behavior that is as recognizable now as it was then.

QUESTIONS

What recent events from our own times spring to mind when we hear Macbeth say about the Scotch nobles, "There's not one of them but in his house/ I keep a servant fee'd"?

COMMENTARY

Many students of this play have agreed that perhaps the most shocking effect of his crimes displayed by Macbeth is a terrible sort of fatigue, a feeling almost akin to boredom.

QUESTIONS

What figure of speech near the end of the scene reveals this shocking (because surprising) attitude of Macbeth?

Part 16 (III, v)

COMMENTARY

Beginning students are often inhibited by a combination of inexperience and modesty from playing the *role of literary critic*. This scene permits you to play this role for once with some confidence. When you have answered the following questions exactly, you should have no difficulty finding your way to a clear-cut judgment.

QUESTIONS

What is the *metrical pattern* of lines 4 to 33? What is the *rhyme pattern*? What *rhythmic effect* is achieved by this particular combination of rhyme and meter? Does it tend toward regularity? Does it have a singsong effect? Is the *diction* in this passage as concrete as in the previous speeches of the three witches? What is the distinction between Hecate's *imagery* and that previously associated with the three sisters? The stage directions immediately following these lines call for music and two songs. Given our previous vivid impressions of the three sisters, does this seem appropriate? On the basis of your answers to these questions can you confidently defend the conclusion that this scene was *not* written by Shakespeare but represents an interpolation by another writer for a performance in which songs and dances by the witches were introduced because someone thought this would be entertaining?

Part 17 (III, vi)

COMMENTARY

Before one can be a good reader of lyric or dramatic poetry, he must be able to catch the *tone* of the utterance. This is indispensable. Yet many students have trouble identifying tone. Here is a good scene to practice on.

QUESTIONS

Lines 1–20 of Lennox's opening remarks serve as a neat summary of most of the important action to date. What is the *tone* of these remarks? What is the precise *pattern* that illustrates how this tone is achieved?

COMMENTARY

We have spoken of Shakespeare's skill at making a scene fulfill more than one purpose. He displays this skill here.

QUESTIONS

In what sense is this a *choral* scene that comments on and interprets the action? In what sense is it a *summary* scene recounting past action? In what sense is it a *foreshadowing* scene that points to future action? Who will be involved in this future action? In what ways, are we led to believe?

Part 18 (IV, i)

COMMENTARY

Here is another test of your skill as *literary critic*.

QUESTIONS

A few of the first 44 lines in this scene were written not by Shakespeare but, presumably, by the same interpolator who supplied III, v. Since all the lines are tetrameters, and since nearly all appear in rhyming couplets, these technical devices alone will not help you to your answer. But other considerations—the metrical "feet," diction, imagery, rhythm, tone—should help you. Which lines are not Shakespeare's? Why do you say so?

COMMENTARY

By now you will have become keenly aware of the significance of *imagery* in conveying the dramatist's intended meanings.

QUESTIONS

Macbeth says to the witches, "I conjure you." He then speaks of many things—winds, churches, navigation, corn, castles, and so on. What do these seemingly very different objects have in common in Macbeth's conjuring speech? Given what Macbeth has become, why is this most appropriate?

COMMENTARY

Perhaps no play of Shakespeare's makes greater use of *spectacle* than does *Macbeth;* and there is no more theatrical scene in the play than this, in which Shakespeare boldly blends the terror of his dark theme with the primitive audience appeal of a puzzle to be solved.

QUESTIONS

In this spectacular sequence, the witches summon up their "masters," three successive apparitions. Whom do each of these apparitions represent? At the end of the play, just before he dies, Macbeth will say,

And be these juggling fiends no more believed,
That palter with us in a double sense.

How do two of the apparitions palter in a double sense with Macbeth in this scene? To what question of Macbeth do the witches provide a truthful and unequivocal answer? How does this mixture of truth and falsehood echo the impression formed in the very first scene of the play when we first met the witches?

COMMENTARY

Still another reminder of Shakespeare's skill at *juxtaposition* is in order at the end of this scene.

QUESTIONS

What Macbeth took to be the galloping off of the witches, Lennox reveals to be the galloping on of messengers. What is the news they bring? Why is this news particularly dramatic reaching Macbeth's ears (and ours) at this moment?

COMMENTARY

From this moment on Macbeth is terribly alone. Until he meets his death at the hands of Macduff, we never again will see him with any of the characters we have come to associate him with—least of all with the one closest to him, Lady Macbeth.

QUESTIONS

What does Shakespeare achieve by thus isolating Macbeth? What does this suggest, once more, about the nature of evil as Shakespeare seems to view it?

Part 19 (IV, ii)

COMMENTARY

The mark of the skillful dramatist is that he always seems to select from among all the possible choices open to him just the right scene to dramatize.

QUESTIONS

Reviewing Macbeth's activities to date, can you explain Shakespeare's purpose in sketching this vignette of a charming boy and his mother only to depict the boy's brutal murder? What role does *contrast* play here? Why is this scene just right coming where it does? We later learn that Lady Macduff was also put to the sword. What did Shakespeare gain by not showing this onstage?

COMMENTARY

We have seen previously in his handling of Banquo that Shakespeare does not oversimplify his good men, making them impossibly virtuous.

QUESTIONS

By permitting Lady Macduff to speak so sharply and eloquently against her husband, a man whom we know to be good, what does Shakespeare suggest about the nature and effect of evil?

COMMENTARY

One of the "givens" in a Shakespearean tragedy is that the ravages of evil seen in his tragic hero (the *microcosm*) will be duplicated by similar horrors in the great world (the *macrocosm*) in which he lives.

QUESTIONS

What lines spoken by Ross and what lines spoken by Macduff's wife are clearly designed to accomplish this particular purpose? Can you trace some rather exact parallels between Scotland under Macbeth's brutal rule and what you have read about life in a twentieth-century police state?

COMMENTARY

One who reads and rereads all of Shakespeare's plays discovers a remarkable consistency in his notion of goodness and in the behavior of his good persons.

QUESTIONS

What is the evidence in the dying words of the man Banquo and again in the words of the little son of Macduff that reveals their unselfish love?

Part 20 (IV, iii)

COMMENTARY

Modern stage and motion picture directors cut this scene heavily or eliminate it altogether, save for the last part where Macduff learns that Macbeth has slaughtered his family. This presents another challenge to *your powers as a literary critic.* What portions, if any, would you cut, and why? The following questions will help you focus on the central problem.

QUESTIONS

Consider the tempo and the action of the scenes immediately preceding and following this one. Do we need a pause between these scenes of furious action and deep appeals to our emotions to give us a little breathing time?

Does Lady Macduff's earlier criticism of her husband's conduct in leaving his family unprotected help prepare us for Malcolm's suspicions that Macduff may be the agent of Macbeth and hence unafraid to leave his family? Does this, in turn, lend some plausibility to the opening exchange of doubts and fears and reassurances between Malcolm and Macduff?

Malcolm's pretense of being a wicked man may seem childish to us at first until we see how he employs this device to test Macduff's true loyalty. To whom or what does Macduff reveal he owes his loyalty? Shakespeare and his audience were fascinated by the good or evil effect of a good or bad king on the kingdom, because they lived at a time when the theory of "the divine right of kings" was more often than not translated into actual policy. Does this help to explain the lengthy catalogs of kingly vices on the one hand, and virtues on the other, recited by Malcolm? Should a twentieth-century audience be spared such long catalogs?

King James I, who ruled England when *Macbeth* was written and performed by Shakespeare's company, was said to be descended from Banquo. Also, he had in 1605 reinstituted the practice, begun by Edward the Confessor many years before, of "curing" the sick by a touch of the royal hand. This doubtless accounts for the dialogue a little past the middle of this scene between Malcolm and the doctor. Is this a functional piece of business; that is, does it advance the action of the play? Or is it something that a modern audience could be spared?

Ross, who has served several times as chorus or messenger, here fills both roles. He gives us yet another picture of suffering Scotland, and he unwillingly reports the murder of Macduff's family. Would you make any "cuts" in these closing lines? If so, where, and what would be your justification?

COMMENTARY

A distinguishing mark of a literary work of art is its astonishing *unity* in every respect.

QUESTIONS

We have already talked about the way Shakespeare associates the Macbeths with death and sterility, as opposed to life and fecundity which we were invited to associate with Duncan. How do the closing lines of this scene reintroduce this motif cunningly while at the same time emphasizing the pathos of Macduff's total loss?

Part 21 (V, i)

COMMENTARY

This is one of the greatest scenes in Shakespeare. It invites the closest reading.

QUESTIONS

How do the opening remarks of the Doctor and the Gentlewoman prepare us, in every way, to understand the subsequent actions and words of Lady Macbeth? Macbeth has complained repeatedly that he cannot sleep. Lady Macbeth, presumably, has been able to sleep. How does this scene give a grimly ironic turn to that seeming contrast? Think back over the light and darkness imagery in the play. What is the painful irony of Lady Macbeth's command that she have light by her continually? Examine lines 32–37 closely. Can you find a precise action that matches and explains each of Lady Macbeth's six different statements? (The first two sentences are really one.) Can you do the same for lines 39–42? Beginning with line 57, and continuing to her final words, Lady Macbeth's concern is not for herself. For whom is she concerned? How does this fit what we have seen of her before? How does it contribute to the poignancy of her last moment before our eyes? Does it give special significance to the Doctor's "God, God forgive us all"? How do the Doctor's summary words illuminate the verdict we are invited to pass on Lady Macbeth? How do his last words to the Gentlewoman foreshadow Lady Macbeth's means of death?

COMMENTARY

Nowhere is the *unity* that is so characteristic of Shakespeare's art better displayed than in the imagery he employs.

QUESTIONS

What image, above all others, dominates the sleepwalking scene? Recalling the appearance of this image elsewhere in the play, why is this—one wants to say—inevitable?

COMMENTARY

An established stage practice of Elizabethan playwrights was to write all speeches spoken by those not in their right minds in prose.

QUESTIONS

Can you think of any reasons, besides this conventional practice, why Shakespeare writes most of this scene in prose? Are you helped to find your answer by an examination of the blank verse spoken by the Doctor in his last speech?

COMMENTARY

Although he did not attempt to trace the psychological nuances of his characters with anything approaching the detail of modern novelists, this does not mean that Shakespeare's principal characters do not display the kind of consistent behavior that makes dramatic characters plausible.

QUESTIONS

How does the breakdown of Lady Macbeth witnessed in this scene support our earlier notion that her fierce invocations to the spirits of evil to render her inhuman prove her humanness rather than the contrary?

Part 22 (V, ii)

COMMENTARY

We have spoken several times of Shakespeare's *economy,* his ability to accomplish several purposes at once.

QUESTIONS

Which of the following tasks demanding his attention does Shakespeare achieve in this scene? Does he provide a choral comment on the state of Scotland at this critical moment? Does he make clear to the audience how the lines of the coming battle are to be drawn and the opposing forces disposed? Does he titillate our ears and contribute to our feeling of suspense by echoing the names "Birnam Wood" and "Dunsinane," recently heard on the skinny lips of the three witches? Does he provide a vivid picture of Macbeth, who has been removed from our sight for some time?

Part 23 (V, iii)

COMMENTARY

In an art form, any special display of *design* demands our careful attention: the artist's pattern is calculated to underscore his meaning.

QUESTIONS

This scene opens and closes with specific references to Birnam Wood and Dunsinane. How does everything in between give the lie to Macbeth's explicitly stated confidence in the prophecies of the apparitions and their supernatural interpreters, the witches?

COMMENTARY

We have observed how Macbeth systematically alienates himself from everyone we associated with him at the outset.

QUESTIONS

Who is the only named retainer left? What is the significance of his name?

COMMENTARY

It has been observed often how brilliantly the older writers have anticipated the discoveries (or rediscoveries) of contemporary psychology.

QUESTIONS

How does Macbeth's dialogue with the Doctor reveal Shakespeare's understanding of that part of a human being vulnerable to a guilty conscience?

COMMENTARY

One of the interestingly difficult problems confronting Shakespeare in this play is how to sustain some genuine sympathy from his audience for his hero-villain, whose evil he must depict in unrelieved colors.

QUESTIONS

Review all of the qualities with which Macbeth was endowed before his first fatal crime. What one remains unimpaired? What examples of this quality does this scene provide?

Part 24 (V, iv)

COMMENTARY

Since he is never interested in writing a "whodunit," but instead wishes to depict the inexorable march of events toward a *foregone conclusion*, Shakespeare must resort to various artful devices to build suspense and sustain interest.

QUESTIONS

How does Shakespeare draw on the earlier scene of the "prophecies" of the apparitions to hold audience interest in this brief scene? What metaphor or analogy comes to mind as we view Macbeth in Dunsinane castle at the center of a narrowing circle of enclosing enemies?

Part 25 (V, v)

COMMENTARY

Single scenes, like entire plays, are often distinguished by a very marked rhythm, a *pattern of movement*.

QUESTIONS

In what sense may we say that about four-fifths of this scene displays a kind of paralysis or stasis, and one-fifth furious motion? What triggers this change?

COMMENTARY

Aural imagery can be very important in a play: Certain sounds, like certain pictures, are often worth many words.

QUESTIONS

What dreadful sound do we and Macbeth hear in this scene? What is Macbeth's reaction? How does it compare with his reaction to other dreadful sounds earlier in the play? What is the significance of this difference in reaction?

COMMENTARY

Some of Shakespeare's most memorable lines suffer a disastrous misinterpretation when torn out of the context of the play and scene for which they were written, and "recited" on a public platform.

QUESTIONS

This scene contains the most famous lines in the play. What do they signify *in context*? Do they signify the same meanings out of context?

COMMENTARY

It is the peculiar property of poetry that often the simplest words are suddenly invested with the deepest of meanings.

QUESTIONS

Here we learn that "The Queen, my lord, is dead." In what sense is Macbeth also dead as he hears these words? In the play's final scene we learn that it is thought Lady Macbeth took her own life. Although the playwright presents this information as speculation, is there any doubt in your mind that this must be the right explanation? Explain your answer to anyone who does not agree.

COMMENTARY

If the phrase "poetic justice" is to have any useful meaning, it can only do so in the light of particular instances.

QUESTIONS

Why is it poetic justice that this couple who, murdered together, should now die apart?

COMMENTARY

Poetic justice is closely related to *irony*: Where one finds the first, he usually will find the second.

QUESTIONS

Macbeth's best chance for survival is to remain within his strongly fortified castle that can "laugh a siege to scorn." What prompts him to abandon this relative security for the certain dangers of a foray outside the walls? Why is this exquisitely ironic?

Part 26 (V, vi)

COMMENTARY

The student should always try to visualize Shakespearean staging when reading a Shakespearean playscript.

QUESTIONS

Where do Scene vi, Scene vii, and the first 35 lines of Scene viii take place? Why do modern motion picture directors give us pictures of the attackers scaling the castle walls, breaking down its gates, leaping its moats, and so forth?

COMMENTARY

Throughout his career, Shakespeare frequently employed rhyming couplets to end a scene, a kind of aural punctuation.

QUESTIONS

What imagery makes Macduff's rhyming couplet at the end of this scene more than a conventional piece of rhetoric to help mark a change in scene?

Part 27 (V, vii)

COMMENTARY

Bearbaiting was a favorite Elizabethan spectacle, and there is evidence that such spectacles took place in theaters like Shakespeare's, with the platform stage removed and the spectators safe in the encircling galleries.

QUESTIONS

How does this fact explain Macbeth's metaphor as he is hemmed in by his enemies? How does a man using such a metaphor view his attackers? Is it in any way a fitting metaphor for Macbeth at this moment in his career?

COMMENTARY

All playwrights must provide suspense and gripping action. The best of them make such scenes perform more than just the function of being exciting, eye-filling physical action.

QUESTIONS

How many functions does Shakespeare succeed in fulfilling by the introduction of Young Siward and his duel to the death with Macbeth? Name them carefully.

COMMENTARY

Modern scholarship, without being arrogant, has corrected some of the traditional notions of scene division. The correct division between scenes is indicated by a cleared stage which, in turn, indicates a shift in time or place or both. Where the action is continuous, the scene is not properly divided.

QUESTIONS

What portion of Scene viii really is an integral part of Scene vii?

Part 28 (V, viii)

For clarity we are preserving the *traditional* scene division here, although dissenting from such a division, as noted in the immediately preceding question.

COMMENTARY

Shakespeare never appears to forget one of his principal problems: How to maintain some sympathy in the minds of his audience for his villainous protagonist.

QUESTIONS

In his final three speeches, what qualities are revealed that somehow echo the better part of Macbeth before he committed the fatal first murder?

COMMENTARY

Despite the complexity of his artistic achievement, Shakespeare never forgot that he was writing to a popular audience and never was consciously obscure.

QUESTIONS

How do Macbeth's final words about the witches disclose with total clarity the nature of the paradoxical statements they made in the first scene of the play?

COMMENTARY

Shakespearean stage directions (as opposed to those interpolated by later editors) are not very numerous and are seldom detailed. Therefore, scholars take them very seriously and are not disposed to quarrel with or seek to explain them away if they do not fit with some preconceived notion of how the scene "should" be staged.

QUESTIONS

Clearly the stage directions establish the fact that Shakespeare intended Macbeth to be killed on stage in the sight of his audience. Why, then, did he have the fighting Macduff and Macbeth exit just before they reenter "fighting and Macbeth slain"? One scholar has suggested that Shakespeare intended to have Macbeth reenter running in terror from the pursuing Macduff, and die ignominiously by being stabbed in the back. Does the attention given to the ensuing conversation in which the elder Siward expresses satisfaction with his son's death because he had "his hurts before" support this notion?

COMMENTARY

There is enough documentary evidence about *Elizabethan staging* practices to give us confidence that the stage direction, "Enter Macduff, with Macbeth's head," signifies an actual piece of stage business.

QUESTIONS

What is the link between this gory business and the earlier apparition scene? How does this visual shocker consort with the verbal imagery that has run through the play? Has Shakespeare once again provided us with a justifiable spectacle that is a means to a larger end, and not just a sensational end in itself?

COMMENTARY

Artistic unity is promoted by echoing imagery that establishes consistency and continuity.

QUESTIONS

Why is it fitting that Malcolm in his speech of thanks engages in such metaphors as, "What's more to do/ Which would be *planted* newly with the time . . ./ We will perform in measure, time, and place"? In what respect does this make him truly his father's son? How does the metaphor befit the present state of Scotland and the hopes of the victors for its future?

COMMENTARY

Shakespearean tragedies, however painful, and however sustained the suffering and disorder, end with the suggestion of order restored, of social wounds healed, of a kind of spiritual restoration, or at least the promise of such.

QUESTIONS

How does the next-to-last couplet of Malcolm, "by the grace of Grace/ We will perform in measure, time, and place," achieve or at least hold out this promise? In your answer take cognizance of the connotative as well as denotative meanings of such words as "grace," "Grace," "measure," "time," and "place."

30
COMPOSITION

So far you have read a long composition on the world of *Macbeth* and many smaller compositions called commentaries, and you have composed, orally or in writing, short answers to a great many questions. You have done these things with the end in view of increasing the range and depth of your understanding of *Macbeth*. Now, in the final chapter you are presented with a number of subjects suitable for a longer composition.

Consult any good dictionary for the definition of the word "*composition*," and you will discover over a dozen denotations listed. Among these is one that would suitably describe *Macbeth*—"an arrangement of the parts of a work of art so as to form a unified, harmonious whole"—and one that might describe what you usually mean by the word—"an exercise in writing done as schoolwork." If to each of these denotative meanings, you were to add their connotations, you would probably find yourself employing adjectives like "wonderful," "stunning," and "impressive" for the former, and "painful," "clumsy," and "unpleasant" for the latter.

This should not be so. It is surely a kind of anomaly to study the composition of a literary masterpiece and then not be able to compose a suitable reaction to that study in one's own prose. A principal reason for any defective composition is the absence in it of any focus. It has no core of meaning, no real organizing principle, no central structure. It has no thesis. It betrays the fact that no mind has been at work shaping the means to make clear an idea.

Insofar as the absence of a controlling idea is responsible for poor compositions, the following subjects should provide a remedy. They are quite different in their concerns, in their scope, and in their intent. But they have one thing in common: They have a central focus, a governing idea. Having read a famous play, a detailed explanation of the working of one of its elements, and a long succession of comments and questions on its other elements, you should be in a position to do two things: to select a single, governing idea about this play, and to compose a coherent and interesting set of statements that develops and clarifies and illustrates that idea.

Here, then, are seven subjects that lend themselves to a *composed* statement about some aspect of *Macbeth*. Each has a one-word caption for immediate identification, followed by a statement that sets forth the thesis to be demonstrated. Read through them, ponder their intent, and select the one you think will permit you to meet the standards of a third definition of composition that falls somewhere between the two definitions quoted earlier: "a putting together of a whole by the combination of its parts."

1. **Theme.** Since a play, like all works of literature, concerns itself with what it means to be human, its theme will take the form of some significant and universal idea about human behavior. Rich and complex masterpieces like *Macbeth* usually have more than one theme. Even when this is so, however, these multiple themes usually will be shown to have a close relationship to each other.

    Here are four well-known quotations which sum up in proverbial fashion some truth about human existence. Write a four-part composition relating each statement to one or more specific characters and actions in the play.
    A. "What is a man profited, if he shall gain the whole world, and lose his own soul?"
    B. "The disease of an evil conscience is beyond all the practice of all the physicians of all the countries in the world."
    C. "Thou shalt not kill."
    D. "Oft hath even a whole city reaped the evil fruit of a bad man."

2. **Hero.** A characteristic of the tragic hero is the distance he falls, from admirable heights to pitiable depths. Macbeth, of course, finally loses his life. But it is a measure of his terrifying fate that death comes to him as a relief. What are his greater losses in the course of the play? Consider among other things his relationship to his king, to his friends, to his state, to his wife, to himself.

3. **Spectacle.** Shakespeare's audiences, we know, had keen appetites for

spectacle: for duels, bloodletting, ghosts, assassinations. Like other play-wrights of his day, Shakespeare gave his audiences what they wanted, and nowhere more extravagantly than in *Macbeth*. Yet he seldom stooped to spectacle for its own sake. He made his spectacular scenes serve a serious purpose in his play. Write a paper demonstrating that Shakespeare did indeed feed the popular appetite for spectacle in *Macbeth* but that he used spectacle as a means to a larger end and never as an end in itself.

4. **Comparison.** Like Shakespeare, Robert Frost understood that the world of any tragic figure operates both inside and outside the sufferer. In a poem appropriately entitled "Desert Places," Frost describes some ter-rifyingly lonely scenes in our physical universe ("empty spaces/ Between stars") and some even more terrifying landscapes locked within a man's soul ("I have it in me . . . my own desert places").

Write a paper in which you show in some detail how Shakespeare in this play created both kinds of "desert places": not only the "blasted heath" where Macbeth first meets the three witches, but also the blasted mind with which Macbeth views his "way of life . . . fall'n into the sear, the yellow leaf."

5. **Allusion.** In IV, iii, 22, Malcolm says: "Angels are bright still, though the brightest fell." The allusion is to Satan, who was once God's brightest angel. Write a paper demonstrating why a comparison of Macbeth and Satan is justified.

6. **Imagery.** You have seen repeated demonstrations of the fact that im-ages that appear and reappear in successive parts of the play have special significance: They illuminate the character associated with them, or the actions to which they are attached. Search through the play for all the clothing images you can find. Having identified all of them, study the contexts in which they appear. Now write a paper demonstrating the spe-cial figurative or symbolic meaning that attaches to each image, and the meaning that all appear to have in common. Having done so, you are in a position to conclude what their special function in the play is.

You may prefer to work with another cluster of images. If so, you will find the images turning on growth, planting, husbandry, and their opposites—sterility, decay, and death—a provocative subject.

7. **Debate.** Great works of literature often give rise to lively disputes. Un-like many everyday arguments, such literary disputes can be pleasant and instructive. Next to the pleasure of reading great literature is the pleasure of talking about it. And some of that talk takes the form of debate.

One such dispute concerns the role of the witches in *Macbeth*. Shake-speare drew his idea for the witches, as he did for much else in this play, from one of his favorite historical sources, Holinshed's *Chronicles*. Here is Holinshed's account of how Macbeth and Banquo first met the three sisters. (Spelling has been modernized.)

Shortly after happened a strange and uncouth wonder, which after-ward was the cause of much trouble in the realm of Scotland, as ye shall hear. It fortuned as Macbeth and Banquo journed toward Forres, where the King then lay, they went sporting by the way together without other company, save only themselves, passing through the woods and fields, when suddenly in the midst of a laund [lawn, open place] there met them three women in strange and wild apparel, resembling creatures of elder world, whom when they attentively beheld, wondering much at the sight, the first of them spake and said: "All hail, Macbeth, Thane of Glammis!" (for he had lately entered into that dignity and office by the death of his father Sinell). The second of them said: "Hail, Macbeth, Thane of Cawder!" But the third said: "All hail, Macbeth, that hereafter shalt be King of Scotland!"

Then Banquo: "What manner of women" (saith he) "are you, that seem so little favorable unto me, whereas to my fellow here, besides high offices, ye assign also the kingdom, appointing forth nothing for me at all?" "Yes," (saith the first of them) "we promise greater benefits unto thee than unto him, for he shall reign indeed, but with an unlucky end; neither shall he leave any issue behind him to succeed in his place, where contrarily thou indeed shalt not reign at all, but of thee those shall be born which shall govern the Scottish kingdom by long order of continual descent." Herewith the foresaid women vanished immediately out of their sight. This was reputed at first but some vain fantastical illusion by Macbeth and Banquo. . . . But afterwards the common opinion was, that these women were either the weird sisters, that is (as ye would say) the goddesses of destiny, or else some nymphs or fairies, endowed with knowledge of prophecy by their necromantical science, because every thing came to pass as they had spoken.

Given this source material, and the play as we have it, the question has arisen: What is the precise function of the witches in *Macbeth*? Are they "goddesses of destiny" and is Macbeth's fate, therefore, predetermined? Or are they more limited "instruments of darkness" who represent evil but who cannot implant evil in the soul of a man who does not will it to be there? We find the issue to be very sharply joined by two professors of English who, interestingly enough, were both distinguished Shakespearean scholars teaching at Harvard University, though at different times.

In 1939, we find Professor George Lyman Kittredge writing:

In adopting the term "Weird Sisters" from Holinshed Shakespeare was obviously adopting also Holinshed's definition—"the goddesses of destiny." The Weird Sisters . . . are the Norns of Scandinavian mythology. The Norns were the goddesses who shaped beforehand the life of every man. . . . Always and everywhere they are great and terrible powers from whose mandate there is no appeal. . . . These were not ordinary witches. . . . They were great powers of destiny, great ministers of fate. . . . The Weird Sisters, then, are not hags in the service of the devil; they are not mere personifications of a man's evil desires or his ruthless craving for power. They are as actual and objective as the Furies. . . .

Yet in 1956, we find Professor Alfred Harbage explaining:

> In Holinshed's *Chronicle,* from which Shakespeare drew his material . . . the Weird Sisters are "goddesses of destiny" derived from a heathen fatalism. In the play they are Elizabethan witches, their predictive powers subtly curtailed; they predict, abet, and symbolize damnation but do not determine it. Any sense that Macbeth is a helpless victim, his crime predestined, his will bound, is canceled as the play proceeds. . . . Nothing in the witches' prophecies would have suggested to an untainted mind that to "be King hereafter" meant to be murdered first. That Macbeth was already tainted would have been apparent to the original audience.

Disregarding the problem of Shakespeare's use of his sources, and focusing exclusively on the evidence presented in the text of the play, write a paper in which you seek to defend one of these interpretations. Perhaps it would be well to conceive of the purpose of this exercise as not so much to come up with "the right answer" as to demonstrate an ability to engage in close reading and to reason from evidence.

SELECTED READINGS

Students who wish to explore the world of *Macbeth*, guided by two of the most keen-eyed pathfinders who ever mapped that terrain, may turn to Sections 1 and 2 of A. C. Bradley's classic "Lecture IX: Macbeth," from his collection of lectures entitled, *Shakespearean Tragedy*, now available in paperback (Meridian Books, 1957), and the chapter entitled *Macbeth* from Mark Van Doren's *Shakespeare* (Doubleday Anchor Books, 1939). Bradley's book, originally published in 1904, is the most eloquent of those that treat Shakespearean characters as though they were living persons. This is a critical viewpoint not much in favor right now, but students who do not automatically equate the contemporary with the correct will find much in it that is illuminating.

Students desiring to compare other, brief scene-by-scene analyses of *Macbeth* with the one set forth in Chapter 29 will find an example of urbane commentary on pages 371–399 of Alfred Harbage's *William Shakespeare: A Reader's Guide* (Noonday Press, 1963). Those who are preparing themselves to become secondary school teachers may wish to read an analysis prepared for high-school students, on pages 52–65 of the *Student Guide* to vol. IV of *Ideas and Patterns in Literature* (Harcourt Brace Jovanovich, 1970), written by the author of this part, who, with Edgar H. Knapp, edited this four-volume series of readers.

The single most famous essay ever written on *Macbeth* is also one of the briefest—Thomas DeQuincey's fine insight into the way Shakespeare can achieve a single moment that is at once electrifying and penetrating—"On the Knocking at the Gate in 'Macbeth.'" Originally published in 1823, this essay is constantly reprinted in current anthologies of British literature of the Romantic period. It will provide today's student with both a good specimen of the romantic writer's finely attuned sensibility and his somewhat overblown style.

Perhaps the best swift transition from nineteenth- to twentieth-century perspectives on *Macbeth* is an essay by the thoughtful British teacher-critic, L. C. Knights, somewhat sardonically entitled, "How Many Children Had Lady Macbeth?" published in *Explorations* (New York University Press, 1947). Knights seeks to render absurd the narrow perspective that views *Macbeth* and other plays of Shakespeare as stories of living human beings, and to assert the importance of the total poetic achievement of which characterization is only a single component. His essay, like the majority of mid-twentieth-century essays on Shakespeare, roots itself in a close study of Shakespeare's language. Close studies of poetic language invariably focus on imagery. A celebrated study of one cluster of poetic images and their structural significance may be found in Cleanth Brooks' *The Well Wrought Urn* (rev. ed., London: Dobson, 1968), in the chapter entitled "The Naked Babe and the Cloak of Manliness."

The link between *language* and *theme* is always close. A book that early asserted this connection is G. W. Knight's *The Wheel of Fire* (Meridian Books, 5th ed., 1964). Like many pioneers, Knight is often excited and sometimes incautious; this makes him both attractive and dangerous. By contrast, the chapter "Macbeth" in Brent Stirling's *Unity in Shakespearean Tragedy* (Gordian Press, 1966) is a model of caution. Stirling explores the workings of "darkness, sleep, raptness, and contradiction" as strands that make up the thematic fabric of the play.

The student should know about and consult two sources of contemporary Shakespearean scholarship and criticism: the American publication, *The Shakespeare Quarterly,* and the British publication, *Shakespeare Survey.* Volume XIX (1966) of the latter is given over entirely to articles on *Macbeth.* Among these, Robert B. Heilman's "The Criminal as Tragic Hero" comes to grips with a question that alert students always raise: How can the criminal Macbeth be at the same time a tragic hero?

The role of the supernatural in *Macbeth* also raises questions. Many satisfying answers may be found by a careful reading of the play. But even an inspired reading will not inform us about the notions of theology and demonology of Shakespeare's own day. W. C. Curry's *Shakespeare's Philosophical Patterns* (Louisiana State University Press, 1937), over half of which is devoted to *Macbeth,* although not easy reading, is regarded as the best full treatment. Curry answers the inevitable question—Does Macbeth have free will?—in the affirmative.

There are five books entirely devoted to *Macbeth.* In the order of their publication they are: Roy Walker's *The Time is Free* (London: Dakers, 1949), whose useful scene-by-scene analysis is partially vitiated for many readers by its author's insistence on reading the play as an exemplum of Christian doctrines; Henry N. Paul's *The Royal Play of Macbeth* (Macmillan, 1950) which exhaustively traces the relationship of the play to King James I; G. R. Elliott's *Dramatic Providence in Macbeth* (Princeton University Press, 1958) which, like Walker's book, provides a scene-by-scene analysis and is also informed by a fascination with the workings of divine providence, but which is free from Walker's doctrinaire Christianity. Students interested in the theatrical history of *Macbeth* will find a full account in Dennis Bartholomeusz's *Macbeth and the Players* (Cambridge University Press, 1969). The most recent of these full-book treatments of *Macbeth,* Paul Jorgensen's *Our Naked Frailties* (University of California Press, 1971), is a demonstration of how scholarship and criticism can be yoked in the service of literary interpretation, in this instance to trace the workings of "sensation" in both Macbeth's ordeal of crime and punishment and the language Shakespeare employs to render vivid that ordeal and to suggest its universal application to the dark, nether side of everyman: "our naked frailties."

The foregoing citations provide the student with a representative sampling of the kinds of inquiries that this play has provoked. A much fuller listing of books and articles about *Macbeth* may be found in convenient form in the paperback, revised edition of Ronald Berman's *A Reader's Guide to Shakespeare's Plays: A Discursive Bibliography* (Scott, Foresman, 1973), and in the older book by Samuel Tannenbaum, *Shakespeare's Macbeth: A Concise Bibliography* (S. A. Tannenbaum, 1939).

PART SEVEN

ANTONY AND CLEOPATRA

R. J. DORIUS

31

LOVE, DEATH, AND THE HEROIC

Antony and Cleopatra is one of the most controversial of Shakespeare's plays. Is it, with its 42 scenes, a "faultily constructed" drama, as Bradley said, or are its realms of Rome and Egypt finally brought within a single imaginative vision? Is it, as many in the rating game now feel, one of the three or four or five greatest of the tragedies? Is it the finest of the histories, perhaps the thirteenth in the remarkable series Shakespeare wrote based upon English chronicle and classical biography? Or is it the first of the romances, a late group of four plays which celebrate a return to life after the preoccupation with death in the tragedies? Is its dominant mood realistic, critical, or triumphant? How indeed can we reach conclusions about a play, many have asked, in which the atmosphere ranges from that of grimly political Rome to flamboyantly self-indulgent Egypt, the tone from cynicism to apotheosis, and the human goals from world domination to fullness of life? Are Antony and Cleopatra consistently drawn throughout, or do they undergo unaccountable changes? Are poetry and drama at odds in *Antony* or do they enrich and deepen each other in ways which are new even for Shakespeare? Clearly, either-or answers will not help us with this drama. We shall have to study it from various points of view.

Let us begin, however, with a tentative assumption and some discriminations. Our critics will shortly question all of these hypotheses.

The heroic, tragic, romantic, and satiric modes form a unity in *Antony*. The play thus achieves an equilibrium which is as subtle and challenging to some readers as it is puzzling or disturbing to others. Defenders of each of these modes emphasize a different Antony and a different response to him. Defenders of (1) the heroic emphasize the hero's cousinship with the gods and our feelings of admiration. Defenders of (2) the tragic emphasize the hero's middle position between the gods and men; this response traditionally combines both sympathy or identification and withdrawal or alienation—or, in Aristotle's terms, pity and terror. Defenders of (3) the romantic emphasize the hero in love in a world of wonders where dreams come true. And finally, defenders of (4) the satiric emphasize the hero mocked and undercut in ways that distance him from our affections. The heroic has often been a component of the tragic, and nowhere more impressively than in this play. Yet critics are divided concerning this alliance, and especially the ways in which the play's soaring Brobdingnagian imagery (to use S. L. Bethell's term) prompts us to admire characters whose "tragic flaws" seem more marked than those of Shakespeare's earlier protagonists. Antony and Cleopatra must either be more fallible than their finest hours suggest or stronger than their weaknesses permit us to acknowledge. Tillyard states the problem succinctly:

The vacillations of Antony and his neglect of duty, the cunning and cruelty of Cleopatra, find no part in the creatures who are transfigured in death; they remain unassimilated, held in tension against the pair's expiring nobilities. The reason why *Antony and Cleopatra* is so baffling a play (and why the rhapsodies it provokes tend to be hysterical) is that the effort to see the two main characters simultaneously in two different guises taxes our strength beyond our capacities. And yet that effort has to be made. Those who see Antony as the erring hero merely, and his final exaltation as ironic infatuation, are as partial in their judgment as those who think that his final heroics wash out his previous frailties. Both sets are part right, but each needs the other's truth to support it.[1]

Isn't a delicate balance of opposing qualities characteristic of Shakespeare's late tragic vision? As Aristotle's catharsis implies, doesn't paradox lie at the heart of the tragic experience? In tragedy we are asked to take complicated journeys through what Pascal called "the grandeur of the misery of man." In this chapter we shall touch upon some of the approaches (beginning with the third listed above) which make it difficult to respond fully to the play's various elements: tragic, heroic, and romantic; pagan and Christian; classical and Renaissance. Predictably perhaps, the divergent opinions we shall survey usually revolve around Shakespeare's treatment of love and Cleopatra, around the relationship of tragedy to romance, especially as it concerns sexual passion.

The central role of Cleopatra, Shakespeare's greatest female protagonist, like that of Falstaff, Shakespeare's greatest clown, has proved to be endlessly fascinating. Both characters are so full of life that they resist all moral categories. This is the heart of the problem.

THE CRITICS AND THE LOVE AFFAIR

In confronting Antony, even those who are well read in Shakespeare finds themselves compelled to reevaluate their expectations and assumptions. In retrospect, we can see why some of the best critics have a qualified response to the play. Samuel Johnson writes of Shakespeare in his Preface to the plays (1765):

> His first defect is that to which may be imputed most of the evil in books or in men. He sacrifices virtue to convenience, and is so much more careful to please than to instruct, that he seems to write without any moral purpose. From his writings indeed a system of social duty may be selected, for he that thinks reasonably must think morally; but his precepts and axioms drop casually from him; he makes no just distribution of good or evil, nor is always careful to shew in the virtuous a disapprobation of the wicked; he carries his persons indifferently through right and wrong, and at the close dismisses them without further care, and leaves their examples to operate by chance. This fault the barbarity of his age cannot extenuate; for it is always a writer's duty to make the world better, and justice is a virtue independent of time or place.

Do we today find that a "just distribution of good or evil" constitutes a "moral purpose"? In what sense do we feel that the writer should "make the world better"? Another assumption of Johnson's is especially awkward in relation to Antony. He is contrasting Shakespeare favorably with other playwrights:

> Upon every other stage the universal agent is love, by whose power all good and devil is distributed, and every action quickened or retarded. . . . But love is only one of many passions; and as it has no great influence upon the sum of life, it has little operation in the dramas of a poet, who caught his ideas from the living world, and exhibited only what he saw before him. He knew, that any other passion, as it was regular or exorbitant, was a cause of happiness or calamity.

Though we might laugh at assertions that love "has no great influence" on life or that Shakespeare feels that "regular" passions lead to happiness, we should nevertheless ask ourselves what preconceptions we have, peculiar to ourselves or our age, that render a sympathetic response to Antony difficult. We shall consider some of these in the next section on tragedy and the heroic.

D. J. Enright—after observing that some of his students view Antony as a "dirty old man" and Cleopatra as an "ageing prostitute"—slyly turns on the teachers:

> It does not seem probable that many academics, either, are fitted by nature or experience to find the play moving, or not in any way other than the detachedly moralistic. Cleopatra in turn has few qualities to fit her for domestic life in an academic community.[2]

This is the crux of the matter. The play demands that we reassess our response to life itself. This of course is not easy. W. K. Wimsatt feels that the play confronts us with "immoral acts" and "evil choices":

> There is no escaping the fact that the poetic splendour of this play, and in particular of its concluding scenes, is something which exists in closest juncture with the acts of suicide and with the whole glorified story of passion. The poetic values are strictly dependent—if not upon the immorality as such—yet upon the immoral acts. Even though, or rather because, the play pleads for certain evil choices, it presents these choices in all their mature interest and capacity to arouse human sympathy.[3]

Though Wimsatt qualifies it carefully, his conclusion is that

> the greatest poems for the Christian will never be . . . the great though immoral. . . . *Antony and Cleopatra* will not be so great as *King Lear*. The testimony of the critical tradition would seem to confirm this. The greatest poetry will be morally right, even though perhaps obscurely so. . . .[4]

Whether Christian or not, we may have deeper doubts concerning what is "morally right," doubts suggested by Wimsatt's "obscurely." Because Una Ellis-Fermor feels that tragedy cannot approximate the final vision of religion, she calls it an "interim reading" of human life. Many modern readers, however, may adopt a position similar to that of I. A. Richards: "Tragedy is only possible to a mind which is for the moment agnostic or Manichean. The least touch of any theology which has a compensating Heaven to offer the tragic hero is fatal."[5] In the light of these varying remarks, how are we to interpret Cleopatra's vision ("Husband, I come") at the end of *Antony*?

Some critics, like Bernard Shaw, have often maintained that questions of truth or falsehood are irrelevant to Shakespeare. And E. E. Stoll, rightly disturbed by those who see Shakespeare chiefly as a philosopher, claims that Shakespeare's purpose "was to reveal not truth but beauty, to imitate and ennoble life, not analyze or expound it." But can such a remark do justice to our experience of the play? Robert Ornstein raises the discussion to a different level when he observes in *Antony* the unity of truth, reason, and imagination:

> We lose the profounder meanings of *Antony and Cleopatra* if we insist that questions of truth and honesty are irrelevant to Cleopatra or that her splendid poetic vision is beyond reason itself. For nothing else is at stake

in the final scene than the honesty of the imagination and the superiority of its truths to the facts of imperial conquest.[6]

Throughout this essay, we shall attempt to determine what is meant by relationships in the play between "truth" and "honesty of the imagination."

Not only is it difficult to place this play in relation to a system of absolutes, it is often difficult to know what its final emphases are. Willard Farnham, who feels that the world is not "well lost" by the lovers and that Antony is at his best in Rome, considers that Antony's struggle for world leadership, not his love, is central. He wonders why, if love is paramount, the play does not open with the scene on the Cydnus![7] But clearly we must accept the play as it is and follow carefully wherever it leads. A few readers feel that the play oversimplifies experience. John Danby finds the drama so sharply polarized that it cannot finally be seen as a unity:

> Cleopatra has been loved by recent commentators not wisely but too well. As Caesar impersonates the world, she, of course, incarnates the flesh. Part of Shakespeare's sleight of hand in the play—his trickery with our normal standards and powers of judgment—is to construct an account of the human universe consisting of only these two terms. There is no suggestion that the dichotomy is resolvable: unless we are willing to take the delusions of either party as a resolution—the "universal peace" of Caesar, the Egypt-beyond-the-grave of Antony and Cleopatra in their autotoxic exaltations before they kill themselves.[8]

Danby's allegorical reading and his "of course" should put us on our guard. Clearly Danby declares a plague on both Rome and Egypt. He speaks further of a "missing third term" in the play: it is

> the deliberate construction of a world without a Cordelia, Shakespeare's symbol for a reality that transcends the political and the personal and "redeems nature from the general curse/ Which twain have brought her to." . . . The excision . . . explains what might be regarded as a diminution of scope in *Antony and Cleopatra*. (We are, of course, only comparing Shakespeare with himself.) The theme of Rome and Egypt, however, is simpler than the theme of "Nature," the trick of using the contraries (again, for Shakespeare) relatively an easy way of organizing the universe.[9]

But how does Shakespeare complicate his use of "contraries"? Why need the structuring through polarities suggest a "trick"? In what ways are these opposites a part of life itself? Is Cordelia primarily a "symbol"? And how are the roles of Cordelia and Cleopatra in the two plays more alike than Danby realizes? Are the perspectives for one Shakespearean play fully appropriate for another?

L. C. Knights finds a willful and contrived quality at the end of the lovers' affair:

Looking back, we can recall how often this love has seemed to thrive on emotional stimulants. They were necessary for much the same reason as the feasts and wine. For the continued references to feasting—and it is not only Caesar and his dry Romans who emphasize the Alexandrian consumption of food and drink—are not simply a means of intensifying the imagery of tasting and savouring that is a constant accompaniment of the love theme; they serve to bring out the element of repetition and monotony in a passion which, centering on itself, is self-consuming, leading ultimately to what Antony himself, in a most pregnant phrase, names as "the heart of loss." . . . The figure that Cleopatra evokes [at the end] may not be fancy—the poetry invests it with a substantial reality; but it is not the Antony that the play has given us; it is something disengaged from, or glimpsed through, that Antony. Nor should the power and beauty of Cleopatra's last great speech obscure the continued presence of something self-deceiving and unreal. She may speak of the baby at her breast that sucks the nurse asleep; but it is not, after all, a baby—new life; it is simply death.

It is, of course, one of the signs of a great writer that he can *afford* to evoke sympathy or even admiration for what, in his final judgement, is discarded or condemned. In *Antony and Cleopatra* the sense of potentiality in life's untutored energies is pushed to its limit, and Shakespeare gives the maximum weight to an experience that is finally "placed." It is perhaps this that makes the tragedy so sombre in its realism, so little comforting to the romantic imagination.[10]

In relation to this love affair, Knights quotes Martin Buber's *I and Thou*: "There is no evil impulse till the impulse has been separated from the being. . . ." But where do we find this separation in the play? What evidence do we have that the love of the pair is "placed"? Do we feel at the end of this tragedy "simply death"? Other critics have even seen Cleopatra's love as a polar evil, associated with death. Benedetto Croce makes assumptions about life and art that we must question. In a passage that might apply to *Antony*, he speaks of a kind of tragedy in which

the will, instead of holding the passions in control—making its footstool of them—allows itself to be dominated by them in their onrush; or it seeks the good, but remains uncertain, dissatisfied as to the path chosen; or finally, when it fails to find its own way, a way of some sort, and does not know what to think of itself or of the world, it preys upon itself in this empty tension.

Croce calls this condition "voluptuousness," which "truly is death, if not physical, yet always internal and moral death, death of the spirit, without which man is already a corpse in process of decomposition. The tragedy of *Antony and Cleopatra* is composed of the violent sense of pleasure, in its power to bind and to dominate, coupled with a shudder at its abject effects of dissolution and death."[11] Anyone who feels that the sensuousness of this play implies the "death of the spirit" is going to find rough weather in *Antony*. Plato was among the first to develop the theory that poetry evokes emotions which cannot be allayed and are therefore dangerous to the state. Norman Holland, however, poses critical questions about views of this kind:

> *Antony and Cleopatra* is the tragedy of two worlds, one bountiful, plenteous; the other competitive, stingy, confining. . . . [T]his play seems closest to *The Merchant of Venice;* there, too, the play juxtaposed two worlds, the world of Shylock's Venice, a man's world, harsh, hard-boiled, realistic, competitive, a scarcity economy; the world of Portia's Belmont, a woman's world, full of plenty, of giving, of love, and feasting. Critics and audiences often talk as though Antony were some sort of a flawed tragic victim, as though it were a flaw in him not to be tending to his warlike business, slaughtering people, starving himself, and fighting Caesar, instead of enjoying himself in Alexandria. Is pleasure wrong? Is it such a right and noble thing to be like Caesar? . . . By contrast with the generous, comfortable world Cleopatra offers, Caesar seems to me simply cold and nasty. It is really better to be a Spartan than an Athenian?[12]

Yet other critics find everything in *Antony* ambiguous. Ernest Schanzer considers it one of Shakespeare's "problem plays," and he sees Shakespeare's strategy here as a "technique of 'dramatic coquetry,' consisting in an alternate enlisting and repelling of the audience's affections."[13] L. C. Knights, as we might expect, contrasts *Antony* unfavorably with plays like *Macbeth,* where "we are never in any doubt of our moral bearings." Knights continues, *"Antony and Cleopatra,* on the other hand, embodies different and apparently irreconcilable evaluations of the central experience."[14] But in what Shakespearean tragedy are our "moral bearings" fully clear from the beginning? If Knights is correct, how are we to arrive at a coherent view of the play? G. K. Hunter sees the values of the play as less ambiguous than frozen: "The later tragedies offer the alternative heroisms of stone or water, of petrifaction or deliquescence; death can be shown to seal the opposite magnificences of Timon and Antony, but in neither case can it conceal the price that has been paid—the abandonment of the good ordinariness of a life lived among compromises."[15] Why do "good ordinariness" and "compromises" suggest the life of a minor character rather than that of a hero? Aware of this problem, Hunter says that nowhere in the last plays "does the individual hero succeed in creating a new world of value inside himself, finding the point of growth which will absorb and transmute the world as it is. The temporizing and compromising society is rejected, but the rejection leaves the hero maimed and incomplete."[16] But has Hunter, like Danby, ignored the contribution of Cleopatra and Act V to *Antony?* Unlike most tragedies, this play has two equally important protagonists. Bradley, referring to Antony in the opening speeches and rejecting sharp dichotomies, says, "Neither the phrase 'a strumpet's fool,' nor the assertion 'the nobleness of life is to do thus,' answers to the total effect of the play. But the truths they exaggerate are equally essential. . . ."[17] Our attempt will be to bring these truths within hailing distance of each other.

Antony portrays the richest relationship between the sexes in Shakespeare. The play shows the qualities that render love of such complexity to be at once doomed and triumphant. Power and love are two of the great polar opposites in Shakespeare; the relationship between these qualities varies throughout his career. Max Weber suggests that this conflict is at the heart of human life: "The genius or demon of politics lives in an inner tension with the god of love. . . . This tension can at any time lead to an irreconcilable conflict." There are few plays in the world in which this *agon* is portrayed with as much force as it is in *Antony*. Since a related struggle is within all of us and is today being sharpened by many crises in our culture, we should find this play particularly interesting. Its portrait of love has often seemed shocking, and yet it has long had defenders. Both the title and emphasis of John Dryden's rewriting of the play, *All for Love; or, The World Well Lost* (1677), point up the puzzles we face in Shakespeare. Are both lovers, or is one, or neither, "all for love"? Throughout the play, sporadically, at the end, or doubtfully, if at any time? Is Caesar's world well lost by the pair or by Shakespeare? Do we concur in its being lost? Does "well" connote "good riddance" or "thoroughly"? As we have seen, many readers have wished to render unto Caesar far more than Dryden did in his play.

Perhaps inevitably, a new appreciation of the "romance" elements in *Antony* begins with the Romantic movement. Coleridge first took the measure of the special character of this tragedy. He writes that Shakespeare "always makes vice odious and virtue admirable," and we wonder how he is using these terms. But his sympathy for the range of experience in the play is remarkable:

> The highest praise or rather form of praise, of this play which I can offer in my own mind, is the doubt which its perusal always occasions in me, whether it is not in all exhibitions of a giant power in its strength and vigor of maturity, a formidable rival of the *Macbeth, Lear, Othello,* and *Hamlet. Feliciter audax* is the motto for its style comparatively with his other works, even as it is the general motto of all his works compared with those of other poets. Be it remembered too, that this happy valiancy of style is but the representative and result of all the material excellencies so exprest.
>
> This play should be perused in mental contrast with Romeo and Juliet; —as the love of passion and appetite opposed to the love of affection and instinct. But the art displayed in the character of Cleopatra is profound in this, especially, that the sense of criminality in her passion is lessened by our insight into its depth and energy, at the very moment that we cannot but perceive that the passion itself springs out of the habitual

craving of a licentious nature, and that it is supported and reinforced by voluntary stimulus and sought-for associations, instead of blossoming out of spontaneous emotion.

But of all perhaps of Shakespeare's plays the most wonderful is the *Antony and Cleopatra*. [There are] scarcely any in which he has followed history more minutely, and yet few even of his own in which he impresses the notion of giant strength so much, perhaps none in which he impresses it more strongly.[18]

Coleridge applies phrases to the play which have been echoed for a century and a half: "a giant power in its strength and vigor" and "happy valiancy of style" ("*Feliciter audax*"). As we have seen, the power of the play has perplexed critics who see it as out of phase with Shakespeare's other tragedies or as a late play which does not conform to earlier and expected patterns. But how can we view a play which so profoundly explores the nature of love as less meaningful than earlier tragedies (through *Macbeth*) which are often more concerned with injustice and evil? To approach the mysteriousness of *Antony*, we must seek, in Coleridge's words, "that willing suspension of disbelief for the moment, which constitutes poetic faith."

A cluster of feelings like those suggested by Blake's proverbs in *The Marriage of Heaven and Hell* (1790) are relevant to our response to *Antony*:

Without Contraries is no progression. Attraction and Repulsion, Reason and Energy, Love and Hate, are necessary to Human existence./ From these contraries spring what the religious call Good & Evil. Good is the passive that obeys Reason. Evil is the active springing from Energy. . . ./ Energy is the only life, and is from the Body; and Reason is the bound or outward circumference of Energy./ Energy is Eternal Delight. . . ./ Those who restrain desire, do so because theirs is weak enough to be restrained. . . ./ The road of excess leads to the palace of wisdom./ Prudence is a rich, ugly, old maid courted by Incapacity. . . ./ If the fool would persist in his folly he would become wise. . . ./ Exuberance is Beauty./ If the lion was advised by the fox, he would be cunning. . . .

These startling proverbs of hell, in which we find a transvaluation of good and evil, confront us with disturbing perspectives similar to those we face in this tragedy. The play's emphasis upon the contraries of power and love, upon energy, the body, excess, folly, and exuberance, is pervasive. Blake's sayings, complicated and often satiric in context, are pertinent to the outrageousness of *Antony*, its flouting of common sense, and its defiance of conventional responses. We all know, of course, that for most of us daily life cannot be lived on the play's terms. We can scarcely turn to *Antony* seeking patterns for ordinary behavior. But why are tragedy and the heroic rarely concerned with such behavior? In a line (which might almost serve as a motto for parts of the play) from Shakespeare's poem concerning the death of true love, *The Phoenix and the Turtle,* he writes that "Love hath reason, reason none." But we must obviously be careful about equating later or even earlier views of love with those of Shakespeare.

TRAGEDY AND THE HEROIC

We have looked at some of the views of *Antony* as a play about love. Two other modes combine to shape the world of *Antony:* the tragic and the heroic. Both here suggest uncompromising attitudes. McFarland says we learn in this play that "one must cast his lot either completely with the world, or completely with love. The moralistic trimmer has no place."[19] Generalizing, Bradley says that the lesser man can easily make compromises impossible for the hero. And Northrop Frye emphasizes that death is the touchstone of the tragic.

> The basis of the tragic vision is being in time, the sense of the one-directional quality of life, where everything happens once and for all, where every act brings unavoidable and fateful consequences, and where all experience vanishes, not simply into the past, but into nothingness, annihilation. In the tragic vision death is, not an incident in life, not even the inevitable end of life, but the essential event that gives shape and form to life. Death is what defines the individual, and marks him off from the continuity of life that flows indefinitely between the past and the future.[20]

In what way is this view of death pertinent to the death of Antony? Of Cleopatra? Frye also says that tragedy is existential:

> The experience of the tragic cannot be moralized or contained within any conceptual world-view. A tragic hero is a tragic hero whether he is a good or a bad man; a tragic action is a tragic action whether it seems to us admirable or villainous, inevitable or arbitrary. And while a religious or philosophical system that answers all questions and solves all problems may find a place for tragedy, and so make it a part of a larger and less tragic whole, it can never absorb the kind of experience that tragedy represents. That remains outside of all approaches to being through thought rather than existence. The remark of the dying Hotspur, "Thought's the slave of life," comes out of the heart of the tragic vision.[21]

How does Frye's statement concerning the independence of tragedy and morality correspond to our experience of *Antony?* Frye objects to anyone's providing a

> justification for a tragic action that comes from something outside tragedy, and so, really, explaining tragedy away. In authentic tragedy what we see as external to us is, first of all, the order of nature, with its servomechanism the wheel of fortune. Nature and fortune, when seen from the point of view of the human situation, constitute a vision of absurdity and anguish,

what design is in them being unintelligible to human imagination, human emotions, and ultimately to human moral instincts.[22]

The relentlessness of Caesar's rising and Antony's falling on fortune's wheel cannot be explained. Even the Soothsayer can only read a little in nature's "infinite book of secrecy." The experience of tragedy is an act of collaboration, Frye continues, a participation so intimate that in the theater the audience becomes part of the "substance" of the hero:

> Tragedy individualizes the audience, nowhere more intensely than in the tragedy of isolation. Man is a creator as an individual; as a member of a society or species, he is a creature. The end of a comedy leaves him creaturely, invited to join a party to celebrate the creation of a new society, from the further fortunes of which he is of course excluded by the ending of the play. The end of a tragedy leaves him alone in a waste and void chaos of experience with a world to remake out of it. It is partly because of this insistent challenge to the spectator's re-creative powers that the great tragedies are so endlessly fascinating to critics: merely to experience them seems to demand commentary as part of one's response.[23]

Paradoxically, the inevitability of defeat in tragedy also releases in the hero an almost superhuman energy, and the inevitability of death evokes the richest resources in human nature. Only the fact of defeat and death makes this spiritual triumph possible. No lesser challenge can have this effect. It is only a Cleopatra committed to death who can make the fallen Antony a cosmic god and the triumphant Caesar an "ass/ Unpolicied." McFarland wonders

> whether the conception of catharsis, of a purgation of pity and terror in the onlooker, is not too negative to account for the magnificence and intensity of the emotional process involved in Antony and Cleopatra. We may inspect our own emotions and conclude that the presence of joy, not the absence of pity and terror, describes our state at the end of the play. We finish the play not with composure but with exhilaration, and the realm toward which we are directed is not the painless but the beatific.
>
> For tragedy does not deal with death; tragedy deals with life. We see in tragedy not the meeting of an end, but the conduct of an existence. If all of us were immortal in this earthly life, then the bare fact of a man's demise would indeed assume awesome proportions; but we all die, and what matters is not the when of death but the how of life.
>
> The theme of tragedy is life, not death. In the great Shakespearean plays the protagonist always has the choice either of accepting a death that defines his life at its highest level, or of avoiding death and descending to a lower level of life, to a level of breathing non-existence. He is always presented with a choice, and we may thus define the tragic protagonist, in his most basic characteristic, as a being who chooses life rather than death. Nietzsche has counseled us not to look too long into the abyss, for fear the abyss begins to look back into us. For most of us the eye of the abyss early begins to exert an hypnotic power, and our very existences are

compromised by its gaze. Man is compounded of being and non-being, and non-being is ever encroaching upon his being. The symbols of the abyss, time and death, ever more powerfully dictate his action. Fear of time causes him to mortgage his present being for the future; fear of death causes him to desert the fullness of life. And in smaller symbols, the abyss, as prudence, as foresight, as all the many trimming virtues of daily life, deludes him with its hypothesis of an existence horizontally extended into unlimited time, rather than an existence vertically elevated into brief eternity. . . .

"We ask," McFarland says,

only one thing of the tragic protagonist, that he be truly alive. In Shakespeare's plays it is always the quality of life, as epitomized by the quality of feeling, that identifies the tragic protagonist. The quality of life, not the quality of thought. . . . We feel no sadness at the death of the tragic protagonist; we feel rather exhilaration at his life. We should speak not of the tragic fall, but of the tragic elevation.[24]

Both McFarland and Frye underline the importance of feeling and experience, rather than thought, in tragedy. Why? Can Frye's emphasis on death and McFarland's on life be reconciled? How does the phrase "tragic elevation" suggest the inadequacy of the familiar "tragic flaw"? In emphasizing not the hero's limitation but his stature, Frye says that because

the heroic is above the normal limits of experience, it also suggests something infinite imprisoned in the finite. This something infinite may be morally either good or bad, for the worst of men may still be a hero if he is big enough to anger or frighten the gods. Man may be infinite if he is infinite only in his evil desires. The hero is an individual, but being so great an individual he seems constantly on the point of being swept into titanic forces he cannot control. The fact that an infinite energy is driving towards death in tragedy means that the impetus of tragedy is *sacrificial*. Sacrifice expresses the principle that in human life the infinite takes the same direction as the finite.

Tragedy, then, shows us the impact of heroic energy on the human situation. The heroic is normally destroyed in the conflict, and the human situation goes on surviving. "A living dog is better than a dead lion," says the Preacher. . . .[25]

Frye's prudent preacher gives the little man's response to the hero's attempt to alter the very nature of things. As scapegoat or sacrificial figure, the hero takes ultimate risks for us. Why?

Almost by definition, tragedy turns worldly defeat into spiritual victory, and yet this play takes a step beyond tragedy. The play is balanced between the emphasis of the earlier tragedies on time and death and that of the last romances on nature and eternity. The conception of the heroic which Shakespeare derived in part from Plutarch (in

North's translation) and other classical writers renders *Antony* a special kind of drama. Eugene Waith refers to the heroic as it was characterized in the Renaissance by the Italian epic poet Tasso. Tasso "distinguishes between moral virtue, which consists in a mean between extremes, and heroic virtue, which is 'I know not what greatness, and an excess, so to speak, of virtue.' [Tasso] supports his argument with references to both Plato and Aristotle, associating heroic virtue closely with understanding and with magnanimity. . . . His essay emphasizes the inclusiveness of this sort of virtue, in which every virtue is represented. . . ."[26] How is this emphasis upon heroic rather than moral virtue, upon an "excess" of virtue, relevant to both of our protagonists? Dorothea Krook further defines the heroic and the magnanimous in the classical tradition:

> If the tragic and the heroic, though connected, are different, what then are the defining virtues of the heroic view of life? They are, I suggest, the virtues subsumed by that virtue which is head and crown of the Aristotelian scheme in the *Nicomachean Ethics,* which in Greek is called *megalopsuchia,* commonly translated *magnanimity* from the Latin *magnanimitas,* but in its full inclusiveness perhaps best rendered in English by the words *greatness* (of soul) or *nobility.*[27]

Antony is Shakespeare's prime example of the heroic man in love. He comes out of a tradition which, as Waith observes, goes back to Hercules and Omphale. Maurice Charney speaks of the language through which the grandeur of the lovers is conveyed.

> The dramatic use of similes and personifications in *Antony and Cleopatra* is part of a larger stylistic purpose very different from the ordered perfection of *Julius Caesar.* The characteristic figure in *Antony and Cleopatra* is the hyperbole, or what Puttenham in his *Arte of English Poesie* (1589) calls "for his immoderate excesse . . . the ouer reacher" or "the loud lyer," and he defines it as "by incredible comparison giuing credit." In Greek, "hyperbole" is "a *throwing beyond: an overshooting, superiority, excess* in anything . . ." (Lidell-Scott Dictionary). It would include the ideas of extravagance and boldness as well as exaggeration and overstatement. In essence, hyperbole is the reaching-out of the imagination for superlatives.[28]

Readers sometimes question whether at the end of the play poetry is doing too much of the work of drama. Is this language merely rhetoric, which Yeats called the will doing the work of the imagination? If we deny that the play's superlatives partly determine its meaning, we risk the fatal separation between matter and manner implied in Dryden's Preface to *Troilus and Cressida:* "If Shakespeare were stripped of all the bombasts in his passion, and dressed in the most vulgar words, we should find the beauties of his thoughts remaining; if his embroideries were burnt down, there would still be silver at the bottom of the melting-pot." The entire critical tradition since Coleridge argues against this divorce between thought and language. Why?

Some readers have felt that the heroic overwhelms the tragic in *Antony,* and they are disturbed by this feeling. Bradley was among the first to pose important questions about our response to the play:

> Why is it that, although we close the book in a triumph which is more than reconciliation, this is mingled, as we look back on the story, with a sadness so peculiar, almost the sadness of disenchantment? Is it that, when the glow has faded, Cleopatra's ecstasy comes to appear, I would not say factitious, but an effort strained and prodigious as well as glorious, not, like Othello's last speech, the final expression of character, of thoughts and emotions which have dominated a whole life? Perhaps this is so, but there is something more, something that sounds paradoxical: we are saddened by the very fact that the catastrophe saddens us so little; it pains us that we should feel so much triumph and pleasure.[29]

The tension between the vaulting heroic and doomed tragic is apparent throughout the play. How can we best respond to it? In what respects might the "triumph and pleasure" which we experience in Act V persuade us to widen our definition of tragedy? Is there a sadistic or masochistic element in our enjoyment of tragedy, as some psychologists have suggested? Are we saddened when we are not pained? We shall examine later whether Cleopatra's final appearances are "strained and prodigious" or the "final expression of character."

Since Aristotle's defense of tragedy against Plato's attack, many critics have commented on the therapeutic effects of tragedy. Morse Peckham takes an unusual position. The reader of a work of art experiences "discontinuity of experience, not continuity; disorder, not order; emotional disturbance, not emotional catharsis." Art exposes man "to the tensions and problems of a false world so that man may endure exposing himself to the tensions and problems of the real world."[30] Walter Slatoff and others have wisely observed that we probably err in assuming that all of the problems in a work of art are solved. Much of the exhilaration that we experience in reading may derive from our attempts to cope with disjunctions or discontinuities in novels or plays.[31] How can we discriminate, however, between what might be unsolved problems in *Antony* and our own failure to read well? In a serio-comic vein, Frye mentions one advantage of our reading:

> One great value of tragedy as a form of art is that it corrupts and weakens our heroism, refining our sensibilities by sapping our courage. It makes a fuss about murder and brutality, instead of accepting them as necessary pleasures of life. The tragedy of passion is in a peculiar sense the audience's tragedy. . . .[32]

Can Frye's position be reconciled with the earlier views?

Roy Morrell, bringing together some of these positions, compares the experience of catharsis in tragedy to that of transference in psycho-analysis:

> The distinctive appeal of Tragedy can only be explained by going beyond the pleasure principle; we suffer an ordeal, face life at its most difficult and complex, but derive pleasure in the new readiness and power we have gained thereby. . . . We feel more deeply and subtly, act more courageously, more passionately, in [the hero], and all the time with the conviction that it is true to life, a fuller life than our own.

Morrell says that we experience courage in tragedy—"not mere tough-ness, nor bravado, nor the will to display power, but simply calmness and readiness, the discovery that even in the harshest experiences there is, to quote Richards, 'no difficulty'; the difficulty arises from the illusions and subterfuges by which we seek to dodge reality, and which we unconsciously fear are going to betray us." Once again, how can Frye's view of the role of heroism and courage in tragedy be recon-ciled with that of Morrell? Morrell phrases his central question thus: "Does Tragedy provide the individual in the audience with a means of expansion through empathy . . . and then, *but only in the destruc-tion of the hero,* free the individual, break his empathy at the point where it is in danger of becoming a fixation, where his fantasies might otherwise usurp the energies required for real life?" And Morrell con-cludes that "Tragedy is man's rehearsal of the harsher realities of life; by it the psyche's cell is forced out of its lethargy, its conservative instinctive life-cycle where it is only delusively secure." In the hero's tragic end, he says, and the end "of the hopes we had in him, there is nothing defeatist; for only in his failure is some connection, some 'transference' between us and our fantasy life in the play, broken, and our own energies set free."[33] Where and how in the play is our identi-fication with Antony and Cleopatra rendered most intense or com-plete? By what means are we distanced from the protagonists and are "our own energies set free"?

Holland compares our psychological response to comedy with that to tragedy:

> It is a necessary condition for tragedy that the defenses it embodies fail, leading to punishment for an impulse toward pleasure; it is a necessary condition for comedy that it build up a defense, leading to gratification without punishment of an impulse toward pleasure. Perhaps this is why tragedy "feels" deeper, more significant to us, comedy much less so: because in one, defense breaks down; in the other, a defense against unconscious material is set up.[34]

How can we compare Holland's view that in tragedy "defense breaks down" with Richards' that we experience in tragedy "no difficulty"? McFarland writes of the transfiguring power of tragedy:

The tragic mirror is . . . a shield of Perseus by whose artifice we look on what would otherwise freeze and congeal our sight. "If in real life," says Cassirer, "we had to endure all those emotions through which we live in Sophocles's *Oedipus* or in Shakespeare's *King Lear* we should scarcely survive the shock and strain. But art turns all these pains and outrages, these cruelties and atrocities, into a means of self-liberation, thus giving us an inner freedom which cannot be attained in any other way."[35]

In what ways are the psychological, philosophical, and aesthetic approaches to tragedy and the heroic similar? In what respects are they at odds?

32

ANTONY, CLEOPATRA, AND CAESAR: ACTS I AND II

BEGINNING THE PLAY

The apparently relaxed and spacious, or, we might almost say, cinematic, construction of *Antony and Cleopatra* and the complexity of its protagonists have generated a library of diverse opinion. Dr. Johnson said that the play's events "are produced without any art of connexion or care of disposition." But like many of Shakespeare's plays, *Antony* is an episodic drama in which the action is organized around key scenes or groups of scenes. Does such a statement imply that the play is poorly organized? By no means. Its movement is organic, it rises and falls, it builds slowly or rapidly toward one climax after another. Can we read the play therefore chiefly in terms of its high points? Again no, for even short transitional scenes afford us valuable insights into character and event. With its seven different settings (Rome, Alexandria, Messina, Misenum, Syria, Athens, and Actium) and its 52 indicated exits and entrances, *Antony* opens before us one of Shakespeare's largest worlds. The word "world," incidentally, occurs more than 40 times in the play, more than in any other.

The tragedy's flouting of the unities of time and space has puzzled many readers. But our first questions should be: What is Shakespeare seeking to convey through this most flexible and seemingly unpredictable of plots? Are the troubling elements—the slow build-up of the action, the many shifts of scene, the juxtapositions of the heroic and comic—signs of a loss of Shakespeare's skill, as some have claimed, or of a new delicacy and subtlety in his study of human life? Are there structural relationships here that are neither casual nor causal? What names should we give to these? Emrys Jones feels that the drama's movements around the Mediterranean world are plotted with great care. In the play's use of "structural syntax, with its nice sense of the temporal measurement of space, *Antony and Cleopatra* is possibly the most sensitive of all the plays; in its care for the nuances of scenic sequence lies much of its formal excellence." What instances do we find of Shakespeare's "temporal measurement of space"? Are there also spacial measurements of time in the play? Jones says that even the apparent off-handedness of the first two acts is part of an overall design: "the fullest answer to the question 'What keeps these scenes from lapsing into formlessness?' is simply that, for all their concern with rendering the random flow of events, they are in fact themselves exquisitely ordered: the sequence is a marvel of minute plotting—and any illusion of life-likeness should not be confused with the reality of formidable artistry. Every small episode is in its place; the order of the sequence cannot be changed without loss."[1]

Experiment with the reordering of these scenes, even with the order of events or speeches within scenes. Only the first act and scene are marked as such in the First Folio of 1623, the only reliable text (and a very good one) for the play. Other act and scene divisions were all added by Rowe and Dyce and later editors. Do the present divisions for Act I and Act II make good dramatic sense? What titles might be appropriate for the first two acts? For later acts? Should the opening group of scenes of exposition run through I, v, or II, i? Should the scenes of attempted reconciliation run through II, vii, or III, i?

If we expect to be confronted at the beginning of the play by the ominous tragic mood that confronts us at the outset in *Hamlet, King Lear,* or *Macbeth,* we shall be disconcerted or disappointed. This play unfolds in an entirely different way. We can guess at Shakespeare's purpose here, as Jones observes, from

> the effect his technique of short scenes has on the audience. At a performance we become aware that our attention is being solicited in a certain way: in the first half of the play particularly, we are being required to look and watch, take notice, compare, essentially to let our understanding play over the scene. What we are not required to do is to become emotionally engaged to any great depth; indeed the structure of the scenes forbids it. For the action is continually breaking off without enlisting any strong emotional allegiance. Not, of course, that the dramatic material is dull or lifeless; it is, on the contrary, everywhere vivacious, full of

personality and quick human awareness. But the rapid succession of little scenes, together with the emotional instability of some of its characters, breeds a sense of irony, even of comedy (again, especially in the first half) which does not allow an emotional response, although—such is the complexity of the play's mode—it does not rule out what might be called an intense affectionate involvement. . . .[2]

How helpful is Jones' distinction between "emotional allegiance" and "affectionate involvement," in our response to the opening scenes? Jones finally says that the tone of the play combines

intimacy with detachment. The style, allusive and particularized ('A certain queen to Caesar in a mattress') permits an intimacy of imaginative response; yet the technique of short scenes enforces a certain detachment. The constant interruptions to the dialogue and the restless shifting of points of view have the effect of encouraging reflection and a tentative evaluation of what is going on before us. The play's irony is of a humane, tolerant kind, not ever as harsh and reductive as that of, say, *Troilus and Cressida*. We are induced to assume a contemplative posture: unsparingly observant but sympathetic, and finally acquiescent. We have the means of passing judgement, but we refrain from doing so. This is the vision of the historical poet, as Shakespeare conceived it in this play.[3]

What else in the play prompts us to be "finally acquiescent" though refraining from "passing judgment"? L. C. Knights points out that the "mildly hypnogenic" effect of Shakespeare's poetry enables us to entertain as hypotheses what our experience would lead us to reject, and he quotes Wilson Knight on the relationship between our past and our present reading: "the memory will always try to reject the imagination." How then can we best approach a play with the unexpected dimensions of *Antony*?

The first scene of the play is a masterpiece of condensation. The play opens and closes with tableaux as formal as Renaissance paintings, as Reuben Brower points out. The ten lines of the first speech, like a ramp up to the play, give us, as in other tragedies (*Julius Caesar, Othello, King Lear,* and *Macbeth*), a complicated or unsympathetic view of the protagonists. What is the dramatic purpose of this initially negative appraisal? Many of the play's characteristic figures of speech and several of its themes are introduced in Philo's speech. The series of antitheses here, distinguishing past from present, heroic from fallen man, soldier from lover, is pervasive throughout the drama. What is the effect of the use of other devices like synecdoche ("goodly eyes," "tawny front," "captain's heart"), the doubling of nouns ("files and musters," "office and devotion"), double meanings ("dotage," "measure," "temper"), and metaphoric oppositions like "triple pillar" and "strumpet's fool"?

King Lear opens with a confusion of quantitative and qualitative, physical and spiritual values ("Nothing will come of nothing"). Antony and Cleopatra enter jesting about similar distinctions ("how much," "reckoned," "bourn"). Antony's manifesto, his dedication to love, is as forceful as Philo's mockery. The Roman arch is seen as the symbol of empire, but Roman (or masculine) forms often "melt" or fall in *Antony*. The "space" or spaciousness of loving is opposed to "kingdoms," mere "clay." The tension between the isolated heroism of the soldier and the mutuality of lovers ("We stand up peerless") is initiated here. In what spirit do we hear Philo's judgment of Antony ("He comes too short of that great property") at the end of this symmetrical first scene? Do we too approve the "common liar," or do we suspend judgment? Demetrius' "better deeds" suggests that the Romans judge their general only in terms of his actions, not the quality of his life. In this tragedy, where character is being perpetually altered and refined, the qualities associated with Antony (Romanness, nobility) dissolve and are redefined. The play penetrates ever more deeply into the meanings of its key words as it unfolds. Are we not therefore asked to see the characters as parts of a continuing process, of a series of subtle changes in which each development gives birth, often surprisingly, to the next?

About a play as great as this, we can be wrong in an embarrassing number of ways, but we can never be sure that we are right. The interpretations that follow, therefore, should be approached as educated guesses or hypotheses. They should never be used as substitutes for the student's own informed intuitions, his thinking or feeling. The play must finally answer its own questions; all critical readings are to be tested repeatedly against the student's own experience with it. Since today all moral and religious sanctions are in question, we are far less confident about external values which have been used as weapons against *Antony*. Indeed, like other ambivalent plays (the tragicomedies), this drama has found a new public in the middle twentieth century. It speaks to us with startling immediacy.

As we have seen, Antony is viewed as both a weakly vacillating general entrapped by the flesh and a heroic soldier who transcends himself in becoming a lover. And Cleopatra is characterized with equal vigor as both an international whore, as destructively manipulative as Lady Macbeth or Volumnia, and a woman of irresistible vitality, who becomes truly a queen, almost a goddess. We might half-humorously term the former group of readers apologists for power and the state or realists and skeptics. We might term the latter apologists for love and private life or romantics and sentimentalists. At times, to be sure, there seems no way of reconciling these two approaches. But to apprehend the play as a successful work of art, the attempt must be made. To clarify the lines of force in the play, we shall now discuss Act I and Act II primarily in terms of the play's three principal characters. Then we shall proceed to study III, IV, and V in greater detail.

ANTONY

The subtlety and complexity of Shakespeare's portrait of Antony are immediately apparent. As we have seen, the play begins with a disturbing Roman view of him before he appears—"this dotage of our General's/ O'erflows the measure"—words which reverberate throughout the play. In the second scene, Antony seems to confirm this view. Though Enobarbus jokes about his remaining in Egypt, Antony speaks of his own bondage and weakness in Roman terms: "These strong Egyptian fetters I must break,/ Or lose myself in dotage." (120–121.) A little later he says, "I must from this enchanting Queen break off." (132.) Notice the repetition of the strong "break," a verb Caesar will use for Antony's death. "Enchanting" implies the witchcraft Antony often associates with Cleopatra: "She is cunning past man's thought." (150.) Antony asks Cleopatra's leave to depart for Rome. He tells her that when he goes "my full heart/ Remains in use with you." (43–44.) And he reassures her by saying, "I go from hence/ Thy soldier, servant, making peace or war/ As thou affect'st." (69–71.) We see that Antony is tragically self-divided from the outset—his body in Rome, his heart and master-mistress in Egypt. What are we to make of Enobarbus' remark—"Hush, here comes Antony"—when Cleopatra enters? (I, ii, 81.) Can we call Antony's relationship to Cleopatra true love, a passionate affair, a flirtation, or enslavement? Are these mutually exclusive possibilities? Only the entire play enables us to answer such questions.

Some critics are troubled about Antony's credibility as an emperor and soldier, since we see him only after he has committed himself to Egypt. Is Shakespeare asking us to take Antony's past glories, chronicled in detail by Plutarch, for granted? In I, iv, when we first meet Caesar, we are given impressive evidence of the respect in which Antony is still held. Lepidus says, "I must not think there are/ Evils enow to darken all his goodness." (10–11.) He speaks of Antony's faults as "what he cannot change/ Than what he chooses," thus reinforcing the note of fatalism prominent in the play. How do we interpret Lepidus' puzzling comparison here of Antony's faults to "the spots of Heaven,/ More fiery by night's blackness"? (12–13.) Unmoved, Caesar compares Antony to those "boys who, being mature in knowledge,/ Pawn their experience to their present pleasure,/ And so rebel to judgment." (31–33.) The implied opposition between man and boy is as demeaning for a Roman soldier as the other antitheses: "knowledge," "experience," and "judgment" versus "present pleasure" and rebellion. We shall be asking repeatedly, however, how and when we can trust the Roman point of view. How does Caesar's report of Antony's receiving a messenger (i, iv, 7), for example, correspond to what we have seen? Caesar contrasts Antony's "lascivious wassails" in Egypt with his heroic earlier days, when he could endure more than "savages" or "beasts." How do these comparisons suggest the kind of man the Romans admire? Referring to the triumvirs, Pompey, a more neutral observer, later says of Antony: "His soldiership/ Is twice the other twain." (II, i, 34–35.) But is it only in the realm of soldiership that Antony's greatness now chiefly lies?

One of the most interesting sequences of scenes in which to study Antony's tragic conflict, caught as he is between two worlds, is that beginning in II, ii, when Antony returns to Rome to meet Caesar. How do Caesar's words, "I do not know,/ Maecenas. Ask Agrippa" (16–17), suggest that this scene has been prearranged? What new signs of Antony's gallantry, honesty, and dignity appear in this Roman ritual, despite the partners' probing suspiciously for one another's weakness and strength? Antony admits that he had neglected Caesar's earlier requests, "when poisoned hours had bound me up/ From mine own knowledge." (90–91.) This is strong language. "Poisoned hours" suggests the "serpent of old Nile." And the play begins to ask insistently what Antony's true self is ("mine own knowledge"): his Roman or Egyptian self, or an unstable combination of the two? The marriage with Octavia is arranged rapidly, and Antony's response to it seems heartfelt:

> May I never
> To this good purpose, that so fairly shows,
> Dream of impediment! Let me have thy hand.
> Further this act of grace, and from this hour
> The heart of brothers govern in our loves
> And sway our great designs! (II, ii, 146–151)

Only after Antony is dead, however, will Caesar speak of him as a "brother," "Friend and companion." (V, i, 42, 44.) We think ironically of Shakespeare's Sonnet 116: "Let me not to the marriage of true minds/ Admit impediments." How does "fairly shows" darken the connotations of "grace" and "loves"? Do the protagonists of the play often say more than they mean, or mean more than they say? How then do we know when we are reading too much into dramatic language? Are the words quoted here from Antony's tongue (to use a favorite Shakespearean opposition) or his heart? Does he intend to respect this bond with Caesar, or is he merely playing a game?

What follows immediately deepens our puzzlement. First Enobarbus describes Antony's meeting with Cleopatra on the Cydnus and prophesies, despite this new marriage, that Antony will not, indeed cannot, leave her: "Other women cloy/ The appetites they feed, but she makes hungry/ Where most she satisfies." (241–243.) Then in II, iii, Antony tells Octavia: "I have not kept my square, but that to come/ Shall all be done by the rule." (6–7.) But almost at once the Soothsayer, again suggesting larger forces behind the play, tells Antony to leave Rome:

"Thy demon, that thy spirit which keeps thee, is/ Noble, courageous, high, unmatchable,/ Where Caesar's is not." (19–21.) How can we speak of a "tragic flaw" in Antony if his chief virtues are threatened by his nearness to Caesar and his old way of life? Is it surprising that Antony soon tells us, in one of his few brief soliloquies, "I will to Egypt./ And though I make this marriage for my peace,/ I' the East my pleasure lies"? (38–40.) What is the first moment in the play when Antony's fall seems inevitable? And is this inevitability a function of the characters of Antony, Caesar, and Cleopatra, of Antony's predicament as soldier and lover, or of all of the forces confronting him?

Ornstein points out the ambiguities in Antony's relationship with Cleopatra in the first two acts:

> At the beginning of the play it is obvious that Antony does not know Cleopatra because he does not yet know what is evident to the audience, that his only desire is to be with this woman. We feel that the hyperbole of his early speeches is strained, because his extravagant professions of love are undercut by his harsh, grating response to news from Rome and by his sensitivity to the Roman view of Cleopatra. Though he says here is my space, he is unable to conceive of a world limited by love; and he is unaware that he uses Cleopatra to excuse his indifference to political issues. We smile at Cleopatra's role of betrayed innocence, but not at her keen perception of the emotional dishonesty of Antony's gestures of devotion and of the callousness that underlies them. She knows how easily an Antony who shrugs off Fulvia's death may desert her in turn. The first scenes show us an Antony who is caught between what he tells Cleopatra, and in part believes, and what he tells himself about her, and in part believes. In Rome he is irritated by every reference to her; he never speaks her name though his is always on her lips, and he never regards her as an equal or as having any claim upon him. When he decides to return to Egypt, he speaks of her as his pleasure.
>
> As Antony's world shrinks, his hyperbole becomes, paradoxically, more convincing. When he is confronted by Octavius' legions, his chivalric pose becomes more than a pose, because at last he does fight for Cleopatra. . . .[4]

How is the "hyperbole" of Antony's first speeches "strained"? Antony is changing the entire direction of his life in middle age (in Plutarch, Cleopatra dies at 38 and Antony in his mid-50s). In what respects, therefore, is the ambivalence described here inevitable?

CLEOPATRA

If the portrait of Antony is complex, how much more complex is that of Cleopatra! The Roman view of her and of Antony's "dotage," with which the play begins, is uncompromising. As we have seen, Philo speaks of Antony as "the bellows and the fan/ To cool a gypsy's lust" and as a "strumpet's fool." (I, i.) In II, i, this note is also sounded by Pompey, who respects Antony's soldiership too much to wish to fight him. He hopes that for Antony "witchcraft join with beauty, lust with both," so "That sleep and feeding may prorogue his honor/ Even till a Lethèd dullness." (22, 26–27.) Even Enobarbus says of women like Cleopatra that "between them and a great cause they should be esteemed nothing." (I, ii, 132.) And yet through Enobarbus' eyes the picture of Cleopatra becomes more subtle. When Antony says he must leave Egypt, Enobarbus says of Cleopatra's play-acting, especially of her "celerity in dying": "We cannot call her winds and waters sighs and tears, they are greater storms and tempests than almanacs can report. . . . she makes a shower of rain as well as Jove." (152.) The mingled tones of this remark—humor, exaggeration, and wonder—characterize much of the masculine uneasiness concerning Cleopatra throughout the play. The Romans frequently convey their contempt or ambiguous feelings about women in the form of jokes.

Cleopatra combines power with unpredictability, a sense of history with a genius for living moment by moment, and she is thus a disturbing paradox for those Romans who wish to cope with an ordered world. The critics' problems with her begin in the first scene. When Antony calls the world to witness that he and Cleopatra are a "mutual pair," and he says that the "nobleness of life" is to embrace her, we wonder how this declaration will be proved or disproved. Is it what Cleopatra later calls a "mouth-made vow"? How are we to interpret her mockery of Antony in I, iii, when he tells her that he must leave and that his wife is dead? With an insight born of her awareness of herself, she asks him to "play one scene/ Of excellent dissembling, and let it look/ Like perfect honor." (78–80.) Antony's mixed feelings render him vulnerable, and Cleopatra anticipates his every move. She neatly collapses the defenses of this descendent of Hercules: "Look, prithee, Charmian,/ How this Herculean Roman does become/ The carriage of his chafe." (84–86.) But when he has left her in II, v, she is obsessed by him. Utterly bored, she wants "music, moody food/ Of us that trade in love." (1–2.) She wants to go to the river, where she will "betray/ Tawny-finned fishes. . . . I'll think them every one an Antony/ And say 'Ah, ha! You're caught.' " (11–15.) Some critics do not forget these verbs. And how do we interpret Cleopatra's later haling the messenger up and down (II, v), as he is forced to repeat five times the news that Antony is married? This bit of theater prompted a legendary Victorian lady to say, "How different from the home life of our own dear queen!" Later, Cleopatra asks for a report of Octavia (III, iii): "What majesty is in her gait? Remember,/ If e'er thou look'st on majesty." (20–21.) These lines probably embody one of the many concealed stage directions in the play which we must project in the mind's eye. Is Cleopatra here outrageously self-indulgent and even self-deceiving, or is she expressing feelings we usually repress? How can we ever draw a clear line between her sincerity and her play-acting?

In *Antony* we are often in a world in which life achieves its highest pitch through theater. For in *Antony,* as in *Hamlet,* the multiple meanings of "act" and "play" are always alive. Enobarbus pays tribute to the range of Cleopatra's powers in II, ii. Once, out of breath after exercise, "she did make defect perfection,/ And breathless, power breathe forth." (236–238.) For even "vilest things/ Become themselves in her, that the holy priests/ Bless her when she is riggish." (243–245.) Some readers do not find themselves as well disposed as the Egyptian priests. In what sense might readers confuse Caesar's sense of public show with Cleopatra's sense of life as play? She can rise to any event. Her occasional moments of grandeur in the early scenes prepare us for the last act. In I, iii, she reminds the departing Antony of their love: "Eternity was in our lips and eyes,/ Bliss in our brows' bent, none our parts so poor/ But was a race of Heaven." (35–37.) "Eternity," "bliss," and "race of Heaven": these suggestions of divinity reach across the entire play to the last scene, where they are finally given richer substance. Plutarch, Shakespeare's principal source for *Antony,* says that there was a rumor at the time of the meeting between Antony and Cleopatra on the Cydnus that "the goddess Venus was come to play with the god Bacchus, for the general good of all Asia." How does Shakespeare transform this rumor into a pervasive feeling or atmosphere?

Frye discusses the mythical implications of Cleopatra:

> Cleopatra, the serpent of the Nile, is a Venus rising from it in Enobarbus'
> speech; she wears the regalia of Isis; she is a *stella maris,* a goddess of
> the moon and the sea. She has affinities with the kind of goddess figure
> that both Hebraic and Classical religions kept trying to subdue by abuse:
> she is a whore and her children are all bastards; she is a snare to men and
> destroys their masculinity, making them degenerate slaves like Circe;
> she is an Omphale dressing her Hercules in women's clothes; she has
> many characteristics of her sister whore of Babylon. . . .
>
> But *Antony and Cleopatra* is not a morality play, and Egypt is not hell:
> it is rather the night side of nature, passionate, cruel, superstitious, barbaric,
> dissolute, what you will, but not to be identified with its vices, any more
> than Rome can be identified with its virtues. . . .[5]

Frye speaks of Prince Hal's rising on Fortune's wheel:

> Antony is on the other side of the wheel: he can only fall out of history
> and action into the anti-historical and mythical world of passion opposite
> it, where the dominating figure is female and the hero is her subordinate.
> The slighter and younger Octavius goes up the wheel and takes command
> of history; Antony goes on to a hero's destruction, yet even in his death

he is upstaged by Cleopatra, who monopolizes the attention of the audience to the end, looking in her death ready to "catch another Antony" and start all over. She is worth the attention, because she is all we can see of a world as big as the Roman world, and not only all we can see of it but that world in herself, a microcosm of passion "whom everything becomes." Her Egypt is able to bring a superhuman vitality out of Antony that Rome cannot equal, not in spite of the fact that it destroys him, but because it destroys him.[6]

What are the differences suggested here between viewing Egypt as hell, as in a morality play, and as the "night side of nature," in mythic terms? In what respects do these archetypal characterizations of Cleopatra seem justified by the play? We shall discuss the queen more fully in the commentary on Act V.

CAESAR

Toward the end of Act II, Shakespeare gives us a deepening insight into the Roman world of power politics. The party celebrating the agreement among the world sharers in II, vii is framed by ironic and satiric commentary. At the outset, an interchange between a soldier and a pirate, the observers who afford us necessary perspectives here, suggests that international robbery on land and sea is taken for granted:

ENOBARBUS: You have been a great thief by sea.
MENAS: And you by land.
ENOBARBUS: . . . give me your hand, Menas. If our eyes had authority, here they might take two thieves kissing.   (II, vi, 97ff.)

The assumption is that eyes will not see, and that agreements like Antony's new bond with Caesar will be of hands, not of hearts. Occupying a position between Antony and Caesar, and thus helping to define them both, Pompey plays an illuminating role in these scenes. When they meet, Caesar comments on a change in Pompey, who replies, "Well, I know not/ What counts harsh Fortune casts upon my face,/ But in my bosom shall she never come/ To make my heart her vassal." (II, vi, 54–57.) This opposition between fortune and the heart is one of several suggesting Antony's predicament near the middle of the play. Menas says of the new peace: "Pompey doth this day laugh away his fortune," and Enobarbus replies, "If he do, sure he cannot weep 't back again." (109 ff.) How do these mixed responses between laughing and weeping point up much that readers find troubling, if they expect in *Antony* a uniformity of tone like that of *Macbeth*? A little later, Menas says of Antony's bond with Octavia: "I think the policy of that purpose made more in the marriage than the love of the parties," and still later Enobarbus says, "Antony will use his affection where it is. He married but his occasion here." (126, 139.) The play echoes throughout with synonyms for these oppositions between "policy" (a word associated with manipulation and Machiavellianism) and love, between "occasion" (suggesting an expedience dictated by time and place) and affection. What is the effect of Shakespeare's organizing his play partly in terms of such polarities?

There follows the marvelous scene on Pompey's galley, a world conference in a situation so vulnerable that it does not augur well for the future, scarcely even for immediate survival. This temptation scene is in ironic contrast to Antony's dismissal of power ("Let Rome in Tiber melt") at the beginning of the play. But it prepares us for Antony's later temporizing question to the Soothsayer, "Whose fortunes shall rise higher, Caesar's or mine?" (II, iii, 16 ff.) Like other scenes in *Antony*, this is a kind of mirror that reflects and compresses much of the movement of the play. First Antony says to his drunken friend, "These quicksands, Lepidus—/ Keep off them, for you sink." (65–66.) And then Menas, thinking the sea pirates might trick the land, takes Pompey aside and, offering to cut the cable, asks him whether he will be the "earthly Jove": "Wilt thou be lord of all the world?" (II, vii, 67.) Pompey had said that he would never be a servant of fortune. But what are we to make of his reply to Menas?

'Tis not my profit that does lead mine honor,
Mine honor, it. . . .
               Being done unknown,
I should have found it afterward well done,
But must condemn it now.   (81–86)

What dominant motive—a delegating of dirty work to subordinates, opportunism, pragmatism, a sense of what's possible or appropriate— is at work here? Only Antony seems comfortable during this Alexandrian feast, keeping his head despite the "conquering wine" and leading the Egyptian bacchanals. He cries to Caesar, perhaps during a toast, "Be a child o' the time," to which Caesar responds, "Possess it, I'll make answer." (106–107.) How does the latter part of the play gloss such telling phrases as "child o' the time" and "Possess it"? How is Caesar's answer ambiguous? (It is also glossed as "have it your way," "enjoy your wish to pledge me," because of "But" in the next line.) Is Antony only taunting Lepidus, in his description of the crocodile— an animal that is as much a mysterious symbol of Egypt as the serpent is of the Nile? What comment do the dancing and singing ("Cup us, till the world go round") make upon the ritual of reconciliation in II, ii?

Dipak Nandy writes of the spirit of Rome and of the scene aboard Pompey's galley, the function of which is "moral definition":

Rome is the world of utilitarian realism ruled by the principle of political self-interest, where values are arrived at by calculation (even the "factions" are "scrupulous"), as opposed to the Egyptian world where "there's beggary in the love that can be *reckon'd*." Now it is not enough, if one wants to make clear that these qualities characterize a whole *society* and not merely an individual, to show only Caesar as their exemplar. It is necessary to have someone sharing the same values and assumptions about ends as Caesar, but *opposed* to him, someone who is a rebel but who nevertheless *abides by the "rules of the game."* This is the function of the scene between Pompey and Menas in Act II scene 7, and the thirty lines or so between them is enough for Shakespeare to show unambiguously how the Roman world ticks. It is governed by elaborate rules and conventions which conceal appalling depth of moral cynicism. . . .[7]

At the end of Act II, Caesar says impatiently, "The wild disguise hath almost/ Anticked us all." (131–132.) This is the only occasion in the play when Caesar permits himself to relax from power politics, to be made in his own eyes a fool or clown (antic). At the opening of Act III, we note the touchy one-upmanship of the Roman world, even when it involves Antony. Ventidius says of him that "ambition,/ The soldier's virtue, rather makes choice of loss/ Than gain which darkens him." (III, i, 22–24.) And in III, ii, the soldier-observers, who had been skeptical before, are now openly satirical about the new unity between the "brothers." They are speaking of Lepidus who, whenever Antony and Caesar did "pinch one another by the disposition," cried out "No more," and took another drink. The passage is one of many in the play that must be read aloud in various ways to catch its tone.

AGRIPPA: 'Tis a noble Lepidus.
ENOBARBUS: A very fine one. Oh, how he loves Caesar!
AGRIPPA: Nay, but how dearly he adores Mark Antony!
ENOBARBUS: Caesar? Why, he's the Jupiter of men.
AGRIPPA: What's Antony? The god of Jupiter.

Lepidus is the weak triumvir who asked Caesar to keep him informed of events and heard the crisp reply, "Doubt not, sir./ I knew it for my bond." (I, iv, 83–84.) What do bonds of friendship mean here, where cables can so easily be cut? Are the soldiers (in III, ii) only speaking of Lepidus in their mocking use of such key words as "noble," "loves," "adores"? Very soon we hear that Pompey has been murdered, and Caesar arrests Lepidus because he "was grown too cruel"! How does Caesar give the game of power away when he says to Octavia, who returns to Rome alone after Antony has left her: "you are come/ A market maid to Rome, and have prevented/ The ostentation of our love, which left unshown/ Is often left unloved"? (III, vi, 50–53.)

Following Plutarch, Shakespeare makes it clear that Caesar is a formidable, probably invincible, rival. The Soothsayer had warned Antony, in an image which transfers Antony's association with the sun or light to Caesar, "Thy luster thickens/ When he shines by." Antony admits that "my better cunning faints/ Under his chance." (II, iii, 27–28, 34–35.) Later, as Antony zigzags across the Mediterranean, Caesar seems at times omniscient: "I have eyes upon him,/ And his affairs come to me on the wind." (III, vi, 61–62.) And a few lines later, he announces to the grieving Octavia, as though he were one of the fates: "let determined things to destiny/ Hold unbewailed their way." (84–85.) Before the first battle, Caesar's efficiency astonishes everyone: "This speed of Caesar's/ Carries beyond belief." (vii, 75–76.) It is scarcely surprising that Caesar says after Antony's death: "We could not stall together/ In the whole world." (V, i, 39–40.) Plutarch says that "it was predestined that the government of all the world should fall into Octavius Caesar's hands." But why is the man of cunning and prudence, who seems to be partly in control of destiny, never the hero of Shakespeare's tragedies? In worldly terms, what advantage over the hero does the politician's freedom from passion give him? Though we hear later that Caesar is the "universal landlord" (III, xiii, 72) and that "The time of universal peace is near" (IV, vi, 5), we have no indication in Shakespeare's play that Caesar later transforms himself into the great Augustus, ruling over the golden age of Roman arts and letters. Why?

Ornstein sees Rome in the play in uncompromising terms:

> The end of an era of nobility was marked in *Julius Caesar* by the execution of a hundred Senators and by the suicides of Portia, Cassius, Titinius, and Brutus. In *Antony and Cleopatra* the decay of Roman idealism is so advanced that it is difficult to say whether a Roman thought is of duty or of disloyalty. Yet the decay of the Roman state is paradoxical, because it is not a melting into Egyptian softness but a hardening into the marble-like ruthlessness of the universal landlord. No trace of Brutus' stoicism remains in Octavius' Rome; the prevailing philosophy is the cynical prudence of the Fool's songs in *Lear*. Weakness is merely despised, misfortune corrupts honest soldiers, and loyalty belongs only to the rising man. . . .

Ornstein continues:

> For more than in the days of Brutus, Rome is bent on empire and ruled by the sword; yet compared to the past, the present is not a time of great soldiery. The continual talk of war only emphasizes that the great military exploits live in memory. All the leaders, including Antony, deal in lieutenantry, and their lieutenants fear to win great victories. Except for the moment when Antony and Scarus beat back Octavius' legions, the battlefield is not a place where honour is won. It is a place where great men defeat themselves; it is the scene of shameful weakness or of the shameless policy that places revolted legions in the van.

The echoes of a nobler past are important because they remind us that the Rome which Octavius rules is not the eternal reality of political life. Only here and now must men like Enobarbus choose between the ways of soldiery and of personal loyalty, that were before a single path. But even as Shakespeare bounds his present scene by placing it in a larger historical framework, his use of archetypal imagery suggests that the worlds of Rome and Egypt are eternal aspects of human experience and form a dichotomy as elemental as that of male and female. The hard masculine world of Rome is imaged in sword, armour, and terms of war, in geometry and stone, and in the engineering that builds or destroys. The soft yielding feminine world of Egypt is poetically imaged as uniting the artifices of sexual temptation to the naturalness of fecundity and to the processes of growth and decay which depend on sun, wind, and water. But the absolute distinctions between Rome and Egypt which the imagery enforces are qualified by the dramatic action, that reveals the extent to which these worlds are mirror images of one another and divergent expressions of the same fundamental human impulses. Although by Roman standards, Antony is unmanned, the Roman standard of masculinity is itself examined by the dramatic action and found deficient. Moreover, although Antony's decline in Egypt is from the Roman measure, his decline also measures the decay of the Roman ideal of soldiery. . . .[8]

This careful summary calls for close attention. Test your responses to the Roman values you discover in your reading against Ornstein's touchstones: "disloyalty" and "cynical prudence." The "absolute distinctions" between the worlds which the "imagery enforces" are qualified by the dramatic action. How? If the Roman standard of masculinity is "itself examined," as it surely is, by what standard can we assess Antony's sense of honor and Romanness in the play?

Is there a transvaluation of sexuality, as of other values, in this tragedy? What are we to make of Caesar's saying that Antony in Egypt "is not more manlike/ Than Cleopatra, nor the Queen of Ptolemy/ More womanly than he"? (I, iv, 5–7.) Or later of Cleopatra's saying that in her games with Antony she "put my tires and mantles on him whilst/ I wore his sword Philippan"? (II, v, 22–23.) Antony takes risks with his Roman identity, risks that disgust the Romans. In the intimacy of his alliance with Cleopatra, in his breaking through his masculine isolation, and in his daring to surrender traditional attributes of his maleness, Antony is exploring the new heaven and earth of the play. For those who can become children of the time, Egypt can turn the instruments of death into life. Even the sword becomes a phallus when Agrippa says of Cleopatra: "She made great Caesar lay his sword to bed./ He plowed her and she cropped." (II, ii, 232–233.) Rome is as lifeless and barren as Octavia (in Shakespeare, not in Plutarch), but everything is generative in Cleopatra's Egypt. This is one of the few Renaissance plays that makes candid sexuality a field for the heroic.

DEFEAT BY SEA: ACTS III AND IV

ANTONY'S FIRST DEFEAT: ACT III

Antony slowly gathers force like a coiled spring, and about the middle of the play we begin to feel its accumulating power. We have seen how the Roman councils in Act II are qualified and undercut by the ironic asides of the soldier-friends of Pompey, Caesar, and Antony. In III, iv and v, we hear first through Antony and then through his soldiers of Antony's anger concerning Caesar's breaking of their agreements. Why do we need both scenes here? And how are we to evaluate the most devastating picture Caesar has yet given of Antony, at the beginning of III, vi? Has Antony lost all judgment, is he mocking Caesar, or are he and Cleopatra play-acting, when they sit "in chairs of gold," in "the common show place," while Antony makes his sons "Kings of Kings," and Cleopatra appears in the "habiliments of the goddess Isis"? Why can't we give either/ or answers to such questions? (Plutarch says that Antony's pageant was in "derision and contempt of the Romans.") Cleopatra later sees Antony's extravagance as munificence: "realms and islands were/ As plates dropped from his pocket." (V, ii, 91–92.)

Scenes III, vii through xiii, form a single movement, the preparation for the first great battle at Actium and its disastrous results. The language and imagery become richer, more complex. Here the Roman and Egyptian Antony face one another for the first time. The oppositions between Antony's two selves, the soldier and the lover, the man of land and sea, are therefore in sharpest focus. When Enobarbus quarrels with Cleopatra about her fighting with Antony, his Roman arguments seem eminently reasonable: "Your presence needs must puzzle Antony,/ Take from his heart, take from his brain, from's time,/ What should not then be spared." (III, vii, 11–13.) Enobarbus says that Antony is "Traduced for levity" in Rome, and Cleopatra responds with a wish like that she has expressed twice before ("Melt Egypt into Nile!"), suggesting the disintegration of solid things:

> Sink Rome, and their tongues rot
> That speak against us! A charge we bear i' the war,
> And as the president of my kingdom will
> Appear there for a man. . . . (17–20)

Notice the many forms in which "man" and its variants occur in this and following scenes. Antony says he will fight at sea because Caesar "dares us to 't." Plutarch emphasizes that Antony is "glued unto" Cleopatra throughout this battle, but Shakespeare explores the polarities involved in the decision more profoundly. The soldiers argue with Antony about a naval battle: "you therein throw away/ The absolute soldiership you have by land . . . and/ Give up yourself merely to chance and hazard/ From firm security." (42–45.) "We/ Have used to conquer standing on the earth/ And fighting foot to foot." (65–67.) Antony's "action grows/ Not in the power on 't. So our leader's led,/ And we are women's men." (69–71.) Clearly the soldiers do see themselves as women's men. They are not fighting, Antaeus-like, on their element, the earth. But the tragic hero always chooses "chance and hazard" over "firm security." Why? (Hecate says in *Macbeth:* "you all know security/ Is mortals' chiefest enemy." [III, v, 32–33.]) Is it meaningful that Antony calls Cleopatra here "Thetis," in Homer the mother of Achilles? How can we compare the relationship of Antony to Cleopatra with that of the poet to the young man in the sonnets? In Sonnet 35, the poet says, "I an accessory needs must be/ To that sweet thief which sourly robs from me."

After the passing of soldiers across the stage, the shocking defeat at sea, which cannot be shown on the stage, is reported to us, first by Antony's soldiers in III, x, and then by Antony himself in xi. We hear that when Antony seems to be winning (a point not made in Plutarch), Cleopatra, in the Egyptian flagship, the *Antoniad,* "Hoists sails and flies," and Antony "flies after her." Why do the soldiers use the imagery of animals (nag, cow) and birds ("doting mallard") here? Notice their repeated references to Antony's losing his identity: his virtues "violate" themselves; "Had our General/ Been what he knew himself, it had gone well." (24, 26–27.) And Antony is yet harder on himself: "The land . . . is ashamed to bear me"; "I/ Have lost my way forever"; "I have fled myself"; "My very hairs do mutiny"; "I have lost command"; "I have offended reputation,/ A most unnoble swerving." (III, xi, 1, 3–4, 8, 13, 23, 49–50.) The former brilliant soldier is "unqualitied with very shame"; shame is an important noun in the latter half of this play. And yet if we trust only the soldier's view, what are we to make of Antony's moving response to Cleopatra's apology?

> Egypt, thou knew'st too well
> My heart was to thy rudder tied by the strings,
> And thou shouldst tow me after .O'er my spirit
> Thy full supremacy thou knew'st, and that
> Thy beck might from the bidding of the gods
> Command me.   (56–61)

How can we encompass the range of feelings here? The first part seems to express the humiliation of a boy. But how does the second suggest the earlier words of Cleopatra in I, iii: "Eternity was in our lips and eyes . . . none our parts so poor/ But was a race of Heaven"? Antony says Cleopatra knew that "My sword, made weak by my affection, would/ Obey it on all cause." (67–68.) The phallic implications of "sword," as we have seen, are pervasive in the play. Before his death, Antony says that Cleopatra has "robbed" him of his sword. (IV, xiv, 23.) And yet after Cleopatra asks for pardon four times, Antony suddenly says, "Fall not a tear, I say. One of them rates/ All that is won and lost. Give me a kiss,/ Even this repays me. . . ." (69–71.) In the light of Antony's loss, this is surely one of the most astonishing acts of forgiveness in Shakespeare, and Antony repeats it in Act IV. At the opening of the play, Antony had defined the "nobleness of life" as embracing Cleopatra, and he dies kissing her. He here poises a tear and a kiss against the world. How is the play slowly working to render Antony's choice of love over empire convincing? In the heroic world the choice is always irrevocable.

Tragedy places the hero in a predicament in which he is tested to the uttermost. The public and private testing of Antony in Act III and Act IV is relentless, often almost unbearable. Caesar's patronizing remark (with its ambiguous second verb) at the end of III, xii—"Observe how Antony becomes his flaw"—may remind us of the interpretation given at the outset of Olivier's film of *Hamlet,* as though a few words could epitomize the play: This is a play about "a man who could not make up his mind." How could a "flaw" help to explain the subtle relationship between character and fate in *Hamlet* or *Antony*? Indeed, how might an emphasis upon the hero's weakness or folly (Aristotle's "error," *hamartia*) result in short-circuiting our response to his dilemma? Can we speak of tragic strength or virtue, as McFarland suggests, rather than of a tragic flaw?

In III, xiii, in response to Cleopatra's question about the defeat, Enobarbus blames "Antony only, that would make his will/ Lord of his reason. . . . The itch of his affection should not then/ Have nicked his captainship. . . .(3–4, 7–8.) Most of the words in these scenes carry multiple meanings. "Will" can have our current meanings, as well as "desire" and "lust"; "nicked" can mean "notched," "impaired," and "got the better of." When Antony enters to find Thidias ("Thyreus," after Plutarch, in some editions) kissing Cleopatra's hand, a new force is released in him. He has just lost the world for a kiss, and now finds Thidias "familiar with/ My playfellow, your hand, this kingly seal/ And plighter of high hearts." (124–126.) In *Antony*, as in other tragedies, the disparity between what the face, tongue, hand, and heart say often lies at the center of the hero's suffering. If in defeat, Antony can trust no "plighter of high hearts," this personal crisis he now confronts is more appalling than both sea battles. He first asks, "what's her name/ Since she was Cleopatra?" and calls her a "morsel" on Caesar's "trencher," a "fragment" of Pompey's, as though she too were falling apart. (98–99, 116, 117.) This language echoes the earlier tone ("Egyptian dish") of the Roman soldiers, who saw Cleopatra as food to be devoured. Then he characterizes tragic infatuation in some of the most terrible words in Shakespeare:

> You have been a boggler ever.
> But when we in our viciousness grow hard—
> Oh, misery on 't!—the wise gods seal our eyes,
> In our own filth drop our clear judgments, make us
> Adore our errors, laugh at 's while we strut
> To our confusion. (110–115)

Is he speaking of himself, of Cleopatra, or of them both here? Why the shift from you to we? Is this very different from Gloucester's fierce remark in *King Lear*, "As flies to wanton boys are we to the gods./ They kill us for their sport"? (IV, i, 38–39.) Antony's remark suggests the hero's walking the gangplank of tragic *hybris*. But is either group of amused or mocking gods wholly representative in either play? Do the words "viciousness," "filth," and "strut" apply to Cleopatra here?

Considering himself a strumpet's fool or cuckold before the world, Antony wishes he could "outroar/ The hornèd herd." (127–128.) Interestingly, this heroic rage, a stage in every hero's experience, is sparked not by the loss at sea but by the fear of losing Cleopatra. He takes his anger out on a messenger, as Cleopatra had earlier. He feels that the "fires" with which he is associated—"my good stars" and the "terrene moon"—portend his fall. After trying to interrupt Antony's rage six times, Cleopatra says that if she has been cold toward Antony, "From

my cold heart let Heaven engender hail/ And poison it in the source,"
a storm that would leave her offspring and Egyptians "graveless, till
the flies and gnats of Nile/ Have buried them for prey." (159–160,
166–167.) Enobarbus' earlier view of Cleopatra as a life-giving force—
"Age cannot wither her"—here becomes a force for death. She is
always aware of both the positive and negative powers of the Nile and
of nature.

Enobarbus now comments minutely on everything that occurs. Why?
When Antony challenges Caesar to fight "sword against sword," Enobarbus, in an aside, says of Antony,

> I see men's judgments are
> A parcel of their fortunes. . . .
> That he should dream,
> Knowing all measures, the full Caesar will
> Answer his emptiness! Caesar, thou hast subdued
> His judgment too. (III, xiii, 31–37)

Philo had said in the opening lines, "this dotage of our General's/
O'erflows the measure." And yet Enobarbus here shrewdly says Antony
knows "all measures." As in *Richard II*, the falling man of power is
emptied as the rising is filled. Protagoras said, "Man is the measure of
all things." Who then serves as the measure of man in tragedy? Enobarbus wonders whether his "faith" in Antony is becoming "folly":

> Yet he that can endure
> To follow with allegiance a fall'n lord
> Does conquer him that did his master conquer,
> And earns a place i' the story. (42–45)

Notice the classical and Renaissance emphasis upon earning a place
in history. In *Antony*, good report through chronicle or art guarantees
the only immortality. Is this speech a portent of Cleopatra's last words
about her outwitting Caesar and rendering him "ass/ Unpolicied"?
When Cleopatra tells Caesar's messenger, "Mine honor was not
yielded,/ But conquered merely," Enobarbus suggests in an aside that
only Cleopatra's fidelity could keep Antony afloat: "Sir, sir, thou art
so leaky/ That we must leave thee to thy sinking, for/ Thy dearest quit
thee." (61–62, 63–65.) The passage may reflect Plutarch's remark that
Antony was "drowned with the love of her." Is Enobarbus right about
Cleopatra, or is she being politic or playing for time?

Act III ends with Antony's deciding to fight again and saying, "The
next time I do fight/ I'll make death love me, for I will contend/ Even
with his pestilent scythe." (192–194.) Where does the play begin to
invest death with a positive, even an erotic, quality? As important as
any event in his life, the hero's death and manner in which he confronts it usually determine his posthumous reputation. But Antony's
case proves to be special. Antony now calls for "one other gaudy

night" and says, "Let's mock the midnight bell." Cleopatra says that it is her birthday, and "since my lord/ Is Antony again, I will be Cleopatra." (183, 185–186.) Why do the two seem to recover energy and their names at this moment? Antony had said at the end of III, xi: "Fortune knows/ We scorn her most when most she offers blows," a characteristic gesture of heroic defiance. Why then does Enobarbus now prepare to leave Antony?

> Now he'll outstare the lightning. To be furious
> Is to be frighted out of fear. . . .
> A diminution in our Captain's brain
> Restores his heart. When valor preys on reason,
> It eats the sword it fights with. I will seek
> Some way to leave him.   (195–201)

To what degree do the mixed emotions we feel for Antony here derive from Enobarbus' struggle with himself over Antony? Antony's behavior would seem to be "dotage" indeed. His sword is·a prey not only to "affection," but to "furious" valor. Is he confusing courage with foolhardiness? When Romeo sees the fates against him, he cries, "Oh, I am fortune's fool." (III, i, 41.) Later Romeo cries, "I defy you, stars!" (V, i, 24.)

In his criticism of his master, Enobarbus seems to be directing Antony's words about strutting to "confusion" (that is, destruction) wholly against Antony. But why should we trust Enobarbus, or anyone else, as the final arbiter of Antony's experience? Is Enobarbus right in IV, ii, for example, when he thinks Antony's emotional address to the soldiers is intended "To make his followers weep"? What is Antony doing in shaking his servants' hands here, and why does he wish to change places with them, speaking of himself as "Married to your good service?" (31.) Throughout, Plutarch emphasizes Antony's closeness to his men. When Antony hears that Enobarbus has abandoned him, he expresses no bitterness but sends his servant's treasure after him and says, "Oh, my fortunes have/ Corrupted honest men." (12–13.) In reporting Antony's "bounty overplus," a soldier tells Enobarbus, "Your Emperor continues still a Jove." And before he dies of grief, Enobarbus says, "O Antony,/ Thou mine of bounty, how wouldst thou have paid/ My better service when my turpitude/ Thou dost so crown with gold." (IV, vi, 31–34.) Though "judgment" and "reason" and the flight of Antony's other captains had prompted Enobarbus' betrayal, he now speaks of Antony as "Nobler than my revolt is infamous. . . ." (ix, 9.) Like Dante, Shakespeare seems to view betrayal, however understandable here, as the darkest crime. What has Enobarbus failed to understand about Antony? What values are beyond reason in tragedy? And why, as with other heroes at a similar point, is Antony now left terribly alone?

Performances of Shakespearean tragedy today are frequently divided into two parts. Where might we best divide this play? Granville-Barker suggests after III, iii (Cleopatra hears about Octavia), III, v (Enobarbus tells about the fates of Romans), or III, vi (Octavia arrives in Rome). He prefers, however, a division after III, vii (the quarrel between Enobarbus and Cleopatra). Jones makes an extraordinarily good case for a break after III, vi, the last of three connected scenes that conclude the first movement of the play. He points out that a

> considerable hiatus separates the scenes leading up to III. vi from III. vii. This scene opens with Cleopatra and Enobarbus quarrelling; and they are shortly joined by Antony. This is the first time that we have seen the lovers together again since Antony's return to Egypt. A good deal has happened in the interim: the wars have already begun. And the new sequence, set going in III. vii, continues without interruption to the end of the play.
>
> *Antony and Cleopatra* divides, then, into two uninterrupted scenic sequences. In the first Antony leaves Cleopatra for Caesar, but in its last scene we learn that he has returned to her. The second movement opens, like the first, with Antony and Cleopatra together; but this time, despite more than one estrangement, he remains with her until his death. Both movements end, not with Antony and Cleopatra themselves, but with Caesar—an arrangement which reflects the historical process. So the first part ends with Caesar's injunction to
>
> > let determin'd things to destiny
> > Hold unbewail'd their way
>
> while the second ends with his final summing-up in which, again transcending his merely historical role, he concludes:
>
> > High events as these
> > Strike those that make them; and their story is
> > No less in pity than his glory which
> > Brought them to be lamented.
>
> He speaks here with the detached, yet all-comprehending voice of the historian, or rather the historical poet; just as in the earlier scene he spoke of future events as if retrospectively—something only granted to the historian who lives later than the events which he describes.

Jones also observes that the kaleidoscopic shifting of scenes of the first part of the play produces an effect very different from that of the second:

> Indeed in the scenes from III. vii to the end of the play we have the impression of something like unity of place: Actium–Alexandria–the Monument are all sufficiently ill defined to be acceptable as different spots in more or less the same locality, an effect quite different from the clearly denoted and far-flung localities of the first half: Egypt, Rome, Misenum, Syria, Athens. Time too is used in a different way in the second

part: it is now no longer possible to ignore it (as it had been in the first), but as far as the lovers are concerned time is now limited and passes with increasing rapidity. It is quite in keeping with this emphasis on continuity that the action of the second part engages the audience's emotions to a far higher degree. The scenic juxtapositions still generate a play of irony, especially where Cleopatra is concerned, but the irony is now deeper, more gravely coloured, more simply tragic, than that of the blander critical mood of the earlier scenes.[1]

How does Jones' emphasis upon the point of view of the "historical poet" seem justified by the play? How could the play be separated into three sequences if a performance required two intermissions? Do the five act divisions which Shakespearean editors traditionally observe seem to be made intelligently in *Antony?* How do they break up continuous sequences of action?

ANTONY'S SECOND DEFEAT AND DEATH: ACT IV

Jones writes of the remarkable group of scenes from the end of Act III through the middle of Act IV:

> The whole of this sequence (III. xiii to IV. viii) has both the sequaciousness and the unpredictability of actual experience. Thus Enobarbus reappears once after he has decided to leave Antony; so Caesar's confident pronouncement is placed immediately before his temporary defeat; so too after the ominous withdrawal of the god Hercules from Antony's side and Cleopatra's murmured admission of her loss of faith in Antony, Antony's day turns out to be victorious. The entire sequence is a succession of small surprises, none of which is forced; it is all natural-seeming and convincing—life is like this.
>
> The technique of short scenes is essential to the effect: for it helps to focus our attention on to the notion of causality, but with a sharp awareness of the true intricacy of the working of cause and effect. There is here a Montaignian sense of the complexity of the process of flux, which the precise ordering of the often very circumscribed scenic units helps to define; indeed without this technique it is hard to see how Shakespeare could have conveyed this sense of combined continuity and discontinuity. Moreover the dialogue of these scenes—the topics of conversation—is such as to confirm us in our concentration on the process of causality and sequence. Nothing distracts us from attending to the present moment and the next, what is and what will be: Caesar, says Antony, makes him angry
>
> > harping on what I am,
> > Not what he knew I was   (III. xiii, 142–3)

and the remark brings out sharply Antony's doomed attempt to swim against the current of time. Cleopatra is more realistic: seeing Antony go out to battle, she says merely, 'Then, Antony—but now' (IV. iv. 38). Granville-Barker is admirable on this battle sequence, and he concludes:

'We have been ideal spectators, we know what happened, and why; and just such an impression has been made on us as the reality would leave behind. It is a great technical achievement, and one of great artistry too.'[2]

How does Jones' emphasis upon the "sense of combined continuity and discontinuity" here—the causality of tragedy and the unpredictability of life—help to explain Shakespeare's flexibility and daring in the structuring of *Antony*?

The many-faceted latter half of Act III—in which Antony moves from a confident insistence upon fighting at sea (vii), through his first defeat (x), his despair and his forgiveness of Cleopatra (xi), his subsequent rage against Cleopatra, his second act of forgiveness, and his decision to fight again (xiii)—is followed at the beginning of Act IV by a welcome lowering of tension. But this act later sharpens the emotions of hope and fear that had seemed to reach a breaking point in Act III. Why is Antony to be put through the tragic wringer again? In the fourth act of many of the tragedies, we see less of the hero and experience a longer relaxation of tension. But in *Antony*, we confront in Act IV the hero's last crisis and death. At the outset, Scarus tells us that Antony "Is valiant, and dejected, and by starts/ His fretted fortunes give him hope, and fear,/ Of what he has, and has not." (xii, 7–9.) There are many ominous portents. Maecenas tells Caesar of Antony's erratic behavior: "When one so great begins to rage, he's hunted/ Even to falling. Give him no breath, but now/ Make boot of his distraction." (i, 7–9.) The hero rages against his fate and, as we have seen, the cool politician, like Iago, manipulates him by means of his passion with surprising ease. The night before battle, Antony makes his followers "onion-eyed." (ii.) His soldiers hear the pervasive sound of the god Hercules abandoning Antony. (iii.) On the morning of battle, Antony hears of Enobarbus' betrayal. (v.) Then Caesar tells of his plan for exhausting and humiliating Antony: "Plant those that have revolted in the van,/ That Antony may seem to spend his fury/ Upon himself." (vi, 9–11.) Antony will later say that his "very force entangles/ Itself with strength." (IV, xiv, 48–49.) In *Troilus*, Shakespeare says of another fighter: "twixt his mental and his active parts/ Kingdom'd Achilles in commotion rages/ And batters down himself." (II, iii, 184–186.)

In the midst of the rapidly moving, cinematic sequences here—the flashing back and forth between Antony's and Caesar's camps and between Antony and Enobarbus—we find a scene with Antony and Cleopatra that is heart-rending, placed as it is between two appalling disasters. We are prepared for the scene in IV, iv, in which Cleopatra helps Eros (the name, like all other names, is in Plutarch) arm Antony for battle. Antony calls Cleopatra the "armorer of my heart," though she is here more efficient than Eros. Why is he fumbling? Antony speaks of his fighting as a "royal occupation" and of himself as a "workman," a "man of steel," as though he were all sword and armor. Despite this splendid recovery of confidence, Cleopatra, deeply apprehensive, wishes that Antony and Caesar might "Determine this great war in single fight." (37.) In IV, vii, we learn that Antony has unexpectedly beaten Caesar in a land battle, and in viii Antony thanks his soldiers for their brilliant fighting, telling them they have fought "Not as you served the cause, but as 't had been/ Each man's like mine. You have shown all Hectors." (6–7.) He had earlier wished to change places with his soldiers. Do we see why, despite their doubts, a thousand soldiers rose before Antony this day to greet him? (iv, 21.) Notice Antony's distinction between a "cause" and personal loyalty; Pompey had told us, on the other hand, that "Caesar gets money where/ He loses hearts." (II, i, 13–14.)

The greeting between Antony and Cleopatra after this brief victory is phrased in language as powerful as that in the last scene of the play. Jones calls this the "most heroic" passage and McFarland the "absolute thematic center of the play." Antony, who had whipped Caesar's messenger for kissing Cleopatra's hand, now commends Scarus to Cleopatra:

> To this great fairy I'll commend thy acts,
> Make her thanks bless thee. O thou day o' the world,
> Chain mine armed neck. Leap thou, attire and all,
> Through proof of harness to my heart, and there
> Ride on the pants triumphing!

And Cleopatra replies, "Lord of lords!/ O infinite virtue, comest thou smiling from/ The world's great snare uncaught?" (viii, 12–16, 16–18.) The bold leaps of this and later metaphoric language prompt many to feel that Shakespeare never surpassed the poetry of this play. With such rhythms in mind, Edith Sitwell said that *Antony* "is one of the greatest miracles of sound that has ever come into this world." The cunning Egyptian serpent here becomes a "great fairy," a magician whose thanks are blessings. She is associated with the golden sun and light, not with the moon and night of the next scene or of Frye's archetypes. She will give Scarus "An armor all of gold," which Antony says he deserves, "were it carbuncled/ Like holy Phoebus' car." How is the earlier imagery of Antony's "heart" as tied to Cleopatra's "rudder" transformed here? In the most astonishing of the images associated with hearts, Antony asks Cleopatra to "Ride . . . triumphing" into Alexandria on his heart. Is this a man who is merely the "bellows and the fan/ To cool a gypsy's lust"? Cleopatra's reply now tells us that the world is a greater trap for Antony than she is. "Infinite virtue" suggests the finest masculine qualities *(virtus)* in inexhaustible supply. In the resonance of its subtly ordered words (try changing the position of "smiling"), this language prepares us for Cleopatra's tribute to the

Emperor Antony in the last scene. The brief passage ends with Antony's plans for a triumphal march, "That Heaven and earth may strike their sounds together,/ Applauding our approach." But Antony's brief victory is not to be ratified by cosmic forces.

In IV, xii, we see at once the ruinous effects on Antony of the second defeat by sea. He bids farewell to the sun and fortune and (repeating one of his favorite nouns) to the "hearts/ That spanieled me at heels," now that he is "Beguiled to the very heart of loss." He cries three times that he is "betrayed" by the "Triple-turned whore," who he thinks has "Packed cards with Caesar, and false-played my glory/ Unto an enemy's triumph." (xiv, 19–20.) What is the evidence for this grave charge? Can we take Cleopatra's disappearance into her monument as proof of any guilt? Antony's anger here is as deeply felt as that near the end of Act. III. In his last hours, Antony seeks the titanic power of his ancestor, Hercules: "Let me lodge Lichas on the horns o' the moon,/ And with these hands that grasped the heaviest club/ Subdue my worthiest self." (xii, 45–47.) In what sense does the rage, however violent, of the cornered tragic hero somehow validate his inner being at moments of crisis and also differentiate his response markedly from other forms of response, whether Stoic or Christian or existential?

Cleopatra wants news of her apparent death worded "piteously" before Antony, and Mardian later tells Antony that as she died "a tearing groan did break/ The name of Antony." (xiv, 31–32.) And yet Antony, unaware of this deceit, now forgives her as suddenly and totally as he did before. Though it is here deepened by Renaissance Christian qualities, as Krook observes, this capacity to forgive is related to the generosity associated with magnanimity, the hero's principal virtue, a characteristic of the "great-souled" or "high-minded" man. For Antony, however, unbearable rage now gives way to unbearable grief. He says, "I will o'ertake thee, Cleopatra, and/ Weep for my pardon." He evokes something like the "new heaven, new earth" that he had referred to in the first scene:

> Eros!—I come, my Queen. Eros!—Stay for me.
> Where souls do couch on flowers, we'll hand in hand,
> And with our sprightly port make the ghosts gaze.
> Dido and her Aeneas shall want troops,
> And all the haunt be ours. Come, Eros, Eros!   (xiv, 50–54)

The repetition of "Eros," like other repetitions in the final scenes, has an incantatory effect. At her death, Cleopatra cries, "Husband, I come." Antony compares his love to that of the greatest epic love affair of antiquity (in Book IV of Virgil's *Aeneid*. Unlike Antony, however, Aeneas abandons Dido to return to Italy to found an empire). In Act V, with something of the wonder with which the "ghosts gaze" here, we watch Cleopatra preparing herself to meet Antony. Readers are often troubled by Cleopatra's sending a false report of her death, as is reported in Plutarch. But are we not concerned here less with what others do than with Antony's responses? How is the "dishonor" he feels in thinking that he has outlived Cleopatra undercut by the fact that she is alive?

Antony's last hours have a strangely ambiguous quality. Antony tells Eros, "I will be/ A bridegroom in my death, and run into 't/ As to a lover's bed" (xiv, 99–101), and Cleopatra later compares the stroke of death to a lover's pinch. But he sees himself as losing his identity. His heart, unlike that of Enobarbus, cannot burst his breast, and he cannot effectively kill himself. Foretelling part of what Cleopatra says in the next scene, he advises his followers with stoic dignity, "Bid that welcome/ Which comes to punish us, and we punish it/ Seeming to bear it lightly." (136–138.) But his death is not easy, for none of his followers dares to give him the final stroke. Of course, as in Plutarch, he must survive for a final scene with Cleopatra. When he hears that she is alive, he asks without surprise to be carried to her. He then tells her, "Not Caesar's valor hath o'erthrown Antony,/ But Antony's hath triumphed on itself" (xv, 14–15), and also that he is "a Roman by a Roman/ Valiantly vanquished." But it is difficult to associate the words "triumphed" and "valiantly" with Antony's last moments. His moving ritual repetitions ("I am dying, Egypt, dying") are haunting, but Cleopatra interrupts his dying words to rail at fortune, he advises her to trust the Roman who betrays her, and he tells her to "please your thoughts/ In feeding them with those my former fortunes/ Wherein I lived the greatest Prince o' the world. . . ." (52–54.)

Why is the death of this prince not more magnificent? Antony is the only titular character in Shakespeare who dies in Act IV. Is his death here an uncompleted episode, part of a dramatic movement that is brought to climax only with the death of Cleopatra? Already in this scene Cleopatra sees him in lofty terms that are in striking contrast to the helplessness of the dying Antony. She wishes she had "great Juno's power" to bid Mercury set Antony "by Jove's side." She goes beyond Antony's farewell to the sun, asking it now to "Burn the great sphere thou movest in," and she says that with his death "there is nothing left remarkable/ Beneath the visiting moon." These impressive tributes to Antony are extended by the Romans in V, i. There is a suggestion of massive dislocation. Cleopatra says, "Young boys and girls/ Are level now with men," and Caesar says that "The round world/ Should have shook lions into civil streets,/ And citizens to their dens." (V, i, 15–17.) Agrippa uses a surprising verb concerning this general who had seemed to lose control of his fate: "A rarer spirit never/ Did steer humanity." He continues with a phrase which beautifully characterizes the tragic (rather than the epic) hero: the gods "will give us/ Some faults to make us men." Though he had pursued Antony relentlessly,

Caesar now calls him "brother," "mate," "The arm of mine own body and the heart/ Where mine his thoughts did kindle. . . ." He is referring perhaps to a period before the play when (in Plutarch) the two had something of the symbiotic relationship of Antony and Cleopatra. We hear that "Caesar is touched" and that he sees himself in the "spacious mirror" of Antony's death. Are the Romans here speaking for the entire play, for themselves, or for both? Can a character step easily in and out of the role of choral commentator?

Nandy says that Enobarbus' dying tribute to Antony prepares us for the ending of the play, with its "tension" between "conviction and suspicion":

> The effect of Enobarbus's awakening to the humanity of Antony tilts the balance towards the Egyptian pole and makes certain that whatever our doubts, our common-sense hesitations about accepting so unearthly an experience as the last act, they will occur within the context of a dominating attitude of acceptance of the validity of Antony and Cleopatra's relationship and their way of life. This does not in the least simplify the play. It provides, on the contrary, a stable framework in these last scenes against which Shakespeare can play off as many ironic insights as he pleases (of which the Seleucus scene is the best example). The case provides, if nothing else, a beautiful exercise in the nice calculation of the tension thus generated between conviction and suspicion. But it is of course much more than this. It makes it possible for us to feel that Cleopatra's "ascension" is, given the history, inevitable, without making us feel that it is *automatic* (which is what a fully romantic view would have it be). She is Cleopatra still, and she *might* have chosen to do what she does. The result is that rich complexity, density almost, of Cleopatra's character that resists analysis into generalized and abstract formulae. Who will say why she does what she does?[3]

Peter Alexander points up the remarkable intensity of Antony's love:

> Having enjoyed all the world can give to unlimited power and the richest physical endowment, he finds in Cleopatra's company a joy beyond anything he has known. And the world, whatever it may say of those who sacrifice reputation and wealth for such a satisfaction, does not readily forget their story, guessing dimly no doubt at the truth with which Aristophanes entertained Socrates and his friends, when he told the fable of the creatures cut in half by Zeus and condemned to go as mere tallies till they find and unite with their counterpart . . . "for surely," he concludes, "it is not satisfaction of sensual appetite that all this great endeavor is after: nay, plainly, it is something other that the soul of each wisheth— something which she cannot tell, but, darkly divining, maketh her end."[4]

The passage in Plato's *Symposium* here referred to is highly illuminating for this play. John Wain suggests in modern terms what the "soul of each wisheth": "Truth is inadequate, and does not satisfy the demands of our nature; we need, and therefore must invent, a greater reality. . . . The needs of love are deeper than the universe can satisfy."[5] And Arnold Stein says that the lovers seek "to be one with their dream, to become it, to be it. They refuse to admit their absurdity. . . ."[6]

In Shakespearean tragedy, the hero always dies, yet his spiritual force transcends itself and endures. Throughout these scenes, we observe a disjunction between Antony's final hours and what is said of him. Only in *Antony* is a woman given most of the final act to place and assess the experience of the hero and her relationship with him. Can she fully comprehend his life without undergoing a change herself? Antony has few brief soliloquies in the play, and the inner meaning of his career cannot be understood without her. Like that of many other heroes in Shakespeare, Antony's function is less to understand his destiny than to live through it, to serve as a vehicle for it. Man can embody his fate, as Yeats says, but he cannot know it. Is not the "recognition" scene in this play reserved for Cleopatra?

When banished, Romeo, awaiting word from Juliet, dreams that she found him dead, "And breathed such life with kisses in my lips/ That I revived and was an emperor." (V, i, 6–7.) As Antony dies, Cleopatra bids him "Die where thou hast lived./ Quicken with kissing. Had my lips that power,/ Thus would I wear them out." (IV, xv, 38–40.) Though he has lost the world for her kisses, they lack the power to revive her emperor. But her language and actions in Act V nearly achieve this miracle. We shall now be concerned with the transfiguring power of Cleopatra's imagination.

34

THE TRIUMPH OF
THE IMAGINATION:
ACT V

In attacking those who read the ending of *Antony* as the triumph of "passion's nobility" over "society or morality," William Rosen recapitulates the position of some of the critics with whom we began.

> However great Cleopatra's appeal, we must question the popular view that Shakespeare advocates the romantic notion of passion's nobility and its power to absolve man from all duty. If we were to concentrate only on the imagery of love, neglecting dramatic context, there would be the danger of extracting Cleopatra's heightened vision of love, so magnificently phrased, to argue that the playwright presents it as life's highest value, more real than society or morality.

There is a tendency today among some Shakespeareans to read the plays backward from the last romances. Rosen sees an equally dangerous procedure in our reading of *Antony*:

> So dazzlingly impressive are Cleopatra's final moments in the play that they have always brought forth excited bravos from spectators and panegyrics from critics. Indeed, many commentators have been so overwhelmed by the ending that they read the play backwards, attempting to reconstruct a consistent characterization so that the final glory of Cleopatra may prevail. Such a reading would maintain that Cleopatra recovers full innocence at her death; that she and Antony are transfigured; therefore,

Shakespeare's play is not about corruption and human weakness but the exaltation of love and its final triumph over death and the world. To interpret the ending this way, however, is to distort what we have seen to be the developing action of the play, Antony's attempt to regain his heroic past.[1]

What evidence do we have that the play is chiefly about "corruption and human weakness" or about "Antony's attempt to regain his heroic past"? It is clear here, as always, that we see what we are looking for. How then can we approximate an "objective" reading of the play, one that takes our own predispositions into account? Art, as Croce said, is life athwart a temperament. What role do our own temperaments play in distorting our reading? In deepening and motivating it?

Janet Adelman speaks of marked differences in our relationship to the protagonists toward the end of *Antony*, a play that is "simultaneously the most tough-minded and the most triumphant of the tragedies":

Throughout most of *Antony and Cleopatra,* we are not permitted to become wholly engaged with the protagonists. In fact, most of the structural devices of the play prevent our engagement. . . . But toward the end of the play the dramatic technique changes radically. We tend more often to accept the lovers' evaluation of themselves, to take them at their word, because we are more often permitted to identify ourselves with them. The entire structure of framing commentary and of shifts of scene had forced us to remain relatively detached from them; after act 4, scene 12, it tends to disappear. No one intervenes between us and lovers; there are no radical and disjunctive shifts in perspective. The final scene of the play is almost twice as long as the next longest scene (364 lines as opposed to 201 in act 3, scene 13): and it is Cleopatra's scene virtually from beginning to end. For once, she is allowed to undercut Caesar by her commentary: "He words me, girls, he words me." . . . We can here take her as seriously as she takes herself, participate with her in the tragic perspective. The critical structure drops away from Antony in act 4, scene 14, in much the same manner. And as we are permitted to become involved with the lovers, their evaluations tend to take on the status of emotional fact even in despite of the literal fact.[2]

The problem of form in *Antony* and of the uniqueness of its final act may be a special instance of the problem of form in all tragedy, the balance between form and subject matter. Murray Krieger, writing in part from an existential position, maintains that ethical values—conservative points of view which confirm and sustain the social fabric—and tragic values—points of view which question or challenge conventional opinion—are always at odds. He sees the catharsis of tragedy in terms of the tension between tragedy's energy and vision of anarchy and its formal order:

The purging of dangerously aroused emotions, following as it does upon the satisfaction, the soothing grace, bestowed upon wayward materials by aesthetic completeness, uses form to overcome the threat of these materials and, consequently, these emotions. This roundedness, this completeness, carrying "aesthetic distance" with it as it brings us the assurances of form, presents us its formal order as a token, a security—something given in hand—to guarantee the cosmic order beyond the turbulence it has conquered. Thus it is that the cathartic principle *is* ultimately a purely formalistic one, even as tragedy, despite its foreboding rumblings, can remain a force for affirmation through its formal powers alone.

How can the "aesthetic distance" and structure of tragedy help to "guarantee the cosmic order" or "remain a force for affirmation"? Krieger feels that the balance achieved in the "classical" tragedy of the Greeks and the Renaissance is no longer possible. The sense of a larger order behind earlier drama made possible

the formal and thematic triumph of tragedy over the errant tragic vision it contained within it. It is as if the security of the older order wanted to test the profundity of its assurances, its capacity to account for the whole of human experience, and thus bred within itself the tragic vision as its *agent provocateur.* And by having the rebellion incarnate in the tragic visionary finally succumb to a higher order which absorbs but never denies the "destructive element," by purifying itself through the cathartic principle, tragedy is asserting the argument a fortiori for the affirmation of its humanistic and yet superhumanistic values. Consequently, it can witness all that befalls its hero without sharing in his disavowal of the meaning of our moral life; without denying, with him, the sensibleness of the universe and of life despite the explosive terrors they can hold in store.[3]

How are these remarks applicable to *Antony?* Do the lovers "succumb to a higher order which absorbs but never denies the 'destructive element'"? What do we feel about the final balance between the play's vision of the "sensibleness of the universe" and of its "explosive terrors"?

Let us return briefly to the scene on the monument. (IV, xv.) In what ways do Cleopatra's remarks, beginning with the last scene of Act IV, suggest a change in language and tone and therefore in spirit? And do such changes imply an alteration or transformation in Cleopatra herself or a shift of emphasis, a deepening of qualities she has always possessed? After she has fled to the monument, Charmian asks her to be comforted, but she replies, "No, I will not./ All strange and terrible events are welcome,/ But comforts we despise." (IV, xv, 3–5.) Cleopatra tells the dying Antony: "Not the imperious show/ Of the full-fortuned Caesar ever shall/ Be brooched with me." (xv, 23–25.) Triumphing Caesar will never wear this jewel as a trophy. When Antony tells her, "Of Caesar seek your honor, with your safety," her response is immediate, "They do not go together." (46–47.) As she always has, she now experiments with her feelings—alternately regal (wishing she had Juno's power), defiant ("let me rail so high/ That the false house-wife Fortune break her wheel"), and self-pitying ("Hast thou no care of me?"). But she faints after Antony dies, a fainting (not now a feint-ing) that her maids think as profound as death, and when she re-covers, she speaks with a new voice: "No more, but e'en a woman, and commanded/ By such poor passion as the maid that milks/ And does the meanest chares." (73–75.) Would the Queen on the Cydnus have understood this "maid" and her chores? She confronts death in terms similar to Antony's: "what's brave, what's noble,/ Let's do it after the high Roman fashion,/ And make death proud to take us." (86–88.) Since we see the "high Roman fashion" rarely in Rome itself, the qualities suggested by "brave," "noble" (now associated four times with Cleopatra), "proud," and "great" are primarily clarified or em-bodied by Antony and Cleopatra as the play unfolds.

The long last scene of the play (V, ii) begins with Cleopatra's defin-ing a new state of mind:

> My desolation does begin to make
> A better life. 'Tis paltry to be Caesar.
> Not being Fortune, he's but Fortune's knave,
> A minister of her will. And it is great
> To do that thing that ends all other deeds,
> Which shackles accidents and bolts up change,
> Which sleeps, and never palates more the dug,
> The beggar's nurse and Caesar's.

How has Cleopatra made the journey from "infinite variety" to the "desolation" which makes a "better life"? Does it only begin after Antony's death? Her dismissal of worldly fortune here prepares us for her address to the asp: "Oh, couldst thou speak,/ That I might hear thee call great Caesar ass/ Unpolicied!" (309–311.) The powerful plac-ing of this last word reminds us that "policy" is associated with oppor-tunistic Caesars throughout Shakespeare's histories and tragedies. The First Folio's reading of "dung" for "dug" suggests not only Antony's opening defiance of Rome's hierarchies ("Our dungy earth alike/ Feeds beast as man") but Hamlet's couplet in the graveyard: "Imperious Caesar, dead and turned to clay,/ Might stop a hole to keep the wind away." (V, i, 236–237.) Can an equally strong case be made for both "dug" and "dung"? When Caesar's soldiers and then Caesar himself enter, we find a language of play-acting which is similar to that used when Antony and Caesar met in II, ii. The play is rich in parallels of this kind. The earlier scene, despite its satiric elements, concludes with Enobarbus' portrait of Cleopatra on the river, and this final scene gives us both Cleopatra's matching portrait of Antony and her prepa-ration for her death. How do the ironic interchanges of both passages help to minimize our skepticism, which might otherwise undercut the exalted poetry of the play? In attempting to assuage Cleopatra's fears, for example, Proculeius here speaks of Caesar as "so full of grace that it flows over/ On all that need." (24–25.) He also speaks of his "master's bounty" and "nobleness." (43, 45.) "Bounty" is associated with Antony, "grace" at times with Cleopatra, and "noble" is taken over from Antony by Cleopatra in the last act. Is it surprising that Cleopatra says of Caesar's use of such language, "He words, me, girls, he words me, that I should not/ Be noble to myself"? (191–192.) Caesar earlier told his soldiers that "her life in Rome/ Would be eternal in our triumph." (V, i, 65–66.) Notice that, as in Plutarch, the asps are "provided" early, before the beginning of V, ii. (i, 195.) How can Cleopatra plan to kill herself and yet ask Dolabella of Caesar, "He'll lead me then in triumph"? (109.)

The Seleucus episode has been interpreted in many different ways: as Cleopatra's play-acting again, as her desire to make a good impression on Caesar, and as her deliberate attempt to make Caesar believe that she wishes to live. Do Cleopatra's motives, here or elsewhere, necessarily exclude one another? Plutarch, never of course the final arbiter for interpreting the play, says that Caesar left, "supposing he had deceived her. But indeed he was deceived himself." Cleopatra says that Seleucus' ingratitude makes her "wild. O slave, of no more trust/ Than love that's hired." (153–154.) She asks, "Must I be unfolded/ With one that I have bred?" (170–171.) Why is Cleopatra being brought to experience how the loss of "pomp is followed" and something of what Antony feared in her? We remember that Antony, in his last fit of anger, accused Cleopatra of selling and betraying him to Caesar. (IV, xii.) Why does the Seleucus passage follow Cleopatra's tribute to Antony?

As with other major passages of the play, the range of interpretations of Cleopatra's speeches concerning Antony and her death is remarkable. She is seen as play-acting again, as vainly attempting to put a good face on what has turned out wretchedly, as entering a realm of fantasy where we can neither follow nor believe her. But she is also seen as creating through her images a level of reality and glory that has not been attained before in the play and rarely even in Shakespeare. Dolabella now partly assumes the role of Enobarbus, at once empathic and critical, and serves as a lightning rod for attitudes that might interfere with our response to Cleopatra. Cleopatra is fully conscious of her soaring and of her audience's possible skepticism, for she asks Dolabella, who addresses her as "Most noble Empress": "You laugh when boys or women tell their dreams. . . ." (74.) Then she says, "I dreamed there was an Emperor Antony./ Oh, such another sleep, that I might see/ But such another man!" She goes on to compare aspects of this colossus with the heavens, the sun, moon, the tunèd spheres and rattling thunder, and then speaks of his mastery of earth and even of water, the element associated with his defeat:

> For his bounty,
> There was no winter in 't, an autumn 'twas
> That grew the more by reaping. His delights
> Were dolphinlike, they showed his back above
> The element they lived in.   (86–90)

Before his death, Enobarbus addressed Antony as "Thou mine of bounty," and he had earlier said that Cleopatra "makes hungry/ Where most she satisfies." Antony's magnanimity is likened not only to a perpetual autumn but his pleasure to the playful prince (dauphin) of the sea. He is at last master of the sea, of women, of life itself. Cleopatra is here, as Waith says, "the final custodian" of Antony's image.[4]

When Cleopatra asks whether "there was, or might be, such a man/ As this I dreamed of," and Dolabella says "Gentle madam, no," she cries:

> You lie, up to the hearing of the gods.
> But if there be, or ever were, one such,
> It's past the size of dreaming. Nature wants stuff
> To vie strange forms with fancy, yet to imagine
> An Antony were nature's piece 'gainst fancy,
> Condemning shadows quite.   (95–100)

Enobarbus had referred to Cleopatra on the Cydnus as "O'er-picturing that Venus where we see/ The fancy outwork nature"—as more magnificent than any work of art. Cleopatra here says that nature is usually worsted by the imagination; yet in *imagining* Antony, nature has outstripped the human mind. Does Cleopatra seem to be speaking for nature? Why is she imagining an Antony, as in a Renaissance painting, on a scale larger than anything we have seen in the play?

In *The Winter's Tale*, Polixenes tells Perdita that "Nature is made better by no mean/ But Nature makes that mean. So, over that art/ Which you say adds to Nature, is an art/ That Nature makes." (IV, iv, 89–92.) Art and nature are seen as functions of each other, though nature is the ultimate creator. But if we are tempted like Dolabella to dismiss Cleopatra's dream of Antony, we remember that Theseus speaks of the poet's eye as glancing

> from heaven to earth, from earth to heaven,
> And as imagination bodies forth
> The forms of things unknown, the poet's pen
> Turns them to shapes, and gives to airy nothing
> A local habitation and a name.   (*A Midsummer Night's Dream*, V, i, 12–16)

Cleopatra names Antony anew as Emperor and gives him his true place in the heavens. She wrests from his humiliating defeat an imperial vision. In *The Tempest,* Prospero calls the actors of the wedding masque which he stages for Ferdinand and Miranda "spirits" in an "insubstantial pageant." Then, moving from his play within a play to "reality," he says,

> We are such stuff
> As dreams are made on, and our little life
> Is rounded with a sleep.   (IV, i, 148–150)

If we ourselves, like actors, are seen as the stuff of dreams, the dreaming of nature, the artist, and God are profoundly allied. What is the relationship between Shakespeare's, Cleopatra's, and the audience's imagining? How is Cleopatra's vision of Antony given substance, conjured into being, by the vitality of the language with which she depicts him?

The ending of the play achieves a unique poetic intensity. And yet the mingling of tones and the multiple perspectives are sustained throughout. Cleopatra tells Iras that if they are taken to Rome she will see "Some squeaking Cleopatra boy my greatness/ I' the posture of a whore." (220–221.) Any dramatist who can afford to remind his audience of the stage conventions of his day (the "squeaking" boy players of women's roles) in an exalted scene such as this is master of the theatrical boldness which Plutarch's historical narrative now inspires. As Sigurd Burckhardt says, "The sense of triumph which the play engenders springs from its immense daring, which, if it were not ultimately made good, would be mere defiance."[5] Cleopatra first tells her servants, "Show me, my women, like a Queen. Go fetch/ My best attires. I am again for Cydnus/ To meet Mark Antony." (227–229.) As Cleopatra prepares for her final journey, she may leave some members of the audience behind her. Indeed, the play is performed infrequently because of the extraordinary demands it makes upon the actress who plays Cleopatra. Now, however, when skeptical observers like Enobarbus have vanished, an unexpected confrontation with a "rural fellow" provides us with a startling perspective on death and helps to validate Cleopatra's image of herself. The comic distance afforded by the Clown on the "worm," women, and the gods limbers up our responses, undercuts our expectations, and prepares us for the transcendent. Why can a passage like this be more appropriately called comic intensification than comic relief? Freud has often associated laughter with moments of heightened emotion. As with Bottom's Pyramus in *The Dream,* the Clown here erases the line between life and death, pleasure and pain: the worm's "biting is immortal"; a dead woman gave "a very good report o' the worm." The Clown twice wishes Cleopatra "joy of the worm." We remember earlier references to Cleopatra as an object, as a "morsel for a monarch." But when Cleopatra asks of the asp, "Will it eat me?" the Clown gives women an even chance for greatness: "a woman is a dish for the gods, if the Devil dress her not." (V, ii, 242 ff.) Cleopatra now dresses (prepares) herself for eternity.

Nandy says that the scene with the asp helps to give credibility to what follows:

> For there *is* a kind of illusion in Cleopatra's moving day-dream of Antony, there is a real sense in which her final ascension, so to speak, is *play-acting*, and Shakespeare breaks the magic with incredible audacity at this point, just because we are in danger of being swept up in her dream and resigning ourselves uncritically to a romantic stupor. The full import of that passage is difficult to explain. What we are witnessing in this scene is the transformation of the "courtesan" (defined in terms of a function) into a person, at once peerless and richly human, and what this passage reveals is a profound and acute perception of the sheer difficulty of any genuine human transformation. The Cleopatra of the last act *is* transformed, but to achieve it she has to *think herself into a new role*. And we are meant to feel simultaneously the reality and wonder of the transformation as well as the artificiality, the play-acting quality, of the means by which it is achieved. . . .

And Nandy denies that Cleopatra's death scene is a form of romantic escapism:

> The significance of Cleopatra's end is not, then, to be dismissed as "escapism." If we are to characterize it, we must describe it as *utopian*, for the vision of death in *Antony and Cleopatra* as a merging into the universe and its processes of life seems to me ultimately to constitute a cosmic act of faith, a belief that in the long run the forces of life, humane values, will reassert themselves because they are a part of the universe and its mode of existence. This is utopian (though not, of course, for that reason false), for it is the sort of proposition that can neither be proved nor disproved this side of utopia.[6]

Just before the Clown enters with the asps, Cleopatra says:

> What poor an instrument
> May do a noble deed! He brings me liberty.
> My resolution's placed, and I have nothing
> Of woman in me. Now from head to foot
> I am marble-constant, now the fleeting moon
> No planet is of mine.

She uses the word "resolution," a surprising term for her, for the third time. The dying Antony had compared himself to a cloud, as "indistinct/ As water is in water" and had felt that he could not hold his "visible shape." (IV, xiv, 10–11, 14.) But Cleopatra, formerly as volatile as water, here prepares for the first time in her life to become marble, "To do that thing that ends all other deeds." And thus she restores to Egypt the clear outlines, the "masculine" forms, that had seemed to "melt" away. ("Melt" is used more frequently here than in any other play.)

After the Clown leaves, Cleopatra arrays herself to meet Antony: "Give me my robe, put on my crown. I have/ Immortal longings in me." (283–284.) We heard earlier, as Plutarch says, that she often dressed as the goddess Isis. But she here abandons her associations with the goddess's moon and water and her Bacchic associations with "Egypt's grape" and becomes "fire and air. My other elements/ I give to baser life." When Antony was absent in Rome, Cleopatra fed herself with "most delicious poison," thinking of the "demi-Atlas of this earth" and wishing to drink mandragora, to "sleep out this great gap of time/ My Antony is away." (I, v.) Now that she faces her final sleep, a life in death, her sense of being close to Antony and about to be united with him is overpowering:

> Methinks I hear
> Antony call. I see him rouse himself
> To praise my noble act, I hear him mock
> The luck of Caesar, which the gods give men
> To excuse their afterwrath. Husband, I come.
> Now to that name my courage prove my title!

The Queen, who has been called everything, from the "gypsy" and "strumpet" of the opening lines to the "foul Egyptian" and "witch" of Antony's indictment, here accepts the simplest name and title and a commitment of woman to man. How do we interpret her previous pursuit, however, of "conclusions infinite/ Of easy ways to die" and her present fear that Iras "first meet the curlèd Antony"? How do such details in fact help to preserve her identity through these changes of role? As Antony had lost the world for a kiss, we now feel that a kiss from Antony would indeed be Cleopatra's "Heaven." All of the imagery of fertility in the play seems epitomized in her lines, "Dost thou not see my baby at my breast,/ That sucks the nurse asleep?" As Cleopatra experiences the "joy of the worm," Eros and Thanatos become one. The movement through the looking glass of death seems organic and inevitable: "The stroke of death is as a lover's pinch/ Which hurts, and is desired." She bids the asp "untie" the "knot intrinsicate/ Of life," and she dies in the middle of a sentence, "As sweet as balm, as soft as air, as gentle . . . ," calling, like Enobarbus, upon Antony. The queen of infinite variety stops moving and faces stillness.

Jones writes of the powerful pictorial effect of Cleopatra's death scene, in which

> we witness a metamorphosis. Cleopatra changes before our eyes from a living human being into an inanimate work of art, "a wonderful piece of work" which men can gaze at as they would at a painting or a piece of sculpture. The metamorphosis is in fact the reverse of what happens at the

end of *The Winter's Tale:* there we witness a "statue" becoming a woman, here a woman becomes a "statue." In Cleopatra's case the sense of the marvellous aroused by the change is very largely due to her extraordinary vitality, which has been so variously evoked throughout the play. Now all that life is translated into this stillness and coldness. But some of the force of the scenic effect derives from the way in which Shakespeare's theatre used *tableaux*. Cleopatra's death is the most deliberate and ceremonious in all Shakespeare's plays, and the *tableau* formed by the dead women is held for fifty lines. With the Romans we look at the formally arranged group; and in no other death scene do we contemplate the dead in so nearly aesthetic a way. This is not, however, like most Shakespeare's *tableau* scenes, merely a figurative or metaphorical one: a stage picture composed of living persons, who for the moment are standing still; instead, it is, so to speak, a literal *tableau*, in which the persons have carefully arranged themselves for exhibition while they were "alive," and have then by "dying" become inanimate objects. They are, for dramatic purposes, as dead as if they were graven images.

Cleopatra's metamorphosis from woman into icon throws light on Shakespeare's purpose in the play as a whole as well as on the poetic and historical vision which he has sought to transmit.[7]

What light is cast upon Shakespeare's "purpose" by Cleopatra's change from "woman into icon"? In *The Winter's Tale,* Paulina, as much of an artist as Cleopatra is here, seems to restore Hermione to life, as Cleopatra restores the image of Antony and the vibrancy of her life with him. In Shakespeare's first narrative poem, *Venus and Adonis* (1593), Venus survives Adonis' death to grieve over her loss and the death of love. What movement in Shakespeare's thought and feeling can be traced from this early poem, through Juliet's grieving over Romeo, to the exalted endings of these late plays? Wilson Knight writes of a deep need of our natures lying behind all of these passages: "no metaphysics, no natural philosophy or art, satisfy the demand that the lost thing, in all its nature-born warmth, be preserved; that it, not only its descendent, shall live; that death be revealed as a sin-born illusion; that eternity be flesh and blood."[8] And Ornstein writes of the "paradox of tragic art, which depicts immeasurable loss and yet preserves forever that which the artist supremely values."[9]

As Cleopatra becomes "marble-constant," life and death, nature and art, become inseparable. Language and theater are the only means available for this unification. What is enacted on a stage before our eyes achieves a heightened reality in our minds. Cleopatra creates for herself and the world an image so indelible that it transforms time into space, into eternity. She creates a monument far more lasting than that which Montague built to memorialize Romeo and Juliet. Death is mastered by language as brilliantly as by the poet in the sonnets, whose verse (as in Sonnet 107) rescues the loved one from time: "thou in this shalt find thy monument,/ When tyrants' crests and tombs of brass are spent."

Even Cleopatra's crown must not be "awry," and Charmian must "mend" it before she too can "play till Doomsday." In a passage close to Plutarch, a Roman Guard enters, sees Cleopatra, and says, "Caesar's beguiled." He asks, "Charmian, is this well done?" She replies, with a fine sense of occasion, "It is well done, and fitting for a Princess/ Descended of so many royal Kings." When Caesar enters, he sees her as still living, as though her force as an earth goddess, the catcher of men, might endure: "she looks like sleep,/ As she would catch another Antony/ In her strong toil of grace." In Roman terms, Antony's turning from the "world's great snare" to Cleopatra's toils has been disastrous. But in the most resonant oxymoron of the play, Cleopatra's power is here seen by her mortal enemy, the man her consummate final act has outwitted, as at once irresistible and benevolent, the power at its best of life itself.

NOTES

CHAPTER 31

[1] E. M. W. Tillyard. *Shakespeare's Last Plays*. Chatto and Windus, London, 1954, p. 22.

[2] D. J. Enright. *Shakespeare and the Students*. Chatto and Windus, London, 1970, p. 70.

[3] W. K. Wimsatt. *The Verbal Icon*. University of Kentucky Press, 1954, p. 97.

[4] Wimsatt, p. 100.

[5] I. A. Richards. *Principles of Literary Criticism*. Harcourt, Brace, and Co., New York, 1924, 1934, p. 246.

[6] Robert Ornstein. "The Ethic of the Imagination: Love and Art in *Antony and Cleopatra*." In *Later Shakespeare*, ed. J. R. Brown and Bernard Harris. Stratford-upon-Avon Studies No. 8. Edward Arnold, London, 1966, p. 32.

[7] Willard Farnham. *Shakespeare's Tragic Frontier*. University of California Press, Berkeley, 1950, p. 175.

[8] John Danby. *Poets on Fortune's Hill*. Faber and Faber, 1952, p. 145.

[9] Danby, pp. 149, 150.

[10] L. C. Knights. "King Lear and the Great Tragedies." in *The Age of Shakespeare*, ed. Boris Ford. (*A Guide to English Literature*, vol. II.) Penguin Books, Baltimore, 1955, pp. 247–248. (Also in *Some Shakespearean Themes*. Stanford University Press, 1959.)

[11] Benedetto Croce. *Ariosto, Shakespeare, and Corneille*. George Allen and Unwin, Ltd., London, 1920, p. 241.

[12] Norman N. Holland. *The Shakespearean Imagination*. The Macmillan Company, 1964; Indiana University Press, Bloomington, 1968, p. 272.

[13] Ernest Schanzer. *The Problem Plays of Shakespeare*. Schocken Books, New York, 1965, p. 146.

[14] L. C. Knights, p. 245.

[15] G. K. Hunter. "The Last Tragic Heroes." In *Later Shakespeare*, ed. J. R. Brown and Bernard Harris. Edward Arnold, London, 1966, p. 25.

[16] Hunter, p. 14. The following quotation from Weber is from "Politics as a Vocation." In *From Max Weber*, ed. H. H. Gerth and C. Wright Mills, 1948, p. 126.

[17] A. C. Bradley. *Oxford Lectures on Poetry*. St. Martin's Press, London, 1909, 1955, p. 293.

[18] T. M. Raysor, ed. *Coleridge's Shakespearean Criticism*. Harvard University Press, Cambridge, 1930, vol. I, p. 86.

[19] Thomas McFarland. *Tragic Meanings in Shakespeare*. Random House, New York, 1966, p. 105. Most quoted passages first appeared in "Antony and Octavius," *The Yale Review*, vol. 48, no. 2 (Winter, 1959), pp. 213–220.

[20] Northrop Frye. *Fools of Time*. University of Toronto Press, 1967, p. 3.

[21] Frye, p. 4.

[22] Frye, p. 116.

[23] Frye, p. 120.

[24] McFarland, pp. 114–115, 115–116.

[25] Frye, p. 5.

[26] Eugene M. Waith. *The Herculean Hero*. Chatto and Windus, London, 1962, pp. 54–55. He is referring to Tasso's essay, "Of Heroic Virtue and of Charity."

[27] Dorothea Krook. *Elements of Tragedy*. Yale University Press, New Haven, 1969, p. 201.

[28] Maurice Charney. *Discussions of Shakespeare's Roman Plays*. D. C. Heath, Boston, 1964, p. 22.

[29] Bradley, p. 304.

[30] Morse Peckham. *Man's Rage for Chaos*. Chilton Books, Philadelphia and New York, 1965, p. 314.

[31] Walter Slatoff. *With Respect to Readers: Dimensions of Literary Response*. Cornell University Press, Ithaca, 1970, chap. 5.

[32] Frye, p. 61.

[33] Roy Morrell. "The Psychology of Tragic Pleasure." In *Essays in Criticism*, vol. VI, no. 1 (January, 1956), pp. 29, 31, 32, 36, 37.

[34] Norman N. Holland. *Psychoanalysis and Shakespeare*. McGraw-Hill, New York, 1964, p. 339.

[35] McFarland, p. 4; Ernst Cassirer. *An Essay on Man*. Yale University Press, New Haven, 1944, p. 149.

CHAPTER 32

[1] Emrys Jones. *Scenic Form in Shakespeare*. Oxford University Press, 1971, pp. 245, 253.

[2] Jones, p. 238.

[3] Jones, pp. 238–239.

[4] Robert Ornstein. "The Ethic of the Imagination: Love and Art in *Antony and Cleopatra*." In *Later Shakespeare*, ed. J. R. Brown and Bernard Harris. Edward Arnold, London, 1966, p. 41.

[5] Northrop Frye. *Fools of Time*. University of Toronto Press, 1967, pp. 71–72.

[6] Frye, pp 72–73.

[7] Dipak Nandy. "The Realism of *Antony and Cleopatra*." In *Shakespeare in a Changing World*, ed. Arnold Kettle. International Publishers, New York, 1964, p. 178.

[8] Ornstein, pp. 35–36, 36–37.

CHAPTER 33

[1] Emrys Jones. *Scenic Form in Shakespeare.* Oxford University Press, 1971, pp. 229–230, 238.

[2] Jones, pp. 254–255.

[3] Dipak Nandy. "The Realism of *Antony and Cleopatra.*" In *Shakespeare in a Changing World,* ed. Arnold Kettle. International Publishers, New York, 1964, p. 186.

[4] Peter Alexander. *Shakespeare's Life and Art.* New York University Press, New York, 1961, p. 176.

[5] John Wain. *The Living World of Shakespeare.* St. Martin's Press, London, 1964, pp. 129ff.

[6] Arnold Stein. "The Image of Antony: Lyric and Tragic Imagination." In *Essays in Shakespearean Criticism,* ed. J. L. Calderwood and H. E. Toliver, Prentice-Hall, 1970, p. 574.

CHAPTER 34

[1] William Rosen. *Shakespeare and the Craft of Tragedy.* Harvard University Press, Cambridge, 1960, pp. 152, 153.

[2] Janet Adelman. *The Common Liar.* Yale University Press, 1973, pp. 109, 158–159.

[3] Murray Krieger. *The Tragic Vision.* The University of Chicago Press, 1960, pp. 4, 17.

[4] Waith, p. 121.

[5] Sigurd Burckhardt. *Shakespearean Meanings.* Princeton University Press, 1968, p. 281.

[6] Dipak Nandy. "The Realism of *Antony and Cleopatra.*" In *Shakespeare in a Changing World,* ed. Arnold Kettle. International Publishers, New York, 1964, pp. 190, 191.

[7] Emrys Jones. *Scenic Form in Shakespeare.* Oxford University Press, 1971, p. 263.

[8] G. Wilson Knight. *The Crown of Life.* Oxford University Press, 1947; Barnes & Noble, New York, 1966, p. 121.

[9] Robert Ornstein. "The Ethic of the Imagination: Love and Art in *Antony and Cleopatra.*" In *Later Shakespeare,* ed. J. R. Brown and Bernard Harris. Edward Arnold, London, 1966, p. 46.

FOR FURTHER READING

Adelman, Janet. *The Common Liar.* Yale, 1973.
Arthos, John. *The Art of Shakespeare.* Barnes & Noble, 1964.
Bradley, A. C. *Oxford Lectures on Poetry.* Macmillan, 1909, 1950.

Brower, R. A. *Hero and Saint: Shakespeare and the Graeco-Roman Heroic Tradition.* Oxford, 1971.

Burckhardt, Sigurd. *Shakespearean Meanings.* Princeton, 1968.

Charney, Maurice, ed. *Discussions of Shakespeare's Roman Plays.* Heath, 1964.

————. *Shakespeare's Roman Plays.* Harvard, 1961.

Coleridge, S. T. *Coleridge's Shakespearean Criticism,* ed. T. M. Raysor. Harvard, 1930; Dutton, 1960.

Danby, John. *Poets on Fortune's Hill.* Faber and Faber, 1952.

Enright, D. J. *Shakespeare and the Students.* Chatto and Windus, 1970.

Farnham, Willard. *Shakespeare's Tragic Frontier.* Univ. of California, Berkeley, 1950.

Frye, Northrop. *Fools of Time.* Toronto, 1967.

Goddard, Harold. *The Meaning of Shakespeare.* Chicago, 1951.

Granville-Barker, Harley. *Prefaces to Shakespeare,* vol. I. Princeton, 1946–1947.

Holland, Norman. *Psychoanalysis and Shakespeare,* McGraw-Hill, 1966.

————. *The Shakespearean Imagination.* Macmillan, 1964; Indiana, 1968.

Holloway, John. *The Story of the Night.* Routledge and Kegan Paul, 1961.

Hunter, G. K. "The Last Tragic Heroes." In *Later Shakespeare,* ed. J. R. Brown and Bernard Harris. Edward Arnold, 1966.

Johnson, Samuel. *Johnson on Shakespeare,* ed. Walter Raleigh. London, 1929.

Jones, Emrys. *Scenic Form in Shakespeare.* Oxford, 1971.

Knight, G. Wilson. *The Crown of Life.* Oxford, 1947; Barnes & Noble, 1966.

————. *The Imperial Theme.* Oxford, 1931; Methuen, 1951.

Knights, L. C. "King Lear and the Great Tragedies." In *The Age of Shakespeare,* ed. Boris Ford. (*A Guide to English Literature,* vol. II.) Penguin, 1955. Also in *Some Shakespearean Themes.* Stanford, 1960.

Krieger, Murray. *The Tragic Vision.* Chicago, 1960.

Krook, Dorothea. *Elements of Tragedy.* Yale, 1969.

MacCallum, M. W. *Shakespeare's Roman Plays and Their Background.* Macmillan, 1910, 1967.

McFarland, Thomas. *Tragic Meanings in Shakespeare.* Random House, 1966.

Nandy, Dipak. "The Realism of *Antony and Cleopatra.*" In *Shakespeare in a Changing World,* ed. Arnold Kettle. International Publishers, 1964.

Nevo, Ruth. *Tragic Form in Shakespeare.* Princeton, 1972.

Ornstein, Robert. "The Ethic of the Imagination: Love and Art in *Antony and Cleopatra.*" In *Later Shakespeare,* ed. Brown and Harris. Edward Arnold, 1966.

Peckham, Morse. *Man's Rage for Chaos.* Chilton Books, 1965.

Phillips, James E., Jr. *The State in Shakespeare's Greek and Roman Plays.* Columbia, 1940.

Proser, M. N. *The Heroic Image in Five Shakespearean Tragedies.* Princeton, 1965.

Rabkin, Norman. *Shakespeare and the Common Understanding.* Free Press, 1967.

Richards, I. A. *Principles of Literary Criticism.* Kegan Paul, Harcourt Brace, 1924.

Rosen, William. *Shakespeare and the Craft of Tragedy.* Harvard, 1960.

Schanzer, Ernest. *The Problem Plays of Shakespeare.* Schocken Books, 1965.

Shakespeare Survey 10, ed. Nicoll. Cambridge, Eng., 1957.

Simmons, J. L. *Shakespeare's Pagan World: the Roman Tragedies.* Univ. of Virginia, 1973.

Speaight, Robert. *Nature in Shakespearian Tragedy.* Hollis and Carter, 1955.

Spencer, T. J. B. *Shakespeare: The Roman Plays.* Longman's, Green, 1963.

————, ed., *Shakespeare's Plutarch.* Penguin, 1964.

Stampfer, Judah. *The Tragic Engagement.* Funk & Wagnalls, 1968.

Stein, Arnold. "The Image of Antony." In *Essays in Shakespearean Criticism,* ed. Calderwood and Toliver. Prentice-Hall, 1970.

Stewart, J. I. M. *Character and Motive in Shakespeare.* Longman's, Green, 1949.

Stoll, E. E. *Poets and Playwrights.* Minneapolis, 1930.

Tillyard, E. M. W. *Shakespeare's Last Plays.* Chatto and Windus, 1938, 1954.

Traversi, D. A. *Shakespeare: The Roman Plays.* Stanford, 1963.

Waith, E. M. *The Herculean Hero.* Chatto and Windus, 1962.

Wilson, H. S. *On the Design of Shakespearian Tragedy.* Toronto, 1957.

Wimsatt, W. K. *The Verbal Icon.* Univ. of Kentucky, 1954.

PART EIGHT

A CONTEMPORARY APPROACH TO TWO SHAKESPEAREAN TRAGEDIES

JAMES J. GREENE

35
POLITICS AND SEX IN JULIUS CAESAR

Julius Caesar, Granville-Barker once pointed out, "is the manliest of plays."[1] The great Shakespearean producer-critic merely asserts the point without explaining what he means. He does not have to. All of us (or virtually all[2]) know exactly what he meant as we watch the plot with its great deeds and events and its bristling Roman politicians unfold before us. This world of politics, intrigue, honor, murder, and war is the world which for centuries has been accepted as the normal arena in which masculinity defines and tests itself. It is a world in which women have no place, or, at best a marginal, subservient one. As one writer describes the Roman society depicted in this play: "This is a world of stout teammates, who pull with spirit. The one or two women nearby don't count."[3] *Julius Caesar* (along with *Coriolanus*) is, without a doubt, the most "Roman" of Shakespeare's plays, and because Rome was the quintessentially masculine or patriarchial society, this play is permeated with Roman notions of *virtus,* that is, the fulfillment of the human (masculine) potential for excellence by adhering to the ideal of honor and heroic actions. And nowhere else in Shakespeare (again with the possible exception of *Coriolanus*) are his characters so obsessed with their honor (that is, their virility). The Roman ideal as it works itself through the action of this play happens to have in this case a distinctly Stoic coloration to it.

This Roman ideal had much to do with the soldierly virtues, with "martial virility and laconic speech." In fact, the general stylistic qualities of the play may be viewed as a fitting linguistic vehicle for conveying the cold, emotionless, "masculine" world of politics, conspiracy, and warfare. The frequently oratorical style of *Julius Caesar,* concerned as it is with exploring the cult of masculinity and horror underlying Roman society, is no accident.

But it is more than the overall stylistic texture of the play, more than its concern with "the . . . idea of Rome," that marks off this play as uniquely concerned with masculinity and its discontents. The words and deeds of the characters reveal their concern to nourish and preserve the inherited definitions of the appropriately masculine and to keep those concepts sharply distinct from what was considered to be appropriately feminine. In the long history of such efforts Shakespeare's play is hardly unique, but it has not really been seriously studied in this light before, and, furthermore, as we might expect, Shakespeare never simply took up the cultural legacies available to him and worked them into his plays without in some way significantly altering or at least questioning them. *Julius Caesar* is no exception.

Consider, for instance, the language employed by Cassius in appealing to his fellow conspirators to throw off the tyrannical yoke of Caesar:

> But woe the while! Our fathers' minds are dead,
> And we are govern'd with our mothers' spirits;
> Our yoke and suff'rance show us womanish. (I, iii, 82–84)[4]

This is more than the merely traditional abuse as cowardly women of those who refuse to take up the sword valiantly, like men. Cassius here appeals to the Romans' deep-rooted sense of patriarchy as he characterizes any refusal to act now as a betrayal of that patriarchy: "Our fathers' minds are dead." For this tradition of allegiance to their "fathers' minds," they have, he says, substituted being "govern'd with our mothers' spirits," a displacement which reveals them as "womanish." Thus by their inaction have they not only unnaturally betrayed their own masculine identities but also the patriarchal idea of Rome, which is, in the final analysis, the same thing. But because the deed Cassius is exhorting the conspirators to perform—namely, the murder of an emperor who has done no actual wrong to the state or the people—is morally ambiguous, it seems fair to conclude that this particular patriarchically inspired political action may be, as Shakespeare presents it, calling into question the very values and traditions which sanction such conduct. But let us postpone a verdict until we examine what other evidence the rest of the play presents.

Again, Cassius' attack on Caesar's physical infirmities is conclusive evidence, as he sees it, of Caesar's unfitness to rule. He recounts the ritual of endurance in which he and Caesar swam the roaring waters of the Tiber and boastfully recalls his rescue of Caesar, who had dared him to leap into the river. The swimming contest is clearly understood by both contestants as a testing of their masculinity. Caesar's reliance on Cassius to rescue him from drowning is presented by Cassius as a humiliation of the Roman leader and as proof of his unreliability as a leader. One could hardly ask for a more convincing example of the Roman alliance of physical strength and valor with moral worth as the definition of virtue or human excellence.

Cassius next describes how Caesar once fell sick in Spain, and the contemptuous simile he employs to characterize Caesar's weakness makes clear with a powerful succinctness that what is at stake here is nothing less than Caesar's masculinity:

> Aye, and that tongue of his that bade the Romans
> Mark him and write his speeches in their books,
> Alas, it cried, "Give me some drink, Titinius,"
> As a sick girl. (I, ii, 125–128)

Sickness, it seems, was an ailment peculiar to Roman women alone; men, by definition, were exempt, or at least men in their symbolically public roles as Roman males, and we must remember that Caesar too insisted on defining himself in this public, official manner. By agreeing to the ground rules (no other course was even imaginable), he made himself vulnerable and to some extent he deserved the scorn of Cassius. It was something the Roman male took for granted.

We must not, however, necessarily assume that, because it is Cassius who invokes the deeply rooted sense of patriarchy and masculinity as he sneers at the physically weak, "feminine" Caesar, we are therefore to conclude that the play is inviting a rejection of that code by the audience. (The syllogism would run: Cassius is an evil conspirator; Cassius justifies the treasonable assassination by appealing to the Roman sense of masculine honor; therefore, we are to condemn that masculine honor to which he appeals.) Shakespeare's plays are rarely, if ever, so simplistically conceived and written. We have only to recall the morally ambiguous light in which Shakespeare presents the conspiracy and the murder of Caesar to see how wrong-headed such an approach would be. No, merely on the basis of Cassius' call for a no-nonsense, straightforward virility, it is not possible to deduce what moral and cultural attitudes are informing and shaping the play's action at this point.

And yet we may perceive, without stretching the textual evidence, the subtle emergence of, at the very least, a serious scrutiny, perhaps even a questioning, of the Roman masculine ideal, as the battlefield standard of manly achievement is moved into more morally and politically complicated spheres of conduct, such as the governing of the state.[5]

Take for instance what every high school student, once having read Mark Antony's funeral oration, knows to be fact: the principle of honor —so closely linked to the heroic ideal of masculine behavior—to which Brutus has dedicated his life is viewed in an ironically ambiguous light by the very character, Mark Antony, who restores order and harmony to the Roman state. Probably no character in Shakespeare has been more closely identified with honor than has Brutus. And honor, we recall, was a major component in the Roman heroic ideal signified by the word "virtus," with its close associations with manliness. But it is that same honor which the events of the play seriously call into question, perhaps even, in the final analysis, undermine. Further examination of the text with this in mind turns up some interesting material.

In the first scene of Act II, which begins with Brutus' dispassionate and thoroughly sophistic justification of the planned murder of Caesar, Brutus berates his fellow conspirators for feeling the need to seal with an oath their commitment to the bloody cause, because honorable men in an honorable cause do not need to swear oaths. His words appeal to their primal fear of being judged unmanly, for they have in their cause, he says, motives for action that would "kindle cowards . . . and the melting spirits of women." Brutus' entire response to Cassius' "And let us swear our resolution," is worth quoting in its entirety:

> No, not an oath! If not the face of men,
> The sufferance of our souls, the time's abuse—
> If these be motives weak, break off betimes,
> And every man hence to his idle bed;
> So let high-sighted tyranny range on,
> Till each man drop by lottery. But if these
> (As I am sure they do), bear fire enough
> To kindle cowards, and to steel with valor
> The melting spirits of women, then, countrymen,
> What need we any spur but our own cause
> To prick us to redress? What other bond
> Than secret Romans, that have spoke the word
> And will not palter? and what other oath
> Than honesty to honesty engag'd
> That this shall be, or we will fall for it?
> Swear priests and cowards, and men cautelous,
> Old feeble carrions, and such suffering souls
> That welcome wrongs; unto bad causes swear
> Such creatures as men doubt; but do not stain
> The even virtue of our enterprise,
> Nor th' insuppressive mettle of our spirits,

To think that or our cause or our performance
Did need an oath; when every drop of blood
That every Roman bears, and nobly bears
Is guilty of a several bastardy
If he do break the smallest particle
Of any promise that bath pass'd from him.   (II, i, 113–140)

This rhetorical manifesto embodies, sometimes implicitly, most of the major themes of the play. The entire speech is based, first of all, on what Granville-Barker has called "the great idea of Rome."[6] In his call for bloodshed Brutus appeals (ironically) to "every drop of blood/ That every Roman bears, and nobly bears." The ultimate sanction for their deed is the fact that to do otherwise is to act in an unmanly fashion, like cowards and women. They need no sacred oath to bind them together, no "other bond/ Than secret Romans, that have spoke the word/ And will not palter." The only ones who need to swear oaths are"priests and cowards, and men cautelous [deceitful]/ Old feeble carrions, and such suffering souls/ That welcome wrongs." For sheer fatuousness and bluster it would be difficult to surpass this primitive, mindless appeal to a vague masculinity as the grounds for the momentous action they are about to undertake: the killing of the head of state.

One image early in this speech is picked up and reechoed several times later in the play, and becomes in fact one of the central symbolic motifs of the play, namely the image of the "idle bed" as the symbol of all those forces opposed to "our own cause," and "the even virtue [there is that word again] of our enterprise." The bed conjures up not only idleness and passivity, but also love and sexuality, those vital forces which always pose such a threat to the ethic of aggressive politics, warfare, and murder.[7] We are dealing here once again with one of the great human antinomies, the mythical encounter between Venus and Mars, love and war, sex and politics, or what has been disastrously defined as the mutually exclusive and respectively appropriate spheres of the feminine and the masculine. That these are the resonances evoked by the image of the bed is amply reinforced by Portia's repeated invocation of the same symbol in her futile attempts to dissuade her husband from his course of action. She literally offers Brutus the choice of life over death, first Caesar's death and ultimately his own. She berates him for stealing from her bed, the place of sexual union, the cradle of life, in order to engage in the murderous intrigue. In fact, the text supports the conclusion that in Shakespeare's portrayal of Portia's character we have the focal point for those moral energies and values by which to judge the play's action. Minor character though she may be, hers is the perspective from which we are to view those momentous events around her from which she has been excluded. No small part of the tragedy of *Julius Caesar* is the failure of that vision to prevail and her literal and symbolic death prior to and apart from the play's denouement. The Portias are finally irrelevant in the Roman world. The old saw about the need for Caesar's wife, unnamed, to be above reproach, is not without point in this connection.

The same scene in which Brutus upbraids those conspirators who think their alliance needs sealing by an oath also contains the moving encounter between Brutus and Portia. She reproaches him, pointing out that his mysterious new enterprise (she does not yet know that it concerns political intrigue and murder) has taken him from the world of her sexuality, or as she puts it, "my bed":

> Y'have ungently, Brutus,
> Stole from my bed; and yesternight at supper
> You suddenly arose and walk'd about,
> Musing and sighing. (II, i, 237–240)

It is clear to Portia, at least, that whatever course her husband has entered upon, it is opposed to those two vital and frequently associated human functions, food and sex. And a few lines later she says to him,

> What, is Brutus sick?
> And will he steal out of his wholesome bed
> And tempt the rheumy and unpurged air
> To add unto his sickness? No, my Brutus;
> You have some sick offence within your mind. (II, i, 263–268)

He has chosen sickness over health, or as she puts it, emphasizing the antisex, antilife nature of his choice, he has left "his wholesome bed/ To dare the vile contagion of the night,/ And tempt the rheumy and unpurged air/ To add unto his sickness." A moment later her desperate entreaties lead her to her knees in appealing to Brutus, who exhorts her to "kneel not, gentle Portia." (II, i, 278.) To which she replies,

> I should not need, if you were gentle Brutus.
> Within the bond of marriage, tell me, Brutus,
> Is it excepted I should know no secrets
> That appertain to you? Am I yourself
> But, as it were, in sort or limitation,
> To keep with you at meals, comfort your bed
> And talk to you sometimes? Dwell I but in the suburbs
> Of your good pleasure? If it be no more,
> Portia is Brutus' harlot, not his wife. (II, i, 279–287)

It would be difficult to surpass the moving eloquence of Portia's depiction of the subjugated woman who exists only in the suburbs of her mate's good pleasure while he concerns himself with the more "important" affairs of life. It should be pointed out, too, that one of her accusations against Brutus, namely that he is not "gentle" (Y'have ungently, Brutus,/ Stole from my bed," and, "I should not need, if you were gentle Brutus"), carried far more weight and impact in Shakespeare's time than it does today. To be gentle in Shakespeare's day meant something a good deal more than kind and soft. It meant nothing less than to act properly and uprightly, both according to one's social position and to the divinely given moral laws governing human conduct. Portia's charge against her husband is, consequently, a serious one. To exclude one's mate from the serious concerns of public, political life, as she accuses him of doing, is to violate both social and ethical canons of decorum, or as Portia puts it, to act "ungently." Such notions of the appropriate male and female marital roles, while probably not terribly startling to most of us, are really rather remarkable for their time. Whether Shakespeare himself is committed to such a view is not the point. The very airing of such ideas, the mere suggestion that they might be listened to and even taken seriously, is what is significant. Now, while we shall never really arrive at any firm conclusions, based on the evidence of Shakespeare's plays as to what he really thought about any given issue, it is nevertheless the proper task of criticism to ask whether a play's action tends to reinforce or to reject the sentiments expressed by any character in that play. To be specific: in what ways is Shakespeare shaping or manipulating an audience's emotional response, both in the first place to Portia's futile pleading with Brutus in the scene just examined, and also from the point of view of the final outcome of the play? Is she, in short, another Dido keeping her Roman man from his important and honorable Roman work, to be pitied, perhaps, but ultimately to be abandoned? Or is she rather the mouthpiece of those who would assert the values of health over sickness, of sexuality over war, of life over death, and thus to be revered as one who carries the message of salvation for her race? This, I suggest, is at least one of the central issues Shakespeare is raising (even if not necessarily answering) in *Julius Caesar*.

There is no question, of course, that Portia is intended to arouse our deepest sympathies. She is strong, loyal, passionate and dignified. Her tragedy is to find herself caught between the crushing forces of her love for Brutus and her sense of herself as a person on the one hand, and a society which defines both that self and that love as inferior and therefore as something less than human on the other. And it is at least plausible to argue that it is her view of Brutus' actions which is finally vindicated by the play's ending. Brutus' choices have, after all, led not only to the death of Caesar (who, we must emphasize, has committed no overt wrongs) and to civil war, but also to the deaths of his fellow conspirators, his wife and finally himself, all because he stole from their "wholesome bed/ To dare the vile contagion of the night,/ And tempt the rheumy and unpurged air."

In Rome, of course, the Portias are without honor. They are reduced to being the passive, unregarded spectators of history's great events. As Brutus' wife puts it, "Ay me! How weak a thing/ The heart of woman is!" (II, iv, 39–40.) And, "I have a man's mind but a woman's might." (III, i, 7–8.) Her very definition of her selfhood, is as a reflection of the men in her life.[8] Her only recourse, if she wishes to be listened to, is to adopt the hollow rhetoric of honor and the mutilating actions of her male contemporaries. Her dilemma is painfully etched in such lines as these:

> I grant I am a woman, but withal
> A woman that Lord Brutus took to wife;
> I grant I am a woman, but withal
> A woman well reputed. Cato's daughter,
> Think you I am no stronger than my sex,
> Being so father'd and so husbanded?
> Tell me your counsels; I will not disclose 'em.
> I have made strong proof of my constancy,
> Giving myself a voluntary wound
> Here in the thigh. Can I bear that with patience
> And not my husband's secrets?   (I, ii, 291–302)

The terrible irony here is that in defining herself exclusively as Cato's daughter and as Lord Brutus' wife, in turning her back on her own feminine humanity and assuming the values of Roman honor and Stoic patience, she inevitably chooses mutilation and death.

It is difficult to view the presence of Portia in this play as anything other than a profound indictment of the ethical norms of the patriarchal society in which she is forced to live out the terms of her existence. The final touch in Shakespeare's moving portrayal of Portia's dilemma and the tragedy of all that she might have stood for had her culture allowed her, is the chilling indifference with which Brutus receives the news of her death:

> Why, farewell, Portia. We must die, Messala.
> With meditating that she must die once,
> I have the patience to endure it now.   (IV, iii, 190–192)

It is difficult to believe that, in the dialectical confrontation of the two world views represented by Brutus and by Portia, Shakespeare is not evoking a good deal of sympathy for Portia and the standards she so eloquently articulated. She may be a secondary character in the play, as she was in Roman society, but through her Shakespeare seems to be holding up to the strong light of critical scrutiny the male cult of violence and death which formed the basis of the Roman patriarchy.

As for Brutus, it is precisely because he abandoned the "wholesome bed" of blessed idleness and a woman's love in obedience to the code of Roman *virtus* that, however exalted his motives, he brought destruction, violence, civil war, and death into the world of political action.

They were, of course, in a very real sense there to begin with. By rejecting Portia's invitation to life, however, Brutus succumbed, like a good Roman male, to what seemed to him to be his unavoidable destiny. Portia argued against such inevitability. She lost the argument, and everything else as well.

36

CORIOLANUS:
THE HERO AS ETERNAL
ADOLESCENT

Coriolanus has always been regarded as a "difficult" play, not so much because it is enigmatic or mysterious or complex, but rather because the stuff of the play is as stern and forbidding as is its protagonist. Even its defenders (with the exception of T. S. Eliot, who eccentrically rhapsodized over its perfections while at the same time attempting to dismiss *Hamlet* as an "artistic failure"[1]) have frequently seemed on the defensive as they go about the task of pointing out the play's strengths and virtues. The play is about power, politics, and war, and because neither of the play's Roman factions (the authoritarian patrician Coriolanus on the one hand, the common people and their Machiavellian leaders on the other) is presented in a particularly attractive light, it is difficult for an audience to form a sympathetic bond with any of the play's major characters. The language of *Coriolanus*, furthermore, is generally harsh, biting, and unemotional—aside from the central character's ranting and raving against the populace, another feature which might be considered as adding to the play's harsh unpleasantness. Such generally untender language, however, is quite appropriate here, because Coriolanus, as a result of dedicating himself completely and exclusively to the Roman ideal of manliness, paradoxically transforms himself into something that is less

366

than a man, in every sense of that word. He becomes a machine, an engine of destruction, or in the words of his military superior Cominius, "He was a thing of blood." (II, ii, 109.) Another character, Menenius, says of him, "When he walks, he moves like an engine, and the ground shrinks before his treading." (V, iv, 18–20.)

This play, consequently, for these and other reasons, has not exactly been a favorite in the Shakespeare canon. Partisan ideologues have occasionally attempted to fashion this political drama into either a pro- or anti-fascist vehicle,[2] but aside from such exercises in critical futility, much of the discussion about this play has been unfavorable. This in turn has provoked a good deal of reaction, with the result that in recent years a wide-ranging critical reexamination of the play has been going on. Little or no attention has been paid, however, to the fact that Shakespeare, in this most severe of his Roman plays, is actually continuing his exploration in depth of the Latin mystique of manliness already undertaken in different ways in *Julius Caesar* and *Antony and Cleopatra. Coriolanus,* as we shall see, is the product of a dramatic vision which critically and unflinchingly examines the myth of masculinity which stood at the very core of Roman society. And the playwright's vision of that myth finds it severely wanting, because the character who tries to embody totally and perfectly the Roman definition of manhood does not become a man, but rather remains a confused and enraged adolescent dominated by a grotesque mother who, in a society that denied its women any outlet for development and creativity, decided to "outman" the men in her ferocious dedication to warfare and killing.

Coriolanus is then, among other things, a devastating indictment of the Roman way, of the mystique of that Roman *virtus* which forces its women to become either mute spectators of the ceremonies of aggression (Coriolanus refers to his wife as his "gracious silence") or, like Volumnia, his mother, to become monstrous caricatures of what was thought of as the manly virtues. This same mystique also destructively narrows the definition of manliness to soldierliness. *Coriolanus,* in short, is Shakespeare's most tellingly direct comment on an ideal of human behavior which, with some slight variations, has governed the conduct of men and women for centuries. It is the purpose of this essay to demonstrate the truth of that assertion.

In making such a claim I am in no sense implying that *Coriolanus* is an ideological tract, a Jacobean version of a nineteenth century *pièce à thèse.* The play is first and foremost and finally just that: a play. But a literary work of art must in some sense concern itself with values, must in some way, however oblique, reflect its creator's ethics and values, not in the way that a sermon or tract does, but by being faithful to its own artistic canons and conventions. I have no intention here of treating Shakespeare's work as a piece of simple-minded didacticism, for any such attempt is doomed to failure. Having said this, I nonetheless remain convinced that Shakespeare, in presenting and exploring a significant aspect of Roman mores and beliefs, has also not recoiled from revealing the weaknesses and failings of those mores and beliefs.

But if it is a distortion to read Shakespeare's plays as though they were legal briefs arguing for or against certain positions, it is hard to escape the conclusion that once he put the eloquent nationalism of *Henry V* behind him, he begins to criticize the martial definition of manhood as ineluctably leading to the denial of love, sex, and even life itself. *Macbeth* and to some extent *Othello*, as well as *Coriolanus*, contain some remarkably clear evidence in support of such a conclusion.

One of the most striking features of this work, and one that has received scant notice from the critics,[3] is that a play so devoid of love and sexuality still contains a surprising amount of erotic language and imagery. Sex, as we shall see, has been perverted from its normal channels and outlets and has been displayed by the false eroticism of power and warfare. Hence the highly charged sexual energy that characterizes much of the play's discourse. As in *Macbeth*, Thanatos is unnaturally worshipped in place of Eros, with equally devastating results in both plays. An examination of those passages containing erotic language suggests that their cumulative effect provides an important clue to the play's direction and meaning.

It is certainly worth remarking that Caius Martius, that bravest and most manly of Roman men, later named Coriolanus for his ferocious exploits against the enemy city of Corioles, employs the language of erotic love in addressing two of his fellow warriors, the Roman general Cominius and later, more subtly, his one time foe and now new ally Aufidius. Greeting his Roman commander on the bloody field of war, his passions stirred by the heat of battle from which they have just emerged, Coriolanus cries out,

> O! let me clip ye
> In arms as sound as when I woo'd, in heart
> As merry as when our nuptial day was done
> And tapers burnt to bedward! (I, vi, 29–32)

There is no mistaking the sexual feeling of that language, although, like every other erotic passage in the play, it is a displaced eroticism which regularly occurs only in a strictly military context. The powerful, creative energy of sex has been diverted, here and elsewhere throughout the play, into the making of war.

An even more striking example of this phenomenon occurs in the scene in which Coriolanus, having been banished by the Roman mob and their tribunes, presents himself to his archenemy Aufidius' remarkable speech of welcome to his former foe:

> Let me twine
> Mine arms about that body, where against
> My grained ash an hundred times hath broke,
> And scarr'd the moon with splinters. Here I cleep
> The anvil of my sword, and do contest
> As hotly and as nobly with thy love
> As ever in ambitious strength I did
> Contend against thy valor. Know thou first,
> I lov'd the maid I married; never man
> Sigh'd truer breath; but that I see thee here,
> Thou noble thing, more dances my rapt heart
> Than when I first my wedded mistress saw
> Bestride my threshold. (IV, v, 106–118)

It is surely no coincidence that in two separate greetings involving military heroes, those perfect symbols of Roman virility, first Coriolanus embraces Cominius, then Aufidius does the same to Coriolanus, while proclaiming their ardent affection in the unmistakably clear accents of passionate sexual love. It is even suggested, if we can trust the backstairs gossip of Aufidius' servants, that their masters' feelings for the former Roman general continue beyond the initial ceremonial welcome. In the words of the Third Servant,

> Our general himself makes a mistress of him,
> sanctifies himself with's hand, and turns up
> the white o' th'eye to his discourse. (IV, v, 194–196)

To suggest, as one psychoanalytically oriented critic does,[4] that the relationship at this point between Coriolanus and Aufidius is an "indirect expression of homosexual needs," is, I believe, too facile an explanation of what is actually a much more complex state of affairs. The overall textual evidence of the play indicates, not that Coriolanus' sexual drives are rooted in homosexual desires—whether suppressed or overt—but rather that for the males in a culture obsessed with defining, redefining and testing masculinity through acts of aggression, through the wielding of power and the slaying of other men, deepseated insecurity about their masculinity is the inevitable result. Heterosexual love, the normal state in which maleness and femaleness are distinguished and defined, does exist for both Coriolanus and Aufidius, but it is rigidly subjugated to the passions of the battlefield and the political forum. The truly powerful drives motivating the characters in this play are military, political, and often murderous: areas that have long been delineated, particularly by Roman society, as distinctively masculine. The strong emotional bonds were those between man and man, regardless of whether the men were allies or enemies. By contrast, the emotional ties between men and women were so weak and tenuous as to be almost nonexistent. That, I believe, is what Shakespeare is getting at when he presents Coriolanus embracing his general with a "heart/ As merry as when our nuptial day was done/ And tapers burnt to bedward! (I, vi, 30–32), and an Aufidius twining his "arms about that body," while exclaiming, "More dances my rapt heart/ Than when I first my wedded mistress saw/ Bestride my threshold" (IV, v, 116–118).

In the few scenes between Coriolanus and his loving wife Virgilia, who is distraught by the carnage by which her husband is continually reasserting his manhood, he is tender, but briefly and fleetingly so. Even the lengthy kiss[5] with which he greets her after their long separation following his exile is described by him in language which discloses the obsessively military-political nature of his concerns. "O, a kiss," he cries out, "Long as my exile, sweet as my revenge!" (V, iii, 44–45.) And earlier in the action, on his triumphant return from the victorious war against the Volsces, he greeted first his mother and then his wife (the order is significant) in these terms:

> Your hand, and yours!
> Ere in our own house I do shade my head,
> The good patricians must be visited,
> From whom I have receiv'd not only greetings,
> But with them change of honors. (II, i, 194–198)

Shakespeare makes clear Coriolanus' affection for his wife; no less clear, however, are the priorities which lead him to attend first to his honor rather than to the love of his mate. Any good Roman would have understood that hierarchy of values. His mother certainly did.

But perhaps the most remarkable outburst of what I have been calling displaced eroticism occurs in the third scene of the first act in a conversation between Coriolanus' mother and his wife. The ferocious Volumnia provides further clues for the sexual origins of the bellicose deeds in this play. Once again the imagery couples the marital bed and the martial performance. In this case the sexual imagery is given a further twist by introducing clearly incestuous resonances into the language:

> I pray you, daughter, sing, or express yourself in a more comfortable sort. If my son were my husband, I should freelier rejoice in that absence wherein he won honor than in the embracements of his bed where he would show most love. When yet he was but tender-bodied and the only son of my womb; when youth with comeliness pluck'd all gaze his way; when for a day of kings' entreaties a mother should not sell him an hour from her beholding; I, considering how honor would become such a

person, that it was no better than picture-like to hang by th'wall, if renown made it not stir, was pleas'd to let him seek danger where he was like to find fame. To a cruel war I sent him, from whence he return'd, his brows bound with oak. I tell thee, daughter, I sprang not more in joy at first hearing he was a man-child than now in first seeing he had prov'd himself a man. (I, iii, 1–17)

Aside from the obviously incestuous thrust, however obliquely stated, of those first few lines, the passage reveals not only a desexualized mother, or rather a mother who has rechanneled her sexual feelings toward her son into areas of military prowess where she can in more socially acceptable ways certify and boast of her son's virility. These lines also powerfully express that code of values whereby valorous deeds (one kind of male performance that ranks second to none) are to be preferred before love, where killing on the battlefield for the maternal city of Rome not only prevails over sex but actually becomes a substitute for it. Volumnia's words also suggest ("When yet he was but tender-bodied") that this was Coriolanus' first battle, his *rite de passage,* his entrance into full manhood through the ritual act of slaying the foe on the battlefield. In making Volumnia the driving force behind Coriolanus' ferocity and the chief mouthpiece in the play for the martial glories and virtues. Shakespeare, it can be argued, has not exactly placed those virtues in a particularly attractive light. It is not a question of Shakespeare blindly following his source here (something he never did any way unless it happened to suit his purposes). With the exception of the embassy of the women to Coriolanus to plead on Rome's behalf, Shakespeare created *ex nihilo* all of the scenes in which Volumnia appears. That fact is hardly without significance.

I pointed out a moment ago that one reason for the almost obsessive concern with manhood which characterizes the central characters in Shakespeare's Roman plays is that these plays in particular deal with a society in which manhood, as defined by the Roman ideal, is not a permanent condition, a state that one achieves once and for all. It must constantly be retested through deeds of valor. Constant performance is all. But because, in the words of one of the play's critics, "Even in ancient Rome there cannot be perpetual war,"[8] any definition of manhood so closely identified with battlefield valor is bound to be flimsy, uncertain, insecure and, in the last analysis, self-deceiving and self-destructive.

In Coriolanus' reply, for example, to his mother's appeal that he should swallow his pride and appeal to the people and the tribunes for the consulship in the time-honored, traditional way, he hints at his anxiety about keeping up the appearances of manhood: "Would you have me/ False to my nature? Rather say, I play/ The man I am." (III, ii, 14–16.) Volumnia responds in kind:

> I would have had you put your power well on
> Before you had worn it out.
>
> You might have been enough the man you are,
> With striving less to be so. (III, ii, 17–20)

Her words, incidentally—"I would have had you put your power well on/ Before you had worn it out"—admit of a sexual interpretation, but like all the other sexuality in this play, it expresses itself in political-military language.

As Coriolanus agrees to what he considers to be the humiliation of begging for the consulship, he describes his forthcoming action in terms which clearly indicate that for him the loss of his virility is involved:

> Away, my disposition, and possess me
> Some harlot's spirit! My throat of war be turn'd,
> Which quier'd with my drum, into a pipe
> Small as an eunuch, or the virgin voice
> That babies lull asleep! The smiles of knaves
> Tent in my cheeks, and schoolboys' tears rake up
> The glasses of my sight! (III, ii, 111–117)

What bothers Coriolanus here is that in prostituting himself, in taking on "some harlot's spirit," he will not only be selling out his integrity, but more significantly in his eyes, he will be yielding up his tenuously held manhood. The phallic imagery of his language is graphic, as he bitterly faces the prospect of transforming "my throat of war . . . into a pipe / Small as an eunuch, or the virgin voice/ That babies lull asleep." There is no question that Roman honor, here as elsewhere, was closely bound up with how one defined one's maleness to oneself and to society.

When, toward the end of the play, his former enemy Aufidius berates Coriolanus for agreeing to save Rome from destruction by the Volsces, he does so in terms which, predictably, impugn Coriolanus' manhood:

> At a few drops of women's rheum, which are
> As cheap as lies, he sold the blood and labor
> Of our great action. (V, vi, 45–46)

And a few lines later,

> You lords and heads a' th' state, perfidiously
> He has betray'd your business, and given up,
> For certain drops of salt, your city Rome,
> I say "your city," to his wife and mother,
> Breaking his oath and resolution like
> A twist of rotten silk, never admitting
> Counsel a' th' war; but at his nurse's tears

He whin'd and roar'd away your victory,
That pages blush'd at him, and men of heart
Look'd wond'ring each at others.   (V, vi, 90–98)

Those sneering references to "a few drops of women's rheum," "certain drops of salt," "his nurse's tears," are Aufidius' way of accusing his rival of having succumbed to womanly feelings and having thereby surrendered his manhood. He follows this up by jeeringly referring to Coriolanus as a boy, the charge which, more than any other, wounds him to the quick and goads him into an uncontrollable fury. But we shall have more to say about that later in this essay.

In his contemptuous references to womanly tears, Aufidius is at once carrying on the long-standing tradition which has always viewed weeping as unmanly and is also wielding a tactically powerful psychological weapon against Coriolanus. (It is interesting to observe, incidentally, how often Shakespeare portrays his heroes weeping without its ever involving any loss of their true masculinity.) Weeping, as those doughty Romans viewed it, betokens weakness and cowardice. It certainly has no place on the battlefield, where only the manly (soldierly) virtues are considered appropriate. As Willard Farnham puts it,

> It is entirely characteristic of Coriolanus to divide all life into war and peace and to judge any man by asking first whether he is a true man of war. The true men of war are of course the warrior aristocrats, who are bred through generations to bear arms, to strive for honor, and never to show cowardice.[7]

Perhaps the clearest and most important statement in the play of this masculine code of honor is to be found in Cominius' address to the commoners in praise of Coriolanus in the second act:

                    The deeds of Coriolanus
Should not be utter'd feebly. It is held
That valor is the chiefest virtue, and
Most dignified the haver; if it be,
The man I speak of cannot in the world
Be singly counterpos'd. At sixteen years,
When Tarquin made a head for Rome, he fought
Beyond the mark of others. Our then dictator
Whom with all praise I point at, saw him fight,
When with his Amazonian chin he drove
The bristled lips before him. He bestrid
An o'erpress'd Roman, and i' the consul's view
Slew three opposers. Tarquin's self he met,
And struck him on his knee. In that day's feats,
When he might act the woman in the scene,
He prov'd best man i' th' field, and for his meed
Was brow-bound with the oak. His pupil age
Man-enter'd thus, he waxed like a sea.   (II, ii, 82–99)

This is a somewhat fuller description of Coriolanus' first battle, his *rite de passage* into full manhood, than Volumnia's speech to Virgilia in Act I already quoted. His youthfulness, his beardlessness ("his Amazonian chin"), might have allowed him to "act the woman in the scene" (the theatrical metaphor indicates he was still young enough to play women's roles in the theater), but he chose instead to prove "the best man i' th' field." He had defined, achieved, and tested his manhood all in one day in the approved Roman fashion: by slaying the foe in battle. Reuben Brower makes clear the significance of this speech by Cominius:

> The meaning of "noble"—as often in Shakespeare, equivalent to "heroic"—is summed up in this tremendous survey of the "deeds of Coriolanus." The theme is anticipated at the start by direct statement: "It is held. . . . That valor is the chiefest virtue" (84–5), "valor" being used here as in Elizabethan translations for ancient Roman "virtue."[8]

And a few pages later Brower continues,

> We recognize—as the more literate and the more theatrically experienced members of Shakespeare's audience would have done more quickly and more certainly—that the core of this speech is an heroic narrative in the Graeco-Roman manner. . . . In "the man I speak of," they might have heard Virgil's *arma virumque cano,* and felt the special force that "man" and "virtue" had acquired through repeated use in heroic contexts of Elizabethan plays and translations.[9]

This is a compelling example of the associative bonds linking that by now familiar word cluster—man, heroic, fame, honor, deeds, virtue—all in the semantic service of Roman masculinity.

This cult of honor is so important that when Coriolanus is about to repudiate the traditional ceremony of asking for the consulship because it would, he feels, violate his honor, his mother, far from questioning the value of her son's exaggerated sense of honor, is forced to conduct her argument on those very same grounds:

> Now, this no more dishonors you at all
> Than to take in a town with gentle words,
> Which else would put you to your fortune and
> The hazard of much blood.
> I would dissemble with my nature where
> My fortunes and my friends at stake requir'd
> I should do so in honor.   (III, ii, 58–64)

If we listen carefully to those words, we will not make the mistake of concluding that honor could ever be tempered or vitiated by compassion simply because Coriolanus has sometimes captured enemy towns through persuasive speech ("gentle words") rather than military might. It is, as Volumnia makes clear, simply a question of policy, of expediency, of achieving the same goal without "the hazard of much blood." Honor and compassion have nothing to do with each other, as Aufidius makes clear later in the play, as he comments on Coriolanus' capitulation to his mother's arguments to save Rome:

> I am glad thou hast set thy mercy and thy honor
> At difference in thee. (V, iii, 200–201)

But before he submits once again to Volumnia's powerful hold over him, he pleads for his honor before yielding to what for him is something akin to compassion. G. Wilson Knight describes the moment: "He tells the ladies not to slay his honour, not to tell him wherein he is 'unnatural.'"[10] As Knight views it, this radical separation between manly honor and the gentler sentiments of love and compassion is a fatal one. And while Knight seems to imply that the fault is Coriolanus' alone, it must be pointed out that while in many ways he is an ethical monster, an unfeeling engine of destruction, he is actually the logical end result of the Roman system of values. Knight's analysis of Coriolanus' moral and psychological flaw might just as validly be applied to the Roman code of honor and to all the people who lived and died— and killed—by it:

> We here watch human excellence, power, valour, even virtue, abstracted from love, or, at the least, overruling love, raised to a high pitch, and pursuing its logical course. That is our hero in his loveless pride. He has never shown love. For love too, whether it be love of mother, wife, friend, or community, is itself a regal mistress: its delicate tyranny tolerates no precedent value. Love subject to any quality quite loveless—pride, ambition, self-concentration of any sort—is not yet love: conversely, "honour" which is not servanted to some quality which is a function of love, becomes rapidly pride, ambition, vainglory.[11]

Or as he puts it more succinctly in another place, "There [is] intrinsic fault in any ambition, or indeed any value, which is not a multiple of love. This is the theme developed in *Coriolanus.*"[12]

One result of establishing this gulf between manly virtue and compassion or love is, as Shakespeare portrays it in this play, the reduction of the military hero to something less than human, to an agent of destruction indifferent to suffering and death. This becomes evident in Cominius' description of his conduct:

> From fact to foot
> He was a thing of blood, whose every motion
> Was tim'd with dying cries. (II, ii, 109–111)

And again,

> He did
> Run reeking o'er the lives of men as if
> 'Twere a perpetual spoil. (II, ii, 118–120)

The response, incidentally, of the congenial mediator Menenius to this catalogue of bloody deeds is, "Worthy man!" (II, ii, 123.) It is difficult not to sympathize with the cry of one of the play's critics, D. J. Enright, who exclaims,

> If only . . . he could be rather more introspective—in the way that Macbeth is—rather more conscious of the cries of his lawful victims! If only we were persuaded that there is more to him than is reflected in his armour.[13]

In keeping with this demythologizing of the military hero which characterizes *Coriolanus*, there is no glorification of war in this play, as there was, for example, in the earlier *Henry V*. The later work is replete with references to the victims, to the survivors, to the widows and orphans left behind after the slaughterous din has subsided. Even the warlike Volumnia, it will be recalled, refers to it as "cruel war." (I, iii, 13.) This same woman has no illusions about the results of her son's deeds, as these lines reveal:

> Before him
> He carries noise, and behind him he leaves tears:
> Death, that dark spirit, in's nervy arm doth lie,
> Which, being advanc'd, declines, and then men die.   (II, i, 158–161)

And Coriolanus, in a rare and very brief soliloquy, paints a grim picture of his battlefield exploits:

> A goodly city is this Antium. City,
> 'Tis I that made thy widows; many an heir
> Of these fair edifices 'fore my wars
> Have I heard groan and drop. Then know me not,
> Lest that thy wives with spits and boys with stones
> In puny battle slay me.   (IV, iv, 1–6)

While it is true that these lines function primarily to establish scene location, as well as the fact of Coriolanus' disguise, it is interesting that Shakespeare works into the passage the point that war results, not in glory, but in carnage and suffering. It is difficult, however, to determine with any precision the speaker's own attitude and feeling toward the scene his memory conjures up. It is hardly remorse, in any case, because not too long after this we see him preparing to level his own beloved Rome to the ground, even though this would involve the deaths of his mother, wife, and son.

On this question of the stance adopted by this play toward war, it might be pointed out that an interesting version of the Shakespearean technique of working minor variations of a major theme in a play into the garbled speech of a comic character (the porter in *Macbeth*, the gravedigger in *Hamlet*) occurs here in the unconsciously ironic discussion by Aufidius' buffoonish servants on the merits of war over peace:

SECOND SERVANT: Why then we shall have a stirring world again. This peace is nothing but to rust iron, increase tailors, and breed ballad makers.

FIRST SERVANT: Let me have war, say I, it exceeds peace as far as day does night; it's sprightly, waking, audible, and full of vent. Peace is a very apoplexy, lethargy, mull'd, deaf, sleepy, insensible, a getter of more bastard children than war's a destroyer of men.

SECOND SERVANT: 'Tis so, and as wars, in some sort, may be said to be a ravisher, so it cannot be denied but peace is a great maker of cuckolds.

(IV, v, 218–229)

If one of the major thematic resonances echoing through the Roman plays is the association of the mystique of masculinity with warfare and destruction and the pitting of that mystique against the forces of love, sexuality, and life, then we are assuredly dealing with a comic version of that theme in this exchange. The first servant, in his insistence that "peace is a . . . getter of more bastard children than war's a destroyer of men," is vigorously supported by his fellow dabbler in clownish philosophy: " 'Tis so, and as wars, in some sort, may be said to be a ravisher, so it cannot be denied but peace is a great maker of cuckolds." I suspect it would be no exaggeration to see in this admirable exchange a strong clue as to the judgmental attitude against war taken by this play, as well as a lucid (although ironic) reiteration of the idea which binds the Roman plays together and justifies our treating them as a group.

It is worth pointing out in passing that while this play paints war as something less than glorious and military heroes as something less than noble and even, at times, less than human, the leaders in the political forum, that other area traditionally associated with exclusively male activities, do not fare well either. Judah Stampfer, commenting on two of the political leaders of the common people, the tribunes Brutus and Sicinius, makes the point that politicians generally do not come off as appealing figures in Shakespeare's plays. (Stampfer does not mention the comically villainous Polonius, but he might have.) After dismissing Brutus and Sicinius as more appropriate to Tammany Hall than to Imperial Rome, Stampfer writes,

> Two-dimensional, a complete instrument of his vocation, the political hero never really gripped Shakespeare's imagination. He is never married or involved with women. Ulysses refuses to kiss Cressida. Sexually, Octavious is an ambiguous neuter; his sister is a political pawn played to advantage. . . . Even-tempered, never angry or impulsive, relaxed or unaware, never in physical combat or gripped by ardor, incessantly at work, they need not control their appetites—they have none to begin with. They hurt no one unnecessarily, but sense each man's weakness, and are utterly without scruple. Steady, systematic, they manipulate for their moment of opportunity, and are politically invincible.[14]

D. J. Enright, who views the play as structured along the lines of a debate, makes a not unrelated point by demonstrating the harm that results when politics and humanity or compassion are separated, in much the same way, as was pointed out earlier, that tragedy ensues when honor and love are kept apart. After remarking that "the voice of Virgilia has no place in the debates which are held. . . . She must remain a 'gracious silence,' " Enright continues,

> And in this sense it may certainly be said to be a "political play," for its final impression of aridness and waste might well be considered a warning against the petrifaction of humanity which occurs when people think exclusively in terms of parties and movements and manifestoes.[15]

The same critic also argues that "the powerful characters of the play all throw in their weight against life—against the kind of love which Virgilia dares to stand up for."[16]

The mention of Virgilia, the wife of Coriolanus, raises the question of the status of women, first in the play itself, and then in that society standing behind and in some way reflected by the action of this work. Aside from Volumnia, whose "masculinized" role we have to some extent already commented on, there is really little to say, because Virgilia herself is given so little to say by the playwright. Coriolanus, in fact, calls her his "gracious silence." (II, i, 175.) But this very muting of the feminine voice can be taken as an eloquent indictment of a patriarchal society which extols the martial values as the true measure of humanity and which silences by edict that half of its population (one cannot with accuracy use the term citizenry in connection with Roman women) which might, however, slightly, have humanized the harshness, and ultimately the inhumanity, of the Roman heroic ideal. One writer even argues that Virgilia's presence in the play accounts for whatever minimal humanity is detectable in Coriolanus.[17] Matthew N. Proser goes so far as to argue that she is the "point of reference from which we can judge the action of the play."[18] I agree that she is, in her relative silence, a kind of negative Sophoclean chorus, providing the emotional and moral focus for observing the events in which she finds herself enmeshed. In view of the general indictment of Roman society and its value code which, as I have been arguing, permeates Coriolanus, this is not an altogether unreasonable way of regarding Virgilia's function in the action.

If Virgilia, in her quiet passivity, represents one available option to the women in an authoritarian society, then it can be argued—and one critic does just that—that Volumnia represents the other choice that that same society offers its women at the other end of the spectrum. Gordon Ross Smith, in an essay entitled "Authoritarian Patterns in Shakespeare's Coriolanus," states the case this way:

In Volumnia we see caricatured this other extreme of feminine authoritarianism: her envy of men is evident first in her unequivocal usurpation of as much of the masculine role as she can manage and later in her living through Coriolanus to enjoy what she cannot seize for herself.[19]

And Charles K. Hofling, approaching the play as a psychoanalytic critic, sees Volumnia as "an extremely unfeminine, non-maternal person, one who sought to mold her son to fit a pre-conceived image gratifying her own masculine (actually pseudo-masculine) striving."[20]

Whether eloquently silent cipher (or more often, probably, merely silent cipher) or grotesque caricature of those hungering for power and fame, the two choices Roman society offered its women have little to recommend them. And Valeria, the functionless third woman in the play—rounding out the three acceptable sex roles assigned to Roman females, virgin, wife, mother[21]—is described by Coriolanus as "The moon of Rome, chaste as the icicle / That's curdied by the frost from purest snow / And hangs on Dian's temple." (V, iii, 65–67.) The imagery is cold and lifeless, suggesting a creature less than human.

And yet these same three women, relegated as they are to roles as spectators, or as instigators of but never actors in the "important" events of history, actually succeed in persuading the battle-lusting, revenge-seeking Coriolanus that the fighting should cease, that peace is greater than war. And ironically and paradoxically it is the eloquence of the pugnacious Volumnia suing for peace that turns the tide of her son's vindictive rage. There are those quick to point out that this is her ultimate manipulation of him, her final act of domination, and one which, fittingly, ends in his death. Furthermore, her probable self-interest must not be forgotten, because she was pleading not only that Rome be spared; she was also pleading for the lives of her grandson, her daughter-in-law, and herself.

And yet there is something splendid and moving in the spectacle of the three women and the young boy interceding with Coriolanus on behalf of peace. For just this once we see Volumnia, whatever her hidden motivation may be, relinquishing her unnatural role and pursuing reconciliation rather than discord. The women succeed in their mission as bringers of peace, but the price is a terrible one: the death of Coriolanus at the hands of the Volsces for having betrayed them by saving Rome. Here are some of Volumnia's stirring words to her son that lead him to perform the one purgative, peace-making deed of his life:

> If it were so that our request did tend
> To save the Romans, thereby to destroy
> The Volsces whom you serve, you might condemn us,
> As poisonous of your honor. No, our suit
> Is that you reconcile them. While the Volsces

> May say, "This mercy we have show'd," the Romans,
> "This we receiv'd: and each in either side
> Give the all hail to thee, and cry, "Be blest
> For making up this peace!" Thou know'st, great son,
> The end of war's uncertain.
>
> (V, iii, 132–141)

There is, to be sure, the same old, familiar appeal to honor in those lines, but the grounds beneath that powerful concept have shifted, significantly. Volumnia appeals to her son's craving for fame and glory: "Each in either/ Give the all hail to thee," but now he will be hailed and blessed "For making up this peace!" We shall never know, for the text remains silent on this subject, whether we are dealing here with a subtle example of that Machiavellian guile she had advised Coriolanus to adopt in seeking the consulship earlier in the play:

> Now it lies you on to speak
> To th' people, not by your own instruction,
> Nor by th' matter which your heart prompts you,
> But with such words that are but roted in
> Your tongue, though but bastards, and syllables
> Of no allowance, to your bosom's truth.
>
> (III, ii, 52–57)

For the true Machiavellian, deception and falsehood can lie down with the lamb, as well as with the lion. Policy (a generally pejorative term in Shakespeare's day) can serve peace, as well as war. Volumnia herself earlier in the play makes the point with great precision and clarity:

> I have heard you say
> Honor and policy, like unsever'd friends,
> I' th' war do grow together; grant that, and tell me
> In peace what each of them by th' other lose
> That they combine not there.

When Coriolanus tries to silence her with his brusque "Tush, tush!" and the eternal mediator Menenius diplomatically comments, "A good demand," Volumnia repeats her argument with no less forcefulness:

> If it be honor in your wars to seem
> The same you are not, which, for your best ends,
> You adopt your policy, how is it less or worse
> That it shall hold companionship in peace
> With honor, as in war, since that to both
> It stands in like request.
>
> (III, ii, 41–51)

In the well-nigh universal revulsion that Volumnia has evoked down through the years, these words of hers have received little attention. As she makes clear in the passage just quoted, honor need not be compromised by political manipulation ("policy"), and both are compatible with peace. This is a critically important deviation from the rigid code of honor by which Roman men, as demonstrations of their manhood, lived and died. Honor, nobility, *virtus,* are now cast in a different light. The undercutting is no less valid because it emanates from the mouth of the ferocious and cunning Volumnia. Coriolanus succumbs and agrees to accept this threat to his Roman-defined masculinity. His commitment is now to peace, not war:

> Ladies, you deserve
> To have a temple built you. All the swords
> In Italy, and her confederate arms
> Could not have made this peace. (V, iii, 206–209)

It is, of course, too late for this boy/warrior to effect such a radical change in his sense of himself as a man. His choices, his actions, his entire life, have made certain consequences inevitable. Death follows quickly upon this climactic turn in the action and the play is over.

Coriolanus' new awareness, suggested by his wish to dedicate a temple to the women for having ended war is, unfortunately, short-lived. A lifetime of Pavlovian responses cannot be undone by one flashing moment of truth, however profound that truth may be. In his masculine insecurity he is still vulnerable, as Aufidius knows full well in the play's final scene. Some have even seen his surrender to Volumnia's rhetoric on behalf of peace as a regression to his habitual boylike submission to a dominating mother which had characterized his entire life up until that moment. In any case the hero's death in the last scene is marked by none of that dignity and meaning attendant upon the deaths of such tragic figures as Lear, Othello, and Macbeth. Coriolanus does not die nobly with a hard-won and new-found vision of himself and his values. His ending is marked by bitterness and futility as he dies by that code which the play's events have disclosed as shallow, truncated, and destructive.

Our final vision of the play's protagonist is of a bad-tempered, pitifully uncontrolled man goaded easily into a ranting and railing by the wily Aufidius, who incites an enraged Volscian mob to hack the Roman general to pieces. In contrast with the final speeches of an Othello or a Lear, there is little dignity in Coriolanus' final outburst. In response to Aufidius' accusations that he is a traitor, Coriolanus incredulously replies, "Hears't thou, Mars?" (V, vi, 99.) The Volscian leader's sneering retort shows that he knows precisely where Coriolanus' vulnerability lies: in his obsessive anxiety over his masculinity, which, as we have seen, underlies all of his actions throughout the play. "Name not the god, thou boy of tears!" (V, vi, 100.) Those four words, "thou boy of tears," more than any charge of treason, are Coriolanus' undoing. The double-barreled charge that he is a boy and a creature susceptible to tears openly challenges his manhood and brings about his immediate collapse. As one critic wisely points out,

> Since the Elizabethans and Jacobeans divided the members of society into two categories, men, and women-and-boys, with much emphasis on virile and effeminate qualities, when a Shakespearean character uses the term "boy" in such an instance as this; it carries the additional implication of "effeminate." There is thus the further irony that Coriolanus should be accused of effeminacy in connection with his nearest approach to a compassionate masculinity.[22]

Having approached the play along the lines traced in this essay, that is, as a study of the destructive consequences resulting from the distorted emphasis on and definition of manhood in the Roman heroic code, we are in a better position to understand more fully why Aufidius' epithet is so devastating to one who has embraced that code so fully and unquestioningly. When, in his final words, Coriolanus reverts to the animal imagery which characterized his arrogant diatribes in the early sections, we understand immediately that he is incapable of escaping the bonds of the behavioral straitjacket into which his society has thrust him, not, of course, without his own consent. Here are his anguished words to the Volsces:

> Boy! False hound!
> If you have writ your annals true, 'tis there,
> Flutter'd your Volscians in Corioli:
> Alone I did it. Boy!   (V, vi, 112–116)

Those lines elicited the following comment from one of the play's critics, who sees this excessive concern with masculinity as linked to the absence of a father for the hero and to the concomitant dominating role played by the mother: "Obviously, this shrill arrogance strives to shout down a passive, feminine sense of himself founded on the only infantile object that was provided him, his mother, for Shakespeare chose to exclude the influence of a father from Coriolanus' life."[23] Other writers have made essentially the same point. Judah Stampfer, for instance, calls him "a precocious, insufferable adolescent, inescapable and unreliable."[24] And John Palmer, referring to Coriolanus as "the splendid oaf who has never come to maturity," goes on to say that "his intolerance of anything outside his special code of honour are more characteristic of an adolescent than a grown man."[25] Even Reuben Brower, who labors mightily to see in the play elements of the tragic (qualified by such phrases as "so poignantly absurd, so tragic in a curiously ironic sense") concedes that this most self-consciously "masculine" of Shakespearean protagonists has never really grown up.[26] Perhaps the best statement of this view of the play's meaning is Stampfer's:

> Throughout the play, he is struggling to escape his "boy" condition. What he wants is manhood, its smell and gesture, but he is jammed in a bind, and blindly flounders, groping toward it. The definition of manhood never

quite comes into focus in Coriolanus. The play has no clarity on manhood, as Coriolanus has none; yet everywhere he gropes toward it, with an intuition vastly different from that of the history plays. This sense of a fresh location for manhood also brings the classical tradegies to a full close. In the early plays, Prince Hal-Henry V achieves manhood when he arrives at complete personal fulfillment in successful public service.[27]

G. Wilson Knight also sees the critique of manly honor as the major theme running through all of the Roman plays. In his view the inadequacy of this code revealed in these plays stems directly from its futile attempt to exclude love and the "womanly" traits from what we might call the Platonic idea of the masculine, as defined officially by Roman civilization.[28]

Viewed in this light, Aufidius' ritualistic funeral speech over the body of the man he has just had murdered becomes a hollow, hypocritical cliché. What is called the conventional genre of the ceremonial, formal closing speech becomes in the context of this play something close to a bitter parody on the tradition:

Beat thou the drum, that it speak mournfully;
Trail your steel pikes. Though in this city he
Hath widowed and unchilded many a one,
Which to this hour bewail the injury,
Yet he shall have a noble memory.   (V, vi, 149–153)

It is significant that Aufidius reminds his hearers that this "hero" has "widowed and unchilded many a one" in Corioles, and somehow we do not believe him when he says that such a man "will have a noble memory" among his people.

This is our final ironic glimpse of the heroic tradition. Its chief votary, in carrying out the terms of that tradition, has never achieved the manhood promised to its adherents, and his heroic attempts to attain to that manhood are viewed as nothing more than the carnage which leaves in its wake the innocent, suffering survivors, the "widowed and unchilded."

A more devastating indictment of the Roman heroic ideal can hardly be imagined.

NOTES

CHAPTER 35

[1] Harvey Granville-Barker, *Prefaces to Shakespeare* (Princeton: Princeton U. Press, 1946), II, p. 160.

[2] G. Wilson Knight argues, somewhat bizarrely, in *The Imperial Theme* (New York: Oxford U. Press, 1936), p. 63, that the play is "charged highly with a general eroticism. All the people are lovers."

[3] Judah Stampfer, *The Tragic Engagement: A Study of Shakespeare's Classical Tragedies* (New York: Funk & Wagnalls, 1968), p. 92.

[4] All quotations from Shakespeare's text are taken from *The Riverside Shakespeare*, ed. G. Blakemore Evans and others (Boston: Houghton Mifflin, 1974).

[5] Reuben Brower, in *Hero and Saint: Shakespeare and the Graeco-Roman Heroic Tradition* (New York: Oxford U. Press, 1971), p. 237, makes essentially the same point: "Shakespeare . . . explores in *Julius Caesar* some of the conflicts that the Graeco-Roman ideal inevitably produces, when the 'noble man' enters a more complex social and political world than the battlefield of ancient epic."

[6] Granville-Barker, p. 160.

[7] A good example of this attitude is to be found in Seneca's Epistle 116, quoted by Otto Kiefer, *Sexual Life in Ancient Rome* (London: Abbey Library, 1934), p. 139: "Love injures us when it is difficult as much as when it is easy: we are bewitched by its easiness, we wrestle with its difficulties. Let us therefore know our own weakness and rest in peace."

[8] One among the many countless examples of this official definition of a woman exclusively in terms of her relationship to men is expressed clearly in a letter written by a Roman named Servius to his friend Cicero to console him on the recent death of his daughter Tullia. Servius writes,

> Tullia lived long enough to satisfy her; she was a contemporary of the *res publica;* she saw you, her father, promoted praetor, then consul, then a member of the college of augurs; she married young men of the best families in the land; she enjoyed almost all the blessings of life; when the *res publica* perished, she died. What complaint can you or she have against fortune on this account.

The passage is found in *Ad Familiares,* IV, 5, 1, in *Res Publica: Roman Politics and Society According to Cicero,* trans. W. K. Lacey and B. W. J. G. Wilson (London: Oxford U. Press, 1970), p. 302.

CHAPTER 36

[1] T. S. Eliot, "Hamlet and His Problems," in *The Sacred Wood* (London: Methuen, 1920), p. 98.

[2] An account of the episode can be found in C. J. Partridge, *Coriolanus* (Oxford: Blackwell, 1970), p. 3.

[3] Northrop Frye, *The Fools of Time* (Toronto: U. of Toronto Press, 1967), p. 56, asserts that Coriolanus' "sexual energy has gone into warfare, and his real mistress is Bellona. . . ."

[4] Robert J. Stoller, "Shakespearean Tragedy: *Coriolanus*," *Psychoanalytic Quarterly*, XXXV (1966), p. 335.

[5] The stage direction, as is so often the case with Shakespeare, is implicit in the dialogue: "O a kiss/ Long as my exile."

[6] D. J. Enright, "*Coriolanus:* Tragedy or Debate," in Maurice Charney, ed., *Discussions of Shakespeare's Roman Plays* (Boston: Heath, 1965), p. 159.

[7] Willard Farnham, *The Tragic Frontier* (Berkeley: U. of California Press, 1950), p. 224.

[8] Reuben A. Brower, *Hero and Saint: Shakespeare and the Graeco-Roman Heroic Tradition* (New York: Oxford U. Press, 1971), p. 356.

[9] Brower, p. 358.

[10] G. Wilson Knight, *The Imperial Theme* (New York: Oxford U. Press, 1931), p. 194.

[11] Knight, p. 190.

[12] Knight, p. 155.

[13] Enright, p. 161.

[14] Judah Stampfer, *The Tragic Engagement: A Study of Shakespeare's Classical Tragedies* (New York: Funk & Wagnalls, 1968), p. 305.

[15] Enright, p. 167.

[16] Enright, p. 165.

[17] Matthew N. Proser, *The Heroic Image in Five Shakespearean Tragedies* (Princeton: Princeton U. Press, 1965), p. 170.

[18] Proser, p. 155.

[19] Gordon Ross Smith, "Authoritarian Patterns in Shakespeare's *Coriolanus*," *Literature and Psychology*, IX (1959), p. 48.

[20] Charles K. Hofling, "An Interpretation of Shakespeare's *Coriolanus*," in *The Design Within* (New York: Science House, 1970), p. 292.

[21] See Otto Kiefer, *Sexual Life in Ancient Rome* (London: Abbey Library, 1934), pp. 60 and 63. Kiefer points out that in ancient Rome prostitutes were nonexistent persons.

[22] Hofling, p. 305, n. 7.

[23] Stoller, p. 335.

[24] Stampfer, pp. 317–318.

[25] Enright, p. 164.

[26] Brower, p. 381.

[27] Stampfer, pp. 322–332.

[28] Knight, p. 196.